Takane & Hana

9

STORY AND ART BY

Yukī Shiwasu

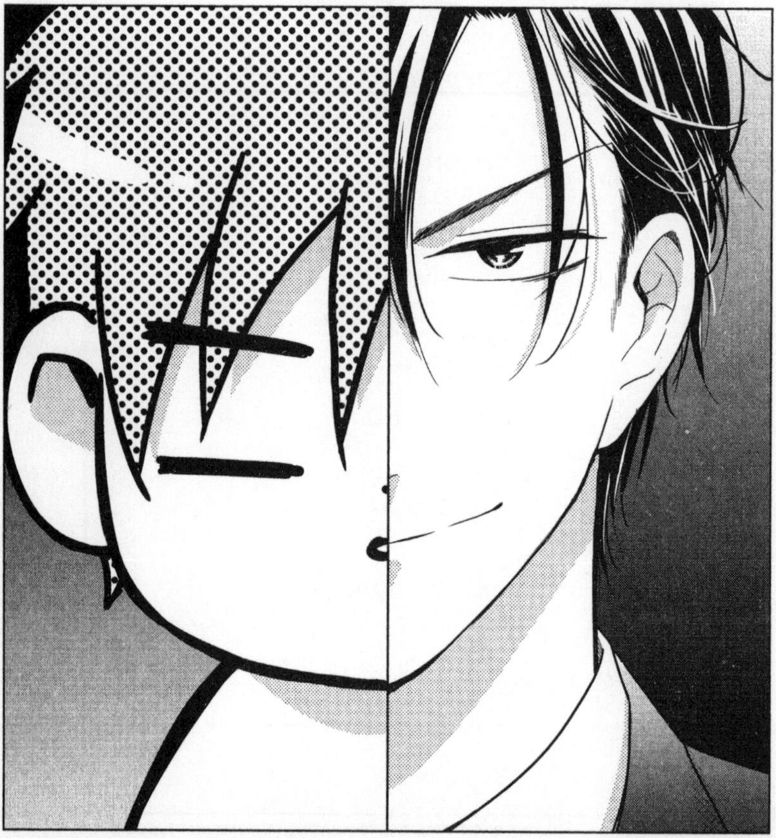

Takane & Hana

9

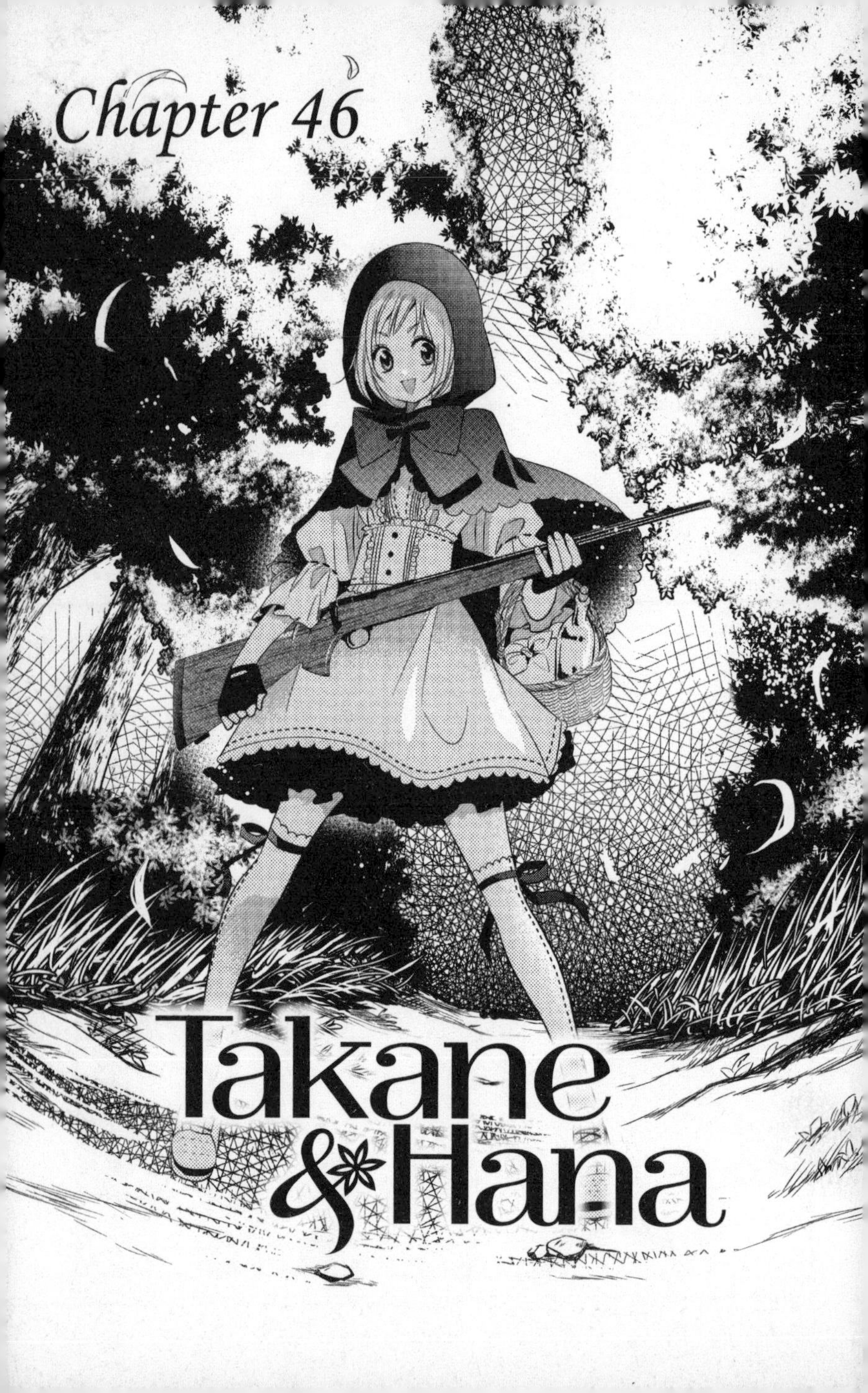
Chapter 46
Takane & Hana

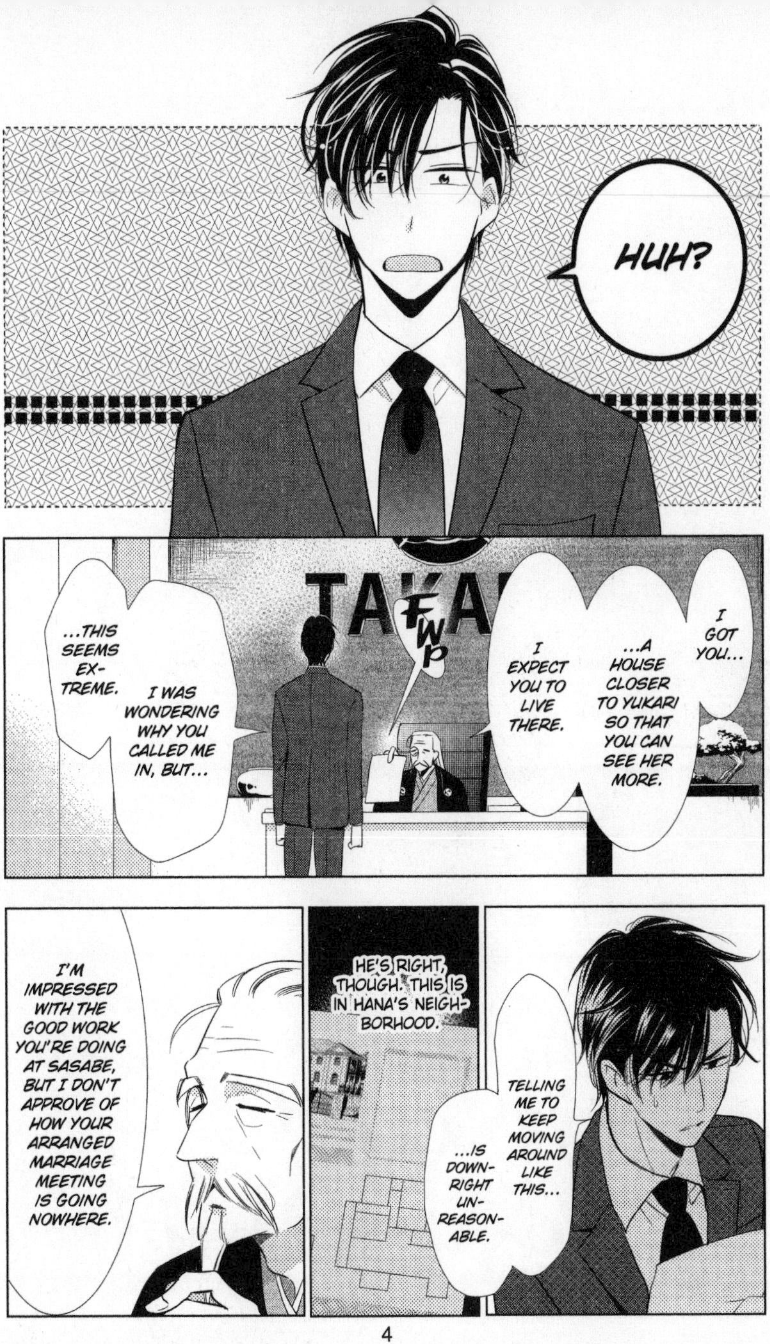
HUH?
I GOT YOU...
...A HOUSE CLOSER TO YUKARI SO THAT YOU CAN SEE HER MORE.
I EXPECT YOU TO LIVE THERE.
FWP
I WAS WONDERING WHY YOU CALLED ME IN, BUT...
...THIS SEEMS EX-TREME.
TELLING ME TO KEEP MOVING AROUND LIKE THIS...
...IS DOWN-RIGHT UN-REASON-ABLE.
HE'S RIGHT, THOUGH. THIS IS IN HANA'S NEIGH-BORHOOD.
I'M IMPRESSED WITH THE GOOD WORK YOU'RE DOING AT SASABE, BUT I DON'T APPROVE OF HOW YOUR ARRANGED MARRIAGE MEETING IS GOING NOWHERE.

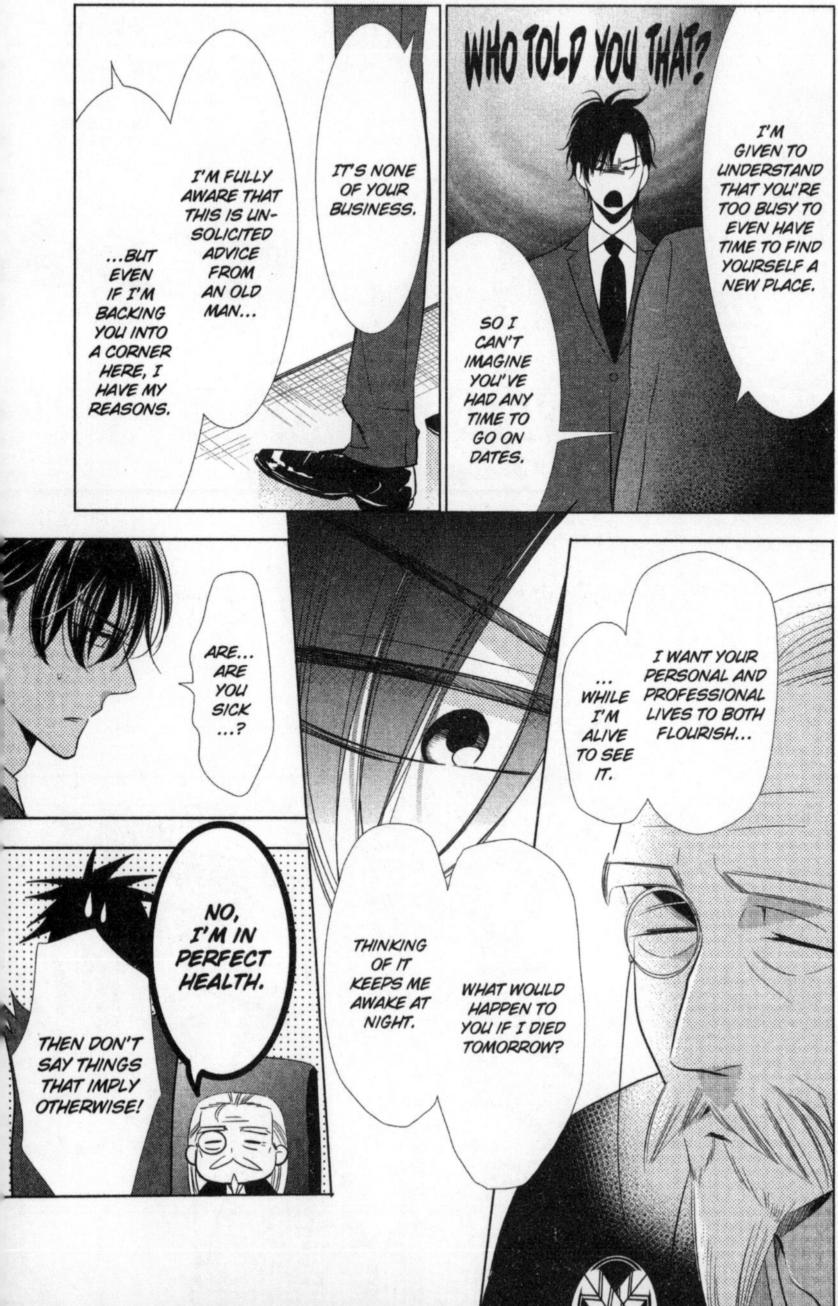
I'M GIVEN TO UNDERSTAND THAT YOU'RE TOO BUSY TO EVEN HAVE TIME TO FIND YOURSELF A NEW PLACE.
SO I CAN'T IMAGINE YOU'VE HAD ANY TIME TO GO ON DATES.
WHO TOLD YOU THAT?
IT'S NONE OF YOUR BUSINESS.
I'M FULLY AWARE THAT THIS IS UNSOLICITED ADVICE FROM AN OLD MAN...
...BUT EVEN IF I'M BACKING YOU INTO A CORNER HERE, I HAVE MY REASONS.
I WANT YOUR PERSONAL AND PROFESSIONAL LIVES TO BOTH FLOURISH...
...WHILE I'M ALIVE TO SEE IT.
WHAT WOULD HAPPEN TO YOU IF I DIED TOMORROW?
THINKING OF IT KEEPS ME AWAKE AT NIGHT.
ARE... ARE YOU SICK...?
NO, I'M IN PERFECT HEALTH.
THEN DON'T SAY THINGS THAT IMPLY OTHERWISE!

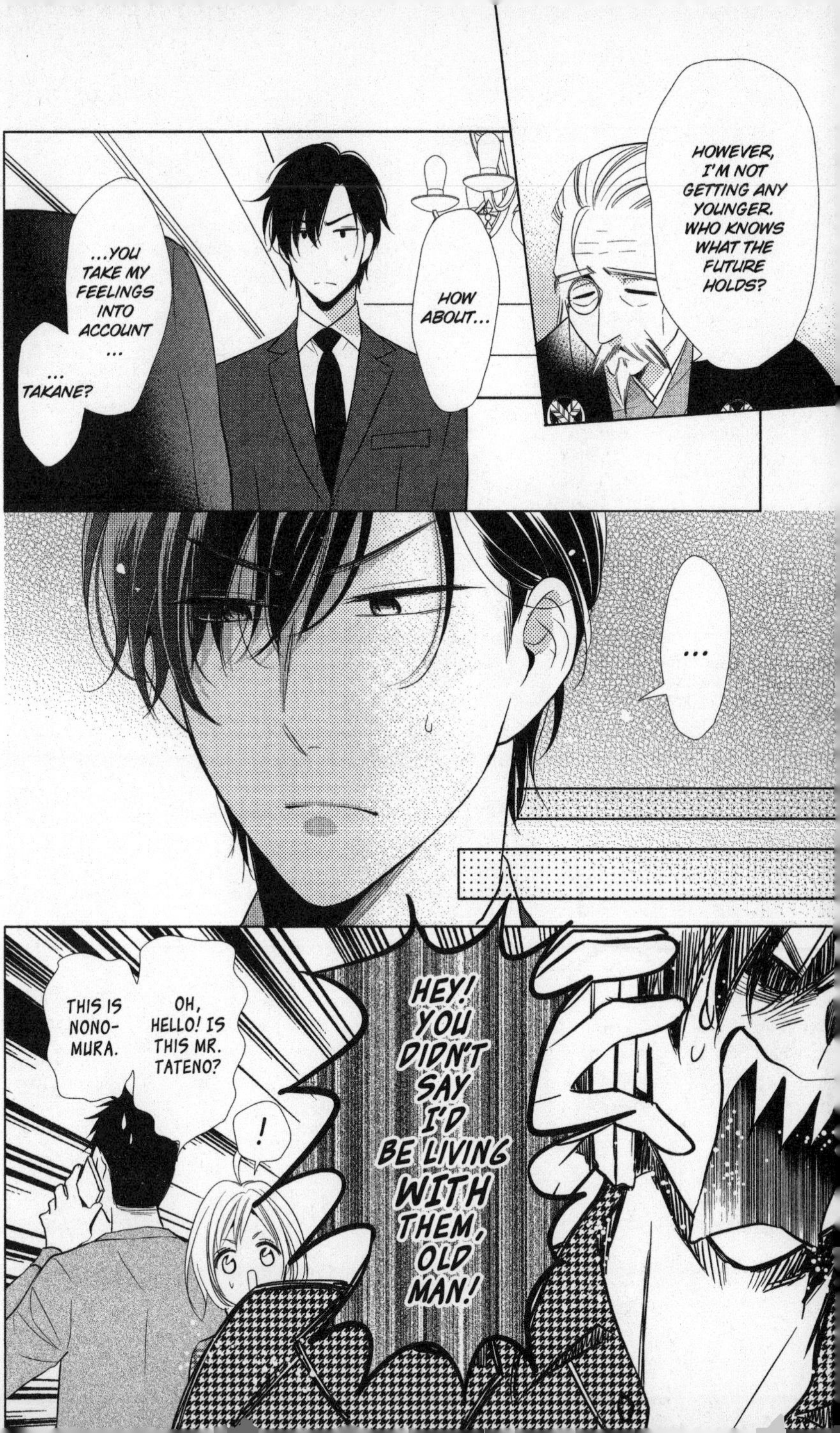
HOWEVER, I'M NOT GETTING ANY YOUNGER. WHO KNOWS WHAT THE FUTURE HOLDS?
HOW ABOUT...
...YOU TAKE MY FEELINGS INTO ACCOUNT...
...TAKANE?
...
HEY! YOU DIDN'T SAY I'D BE LIVING WITH THEM, OLD MAN!
OH, HELLO! IS THIS MR. TATENO?
THIS IS NONO-MURA.
!

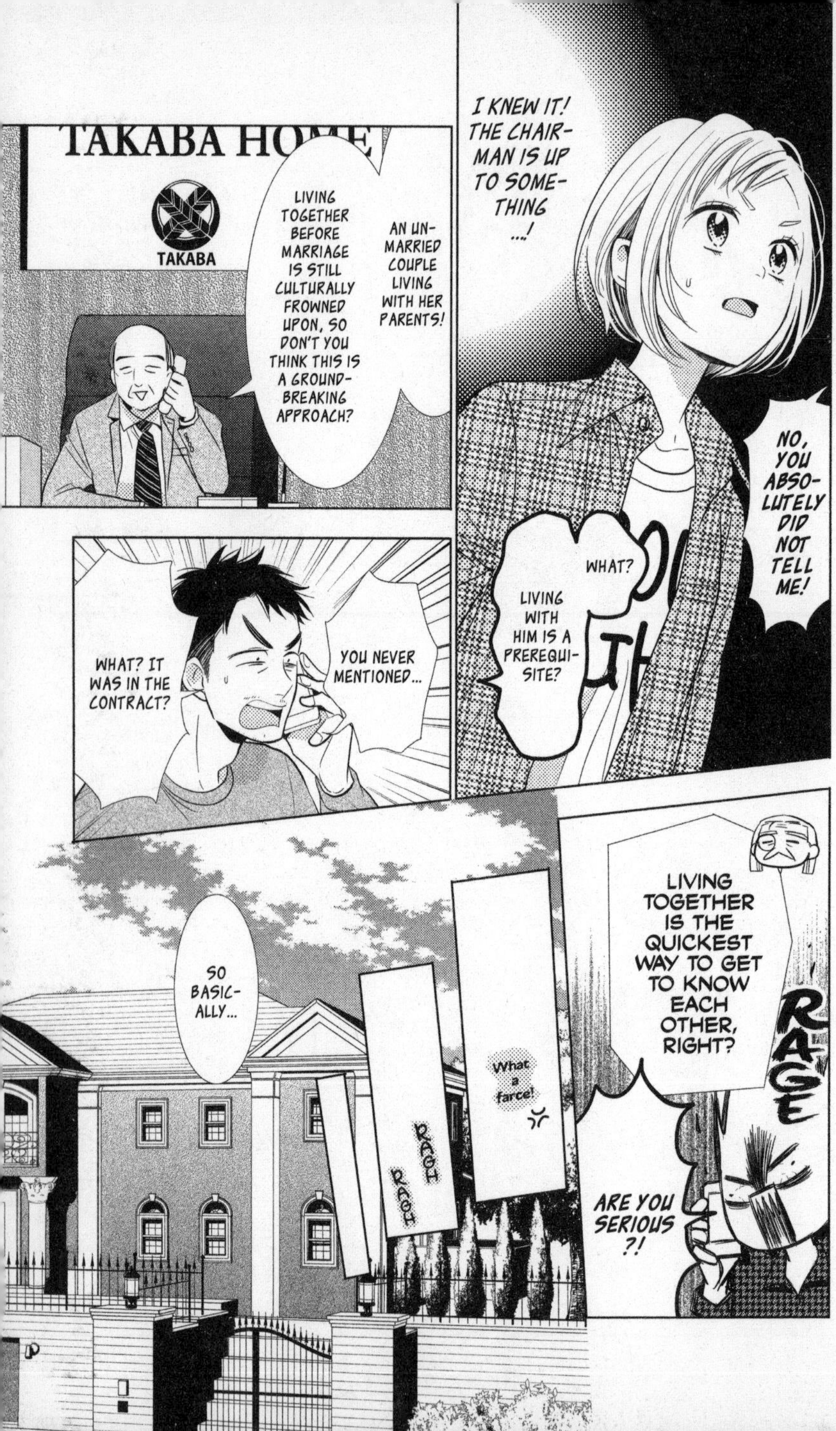
I KNEW IT! THE CHAIR-MAN IS UP TO SOME-THING ...!
NO, YOU ABSO-LUTELY DID NOT TELL ME!
WHAT?
LIVING WITH HIM IS A PREREQUI-SITE?
TAKABA HOME
TAKABA
AN UN-MARRIED COUPLE LIVING WITH HER PARENTS!
LIVING TOGETHER BEFORE MARRIAGE IS STILL CULTURALLY FROWNED UPON, SO DON'T YOU THINK THIS IS A GROUND-BREAKING APPROACH?
YOU NEVER MENTIONED...
WHAT? IT WAS IN THE CONTRACT?
LIVING TOGETHER IS THE QUICKEST WAY TO GET TO KNOW EACH OTHER, RIGHT?
RAGE
ARE YOU SERIOUS ?!
What a farce!
RAGH
RAGH
SO BASIC-ALLY...

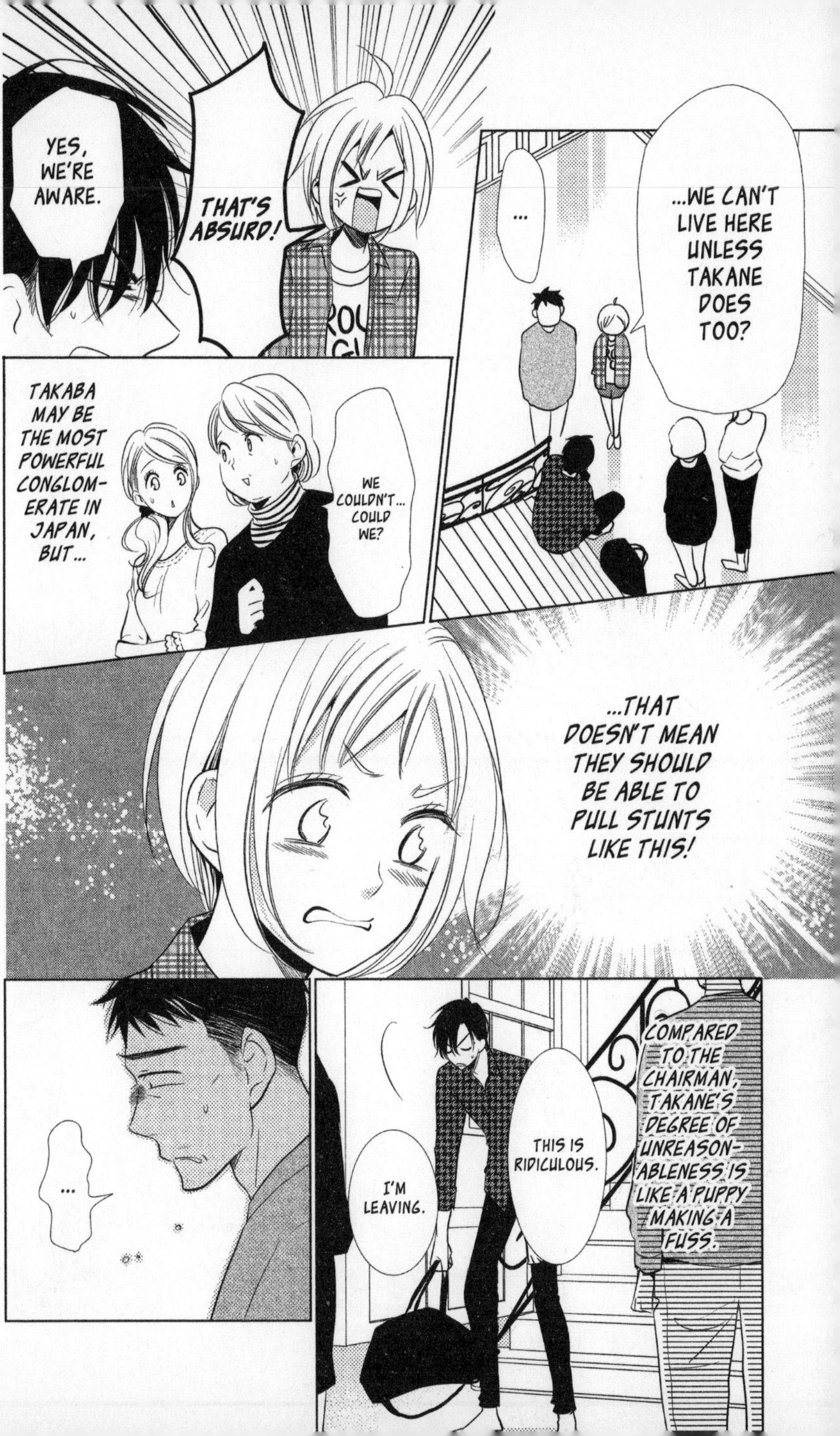
...WE CAN'T LIVE HERE UNLESS TAKANE DOES TOO?
...
THAT'S ABSURD!
YES, WE'RE AWARE.
WE COULDN'T... COULD WE?
TAKABA MAY BE THE MOST POWERFUL CONGLOMERATE IN JAPAN, BUT...
...THAT DOESN'T MEAN THEY SHOULD BE ABLE TO PULL STUNTS LIKE THIS!
COMPARED TO THE CHAIRMAN, TAKANE'S DEGREE OF UNREASONABLENESS IS LIKE A PUPPY MAKING A FUSS.
THIS IS RIDICULOUS.
I'M LEAVING.
...

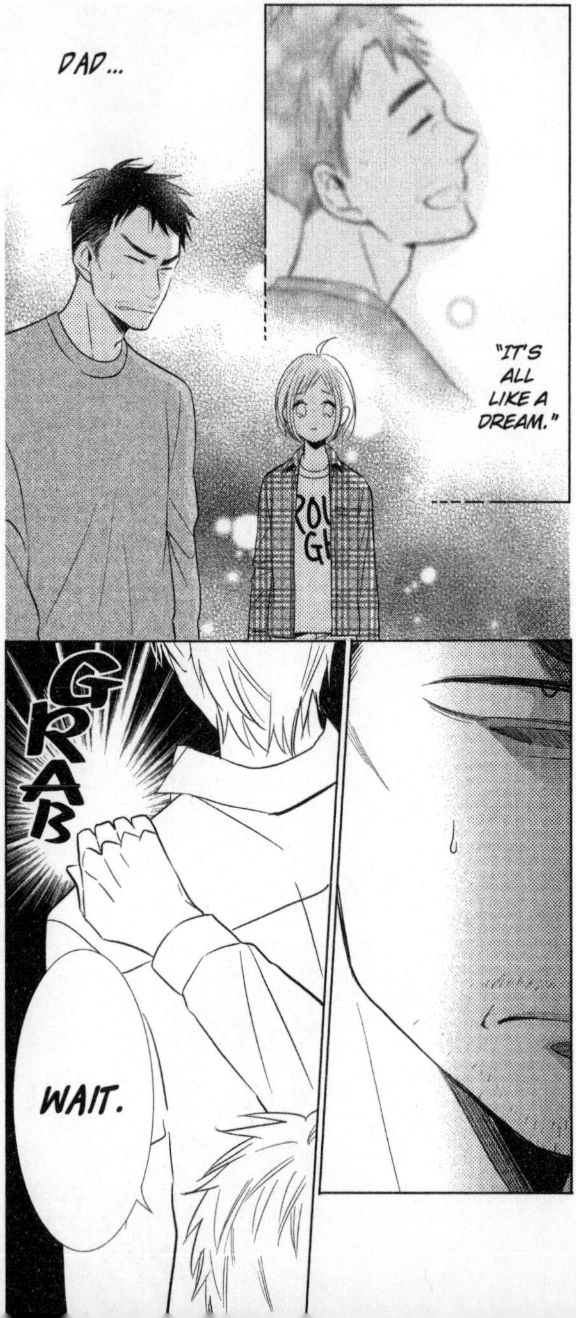
"IT'S ALL LIKE A DREAM."
DAD...
GRAB
WAIT.

• Suit •

Hello, it's me, the author. Lately, I find myself getting more excited at the sight of a man's suit on its own rather than a man wearing a suit. And that's all thanks to...

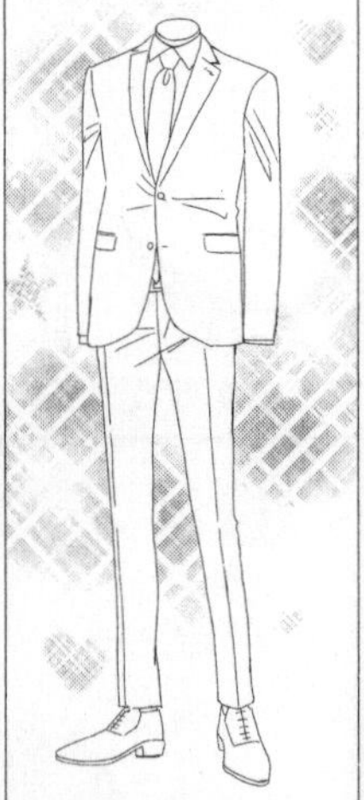

The mannequin!

A mannequin designed for suits, wearing a suit. And the suit it's wearing is just so cool.

It goes without saying, right? After all, it was made specifically to wear a suit. That's its whole reason for existence. I guess you can say I'm hot for the mannequin.

The mannequin's proportions are similar to a manga character's, so it serves as a useful reference.

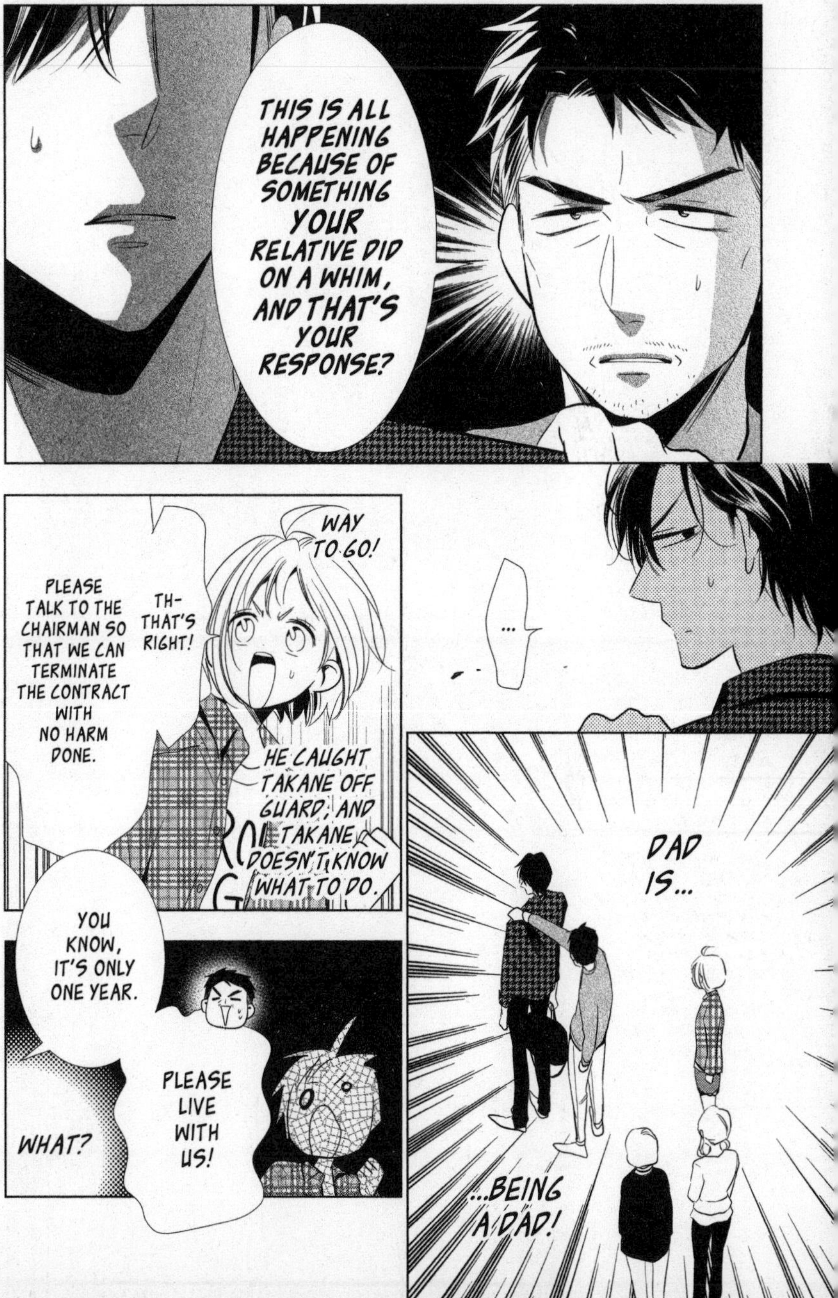
THIS IS ALL HAPPENING BECAUSE OF SOMETHING YOUR RELATIVE DID ON A WHIM, AND THAT'S YOUR RESPONSE?
...
WAY TO GO!
TH- THAT'S RIGHT!
PLEASE TALK TO THE CHAIRMAN SO THAT WE CAN TERMINATE THE CONTRACT WITH NO HARM DONE.
HE CAUGHT TAKANE OFF GUARD, AND TAKANE DOESN'T KNOW WHAT TO DO.
YOU KNOW, IT'S ONLY ONE YEAR.
PLEASE LIVE WITH US!
WHAT?
DAD IS...
...BEING A DAD!

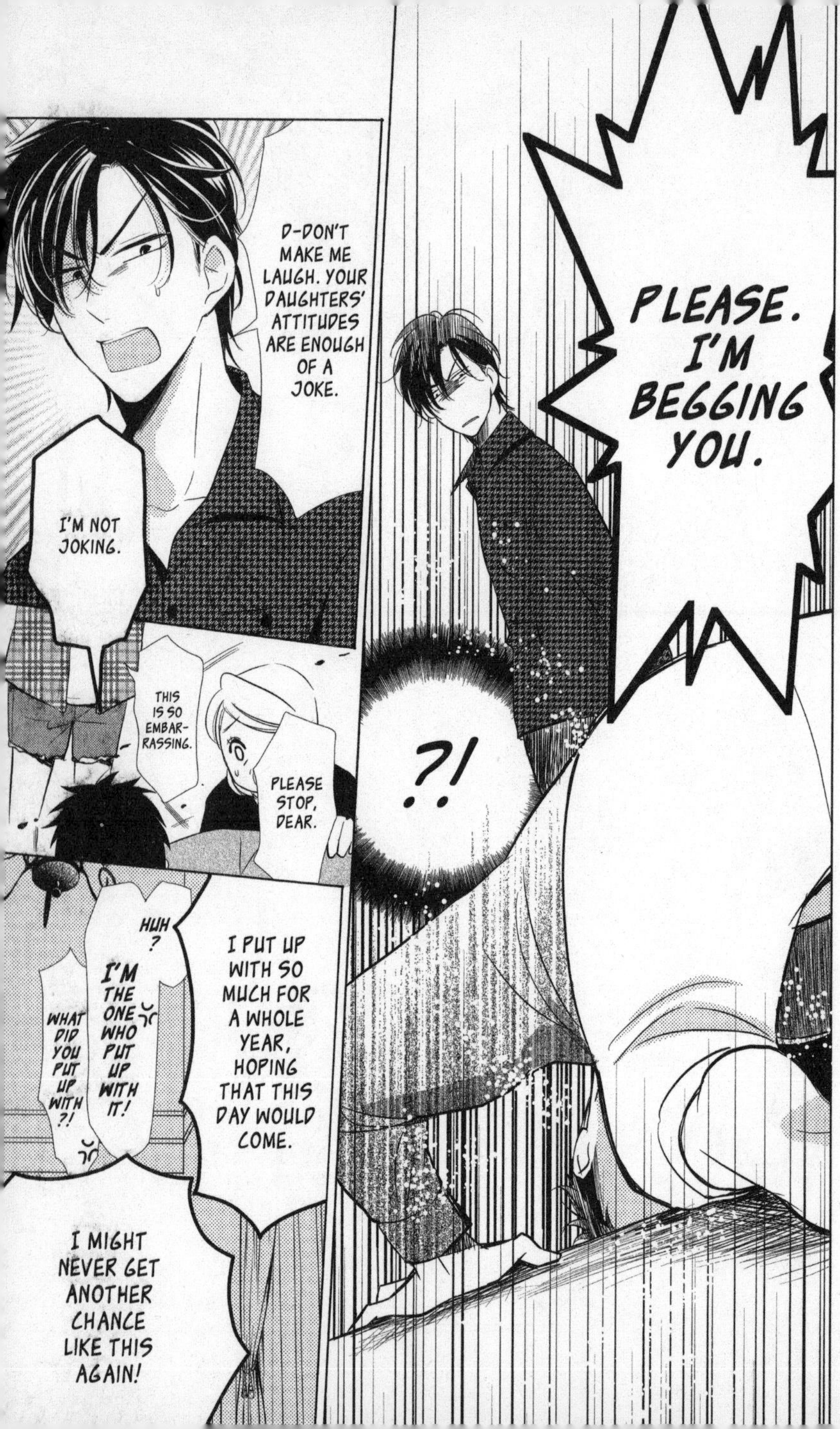
PLEASE. I'M BEGGING YOU.
?!
D-DON'T MAKE ME LAUGH. YOUR DAUGHTERS' ATTITUDES ARE ENOUGH OF A JOKE.
I'M NOT JOKING.
PLEASE STOP, DEAR.
THIS IS SO EMBAR-RASSING.
I PUT UP WITH SO MUCH FOR A WHOLE YEAR, HOPING THAT THIS DAY WOULD COME.
HUH?
I'M THE ONE WHO PUT UP WITH IT!
WHAT DID YOU PUT UP WITH?!
I MIGHT NEVER GET ANOTHER CHANCE LIKE THIS AGAIN!

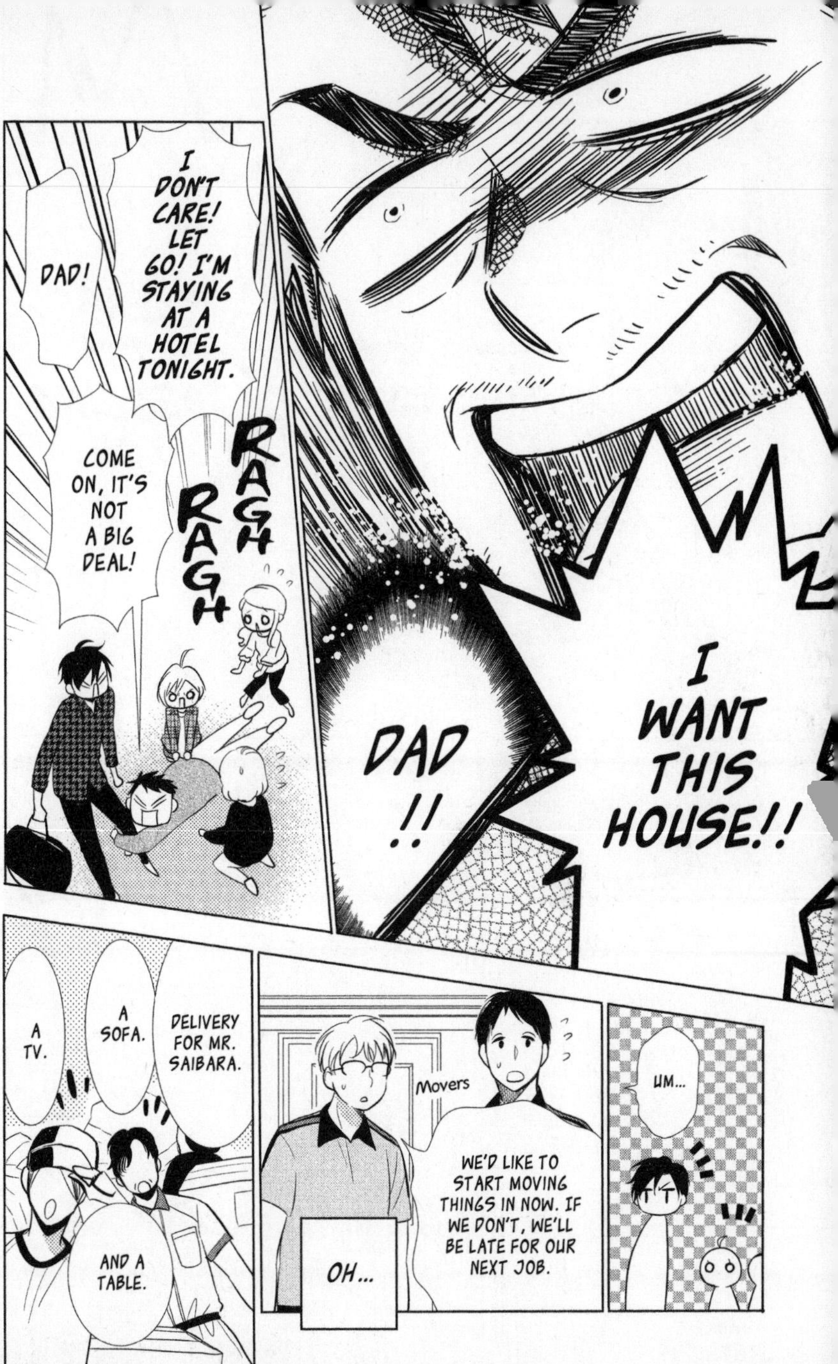
I WANT THIS HOUSE!!
DAD !!
I DON'T CARE! LET GO! I'M STAYING AT A HOTEL TONIGHT.
DAD!
RAGH RAGH
COME ON, IT'S NOT A BIG DEAL!
UM...
Movers
WE'D LIKE TO START MOVING THINGS IN NOW. IF WE DON'T, WE'LL BE LATE FOR OUR NEXT JOB.
OH...
DELIVERY FOR MR. SAIBARA.
A SOFA.
A TV.
AND A TABLE.

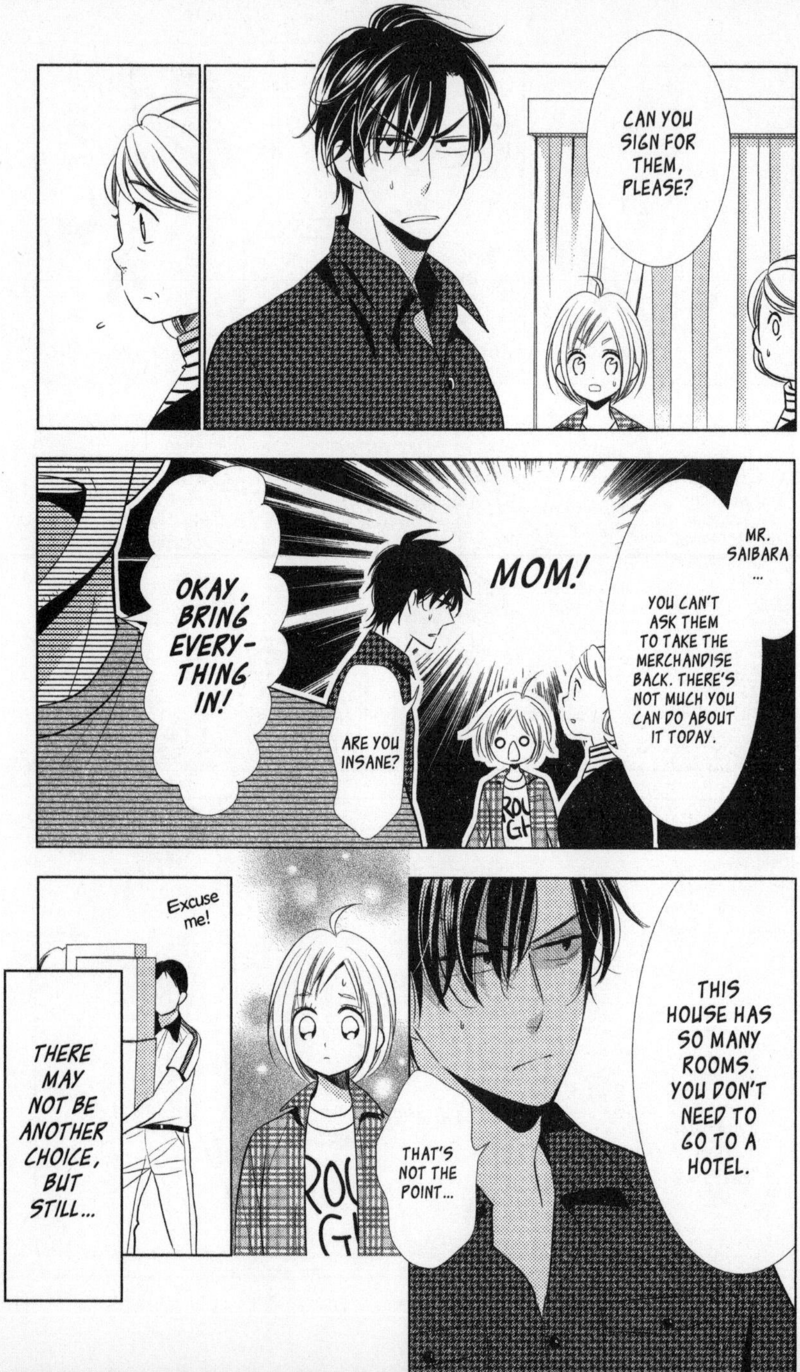
CAN YOU SIGN FOR THEM, PLEASE?
MR. SAIBARA ... YOU CAN'T ASK THEM TO TAKE THE MERCHANDISE BACK. THERE'S NOT MUCH YOU CAN DO ABOUT IT TODAY.
MOM!
OKAY, BRING EVERY-THING IN!
ARE YOU INSANE?
THIS HOUSE HAS SO MANY ROOMS. YOU DON'T NEED TO GO TO A HOTEL.
THAT'S NOT THE POINT...
Excuse me!
THERE MAY NOT BE ANOTHER CHOICE, BUT STILL...

Wow, every single thing...
...is imported.
That goes over there.
Careful with it.
IS THIS REALLY OKAY?
IT'S LIKE WE'RE FORCING HIM INTO THIS.
WHOA—! THE CAR!
GLEAM
I REFUSED TO MOVE HERE IF HE DIDN'T GIVE IT BACK. I'M WAY FARTHER FROM THE STATION NOW.
I refuse to keep taking things lying down.
NOT THAT THIS IS NEW, BUT COMMUTING IN THAT THING IS ABSURD.
JINGLE
HMPH.
I DON'T MEAN IT IN A GOOD WAY!
Wel-come back ... Macho Daruma.
TAKANE! ♡
I MADE YOU SOME COFFEE.
YOU'RE SUPPOSED TO BE HELPING US!

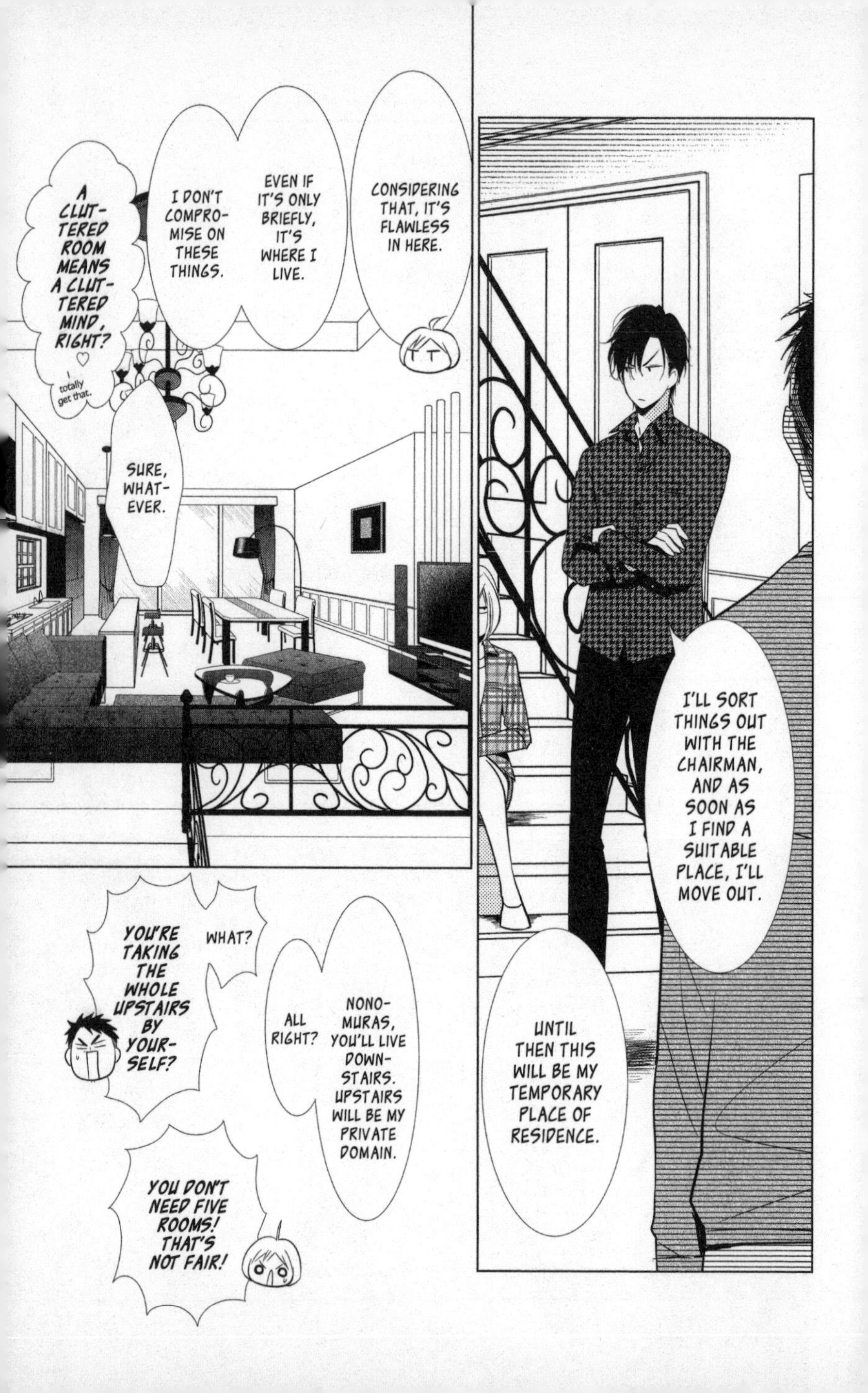
CONSIDERING THAT, IT'S FLAWLESS IN HERE.
EVEN IF IT'S ONLY BRIEFLY, IT'S WHERE I LIVE.
I DON'T COMPRO-MISE ON THESE THINGS.
A CLUT-TERED ROOM MEANS A CLUT-TERED MIND, RIGHT? ♡
I totally get that.
SURE, WHAT-EVER.
I'LL SORT THINGS OUT WITH THE CHAIRMAN, AND AS SOON AS I FIND A SUITABLE PLACE, I'LL MOVE OUT.
UNTIL THEN THIS WILL BE MY TEMPORARY PLACE OF RESIDENCE.
NONO-MURAS, YOU'LL LIVE DOWN-STAIRS. UPSTAIRS WILL BE MY PRIVATE DOMAIN.
ALL RIGHT?
WHAT?
YOU'RE TAKING THE WHOLE UPSTAIRS BY YOUR-SELF?
YOU DON'T NEED FIVE ROOMS! THAT'S NOT FAIR!

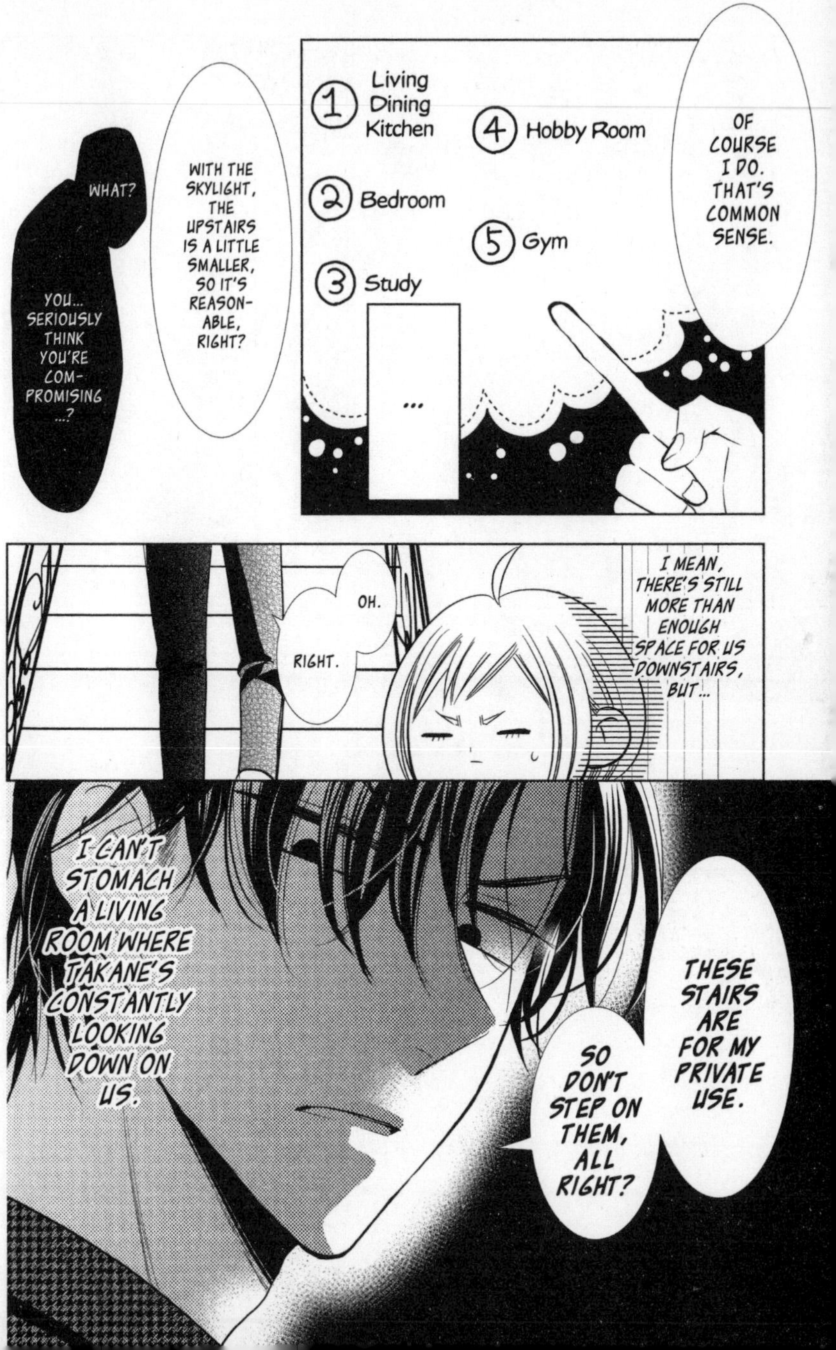
OF COURSE I DO. THAT'S COMMON SENSE.
1 Living Dining Kitchen
4 Hobby Room
2 Bedroom
5 Gym
3 Study
...
WITH THE SKYLIGHT, THE UPSTAIRS IS A LITTLE SMALLER, SO IT'S REASON-ABLE, RIGHT?
WHAT?
YOU... SERIOUSLY THINK YOU'RE COM-PROMISING ...?
I MEAN, THERE'S STILL MORE THAN ENOUGH SPACE FOR US DOWNSTAIRS, BUT...
OH.
RIGHT.
THESE STAIRS ARE FOR MY PRIVATE USE.
SO DON'T STEP ON THEM, ALL RIGHT?
I CAN'T STOMACH A LIVING ROOM WHERE TAKANE'S CONSTANTLY LOOKING DOWN ON US.

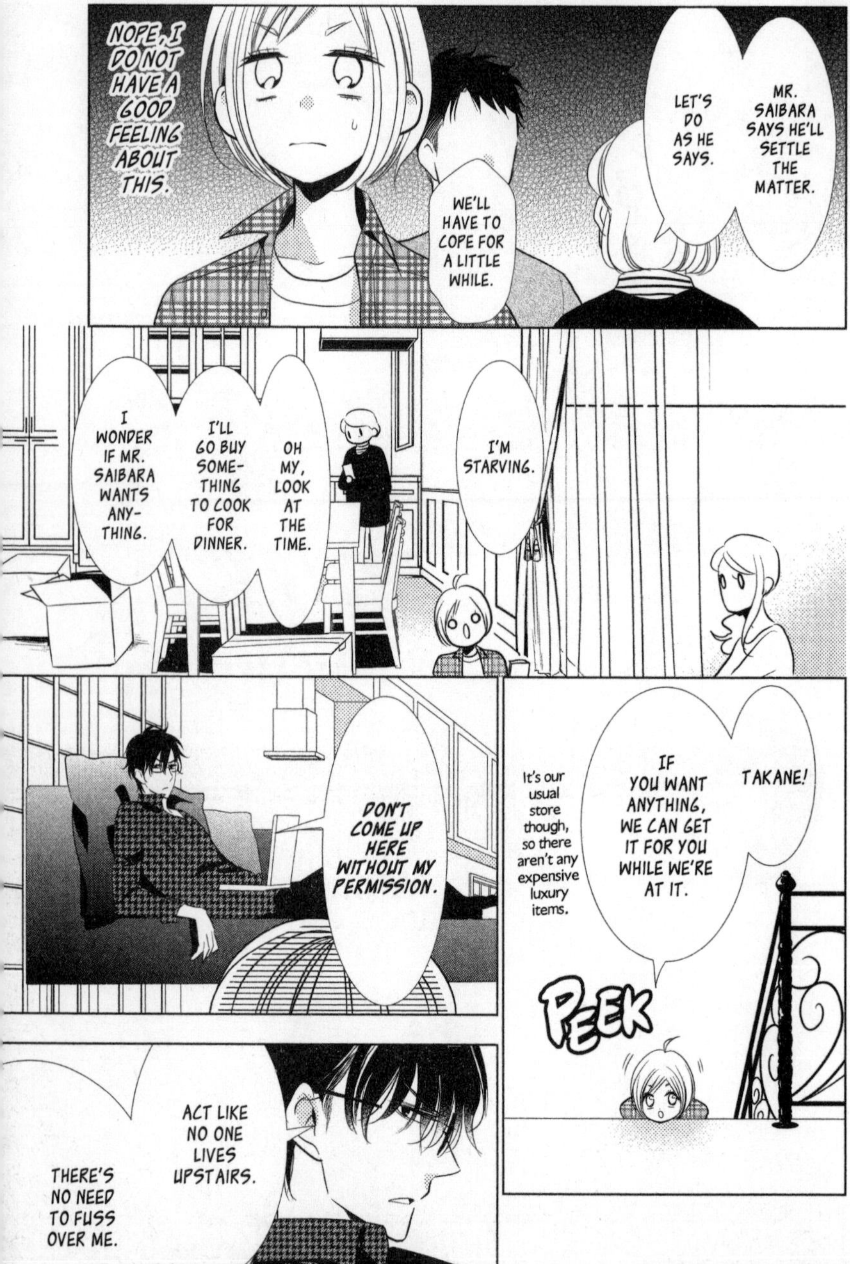
MR. SAIBARA SAYS HE'LL SETTLE THE MATTER.
LET'S DO AS HE SAYS.
WE'LL HAVE TO COPE FOR A LITTLE WHILE.
NOPE, I DO NOT HAVE A GOOD FEELING ABOUT THIS.
I'M STARVING.
OH MY, LOOK AT THE TIME.
I'LL GO BUY SOME-THING TO COOK FOR DINNER.
I WONDER IF MR. SAIBARA WANTS ANY-THING.
TAKANE!
IF YOU WANT ANYTHING, WE CAN GET IT FOR YOU WHILE WE'RE AT IT.
It's our usual store though, so there aren't any expensive luxury items.
PEEK
DON'T COME UP HERE WITHOUT MY PERMISSION.
ACT LIKE NO ONE LIVES UPSTAIRS.
THERE'S NO NEED TO FUSS OVER ME.

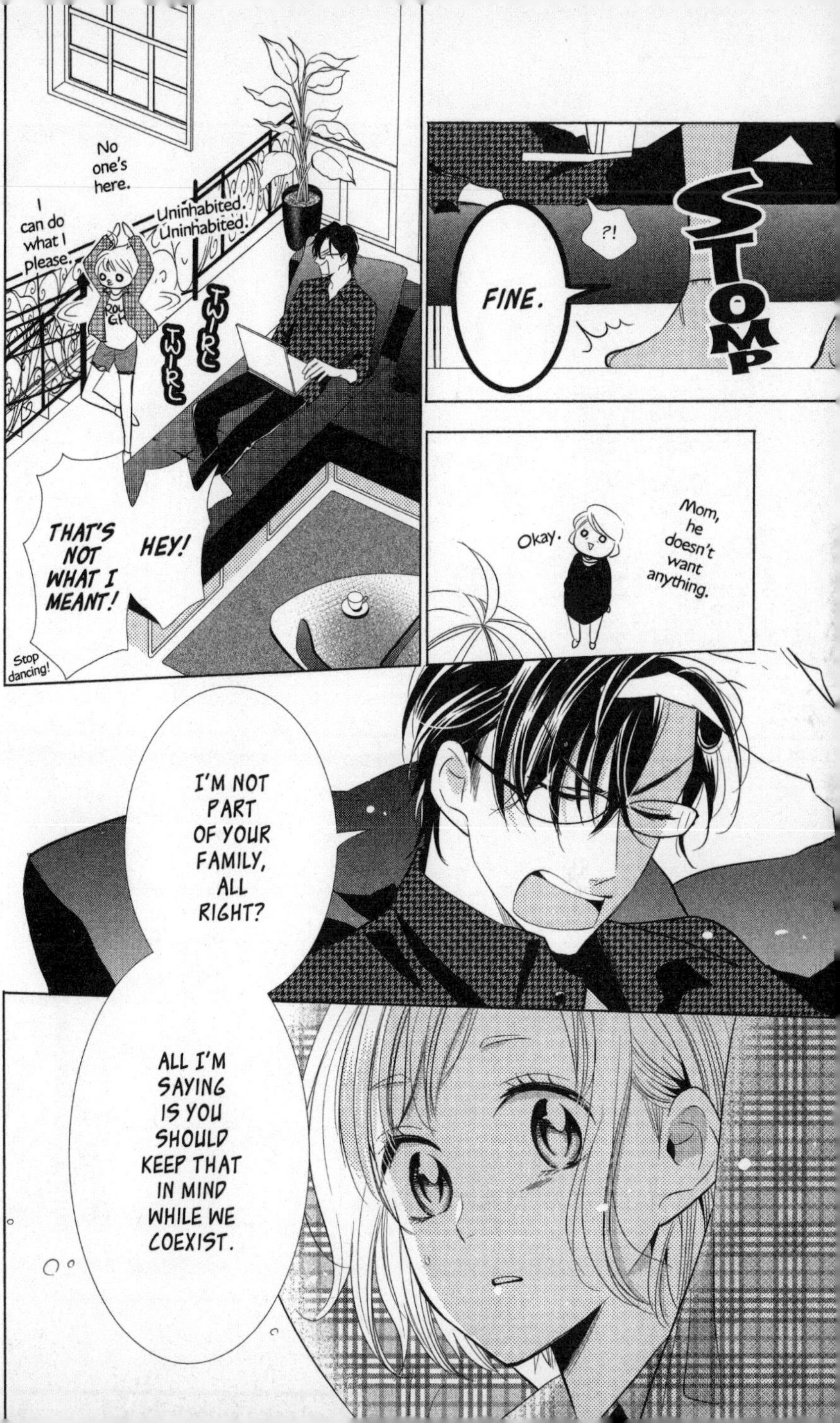

STOMP
?!
FINE.
Mom, he doesn't want anything.
Okay.
Uninhabited. Uninhabited!
No one's here.
I can do what I please.
TWIRL
TWIRL
HEY!
THAT'S NOT WHAT I MEANT!
Stop dancing!
I'M NOT PART OF YOUR FAMILY, ALL RIGHT?
ALL I'M SAYING IS YOU SHOULD KEEP THAT IN MIND WHILE WE COEXIST.

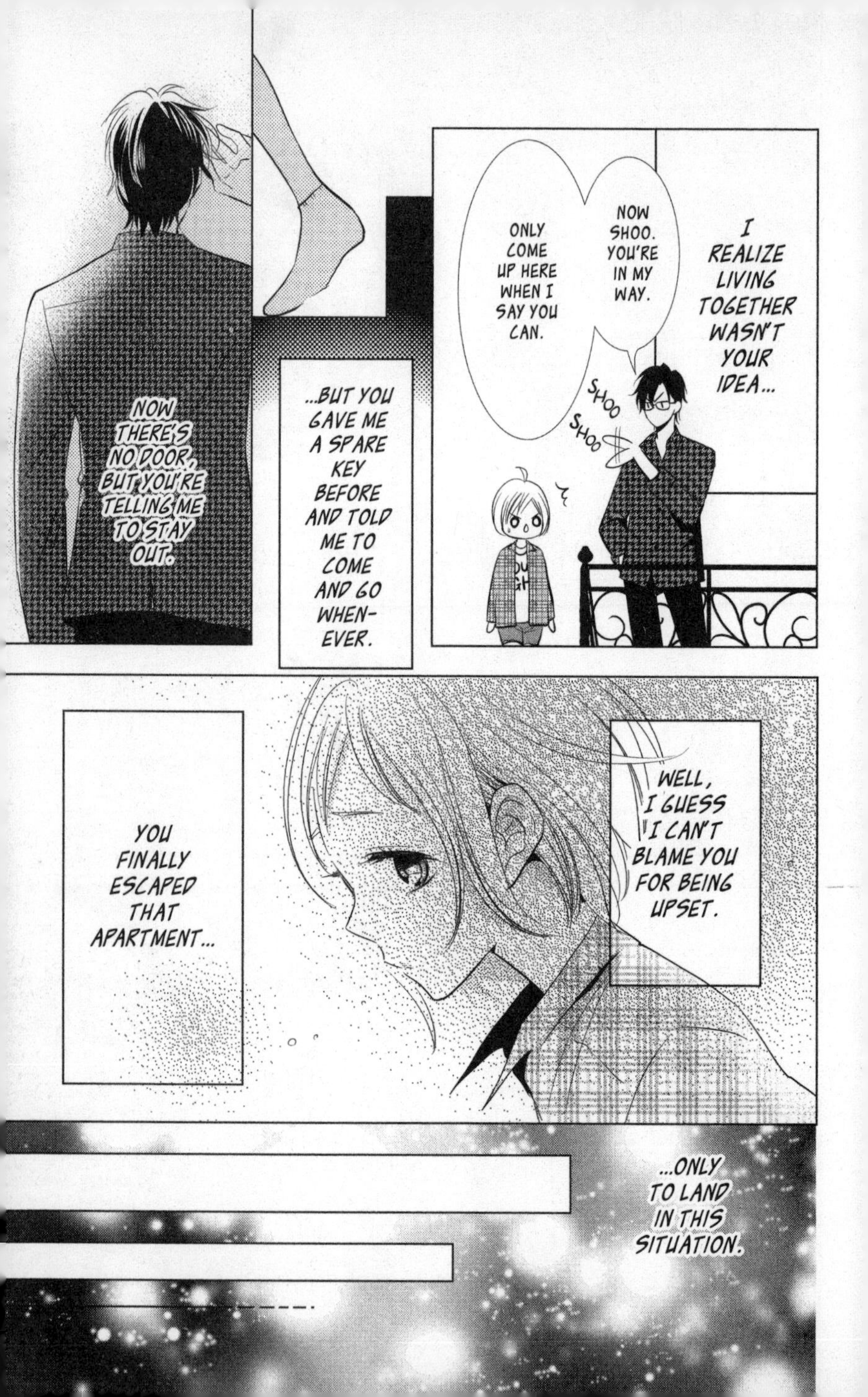
I REALIZE LIVING TOGETHER WASN'T YOUR IDEA...
NOW SHOO. YOU'RE IN MY WAY.
ONLY COME UP HERE WHEN I SAY YOU CAN.
SHOO SHOO
...BUT YOU GAVE ME A SPARE KEY BEFORE AND TOLD ME TO COME AND GO WHENEVER.
NOW THERE'S NO DOOR, BUT YOU'RE TELLING ME TO STAY OUT.
WELL, I GUESS I CAN'T BLAME YOU FOR BEING UPSET.
YOU FINALLY ESCAPED THAT APARTMENT...
...ONLY TO LAND IN THIS SITUATION.

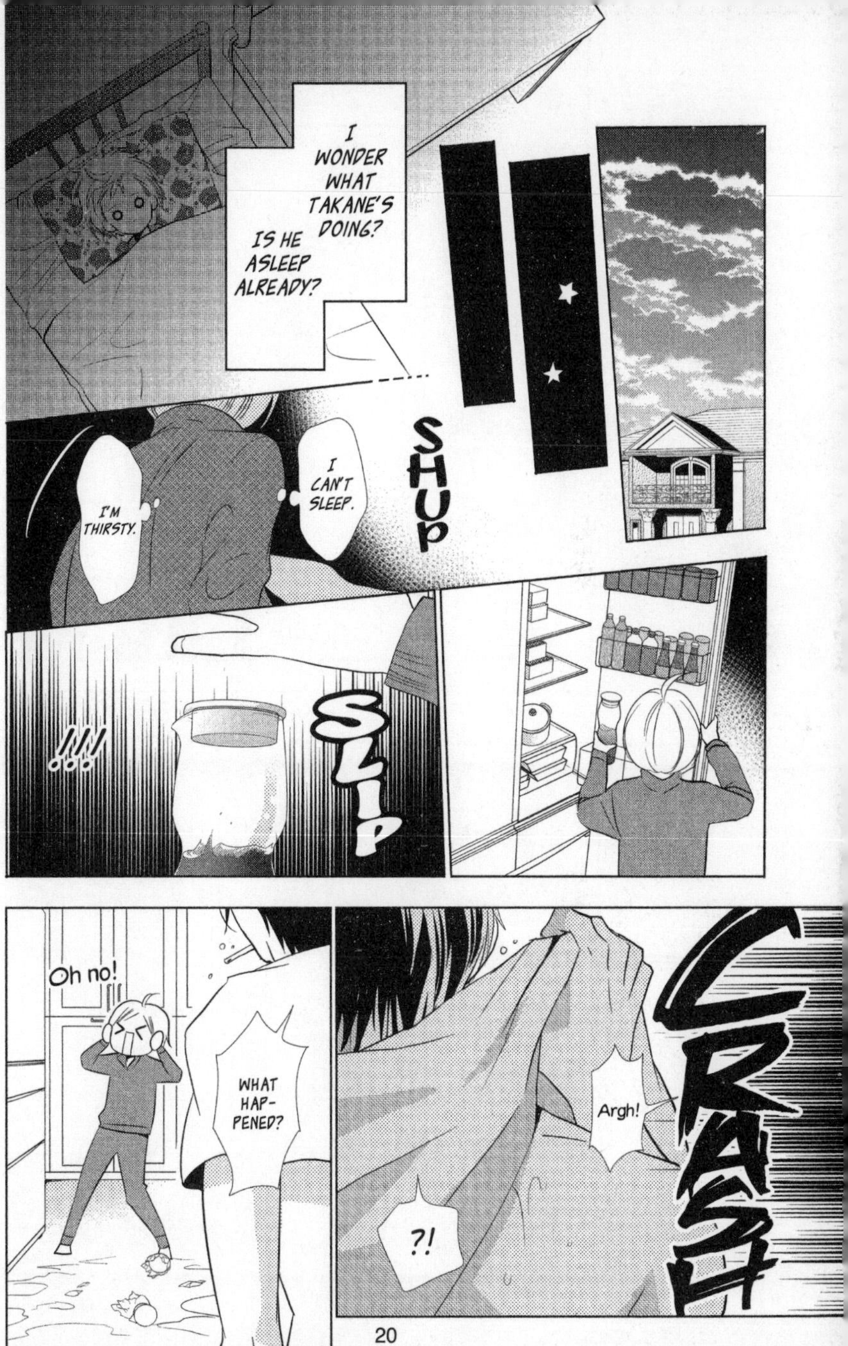
I WONDER WHAT TAKANE'S DOING?
IS HE ASLEEP ALREADY?
SHUP
I CAN'T SLEEP.
I'M THIRSTY.
SLIP
!!!
CRASH
Argh!
?!
Oh no!
WHAT HAP-PENED?

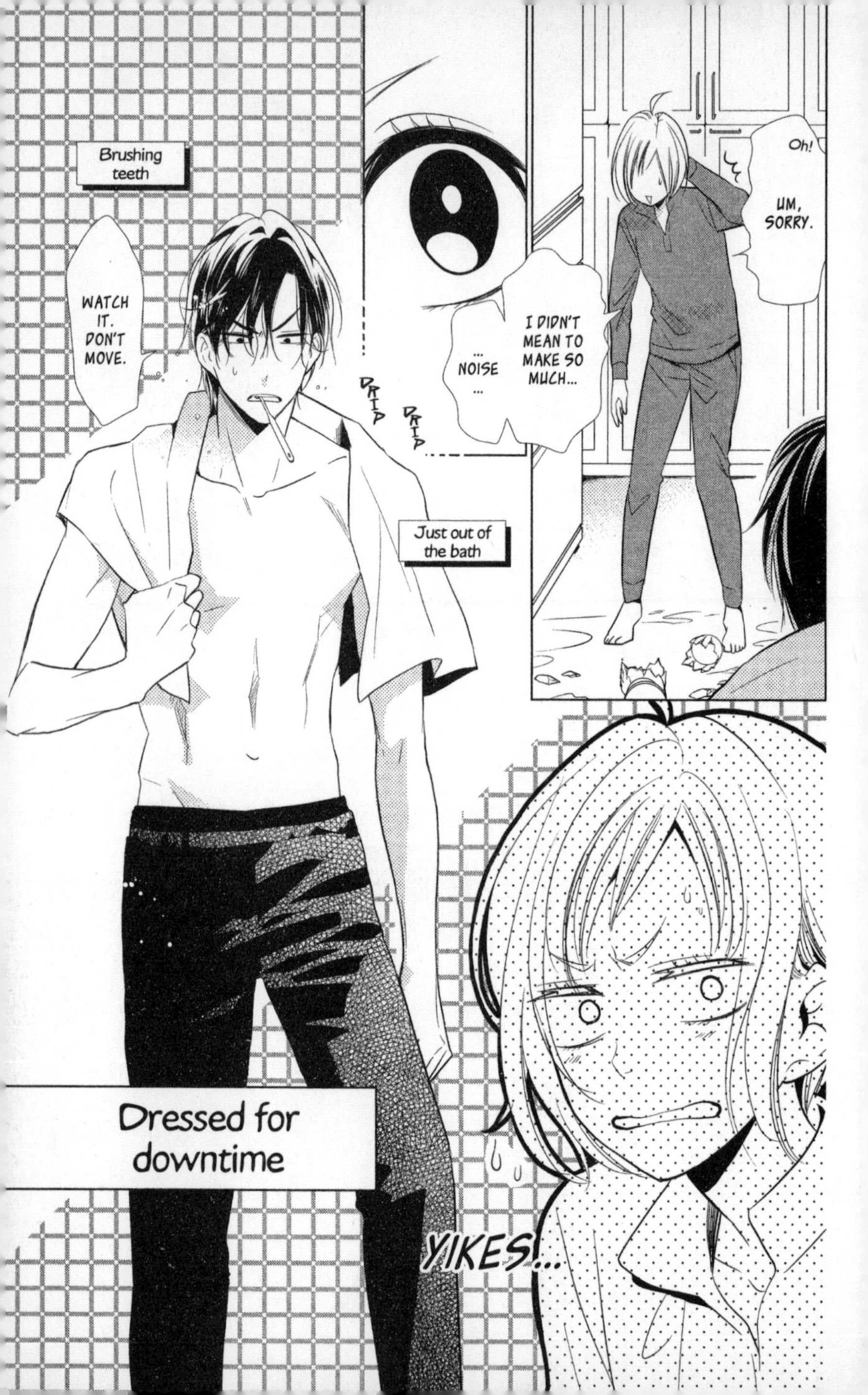
Oh!
UM, SORRY.
I DIDN'T MEAN TO MAKE SO MUCH...
... NOISE ...
DRIP DRIP
YIKES...
Brushing teeth
WATCH IT. DON'T MOVE.
Just out of the bath
Dressed for downtime

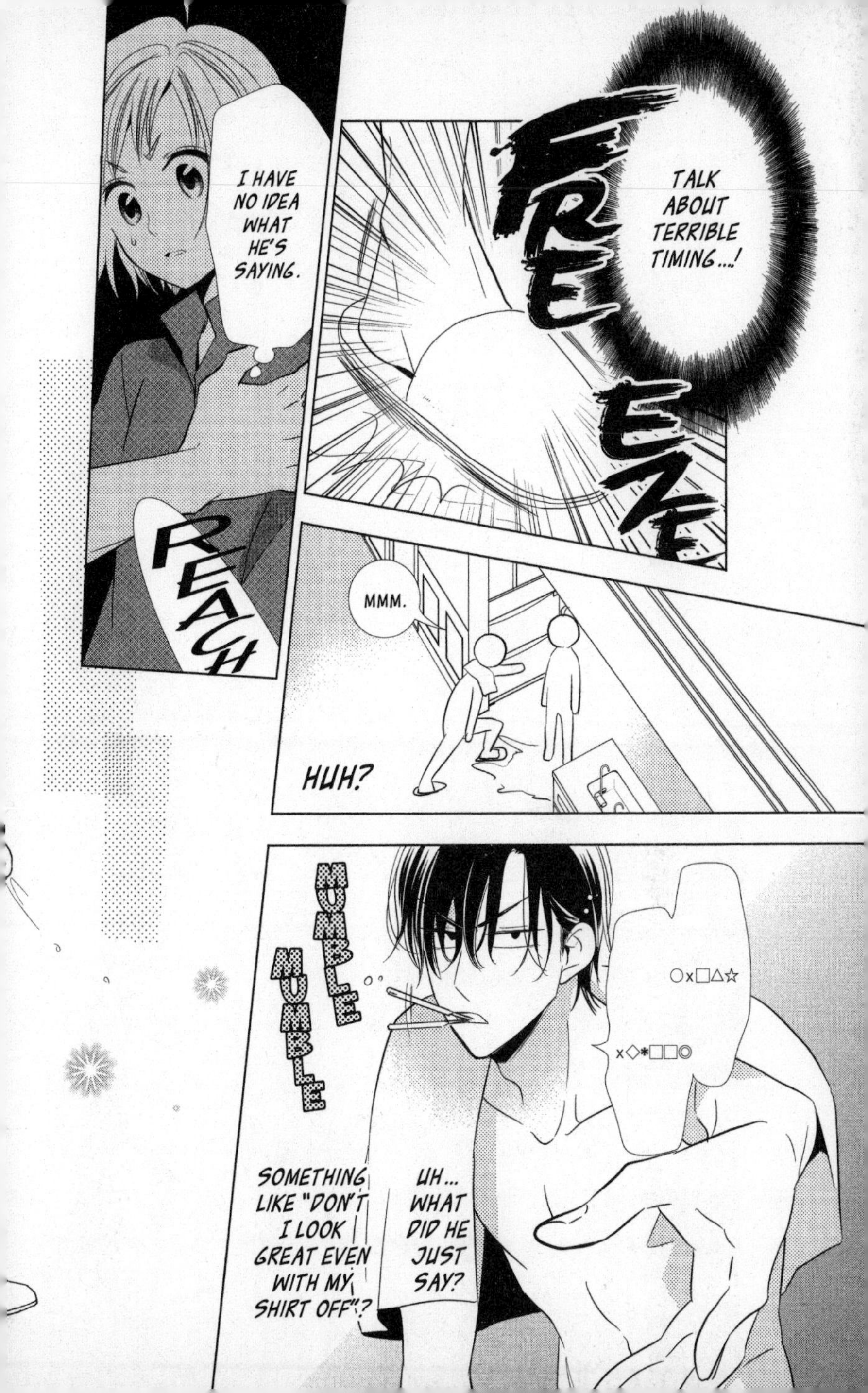
FREEZE
TALK ABOUT TERRIBLE TIMING...!
MMM.
HUH?
I HAVE NO IDEA WHAT HE'S SAYING.
REACH
○x□△☆
x◇*□□◎
MUMBLE
MUMBLE
UH... WHAT DID HE JUST SAY?
SOMETHING LIKE "DON'T I LOOK GREAT EVEN WITH MY SHIRT OFF"?

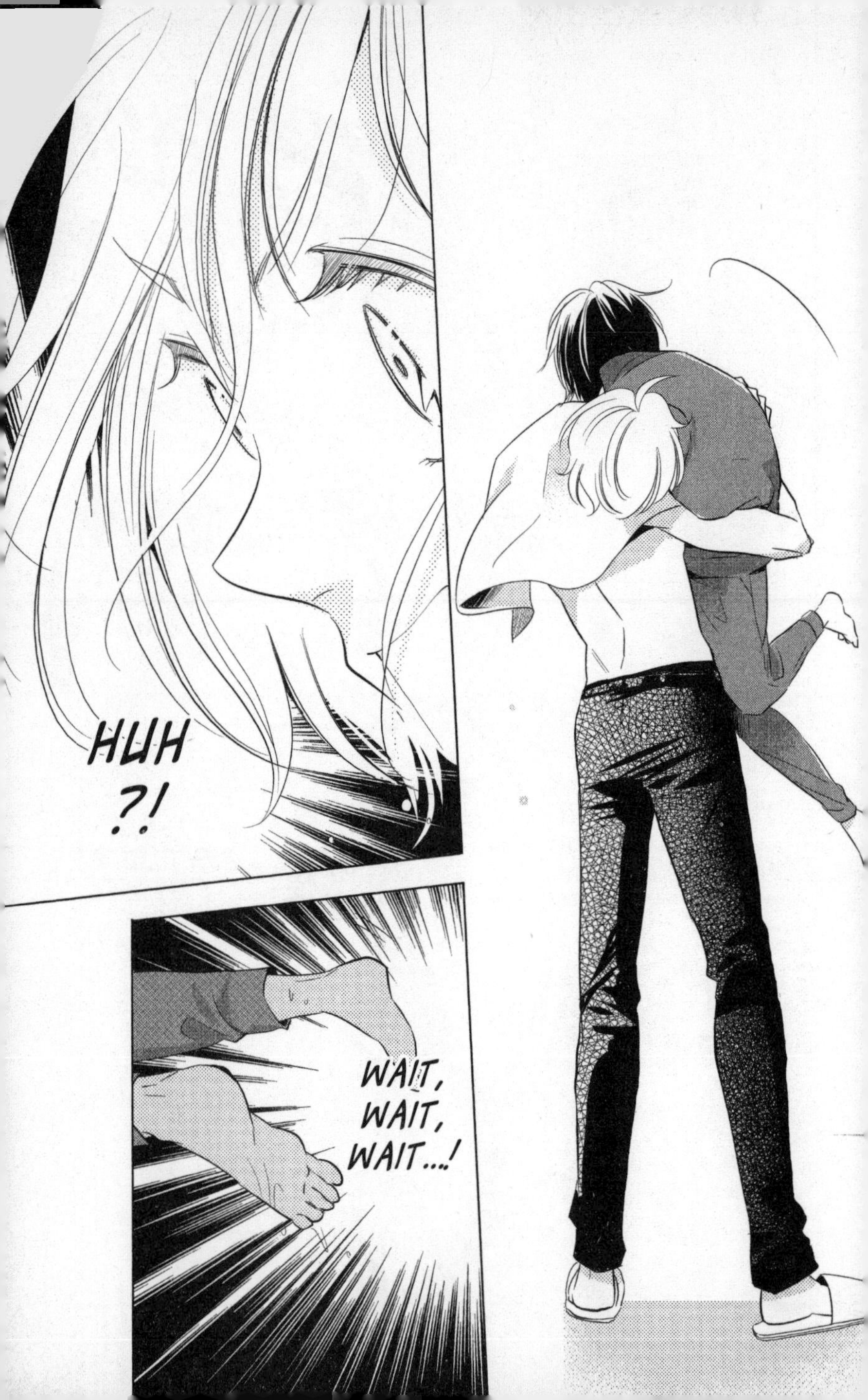
HUH ?!
WAIT, WAIT, WAIT...!

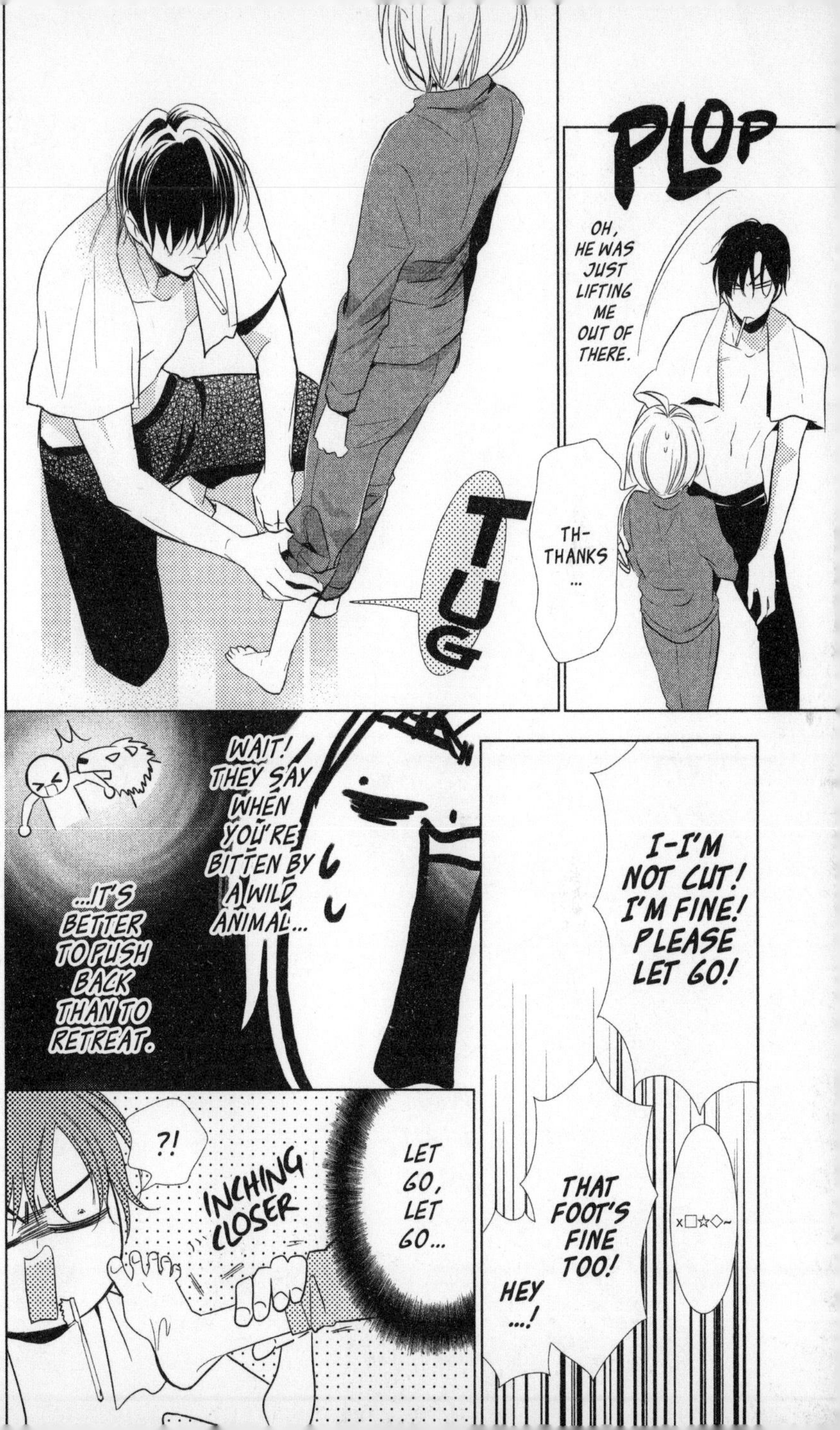
PLOP
OH, HE WAS JUST LIFTING ME OUT OF THERE.
TH-THANKS...
TUG
I-I'M NOT CUT! I'M FINE! PLEASE LET GO!
x□☆◇~
THAT FOOT'S FINE TOO!
HEY...!
WAIT! THEY SAY WHEN YOU'RE BITTEN BY A WILD ANIMAL...
...IT'S BETTER TO PUSH BACK THAN TO RETREAT.
LET GO, LET GO...
INCHING CLOSER
?!

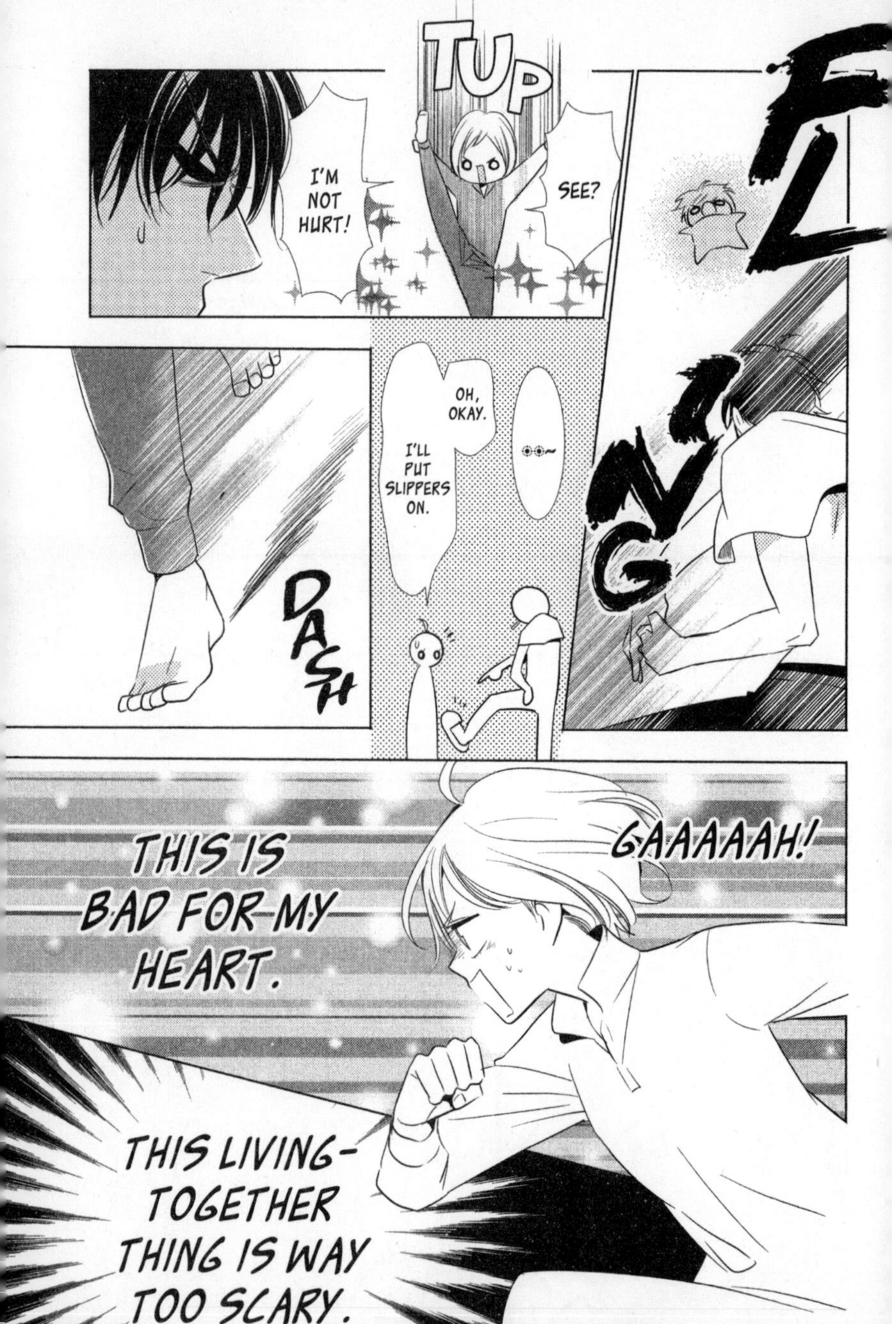
FLING
TUP
SEE?
I'M NOT HURT!
OH, OKAY.
I'LL PUT SLIPPERS ON.
DASH
GAAAAAH!
THIS IS BAD FOR MY HEART.
THIS LIVING-TOGETHER THING IS WAY TOO SCARY.

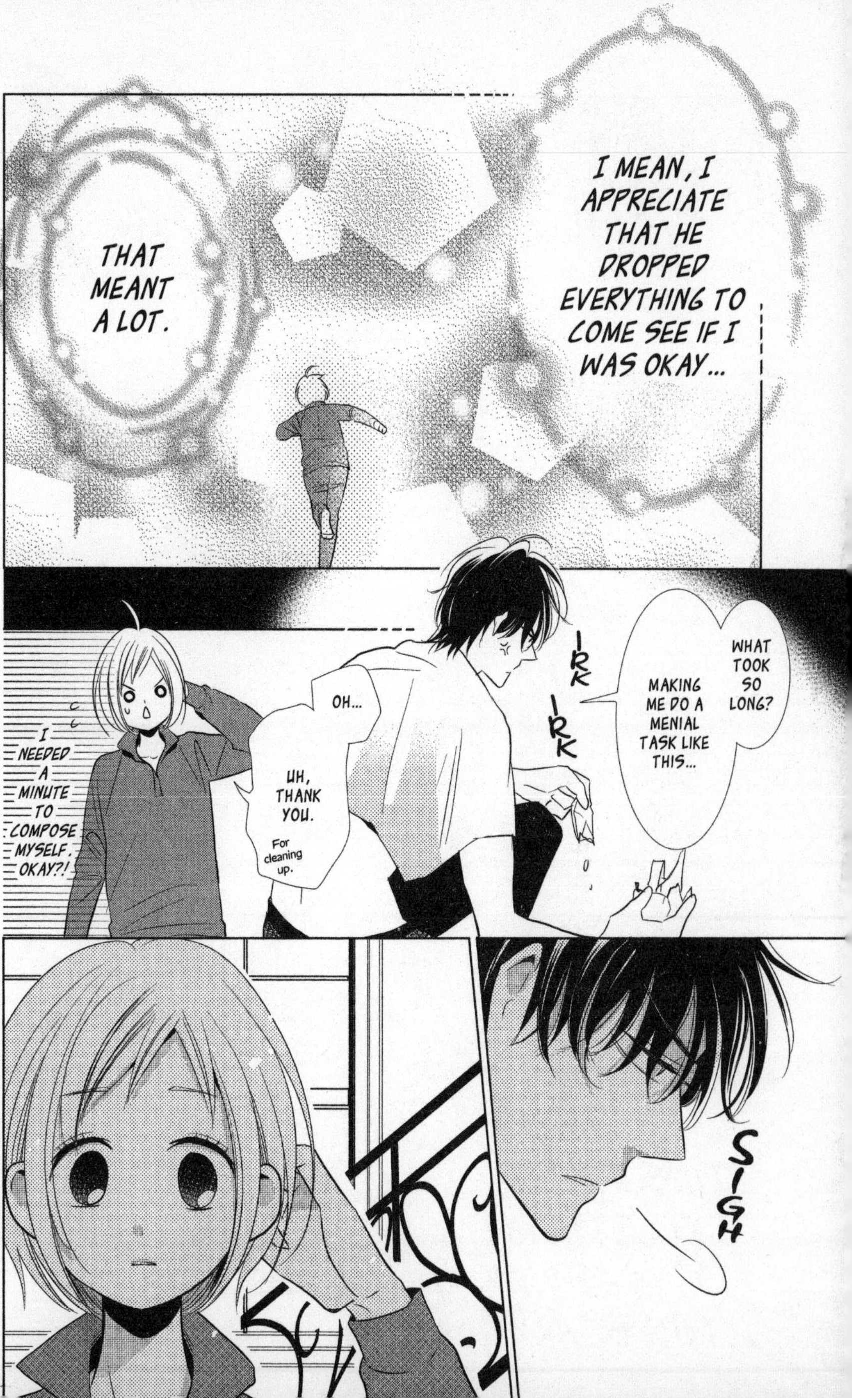
I MEAN, I APPRECIATE THAT HE DROPPED EVERYTHING TO COME SEE IF I WAS OKAY...
THAT MEANT A LOT.
WHAT TOOK SO LONG?
MAKING ME DO A MENIAL TASK LIKE THIS...
IRK IRK
OH...
UH, THANK YOU.
For cleaning up.
I NEEDED A MINUTE TO COMPOSE MYSELF. OKAY?!
SIGH

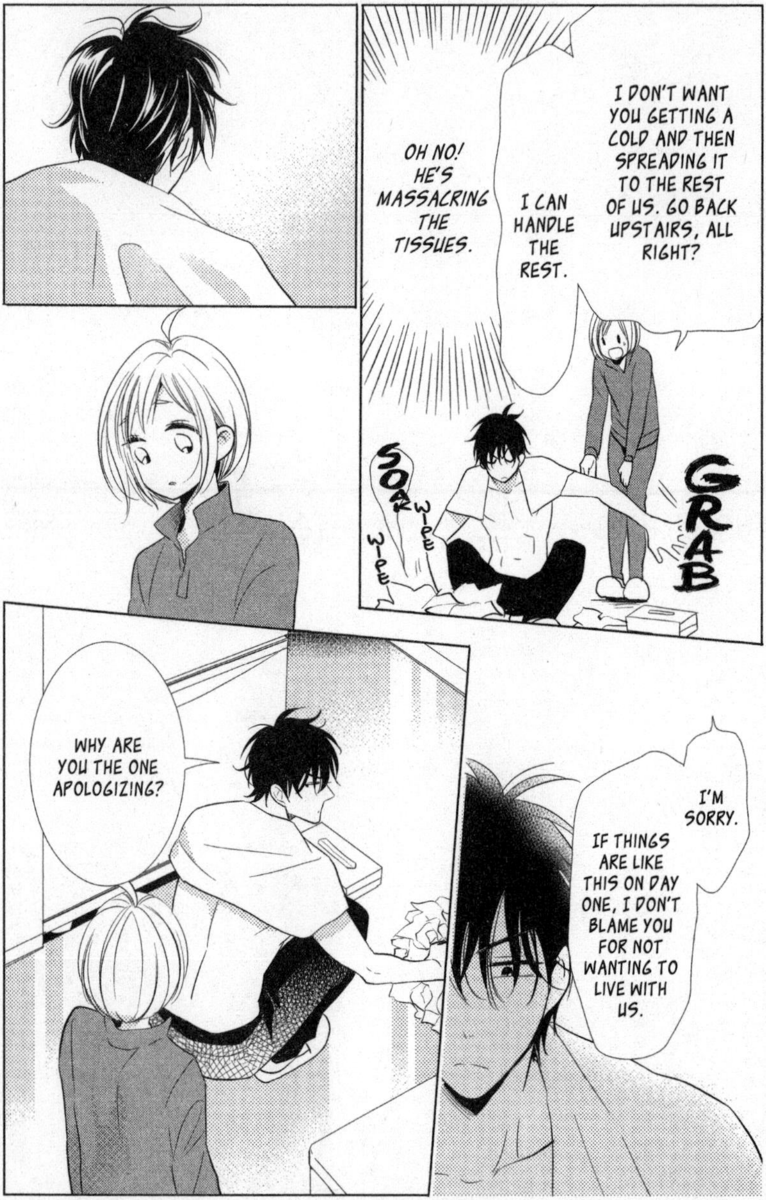
I DON'T WANT YOU GETTING A COLD AND THEN SPREADING IT TO THE REST OF US. GO BACK UPSTAIRS, ALL RIGHT?
I CAN HANDLE THE REST.
OH NO! HE'S MASSACRING THE TISSUES.
GRAB
SOAK
WIPE
WIPE
I'M SORRY.
IF THINGS ARE LIKE THIS ON DAY ONE, I DON'T BLAME YOU FOR NOT WANTING TO LIVE WITH US.
WHY ARE YOU THE ONE APOLOGIZING?

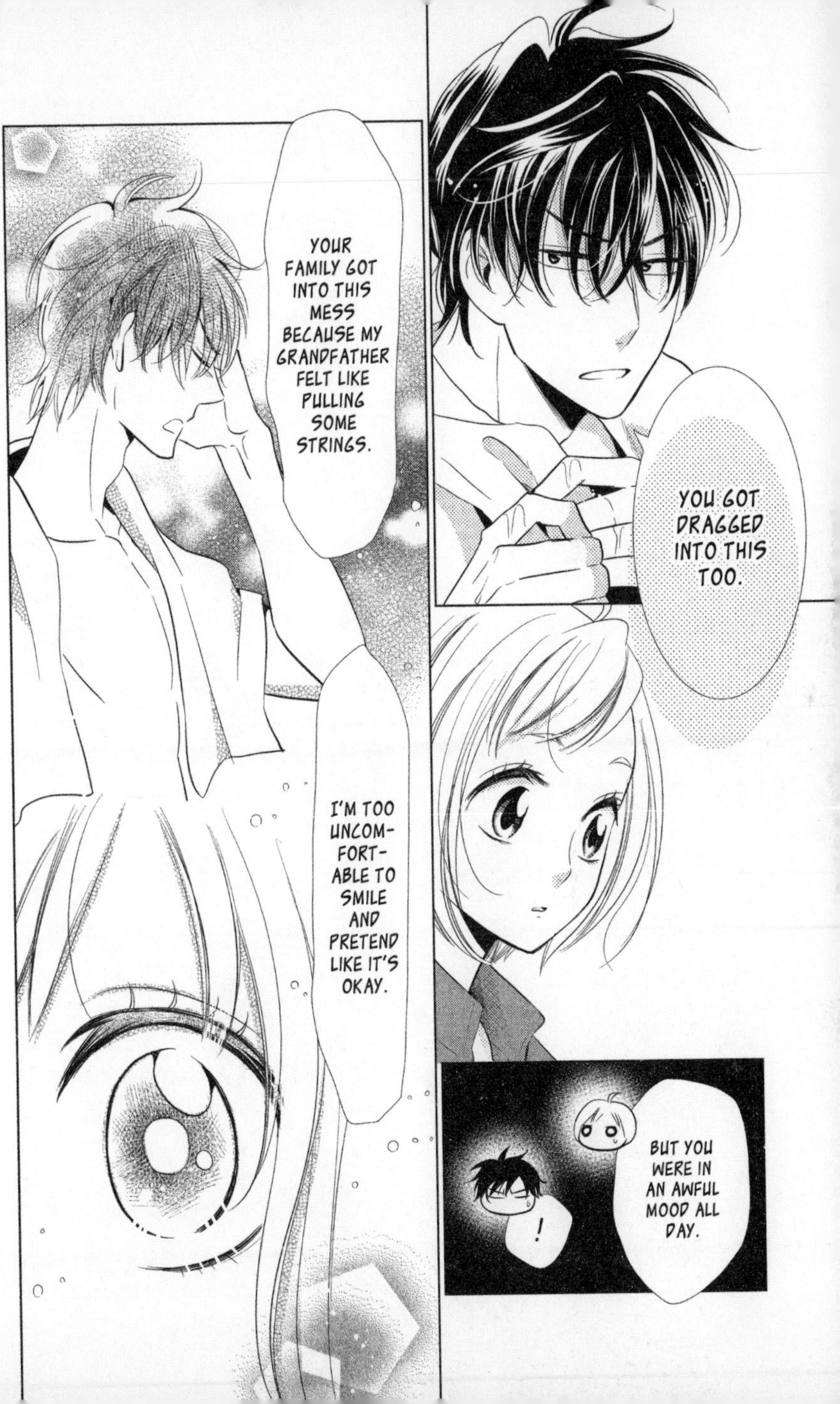
YOU GOT DRAGGED INTO THIS TOO.
!
BUT YOU WERE IN AN AWFUL MOOD ALL DAY.
YOUR FAMILY GOT INTO THIS MESS BECAUSE MY GRANDFATHER FELT LIKE PULLING SOME STRINGS.
I'M TOO UNCOM-FORT-ABLE TO SMILE AND PRETEND LIKE IT'S OKAY.

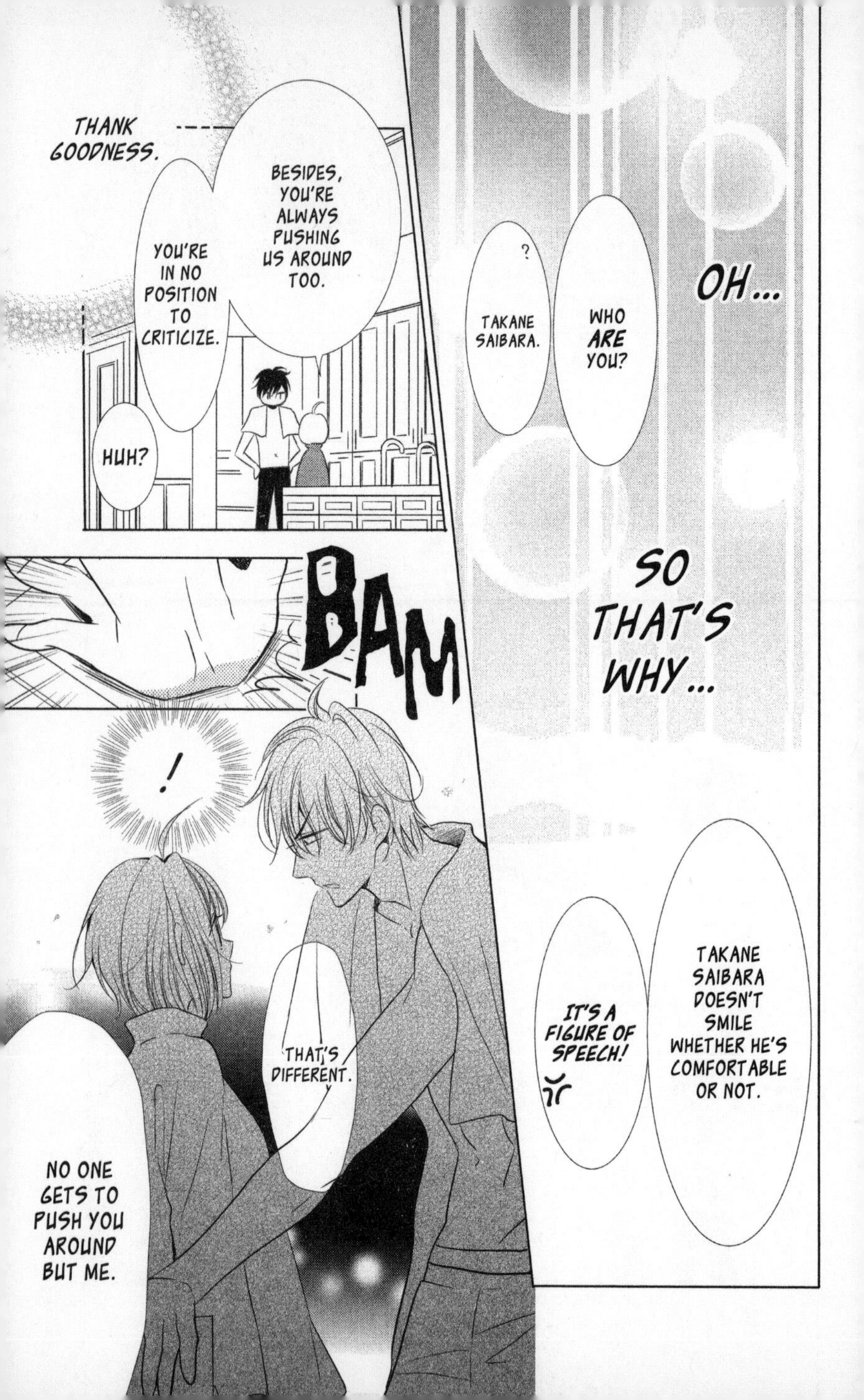
OH...
WHO ARE YOU?
TAKANE SAIBARA.
?
SO THAT'S WHY...
TAKANE SAIBARA DOESN'T SMILE WHETHER HE'S COMFORTABLE OR NOT.
IT'S A FIGURE OF SPEECH!
THANK GOODNESS.
BESIDES, YOU'RE ALWAYS PUSHING US AROUND TOO.
YOU'RE IN NO POSITION TO CRITICIZE.
HUH?
BAM
!
THAT'S DIFFERENT.
NO ONE GETS TO PUSH YOU AROUND BUT ME.

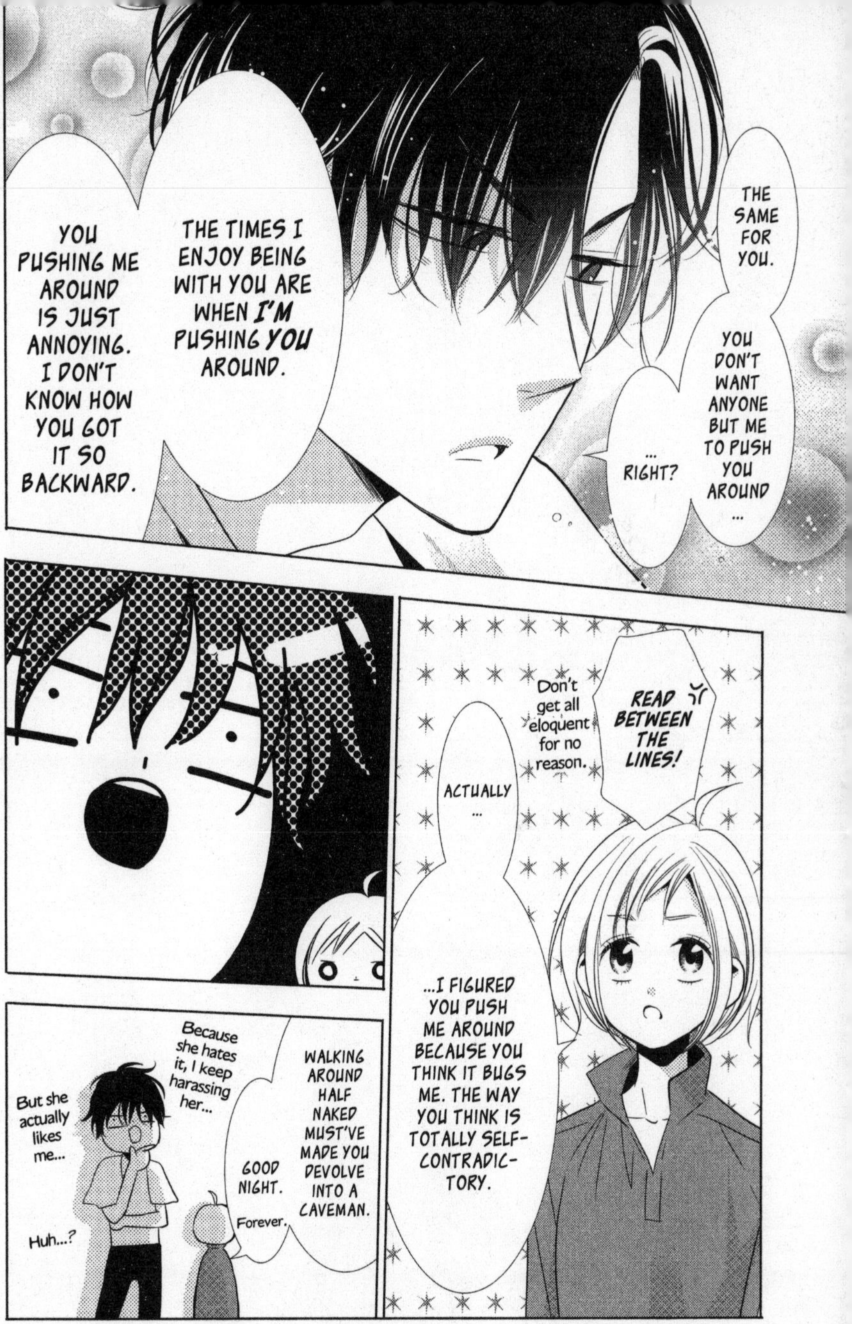
THE SAME FOR YOU.
YOU DON'T WANT ANYONE BUT ME TO PUSH YOU AROUND...
...RIGHT?
THE TIMES I ENJOY BEING WITH YOU ARE WHEN I'M PUSHING YOU AROUND.
YOU PUSHING ME AROUND IS JUST ANNOYING. I DON'T KNOW HOW YOU GOT IT SO BACKWARD.
READ BETWEEN THE LINES!
Don't get all eloquent for no reason.
ACTUALLY...
...I FIGURED YOU PUSH ME AROUND BECAUSE YOU THINK IT BUGS ME. THE WAY YOU THINK IS TOTALLY SELF-CONTRADICTORY.
WALKING AROUND HALF NAKED MUST'VE MADE YOU DEVOLVE INTO A CAVEMAN.
GOOD NIGHT.
Forever.
Because she hates it, I keep harassing her...
But she actually likes me...
Huh...?

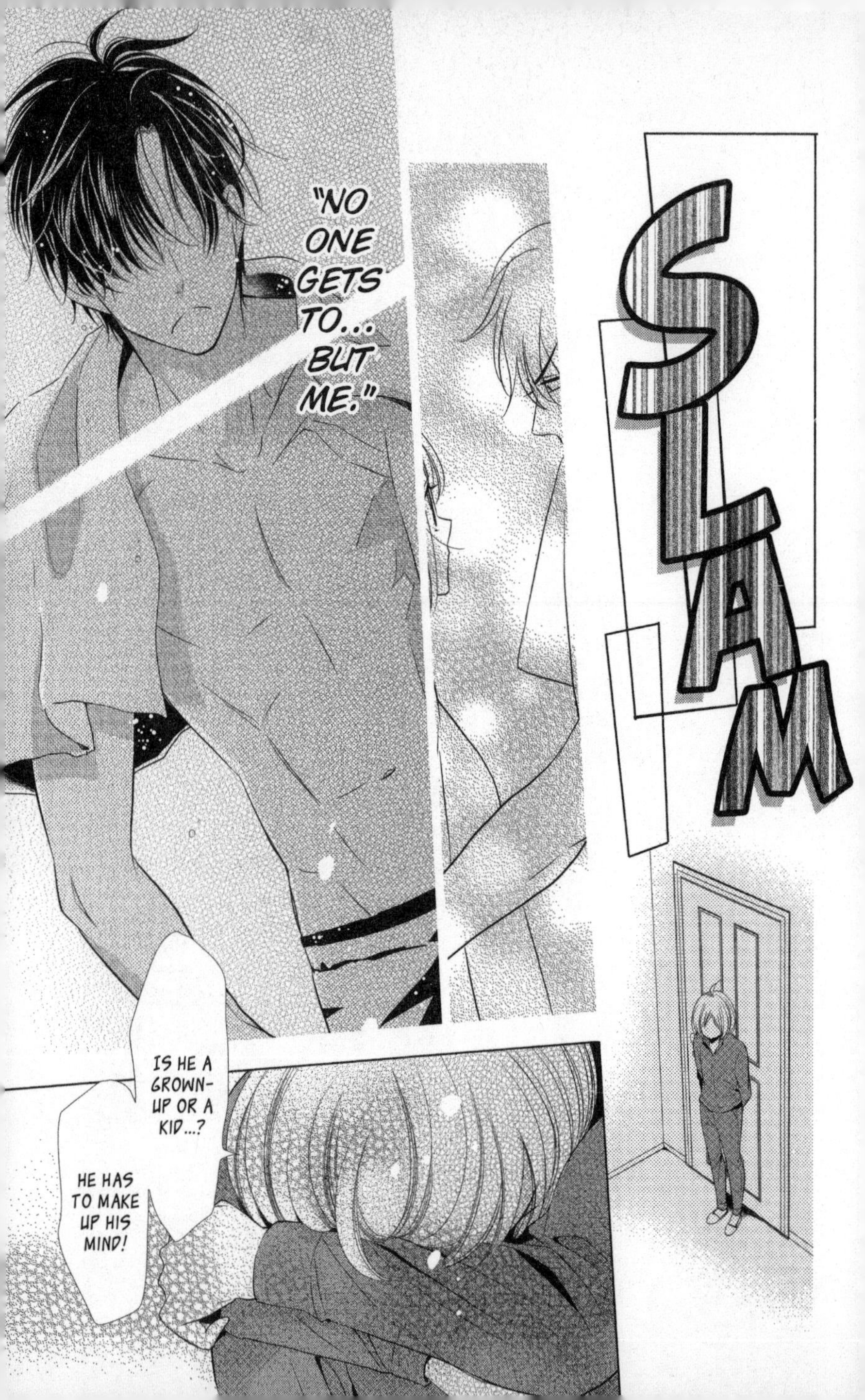
SLAM
"NO ONE GETS TO... BUT ME."
IS HE A GROWN-UP OR A KID...?
HE HAS TO MAKE UP HIS MIND!

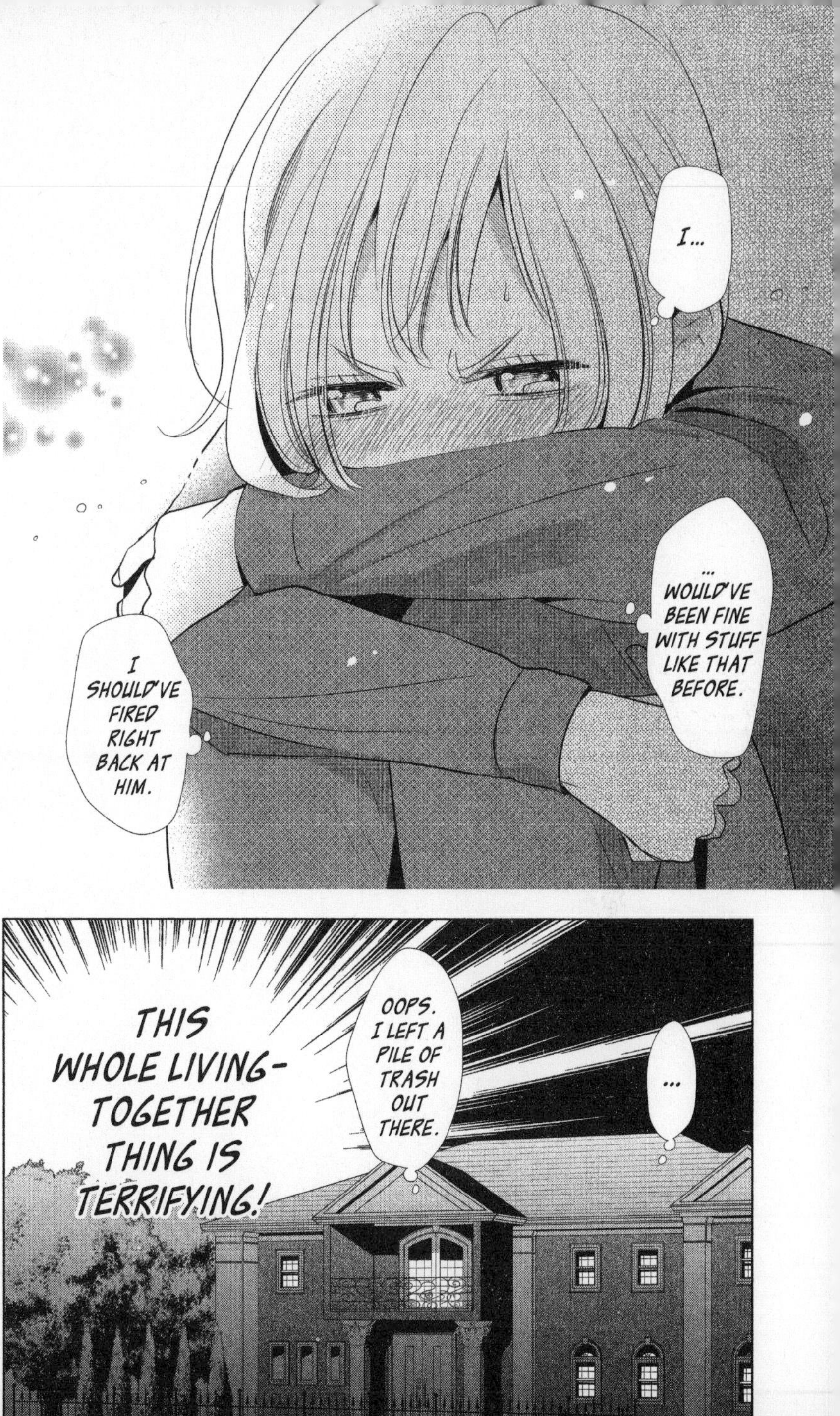
I...
...WOULD'VE BEEN FINE WITH STUFF LIKE THAT BEFORE.
I SHOULD'VE FIRED RIGHT BACK AT HIM.
...
OOPS. I LEFT A PILE OF TRASH OUT THERE.
THIS WHOLE LIVING-TOGETHER THING IS TERRIFYING!

Chapter 47

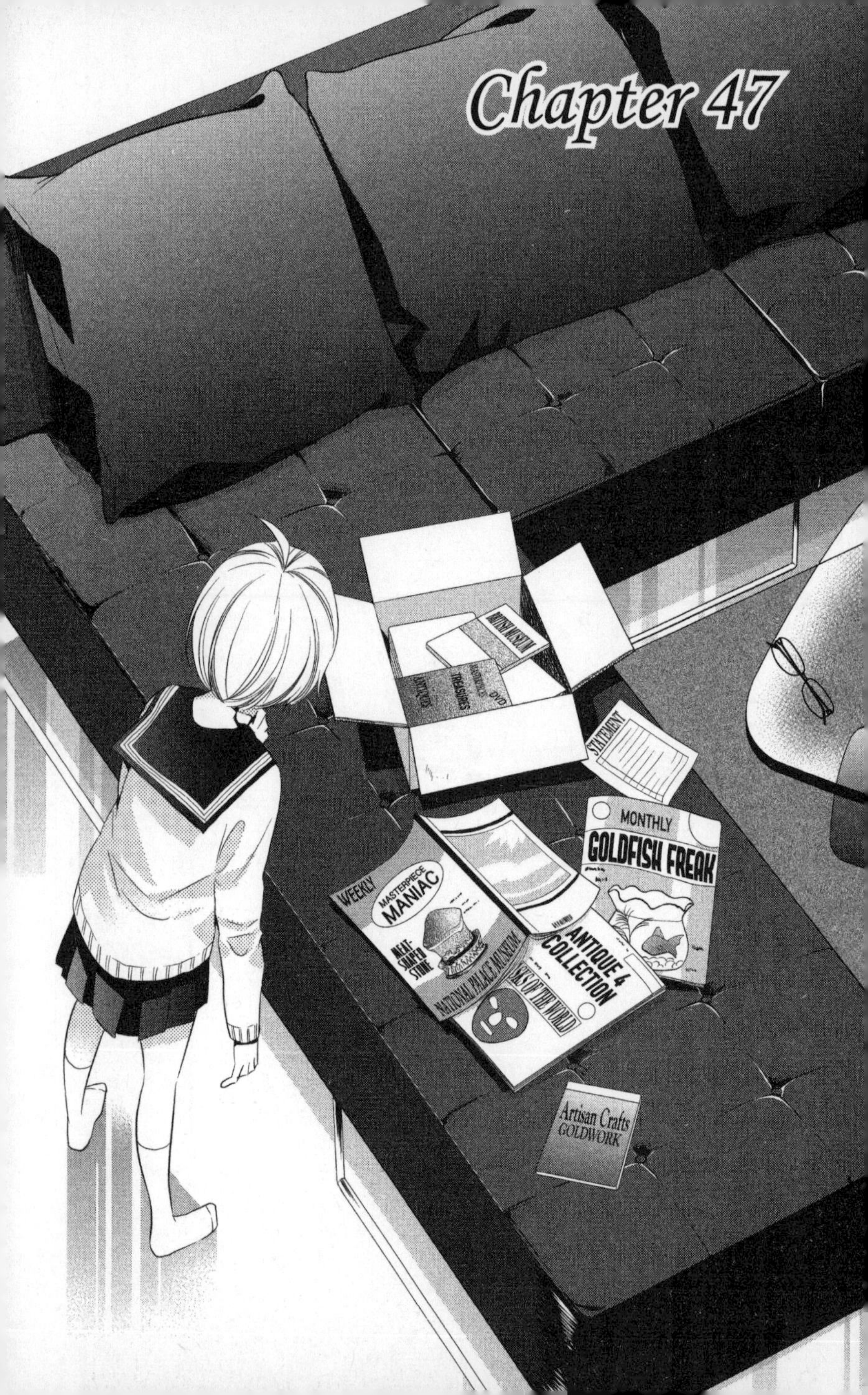

BRITISH MUSEUM
TREASURES
ANTIQUES
DVD
STATEMENT
MONTHLY
GOLDFISH FREAK
WEEKLY
MASTERPIECE MANIAC
MEAT-SHAPED STONE
NATIONAL PALACE MUSEUM
ANTIQUE 4 COLLECTION
Artisan Crafts
GOLDWORK

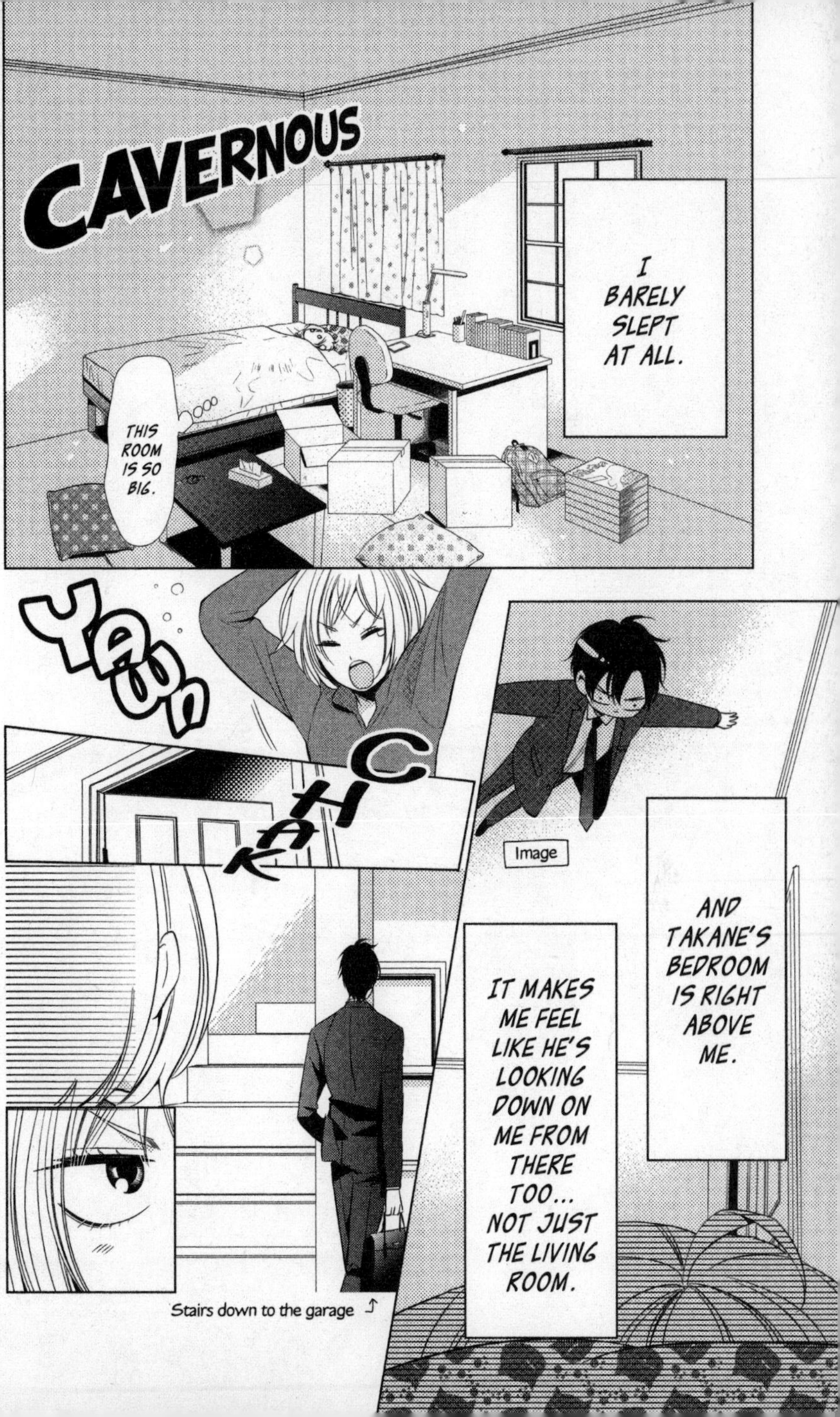
I BARELY SLEPT AT ALL.
CAVERNOUS
THIS ROOM IS SO BIG.
Image
AND TAKANE'S BEDROOM IS RIGHT ABOVE ME.
IT MAKES ME FEEL LIKE HE'S LOOKING DOWN ON ME FROM THERE TOO... NOT JUST THE LIVING ROOM.
YAWN
CHAK
Stairs down to the garage

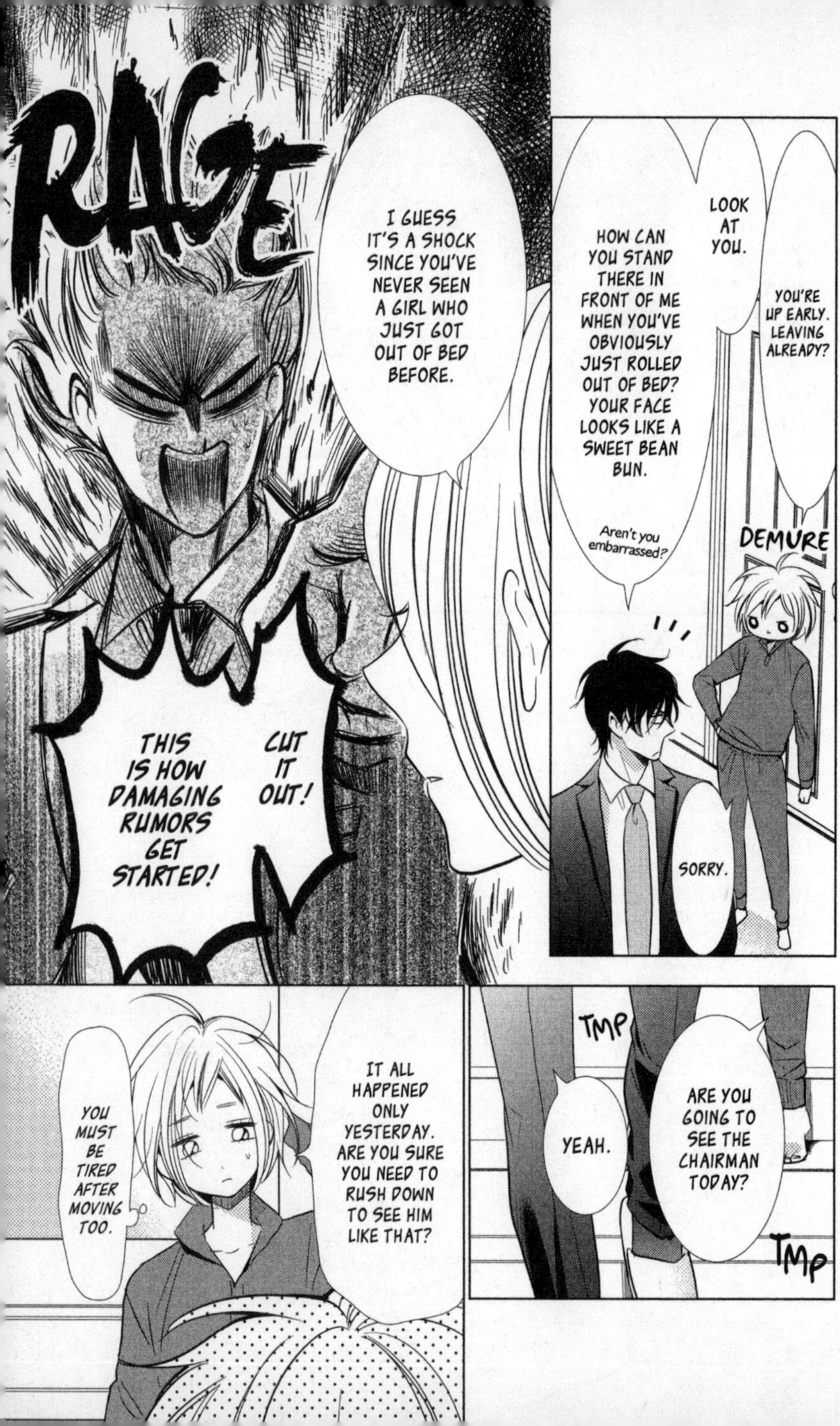
YOU'RE UP EARLY. LEAVING ALREADY?
LOOK AT YOU.
HOW CAN YOU STAND THERE IN FRONT OF ME WHEN YOU'VE OBVIOUSLY JUST ROLLED OUT OF BED? YOUR FACE LOOKS LIKE A SWEET BEAN BUN.
Aren't you embarrassed?
DEMURE
SORRY.
I GUESS IT'S A SHOCK SINCE YOU'VE NEVER SEEN A GIRL WHO JUST GOT OUT OF BED BEFORE.
RAGE
CUT IT OUT!
THIS IS HOW DAMAGING RUMORS GET STARTED!
TMP
ARE YOU GOING TO SEE THE CHAIRMAN TODAY?
YEAH.
TMP
IT ALL HAPPENED ONLY YESTERDAY. ARE YOU SURE YOU NEED TO RUSH DOWN TO SEE HIM LIKE THAT?
YOU MUST BE TIRED AFTER MOVING TOO.

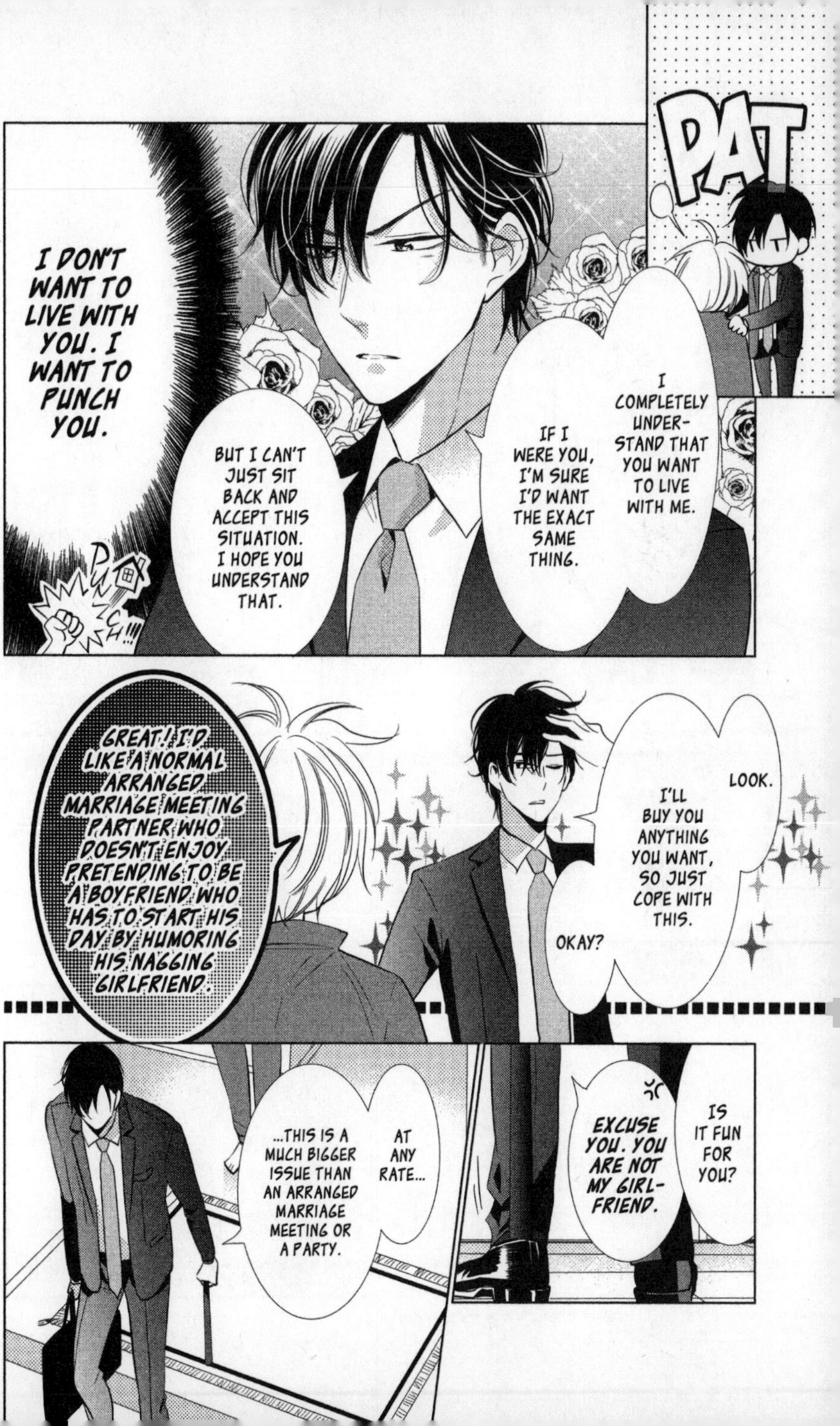
PAT
I COMPLETELY UNDERSTAND THAT YOU WANT TO LIVE WITH ME.
IF I WERE YOU, I'M SURE I'D WANT THE EXACT SAME THING.
BUT I CAN'T JUST SIT BACK AND ACCEPT THIS SITUATION. I HOPE YOU UNDERSTAND THAT.
I DON'T WANT TO LIVE WITH YOU. I WANT TO PUNCH YOU.
PUNCH!!!
LOOK.
I'LL BUY YOU ANYTHING YOU WANT, SO JUST COPE WITH THIS.
OKAY?
GREAT! I'D LIKE A NORMAL ARRANGED MARRIAGE MEETING PARTNER WHO DOESN'T ENJOY PRETENDING TO BE A BOYFRIEND WHO HAS TO START HIS DAY BY HUMORING HIS NAGGING GIRLFRIEND.
IS IT FUN FOR YOU?
EXCUSE YOU. YOU ARE NOT MY GIRLFRIEND.
AT ANY RATE...
...THIS IS A MUCH BIGGER ISSUE THAN AN ARRANGED MARRIAGE MEETING OR A PARTY.

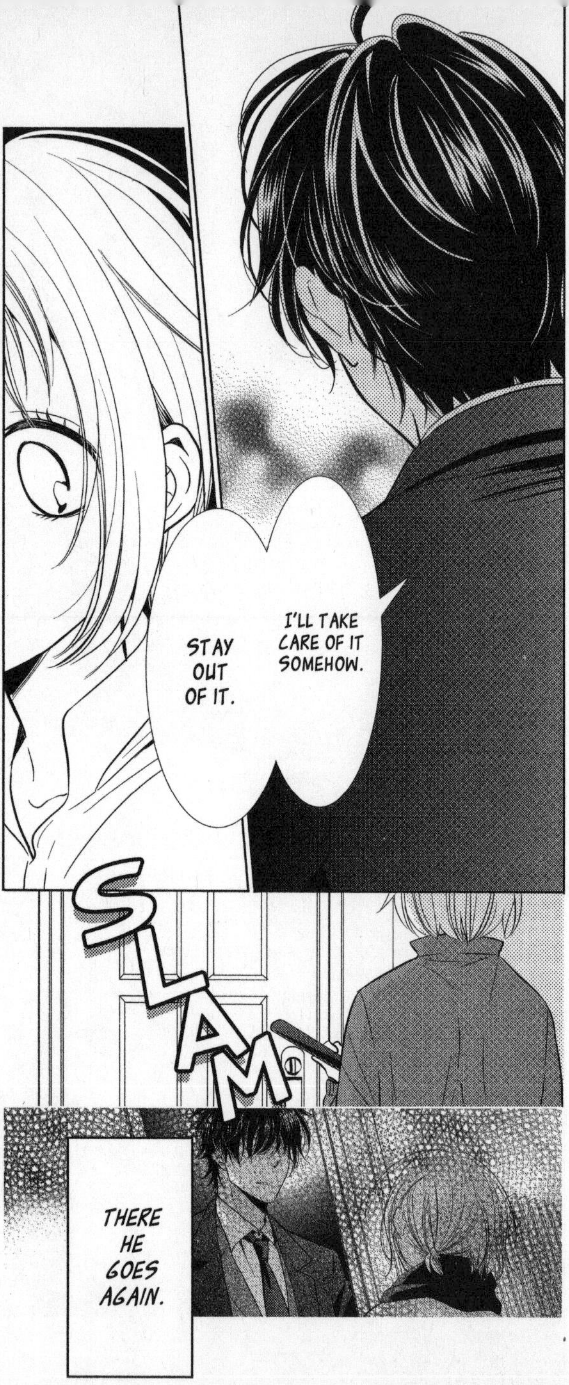
I'LL TAKE CARE OF IT SOMEHOW.
STAY OUT OF IT.
SLAM
THERE HE GOES AGAIN.

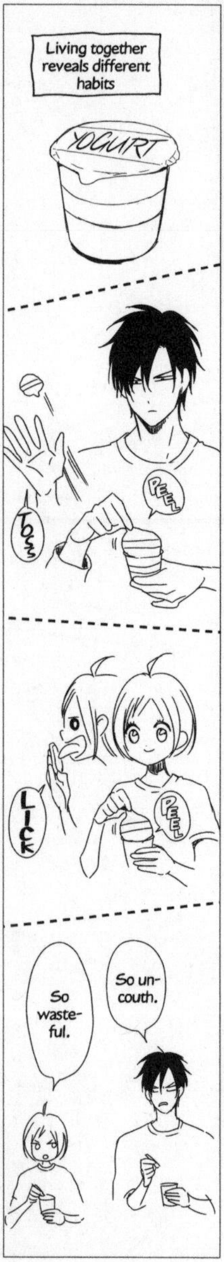
Living together reveals different habits
YOGURT
PEEL
TOSS
PEEL
LICK
So un-couth.
So waste-ful.

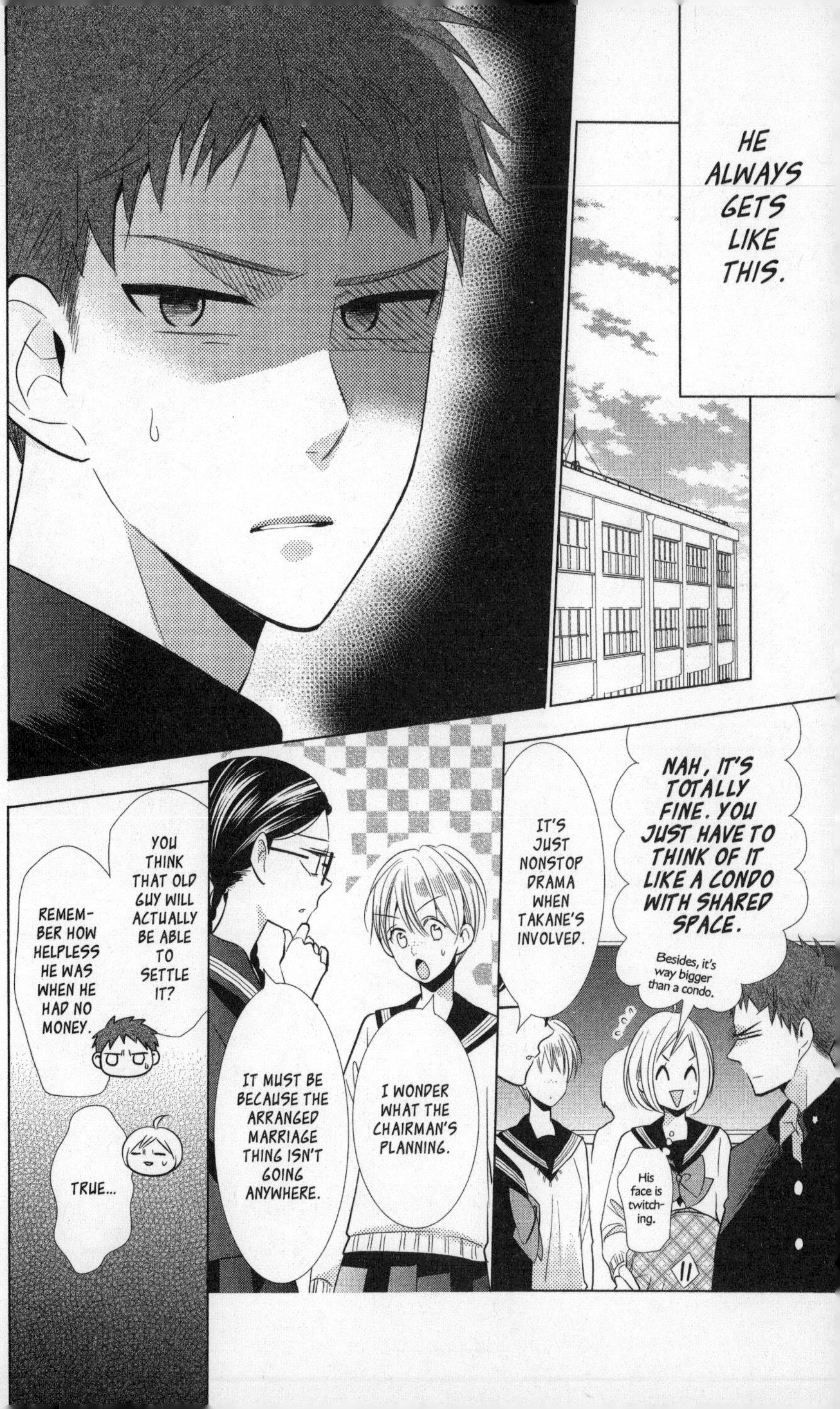
HE ALWAYS GETS LIKE THIS.
NAH, IT'S TOTALLY FINE. YOU JUST HAVE TO THINK OF IT LIKE A CONDO WITH SHARED SPACE.
Besides, it's way bigger than a condo.
IT'S JUST NONSTOP DRAMA WHEN TAKANE'S INVOLVED.
His face is twitch-ing.
I WONDER WHAT THE CHAIRMAN'S PLANNING.
IT MUST BE BECAUSE THE ARRANGED MARRIAGE THING ISN'T GOING ANYWHERE.
YOU THINK THAT OLD GUY WILL ACTUALLY BE ABLE TO SETTLE IT?
REMEM-BER HOW HELPLESS HE WAS WHEN HE HAD NO MONEY.
TRUE...

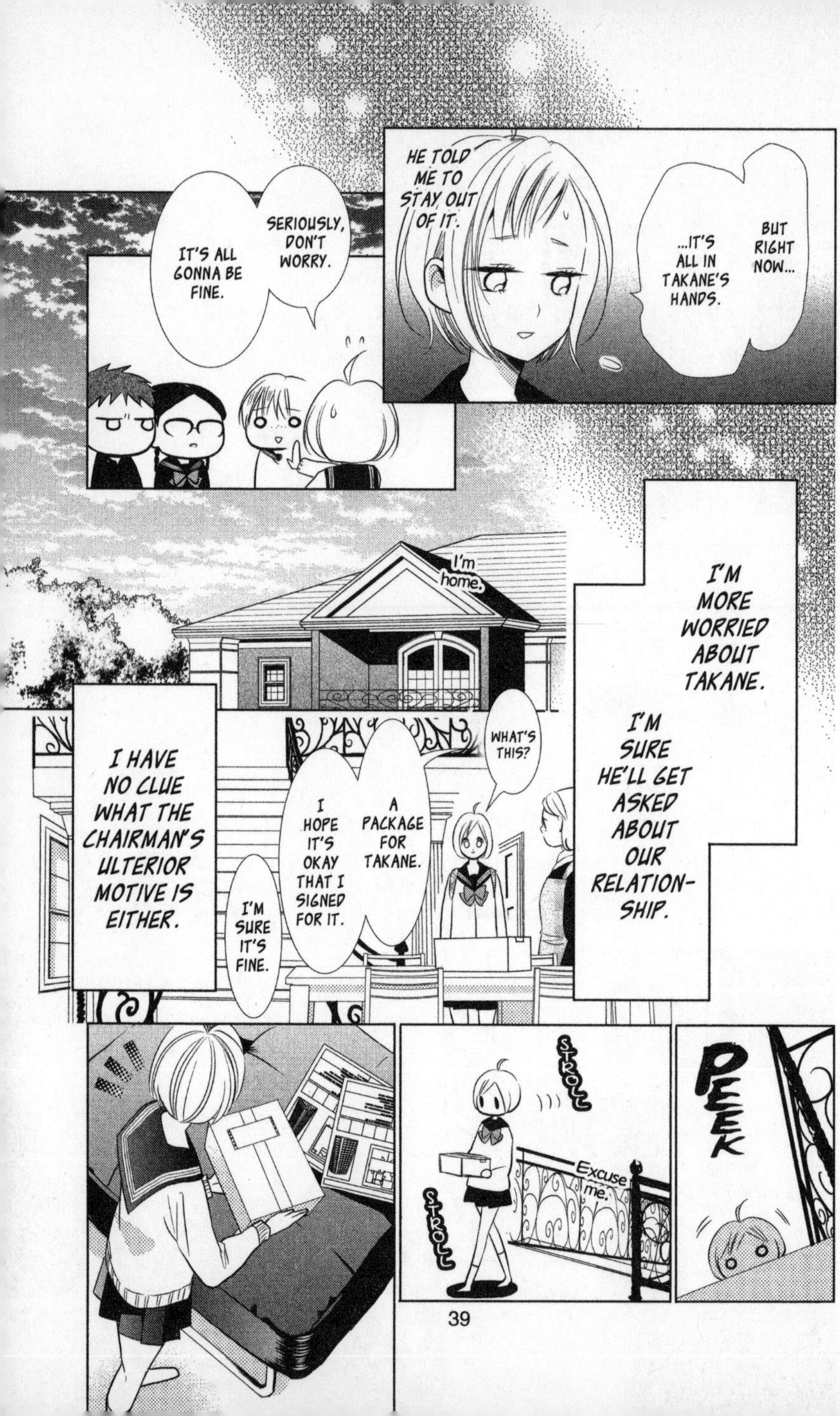
BUT RIGHT NOW...
...IT'S ALL IN TAKANE'S HANDS.
HE TOLD ME TO STAY OUT OF IT.
SERIOUSLY, DON'T WORRY.
IT'S ALL GONNA BE FINE.
I'm home.
I'M MORE WORRIED ABOUT TAKANE.
I'M SURE HE'LL GET ASKED ABOUT OUR RELATION-SHIP.
WHAT'S THIS?
A PACKAGE FOR TAKANE.
I HOPE IT'S OKAY THAT I SIGNED FOR IT.
I'M SURE IT'S FINE.
I HAVE NO CLUE WHAT THE CHAIRMAN'S ULTERIOR MOTIVE IS EITHER.
PEEK
STROLL
Excuse me.
STROLL

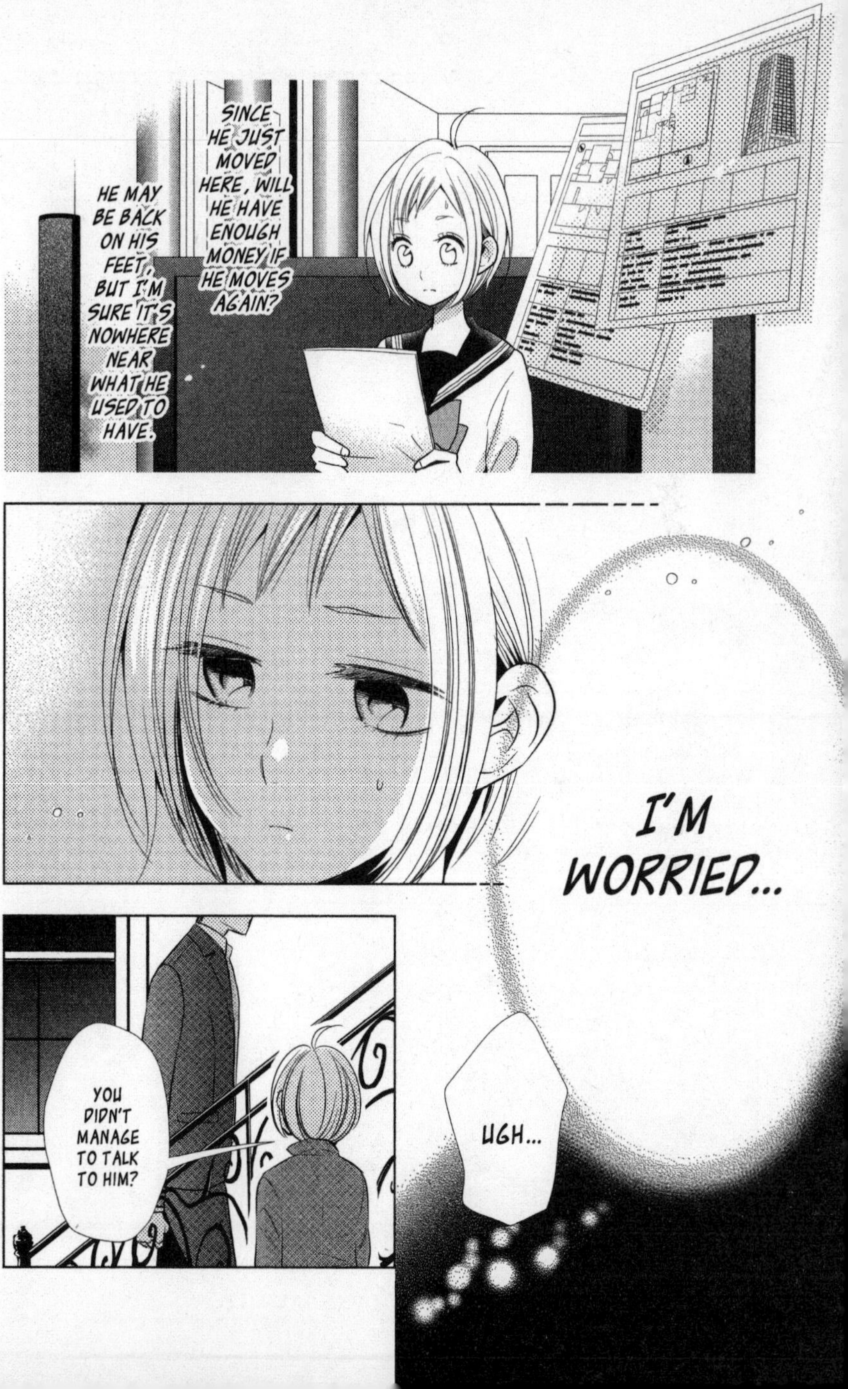

SINCE HE JUST MOVED HERE, WILL HE HAVE ENOUGH MONEY IF HE MOVES AGAIN?
HE MAY BE BACK ON HIS FEET, BUT I'M SURE IT'S NOWHERE NEAR WHAT HE USED TO HAVE.
I'M WORRIED...
UGH...
YOU DIDN'T MANAGE TO TALK TO HIM?

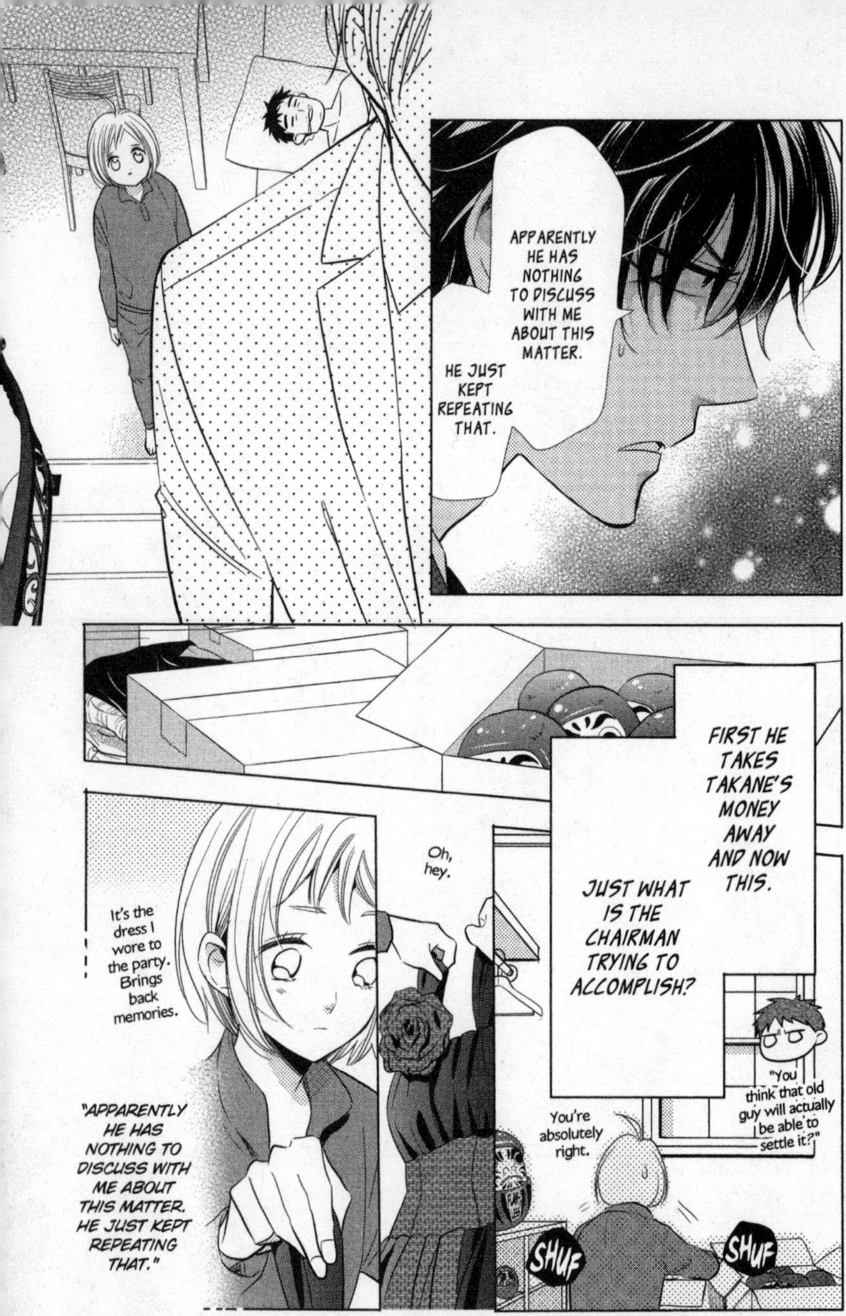
APPARENTLY HE HAS NOTHING TO DISCUSS WITH ME ABOUT THIS MATTER.
HE JUST KEPT REPEATING THAT.
FIRST HE TAKES TAKANE'S MONEY AWAY AND NOW THIS.
JUST WHAT IS THE CHAIRMAN TRYING TO ACCOMPLISH?
Oh, hey.
"You think that old guy will actually be able to settle it?"
You're absolutely right.
SHUF
SHUF
It's the dress I wore to the party. Brings back memories.
"APPARENTLY HE HAS NOTHING TO DISCUSS WITH ME ABOUT THIS MATTER. HE JUST KEPT REPEATING THAT."

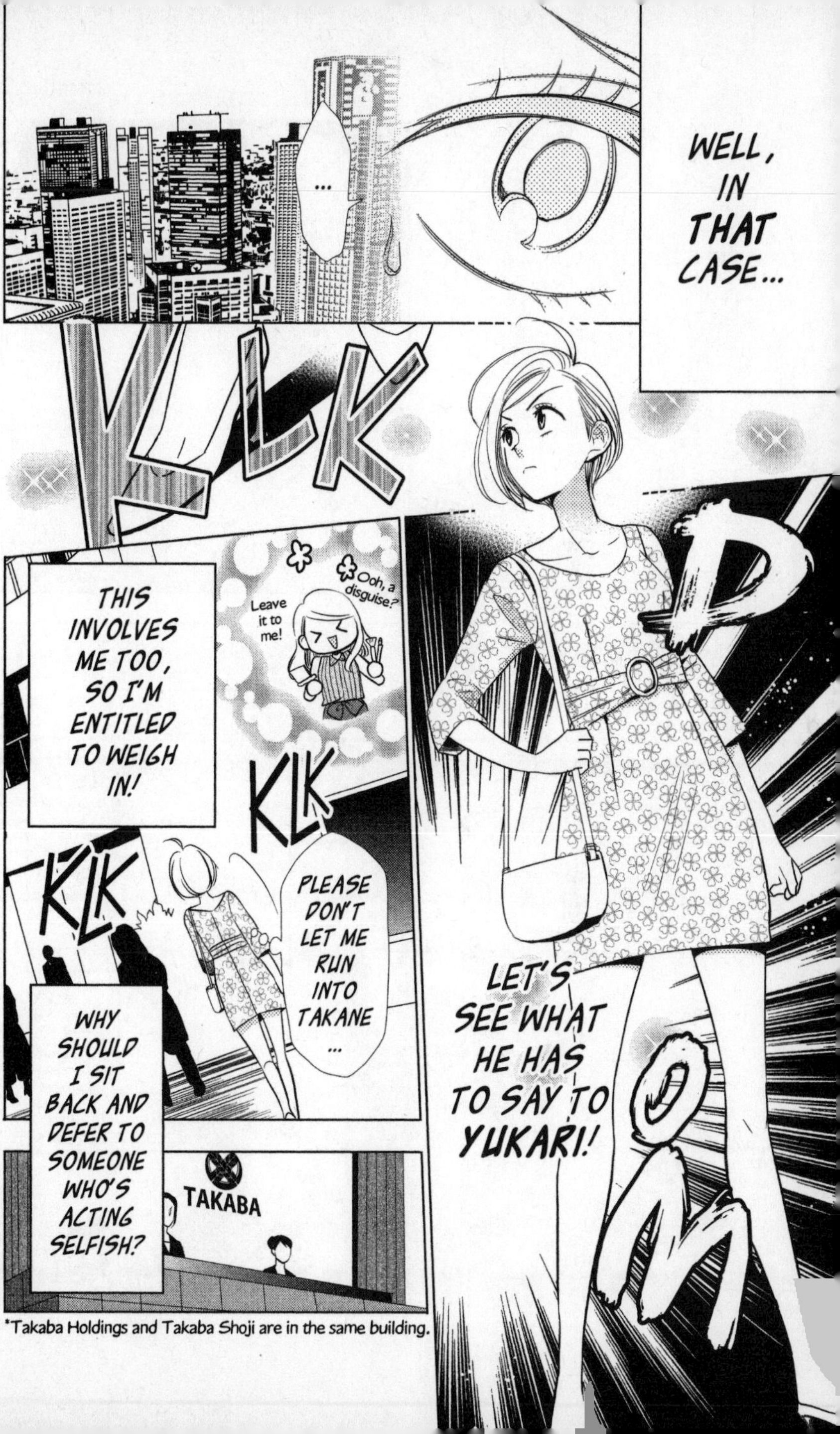
WELL, IN THAT CASE...
...
KLLK
LET'S SEE WHAT HE HAS TO SAY TO YUKARI!
THIS INVOLVES ME TOO, SO I'M ENTITLED TO WEIGH IN!
Ooh, a disguise?
Leave it to me!
KLK
PLEASE DON'T LET ME RUN INTO TAKANE...
KLK
WHY SHOULD I SIT BACK AND DEFER TO SOMEONE WHO'S ACTING SELFISH?
TAKABA

*Takaba Holdings and Takaba Shoji are in the same building.

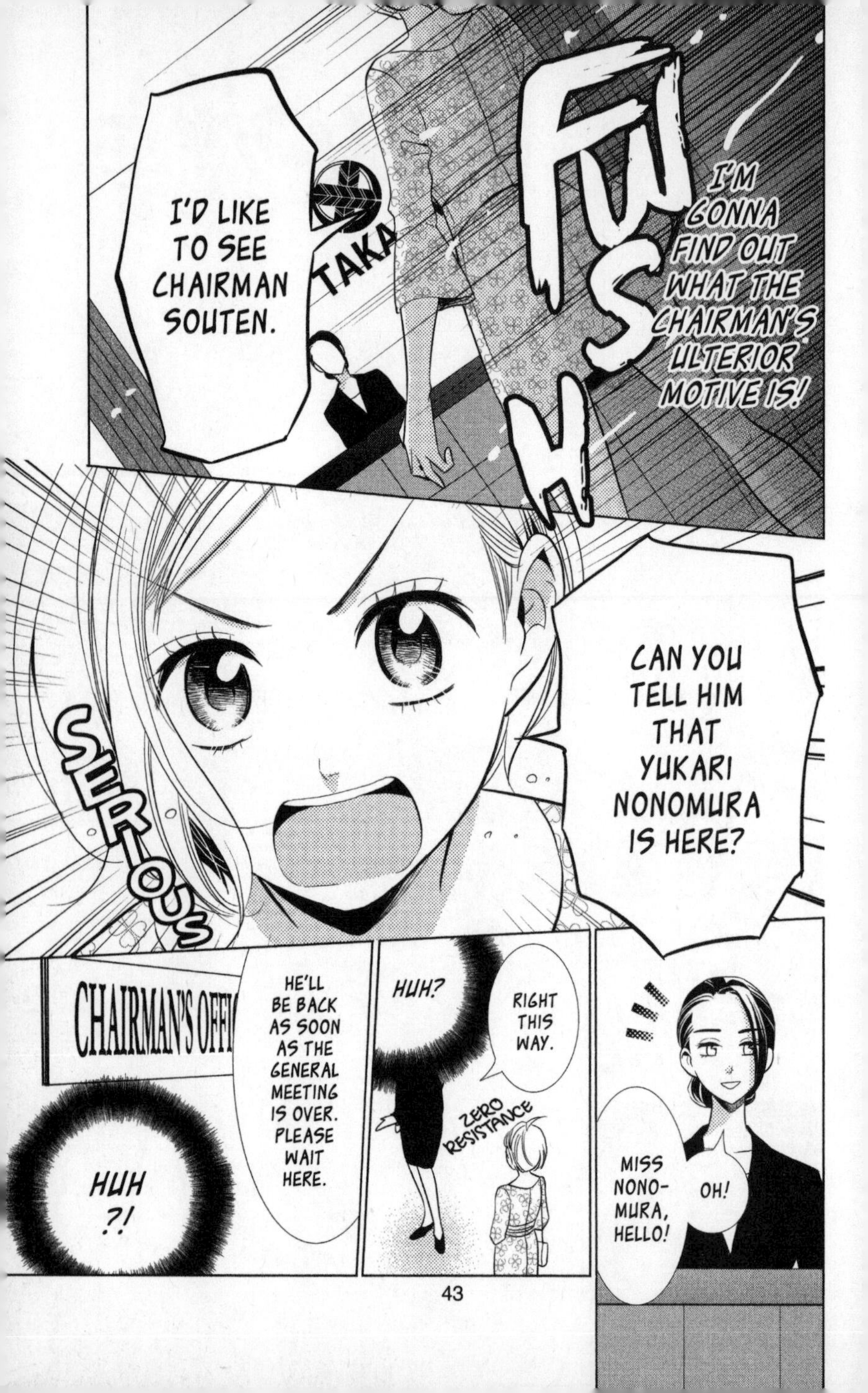
I'M GONNA FIND OUT WHAT THE CHAIRMAN'S ULTERIOR MOTIVE IS!
FUSH
TAKA
I'D LIKE TO SEE CHAIRMAN SOUTEN.
CAN YOU TELL HIM THAT YUKARI NONOMURA IS HERE?
SERIOUS
!!!
OH!
MISS NONOMURA, HELLO!
RIGHT THIS WAY.
HUH?
ZERO RESISTANCE
CHAIRMAN'S OFFIC
HE'LL BE BACK AS SOON AS THE GENERAL MEETING IS OVER. PLEASE WAIT HERE.
HUH?!

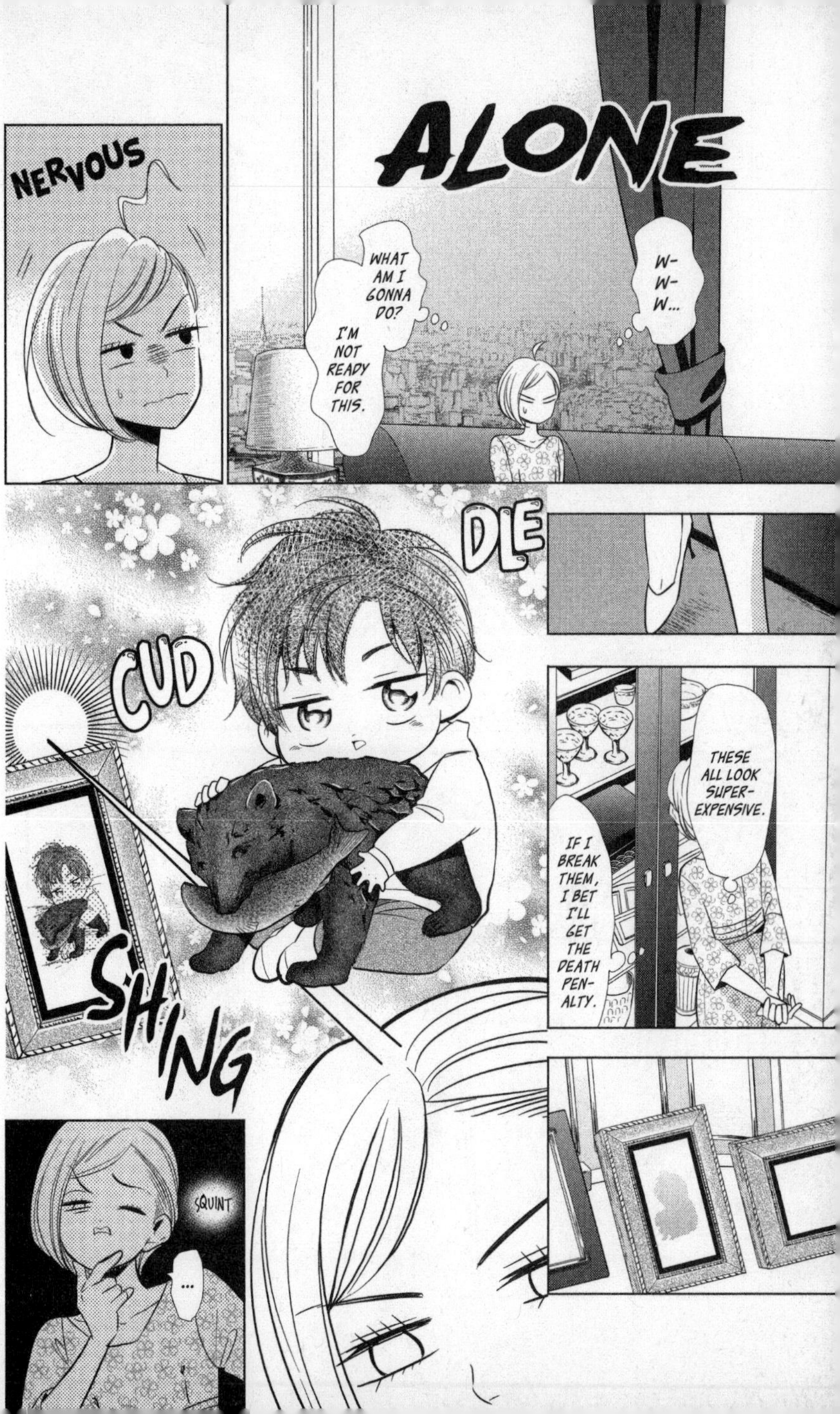
ALONE
W-W-W...
WHAT AM I GONNA DO?
I'M NOT READY FOR THIS.
NERVOUS
THESE ALL LOOK SUPER-EXPENSIVE.
IF I BREAK THEM, I BET I'LL GET THE DEATH PEN-ALTY.
DLE
CUD
SHING
SQUINT
...

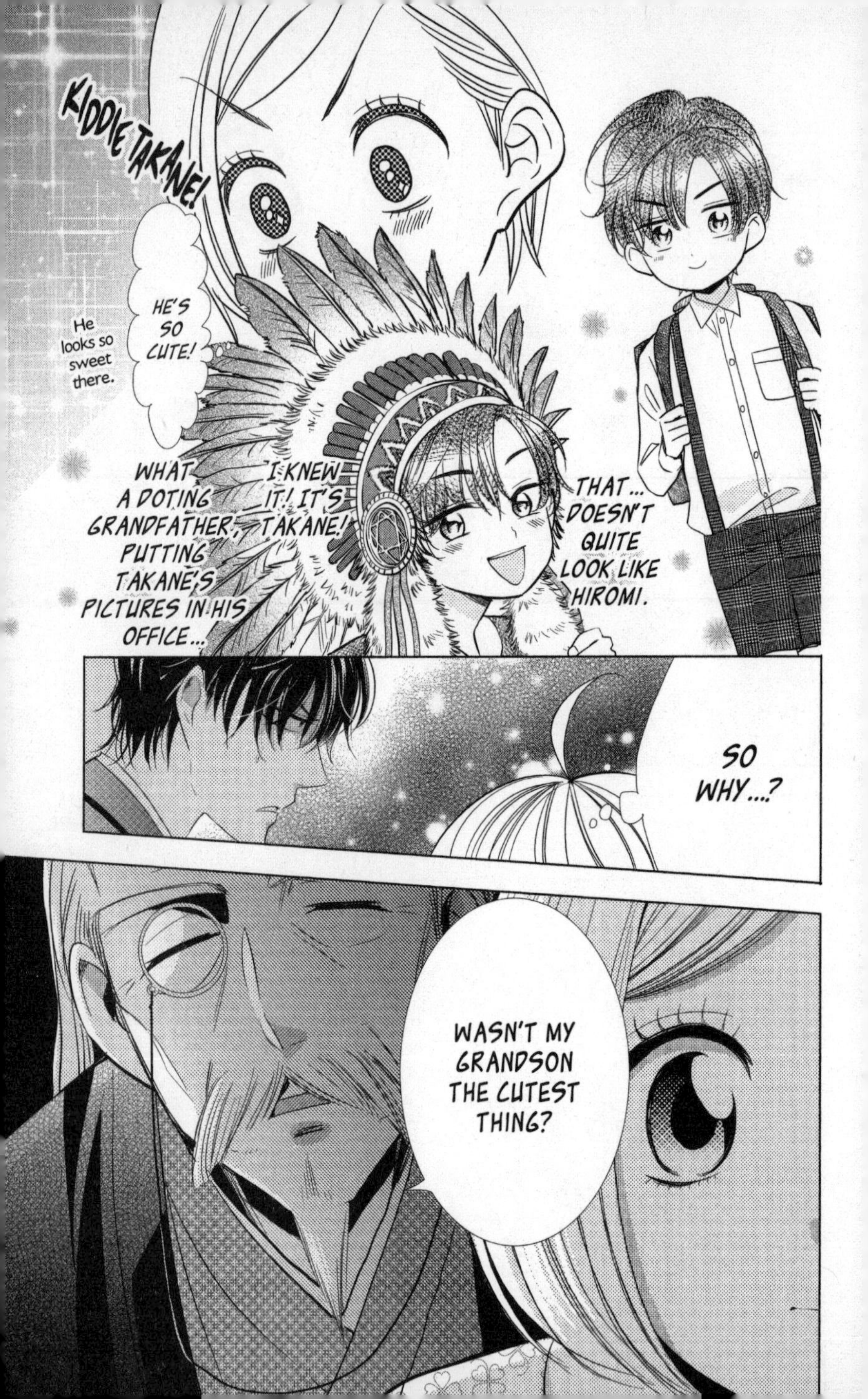
KIDDIE TAKANE!
HE'S SO CUTE!
He looks so sweet there.
THAT... DOESN'T QUITE LOOK LIKE HIROMI.
I KNEW IT! IT'S TAKANE!
WHAT A DOTING GRANDFATHER, PUTTING TAKANE'S PICTURES IN HIS OFFICE...
SO WHY...?
WASN'T MY GRANDSON THE CUTEST THING?

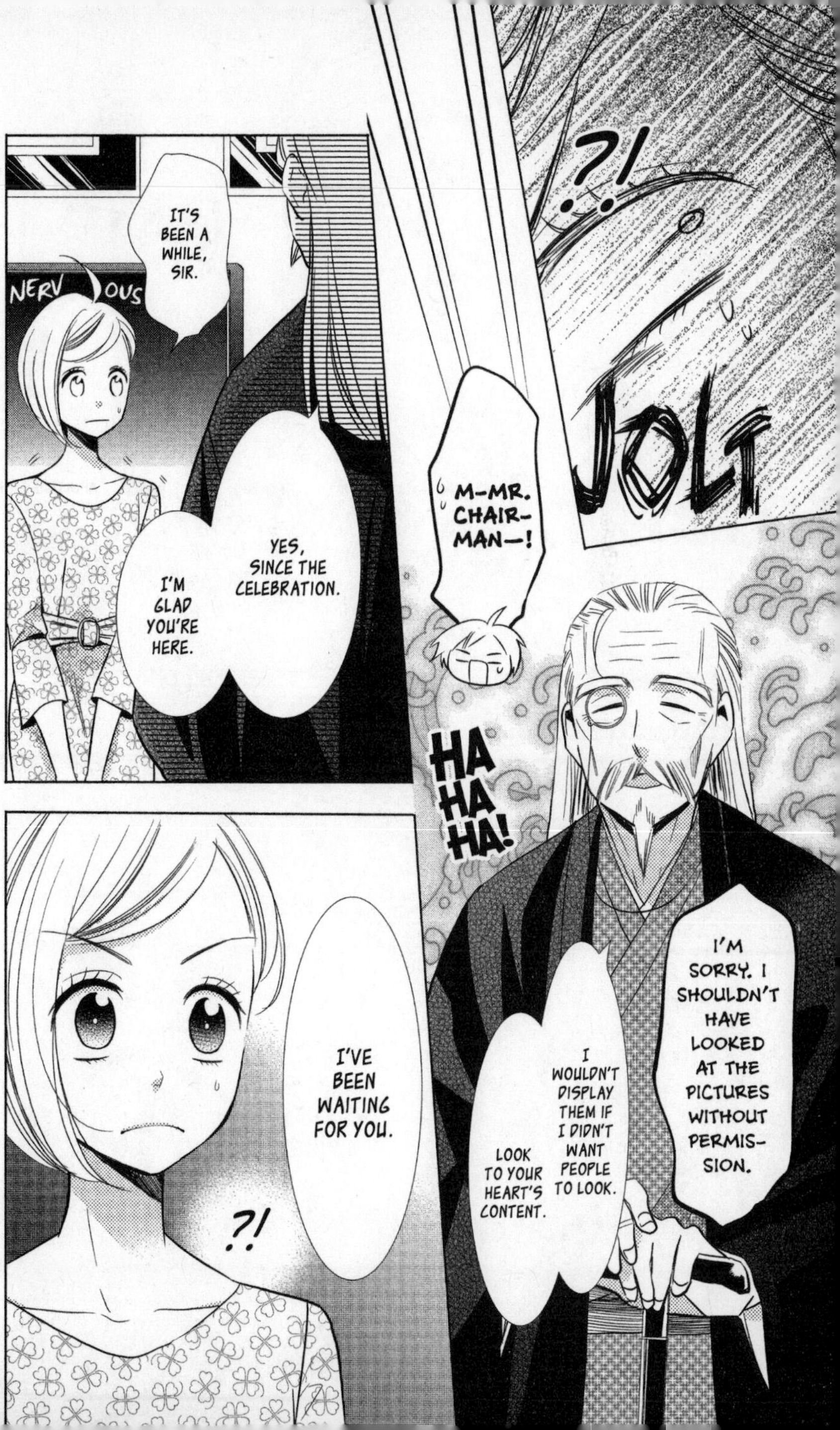
?!
JOLT
M-MR. CHAIRMAN—!
HA HA HA!
I'M SORRY. I SHOULDN'T HAVE LOOKED AT THE PICTURES WITHOUT PERMISSION.
I WOULDN'T DISPLAY THEM IF I DIDN'T WANT PEOPLE TO LOOK.
LOOK TO YOUR HEART'S CONTENT.
IT'S BEEN A WHILE, SIR.
NERVOUS
YES, SINCE THE CELEBRATION.
I'M GLAD YOU'RE HERE.
I'VE BEEN WAITING FOR YOU.
?!

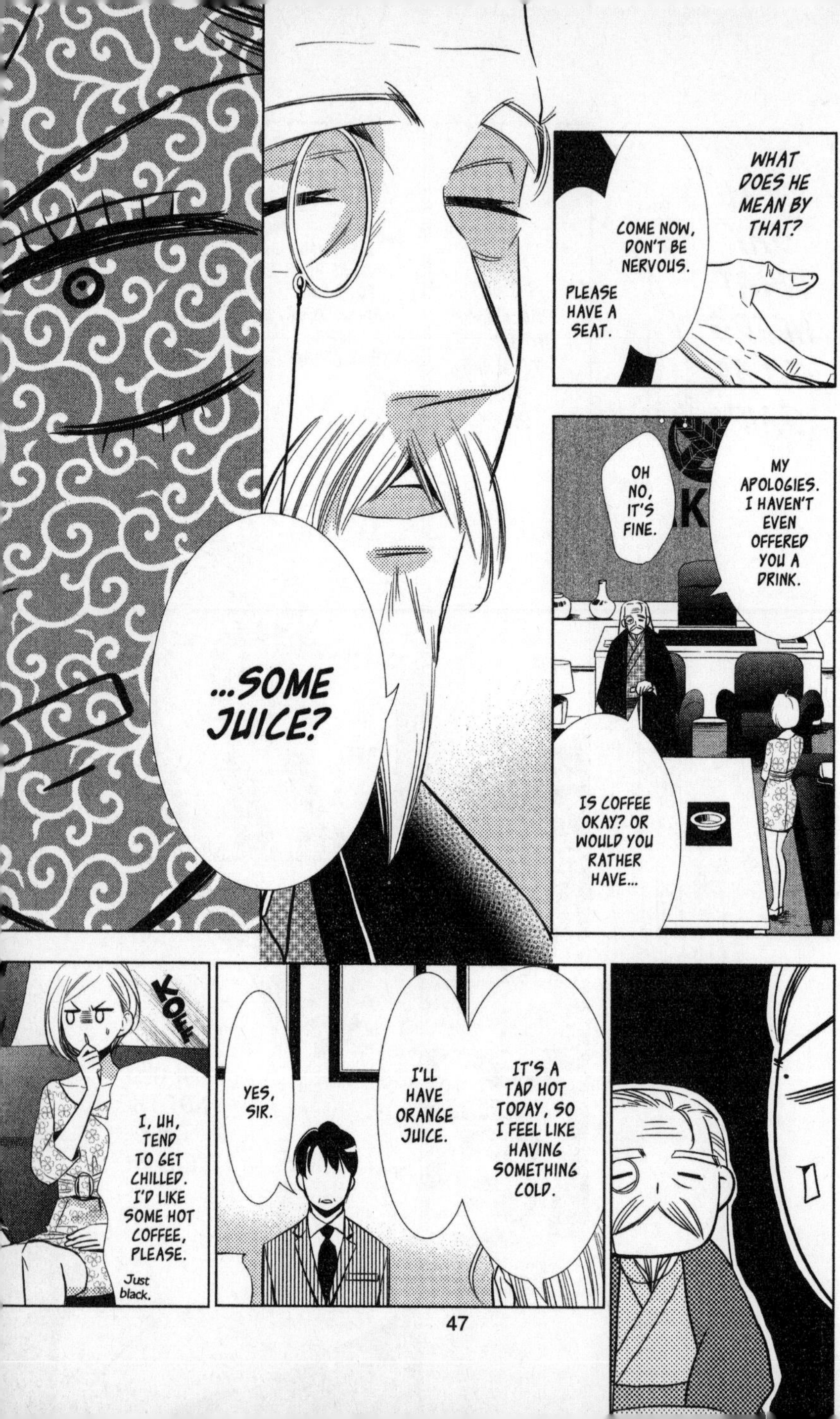
WHAT DOES HE MEAN BY THAT?
COME NOW, DON'T BE NERVOUS.
PLEASE HAVE A SEAT.
MY APOLOGIES. I HAVEN'T EVEN OFFERED YOU A DRINK.
OH NO, IT'S FINE.
IS COFFEE OKAY? OR WOULD YOU RATHER HAVE...
...SOME JUICE?
IT'S A TAD HOT TODAY, SO I FEEL LIKE HAVING SOMETHING COLD.
I'LL HAVE ORANGE JUICE.
YES, SIR.
KOH
I, UH, TEND TO GET CHILLED. I'D LIKE SOME HOT COFFEE, PLEASE.
Just black.

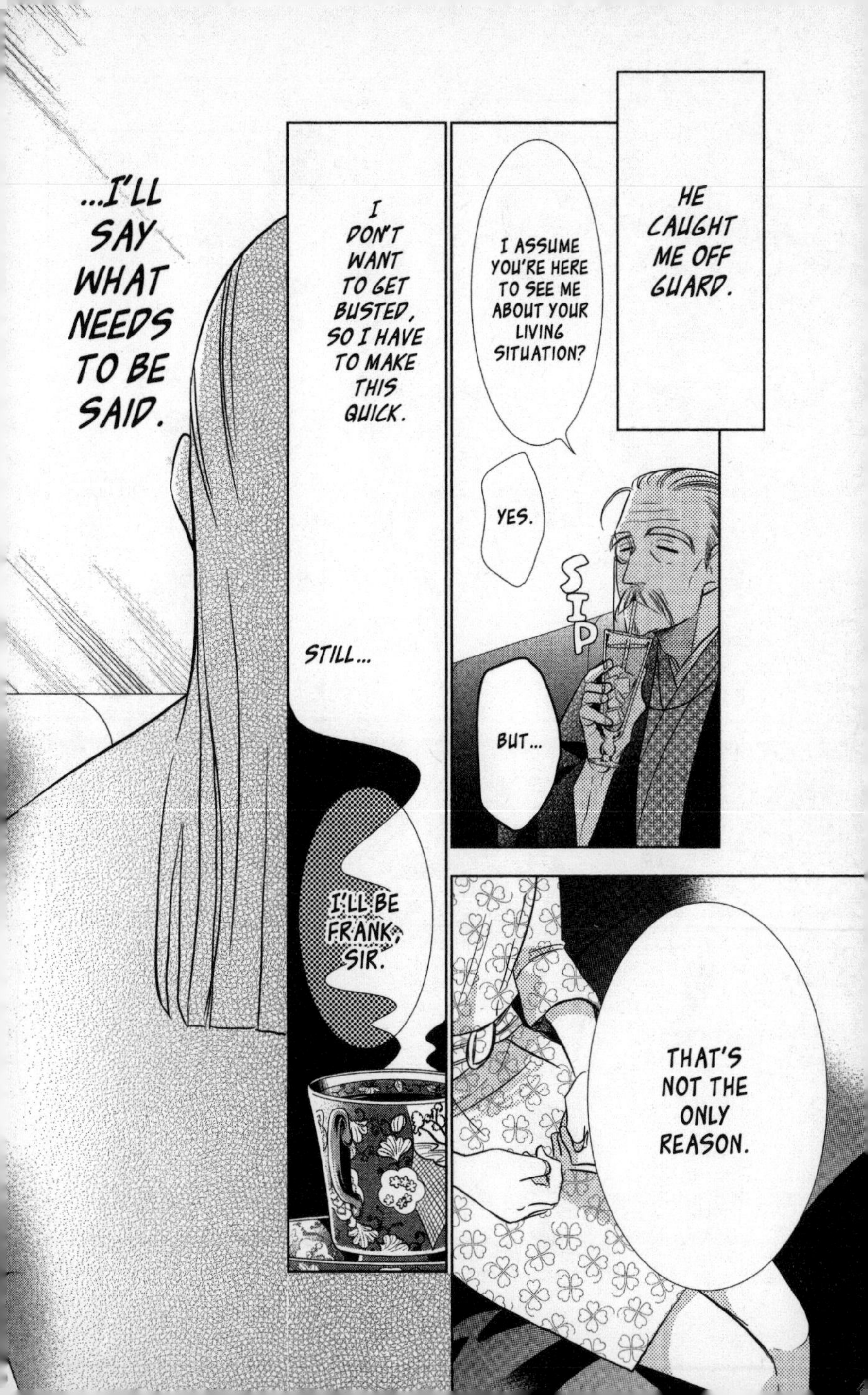
HE CAUGHT ME OFF GUARD.
I ASSUME YOU'RE HERE TO SEE ME ABOUT YOUR LIVING SITUATION?
YES.
SIP
BUT...
THAT'S NOT THE ONLY REASON.
I DON'T WANT TO GET BUSTED, SO I HAVE TO MAKE THIS QUICK.
STILL...
I'LL BE FRANK, SIR.
...I'LL SAY WHAT NEEDS TO BE SAID.

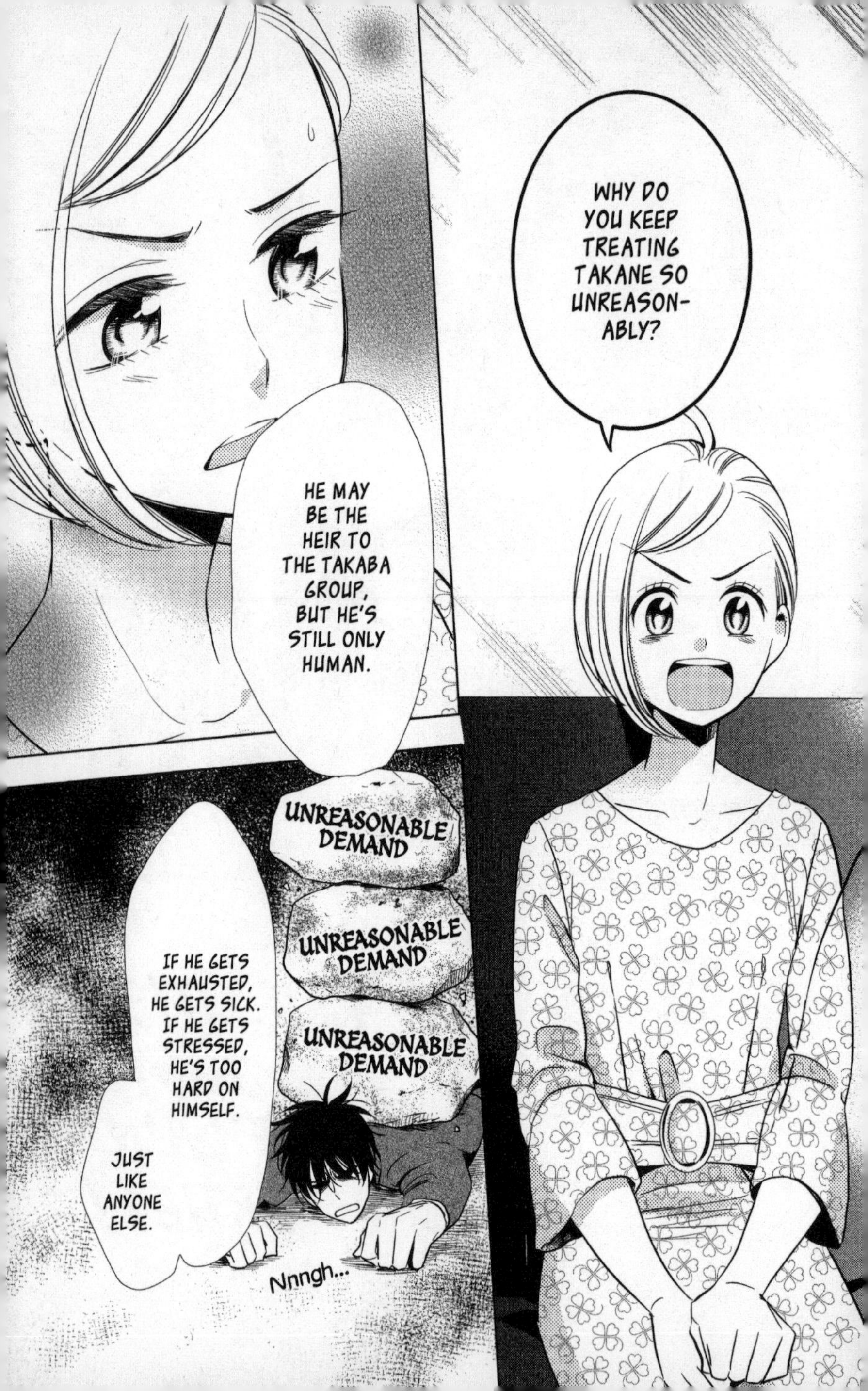
WHY DO YOU KEEP TREATING TAKANE SO UNREASON-ABLY?
HE MAY BE THE HEIR TO THE TAKABA GROUP, BUT HE'S STILL ONLY HUMAN.
UNREASONABLE DEMAND
UNREASONABLE DEMAND
UNREASONABLE DEMAND
IF HE GETS EXHAUSTED, HE GETS SICK. IF HE GETS STRESSED, HE'S TOO HARD ON HIMSELF.
JUST LIKE ANYONE ELSE.
Nnngh...

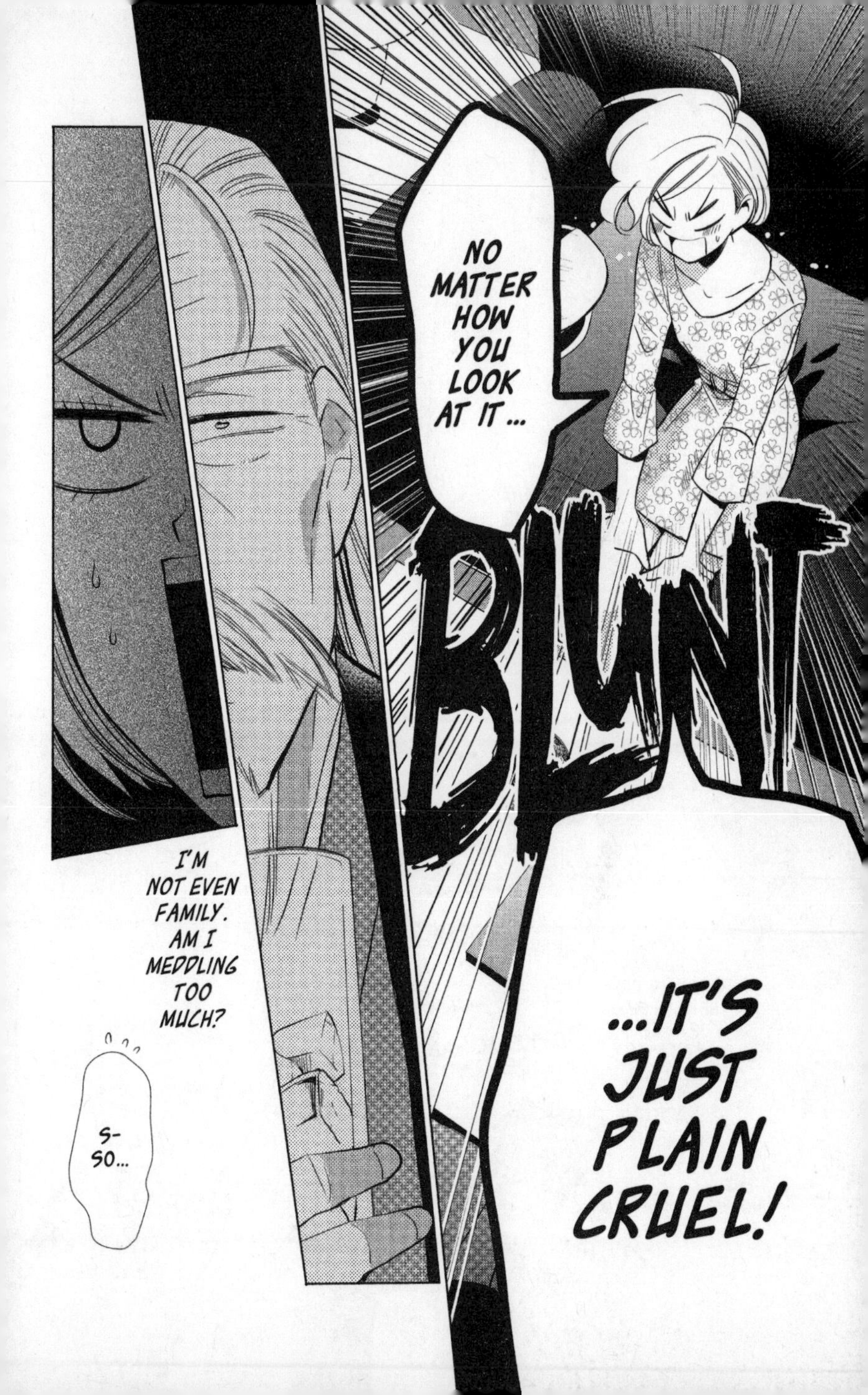
NO MATTER HOW YOU LOOK AT IT...
BLUNT
...IT'S JUST PLAIN CRUEL!
I'M NOT EVEN FAMILY. AM I MEDDLING TOO MUCH?
S-SO...

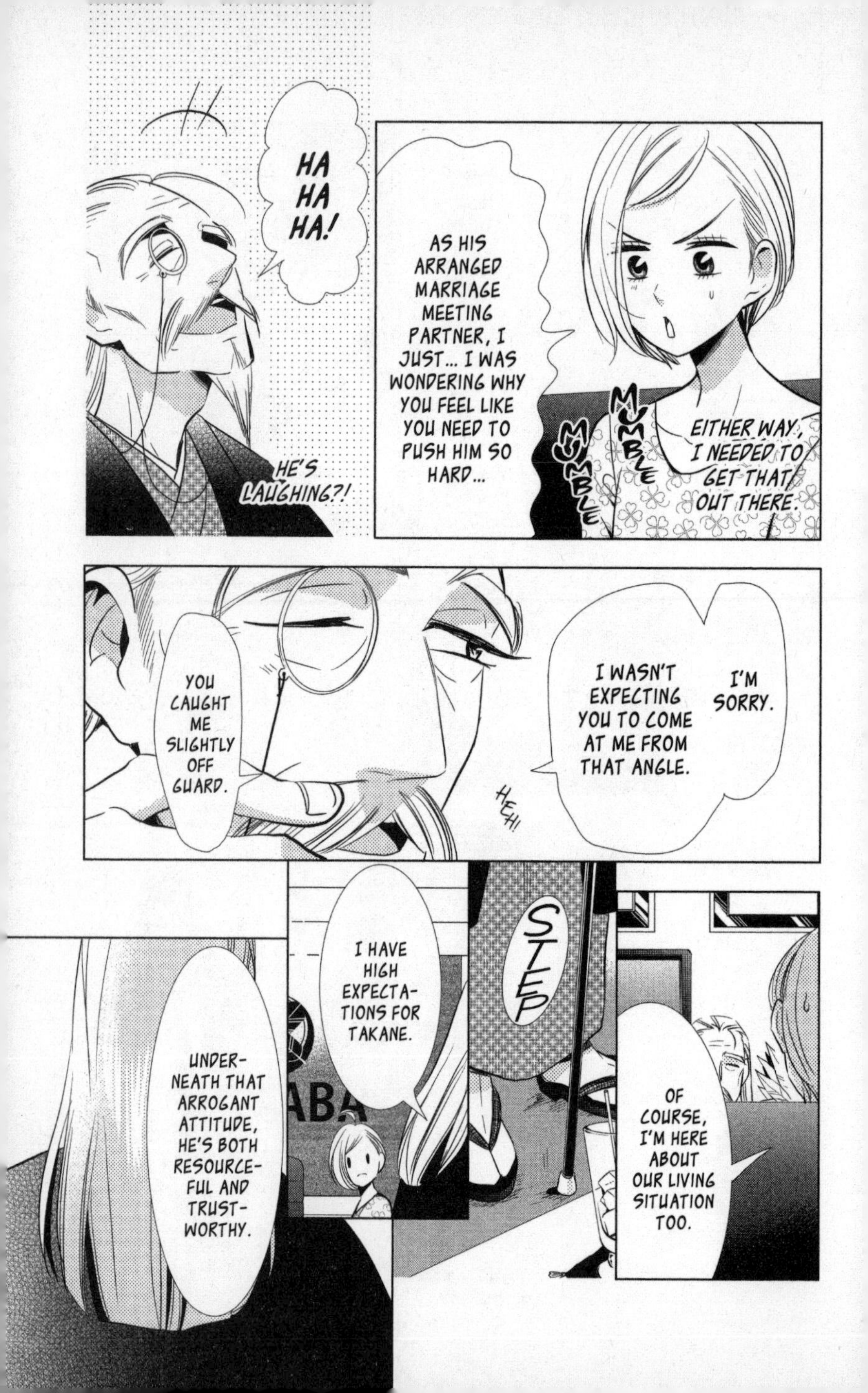
AS HIS ARRANGED MARRIAGE MEETING PARTNER, I JUST... I WAS WONDERING WHY YOU FEEL LIKE YOU NEED TO PUSH HIM SO HARD...
MUMBLE MUMBLE
EITHER WAY, I NEEDED TO GET THAT OUT THERE.
HA HA HA!
HE'S LAUGHING?!
I'M SORRY.
I WASN'T EXPECTING YOU TO COME AT ME FROM THAT ANGLE.
HEH!
YOU CAUGHT ME SLIGHTLY OFF GUARD.
OF COURSE, I'M HERE ABOUT OUR LIVING SITUATION TOO.
STEP
I HAVE HIGH EXPECTA-TIONS FOR TAKANE.
UNDER-NEATH THAT ARROGANT ATTITUDE, HE'S BOTH RESOURCE-FUL AND TRUST-WORTHY.

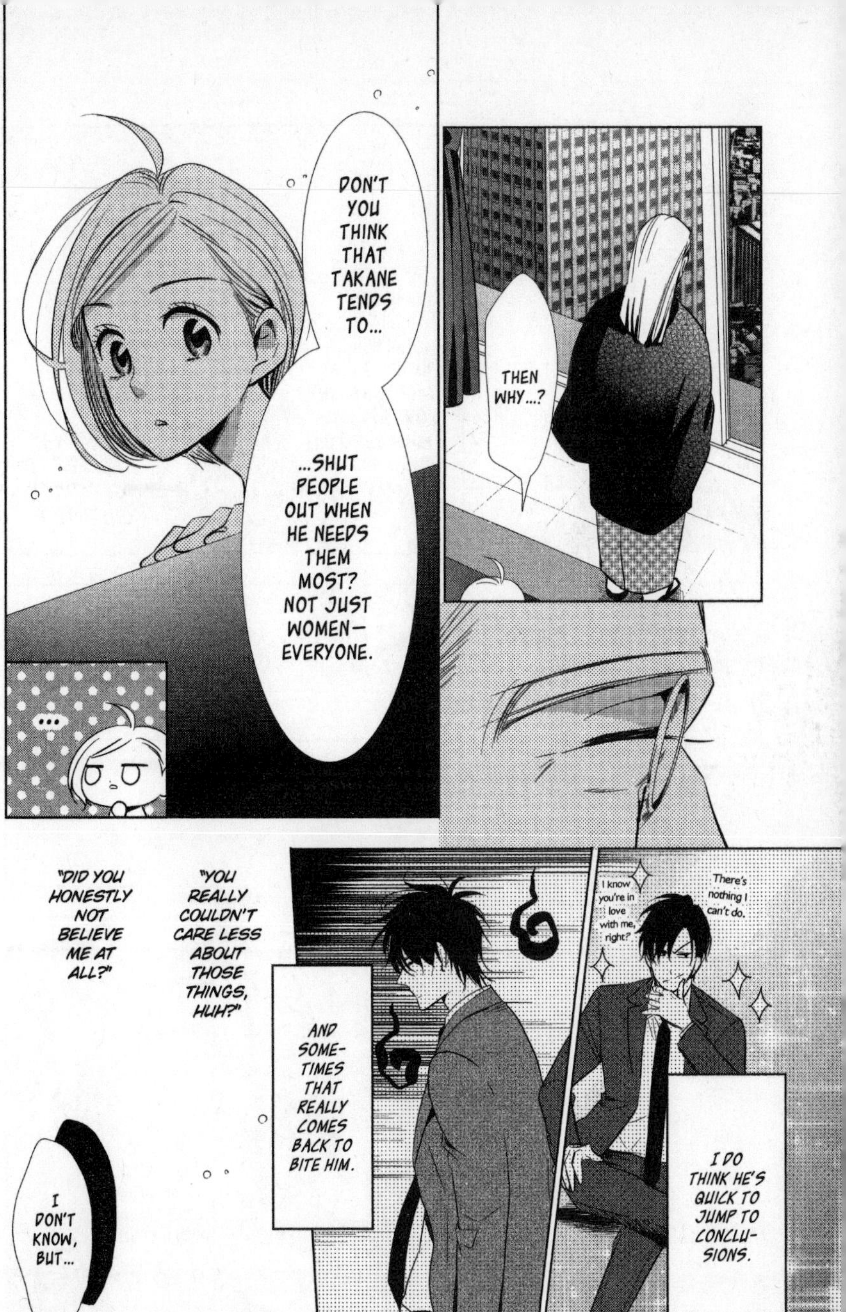
THEN WHY...?
DON'T YOU THINK THAT TAKANE TENDS TO...
...SHUT PEOPLE OUT WHEN HE NEEDS THEM MOST? NOT JUST WOMEN— EVERYONE.
...
There's nothing I can't do.
I know you're in love with me, right?
I DO THINK HE'S QUICK TO JUMP TO CONCLU-SIONS.
AND SOME-TIMES THAT REALLY COMES BACK TO BITE HIM.
"YOU REALLY COULDN'T CARE LESS ABOUT THOSE THINGS, HUH?"
"DID YOU HONESTLY NOT BELIEVE ME AT ALL?"
I DON'T KNOW, BUT...

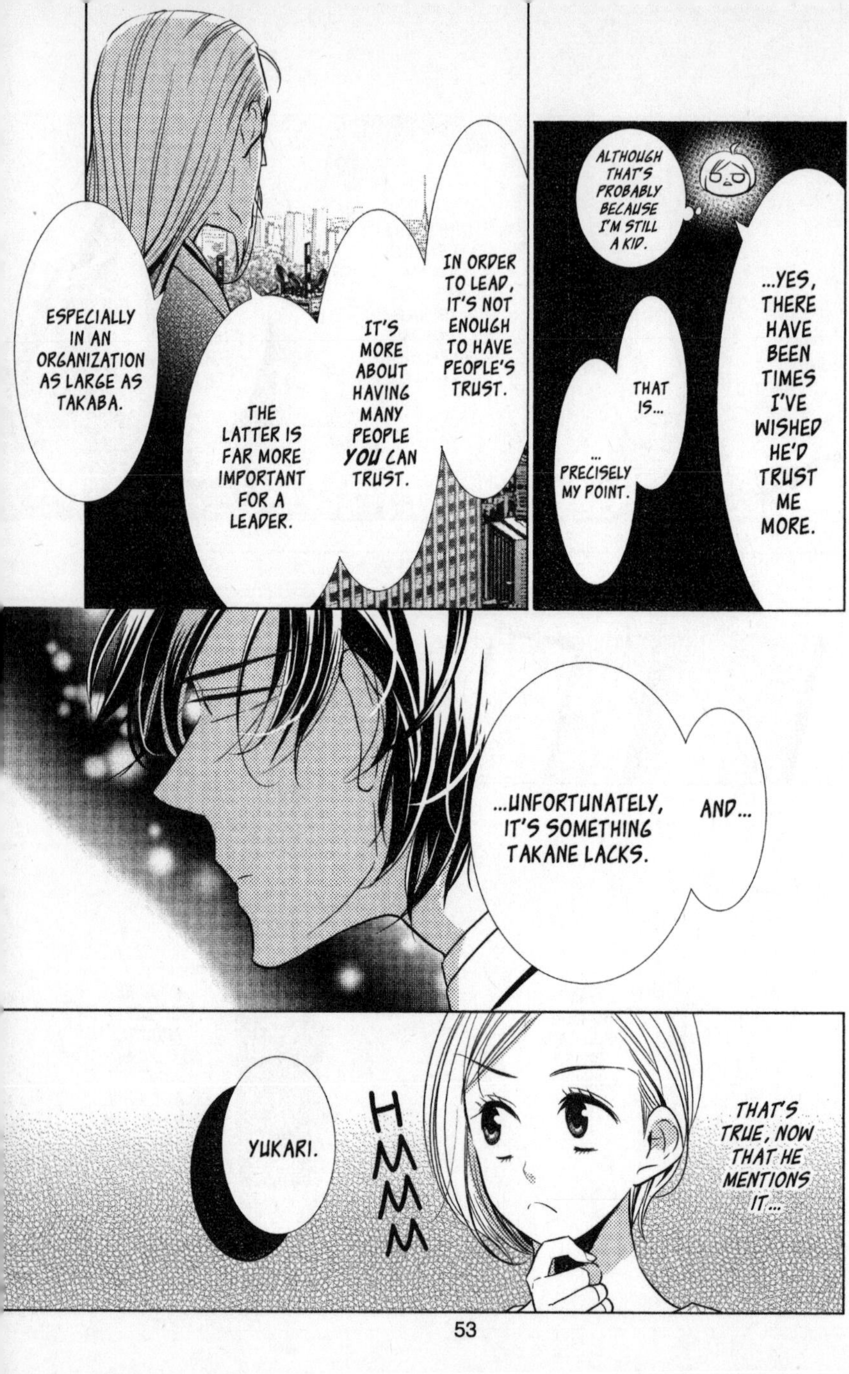
...YES, THERE HAVE BEEN TIMES I'VE WISHED HE'D TRUST ME MORE.
ALTHOUGH THAT'S PROBABLY BECAUSE I'M STILL A KID.
THAT IS...
...PRECISELY MY POINT.
IN ORDER TO LEAD, IT'S NOT ENOUGH TO HAVE PEOPLE'S TRUST.
IT'S MORE ABOUT HAVING MANY PEOPLE *YOU* CAN TRUST.
THE LATTER IS FAR MORE IMPORTANT FOR A LEADER.
ESPECIALLY IN AN ORGANIZATION AS LARGE AS TAKABA.
AND...
...UNFORTUNATELY, IT'S SOMETHING TAKANE LACKS.
THAT'S TRUE, NOW THAT HE MENTIONS IT...
HMMM
YUKARI.

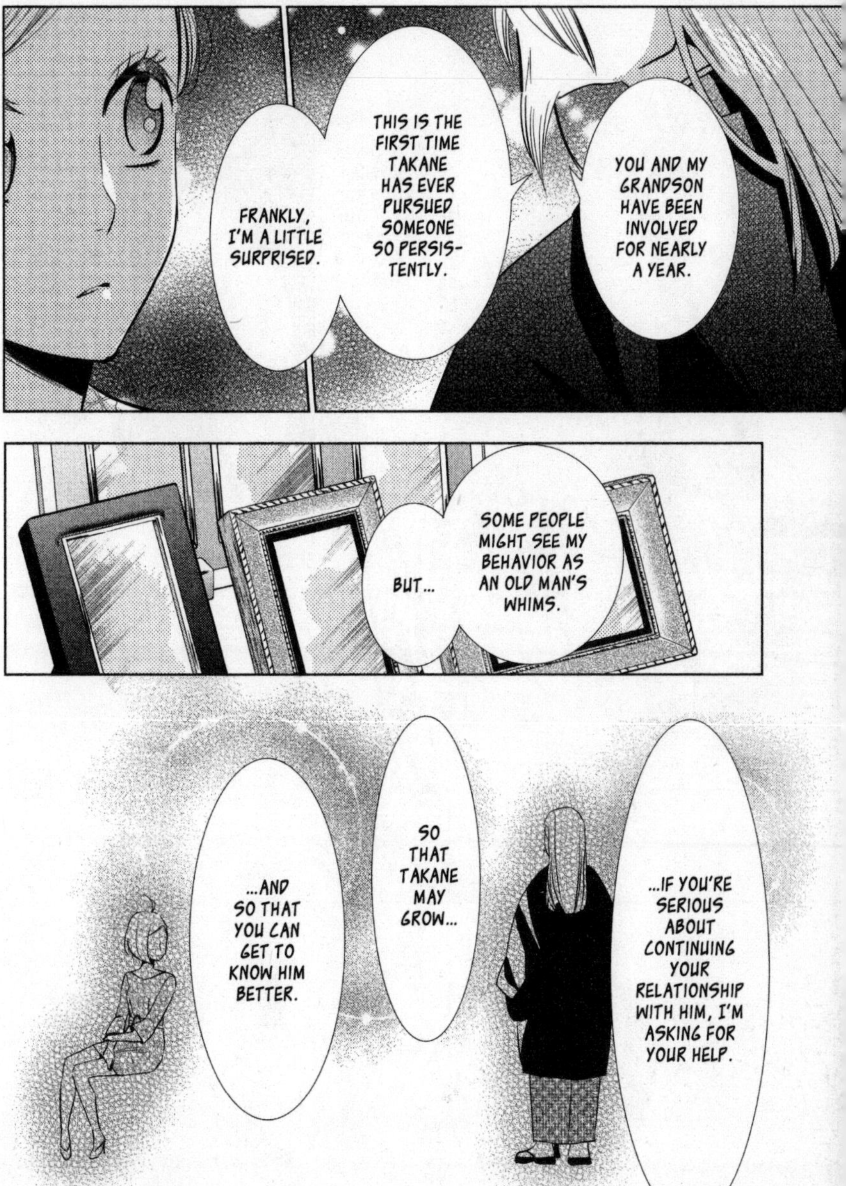
YOU AND MY GRANDSON HAVE BEEN INVOLVED FOR NEARLY A YEAR.
THIS IS THE FIRST TIME TAKANE HAS EVER PURSUED SOMEONE SO PERSIS-TENTLY.
FRANKLY, I'M A LITTLE SURPRISED.
SOME PEOPLE MIGHT SEE MY BEHAVIOR AS AN OLD MAN'S WHIMS.
BUT...
...IF YOU'RE SERIOUS ABOUT CONTINUING YOUR RELATIONSHIP WITH HIM, I'M ASKING FOR YOUR HELP.
SO THAT TAKANE MAY GROW...
...AND SO THAT YOU CAN GET TO KNOW HIM BETTER.

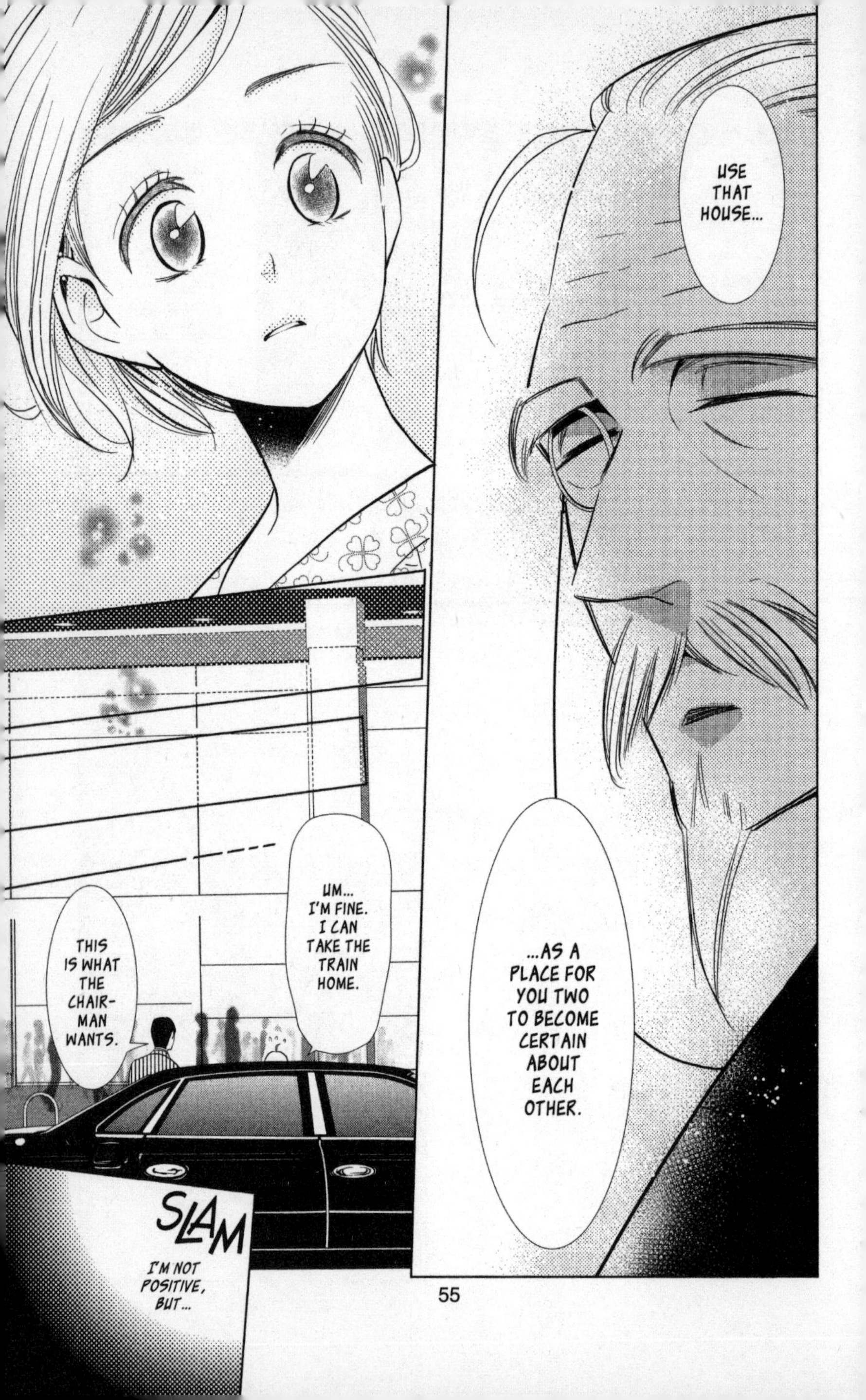
USE THAT HOUSE...
...AS A PLACE FOR YOU TWO TO BECOME CERTAIN ABOUT EACH OTHER.
UM... I'M FINE. I CAN TAKE THE TRAIN HOME.
THIS IS WHAT THE CHAIR-MAN WANTS.
SLAM
I'M NOT POSITIVE, BUT...

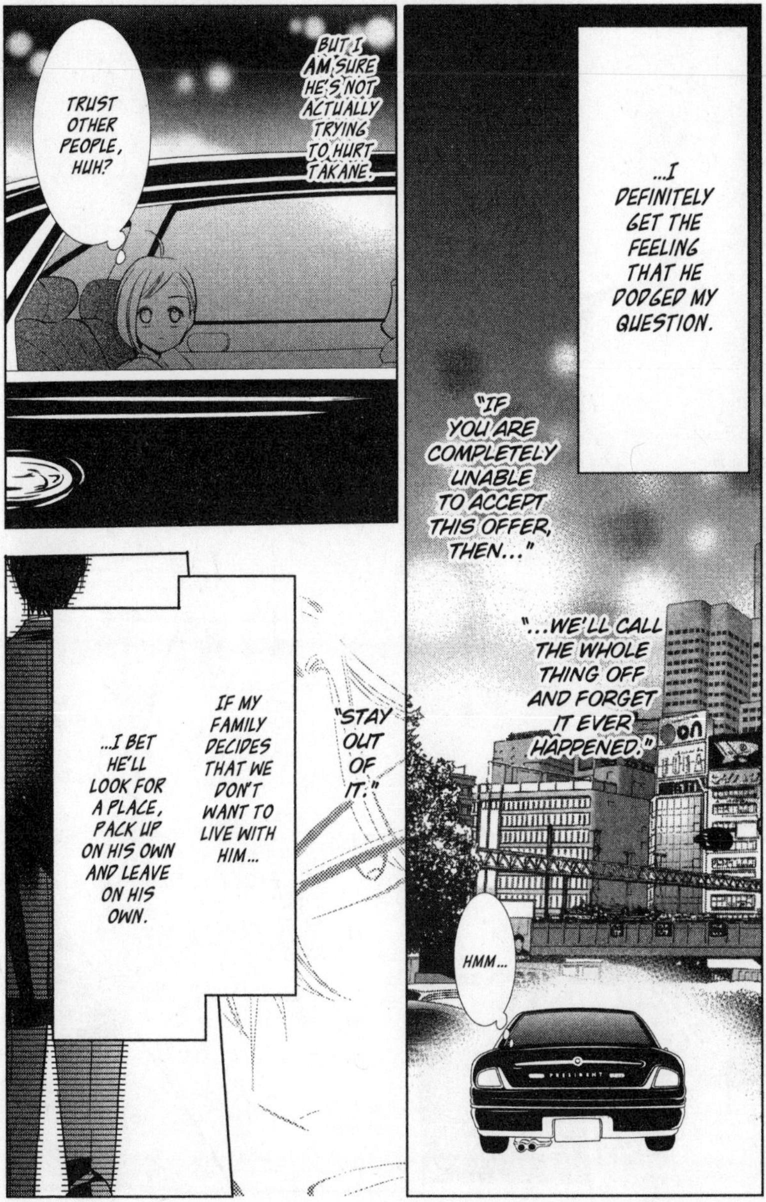
...I DEFINITELY GET THE FEELING THAT HE DODGED MY QUESTION.
"IF YOU ARE COMPLETELY UNABLE TO ACCEPT THIS OFFER, THEN..."
"...WE'LL CALL THE WHOLE THING OFF AND FORGET IT EVER HAPPENED."
HMM...
BUT I AM SURE HE'S NOT ACTUALLY TRYING TO HURT TAKANE.
TRUST OTHER PEOPLE, HUH?
"STAY OUT OF IT."
IF MY FAMILY DECIDES THAT WE DON'T WANT TO LIVE WITH HIM...
...I BET HE'LL LOOK FOR A PLACE, PACK UP ON HIS OWN AND LEAVE ON HIS OWN.

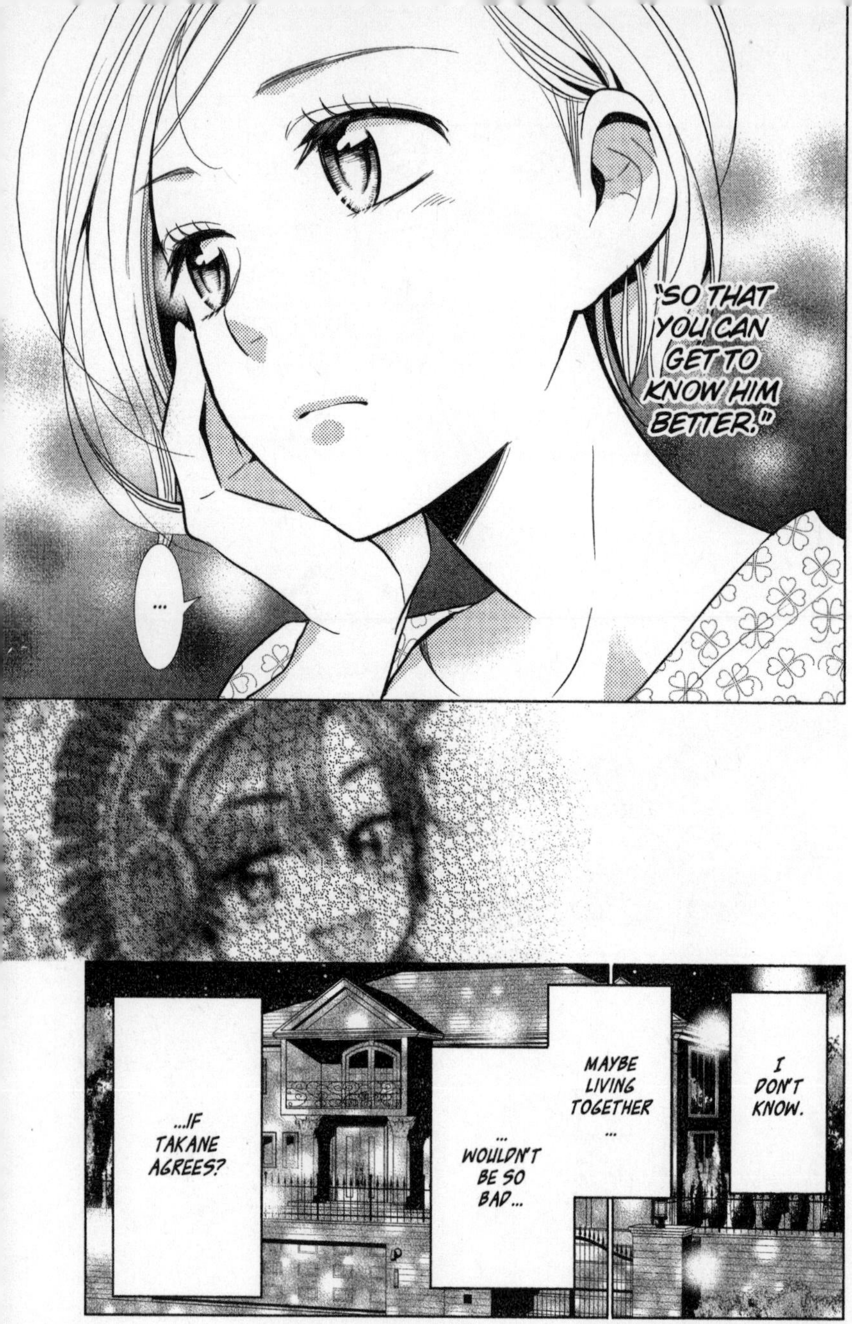
"SO THAT YOU CAN GET TO KNOW HIM BETTER."
...
I DON'T KNOW.
MAYBE LIVING TOGETHER ...
... WOULDN'T BE SO BAD...
...IF TAKANE AGREES?

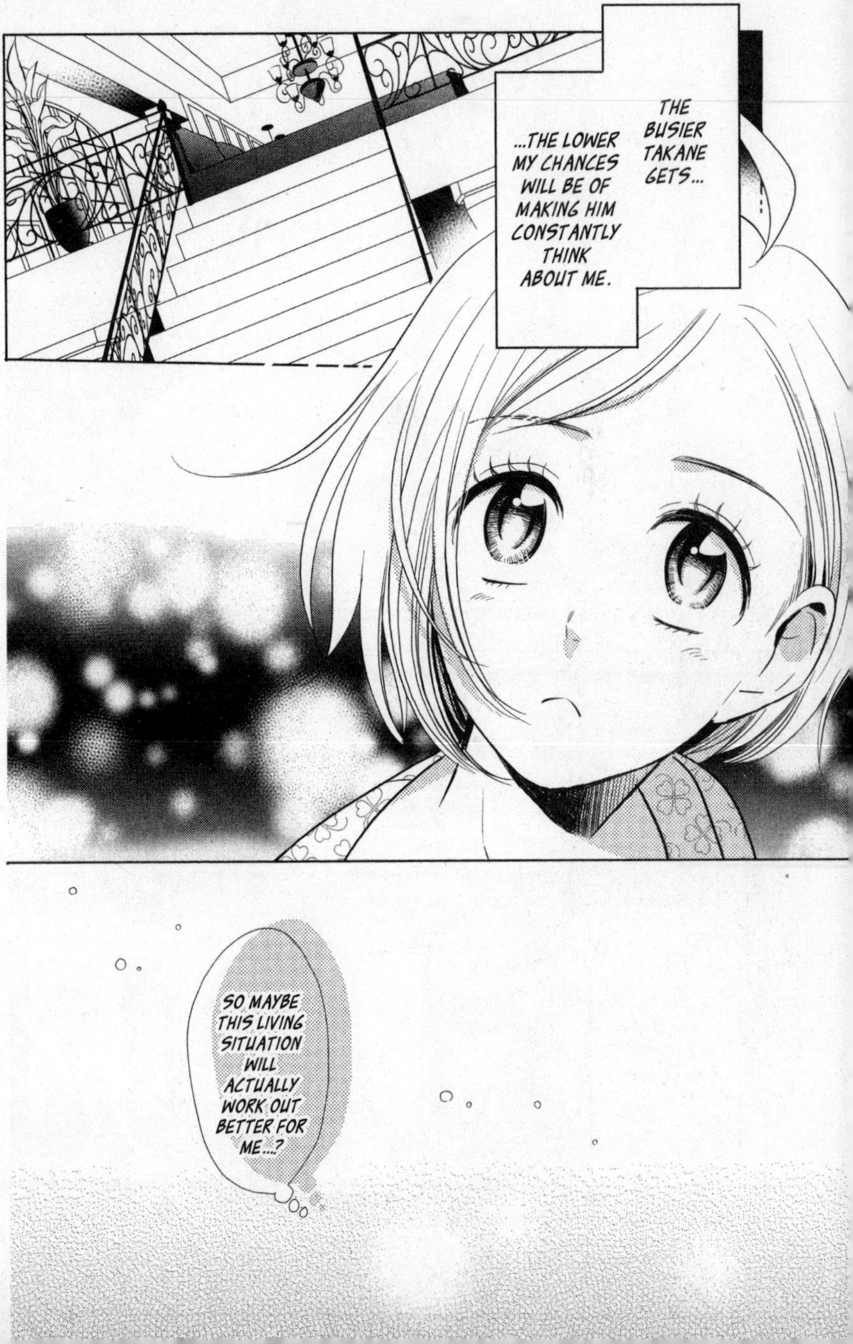
THE BUSIER TAKANE GETS...
...THE LOWER MY CHANCES WILL BE OF MAKING HIM CONSTANTLY THINK ABOUT ME.
SO MAYBE THIS LIVING SITUATION WILL ACTUALLY WORK OUT BETTER FOR ME...?

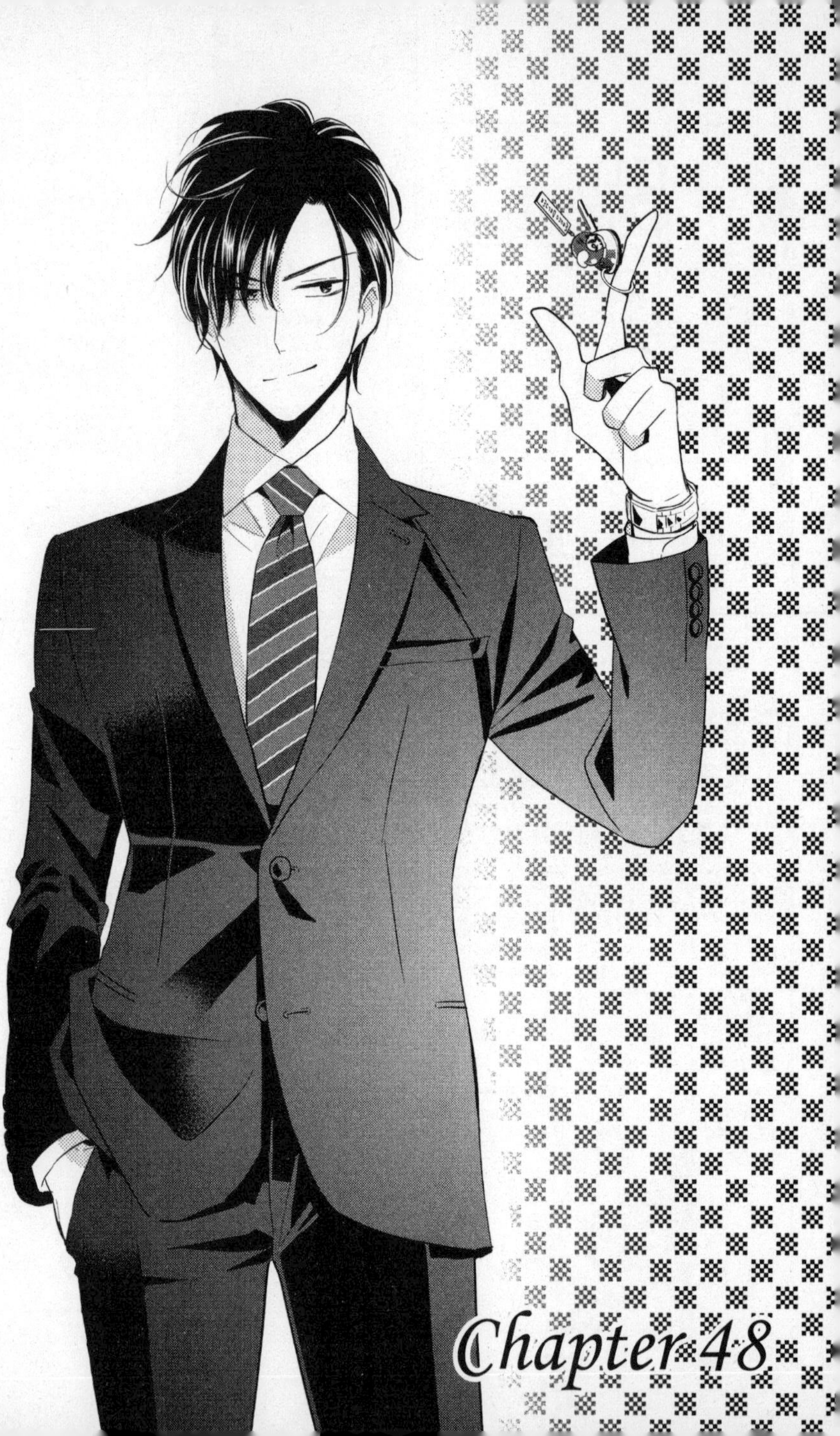

Chapter 48

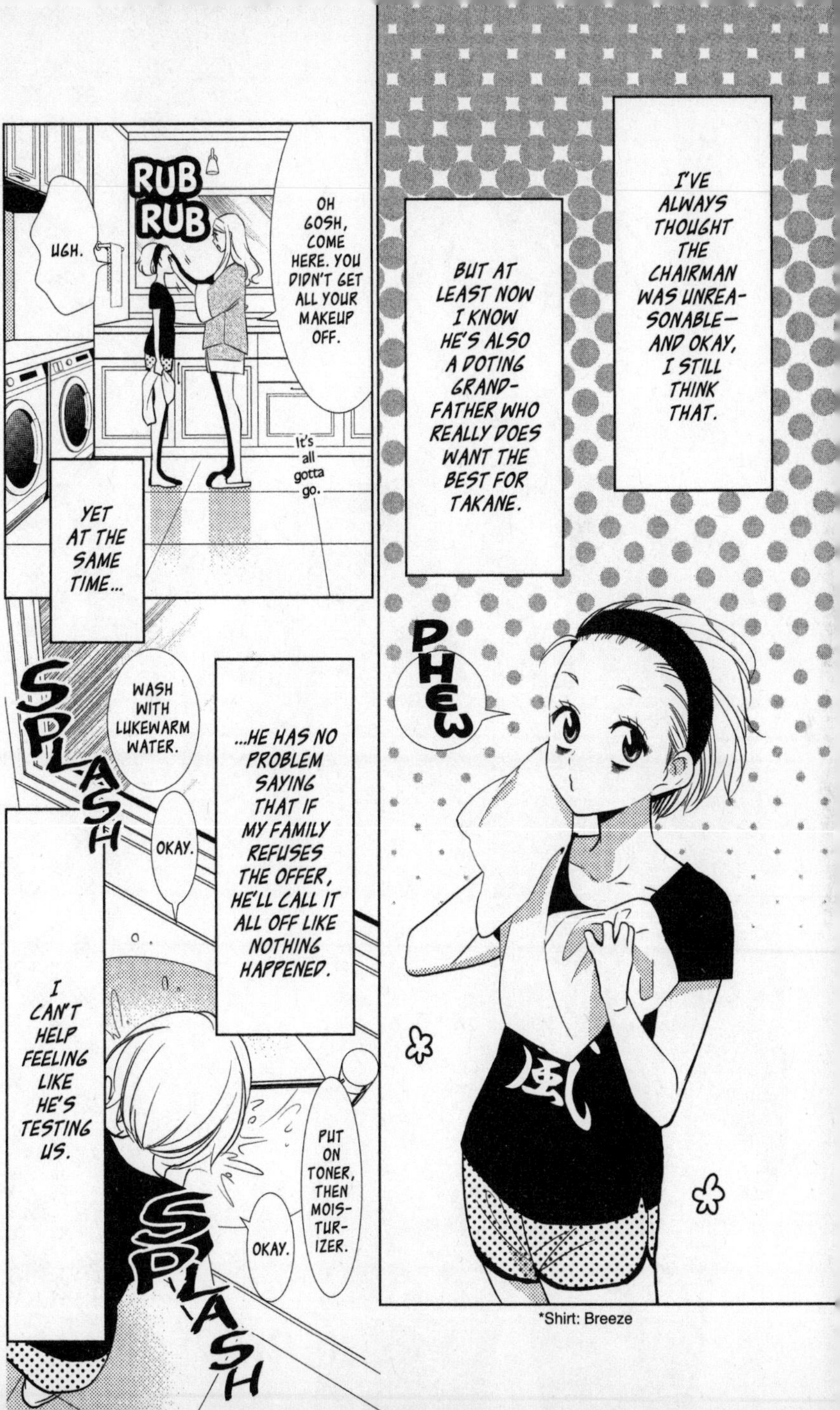
I'VE ALWAYS THOUGHT THE CHAIRMAN WAS UNREASONABLE—AND OKAY, I STILL THINK THAT.
BUT AT LEAST NOW I KNOW HE'S ALSO A DOTING GRANDFATHER WHO REALLY DOES WANT THE BEST FOR TAKANE.
PHEW
OH GOSH, COME HERE. YOU DIDN'T GET ALL YOUR MAKEUP OFF.
RUB RUB
UGH.
It's all gotta go.
YET AT THE SAME TIME...
...HE HAS NO PROBLEM SAYING THAT IF MY FAMILY REFUSES THE OFFER, HE'LL CALL IT ALL OFF LIKE NOTHING HAPPENED.
WASH WITH LUKEWARM WATER.
SPLASH
OKAY.
PUT ON TONER, THEN MOISTURIZER.
OKAY.
SPLASH
I CAN'T HELP FEELING LIKE HE'S TESTING US.
*Shirt: Breeze

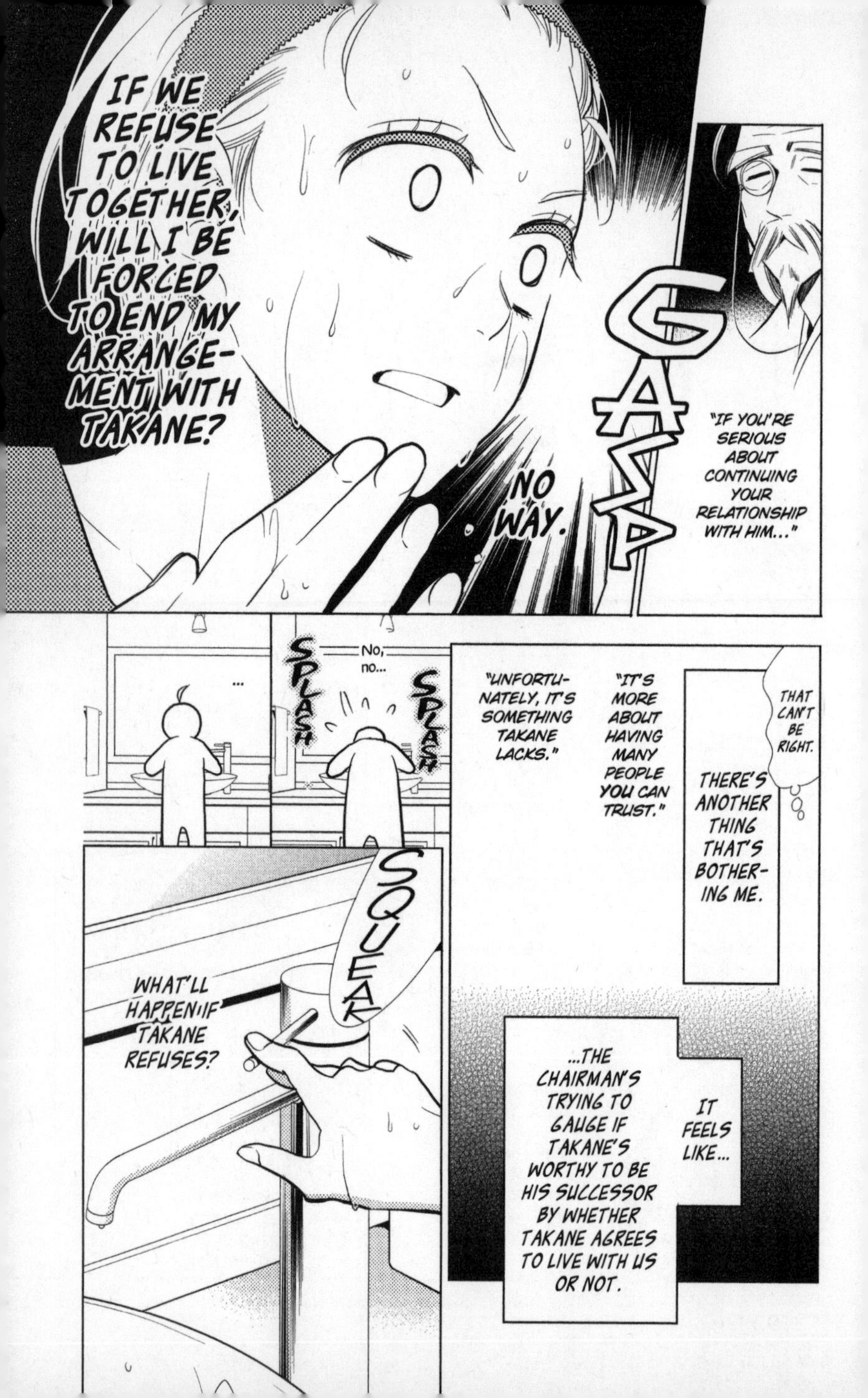
"IF YOU'RE SERIOUS ABOUT CONTINUING YOUR RELATIONSHIP WITH HIM..."
GASP
NO WAY.
IF WE REFUSE TO LIVE TOGETHER, WILL I BE FORCED TO END MY ARRANGEMENT WITH TAKANE?
THAT CAN'T BE RIGHT.
THERE'S ANOTHER THING THAT'S BOTHERING ME.
"IT'S MORE ABOUT HAVING MANY PEOPLE YOU CAN TRUST."
"UNFORTUNATELY, IT'S SOMETHING TAKANE LACKS."
IT FEELS LIKE...
...THE CHAIRMAN'S TRYING TO GAUGE IF TAKANE'S WORTHY TO BE HIS SUCCESSOR BY WHETHER TAKANE AGREES TO LIVE WITH US OR NOT.
SPLASH
SPLASH
No, no...
...
SQUEAK
WHAT'LL HAPPEN IF TAKANE REFUSES?

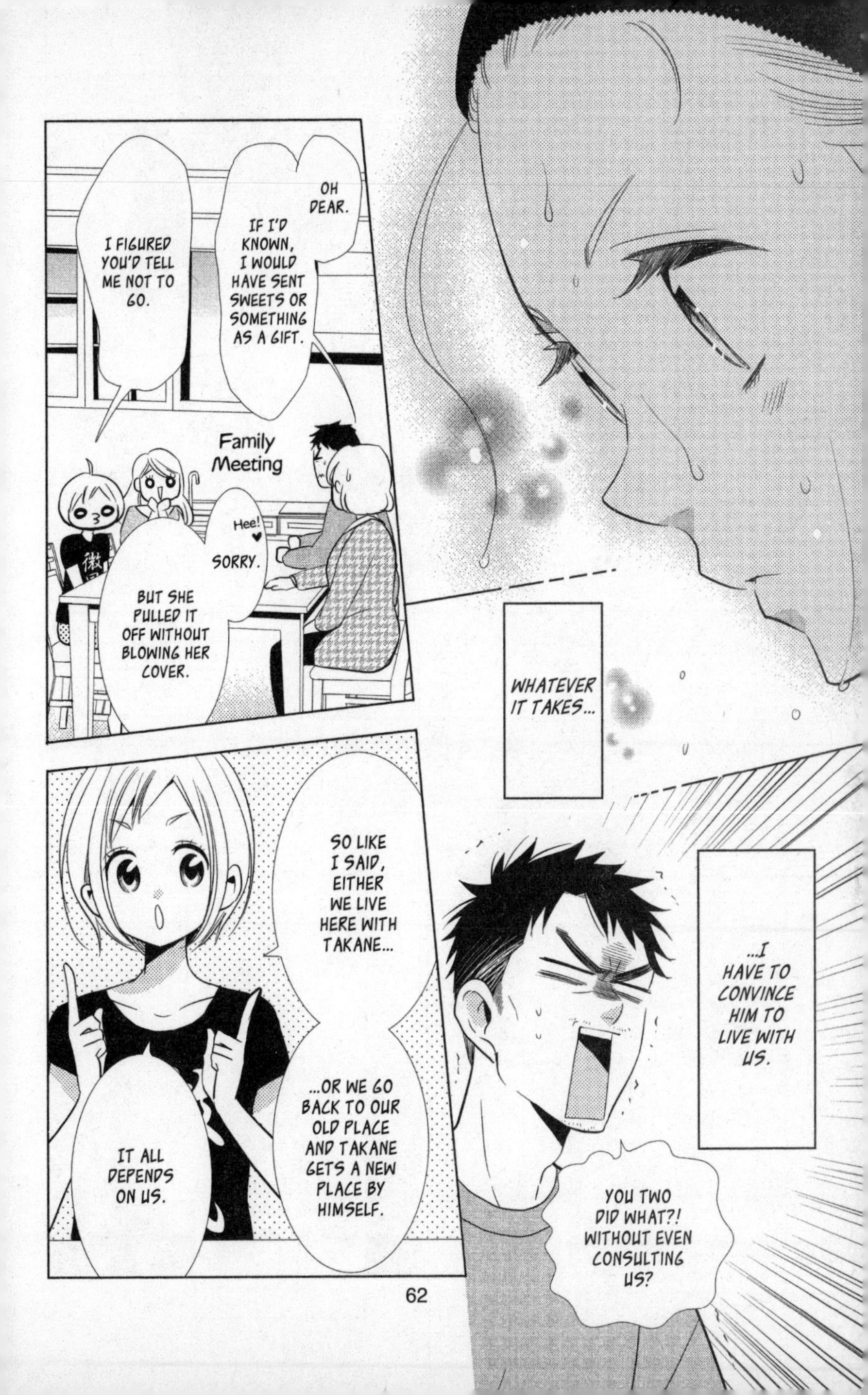
WHATEVER IT TAKES...
OH DEAR.
IF I'D KNOWN, I WOULD HAVE SENT SWEETS OR SOMETHING AS A GIFT.
I FIGURED YOU'D TELL ME NOT TO GO.
Family Meeting
Hee! ♥
SORRY.
BUT SHE PULLED IT OFF WITHOUT BLOWING HER COVER.
...I HAVE TO CONVINCE HIM TO LIVE WITH US.
YOU TWO DID WHAT?! WITHOUT EVEN CONSULTING US?
SO LIKE I SAID, EITHER WE LIVE HERE WITH TAKANE...
...OR WE GO BACK TO OUR OLD PLACE AND TAKANE GETS A NEW PLACE BY HIMSELF.
IT ALL DEPENDS ON US.

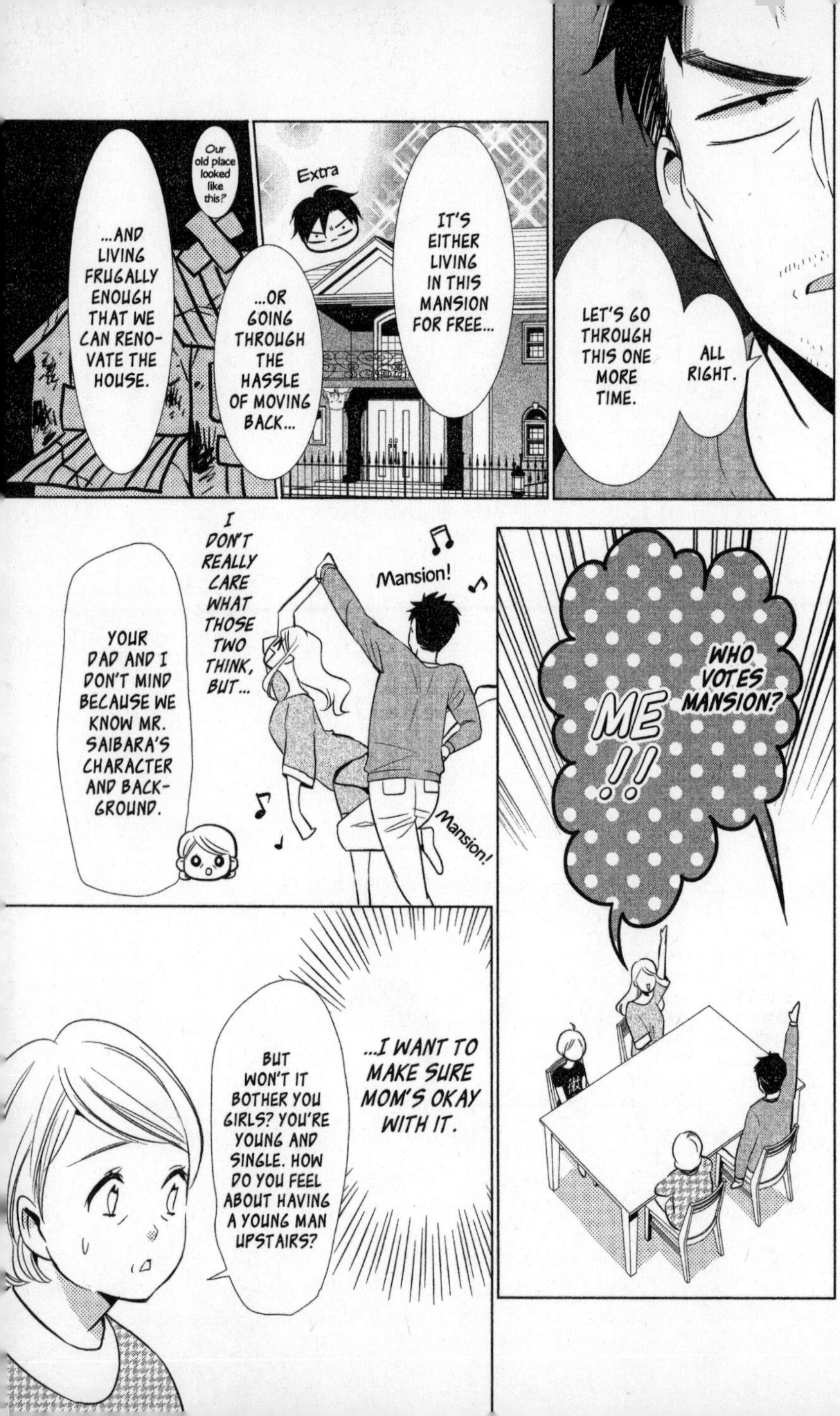
ALL RIGHT.
LET'S GO THROUGH THIS ONE MORE TIME.
IT'S EITHER LIVING IN THIS MANSION FOR FREE...
Extra
...OR GOING THROUGH THE HASSLE OF MOVING BACK...
Our old place looked like this?
...AND LIVING FRUGALLY ENOUGH THAT WE CAN RENOVATE THE HOUSE.
WHO VOTES MANSION?
ME!!
Mansion!
I DON'T REALLY CARE WHAT THOSE TWO THINK, BUT...
Mansion!
YOUR DAD AND I DON'T MIND BECAUSE WE KNOW MR. SAIBARA'S CHARACTER AND BACKGROUND.
...I WANT TO MAKE SURE MOM'S OKAY WITH IT.
BUT WON'T IT BOTHER YOU GIRLS? YOU'RE YOUNG AND SINGLE. HOW DO YOU FEEL ABOUT HAVING A YOUNG MAN UPSTAIRS?

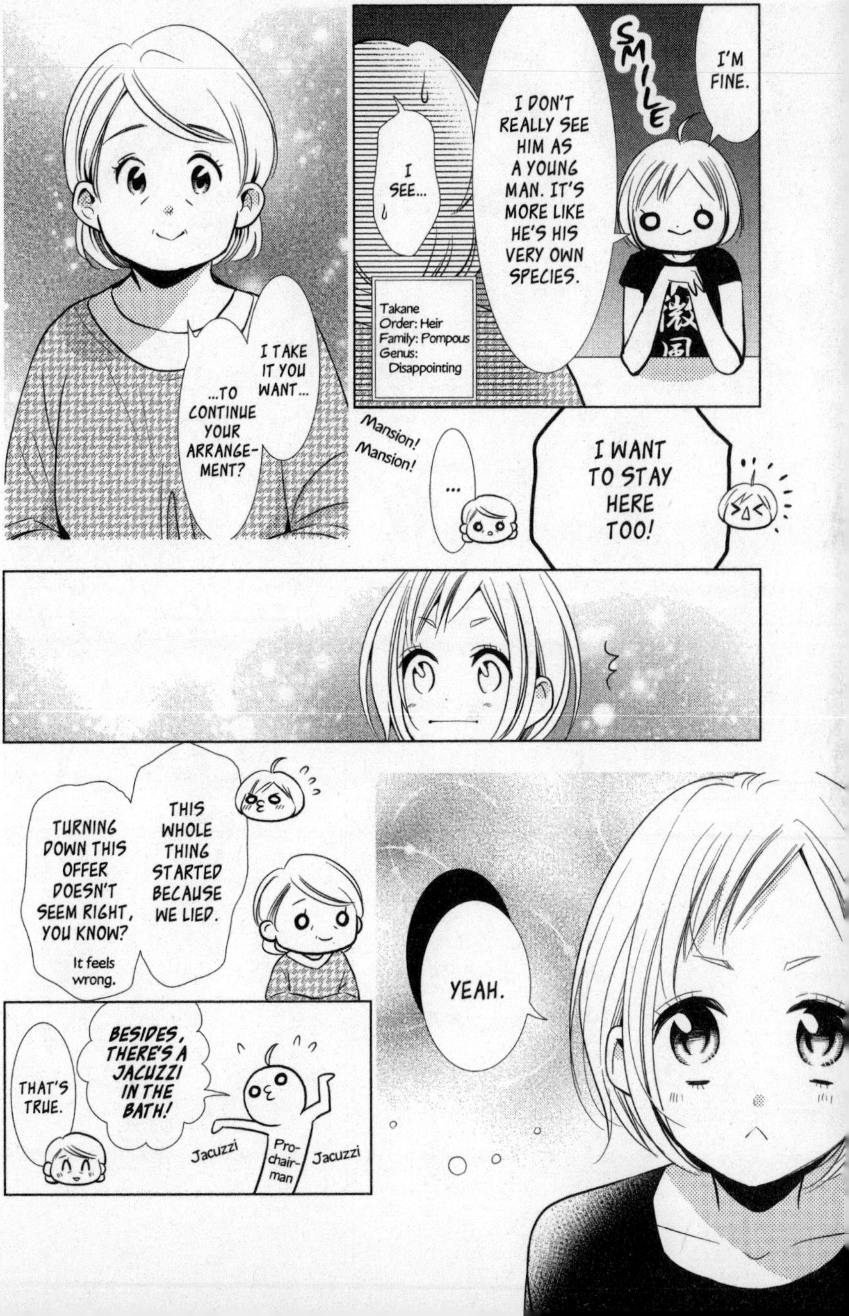
I'M FINE.
SMILE
I DON'T REALLY SEE HIM AS A YOUNG MAN. IT'S MORE LIKE HE'S HIS VERY OWN SPECIES.
I SEE...
Takane
Order: Heir
Family: Pompous
Genus: Disappointing
I WANT TO STAY HERE TOO!
Mansion! Mansion!
...
I TAKE IT YOU WANT...
...TO CONTINUE YOUR ARRANGEMENT?
YEAH.
THIS WHOLE THING STARTED BECAUSE WE LIED.
TURNING DOWN THIS OFFER DOESN'T SEEM RIGHT, YOU KNOW?
It feels wrong.
BESIDES, THERE'S A JACUZZI IN THE BATH!
Jacuzzi
Pro-chairman
Jacuzzi
THAT'S TRUE.

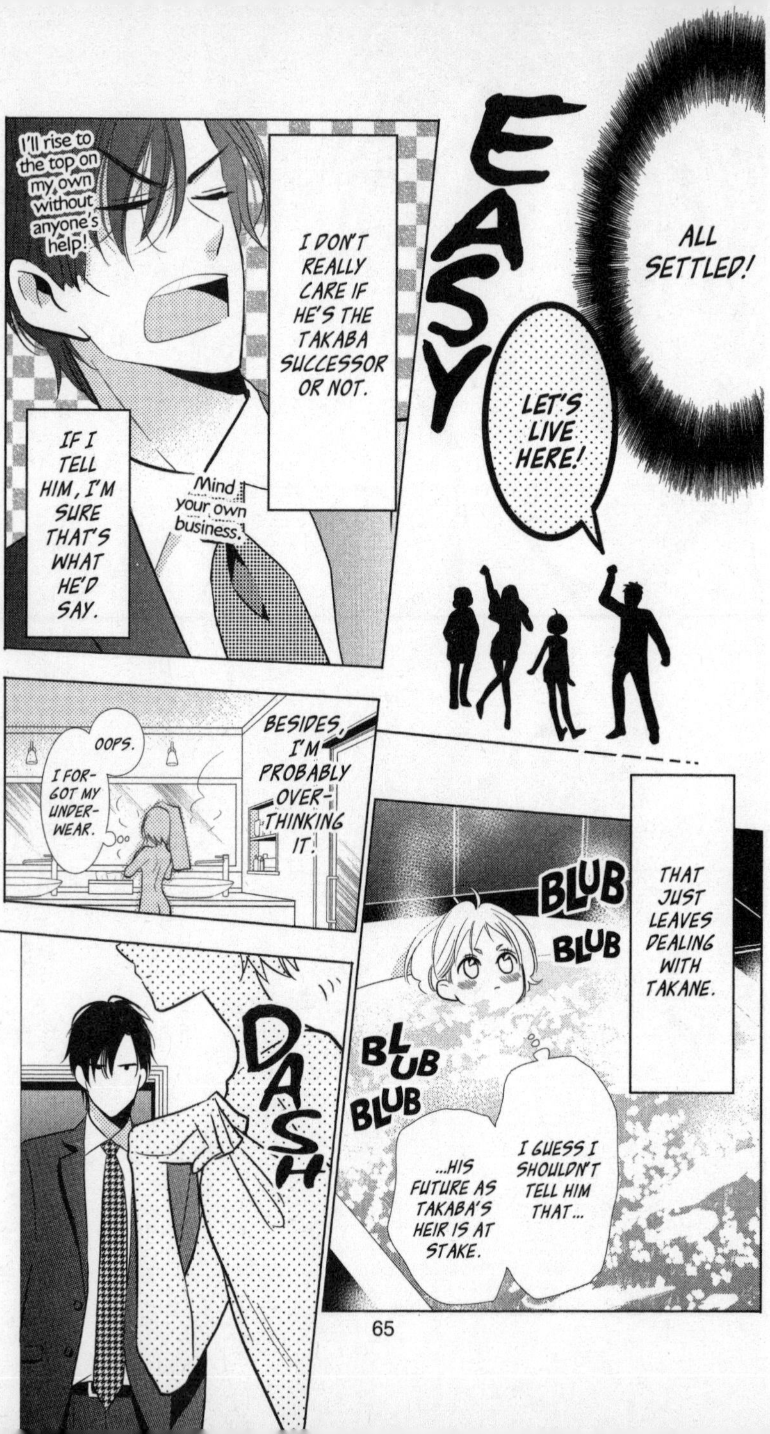
ALL SETTLED!
EASY
LET'S LIVE HERE!
I DON'T REALLY CARE IF HE'S THE TAKABA SUCCESSOR OR NOT.
I'll rise to the top on my own without anyone's help!
Mind your own business.
IF I TELL HIM, I'M SURE THAT'S WHAT HE'D SAY.
THAT JUST LEAVES DEALING WITH TAKANE.
BLUB
BLUB
BLUB
BLUB
I GUESS I SHOULDN'T TELL HIM THAT...
...HIS FUTURE AS TAKABA'S HEIR IS AT STAKE.
BESIDES, I'M PROBABLY OVER-THINKING IT.
OOPS.
I FOR-GOT MY UNDER-WEAR.
DASH

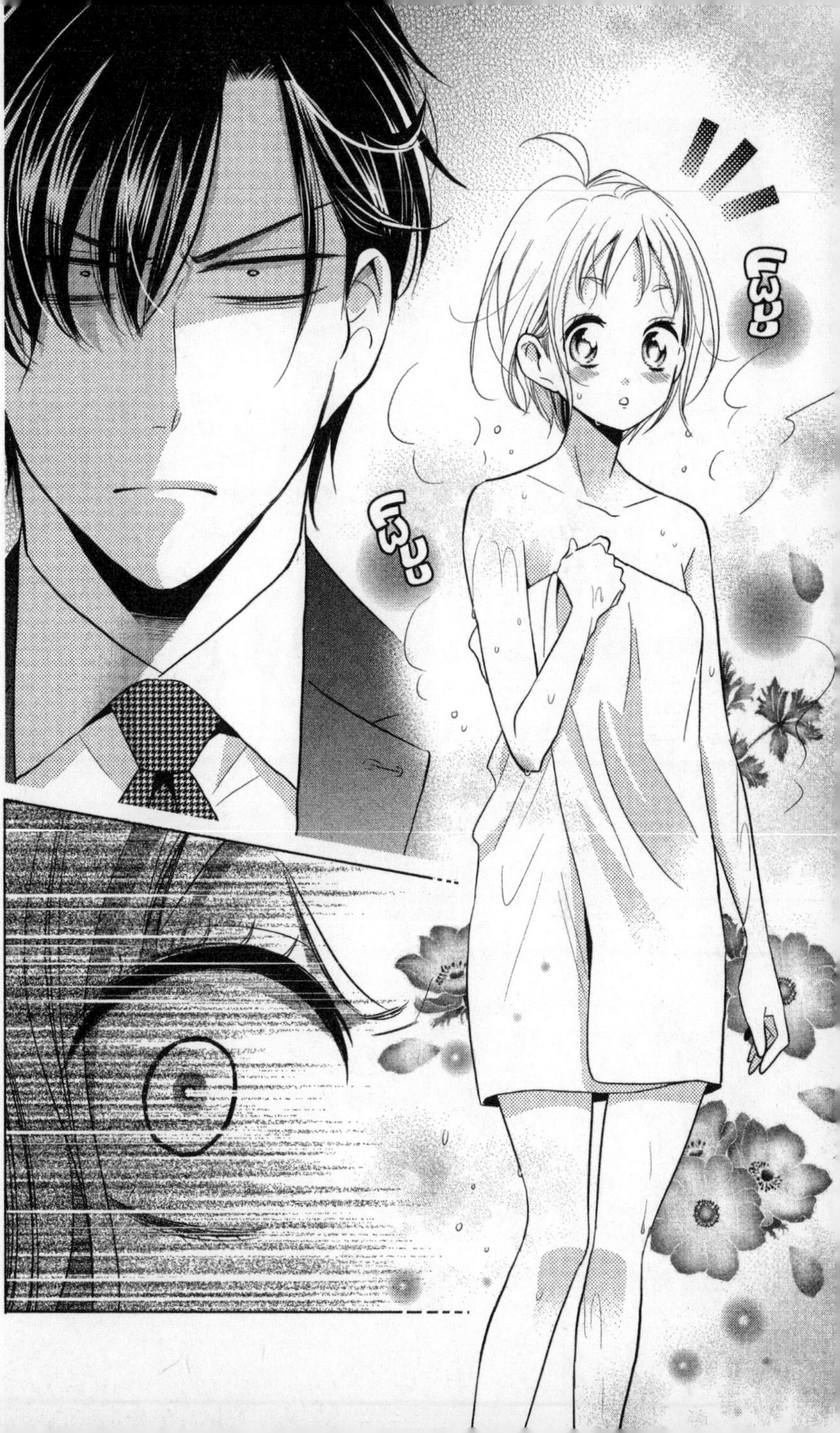

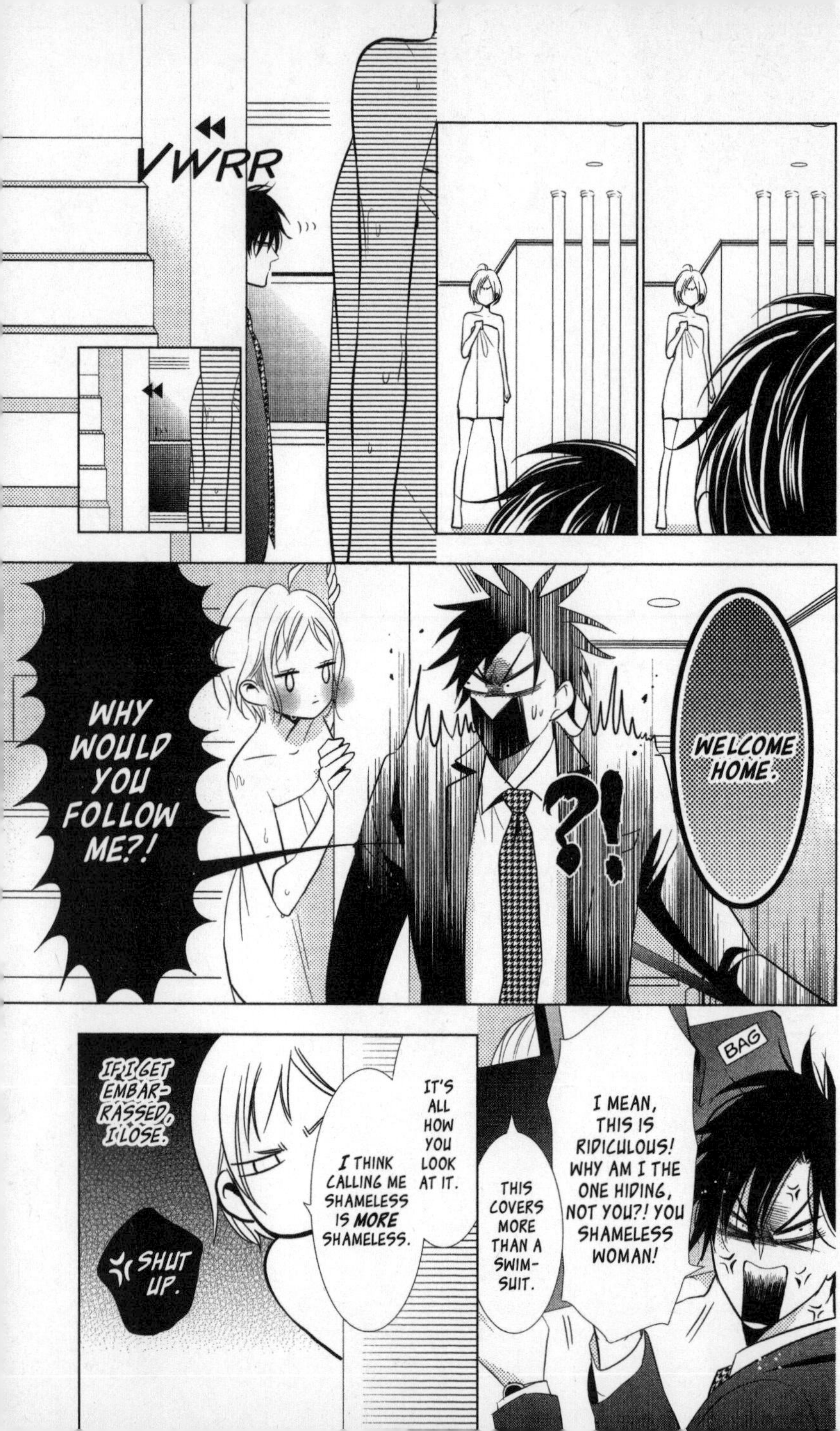
VWRR
WELCOME HOME.
?!
WHY WOULD YOU FOLLOW ME?!
BAG
I MEAN, THIS IS RIDICULOUS! WHY AM I THE ONE HIDING, NOT YOU?! YOU SHAMELESS WOMAN!
THIS COVERS MORE THAN A SWIM-SUIT.
IT'S ALL HOW YOU LOOK AT IT.
I THINK CALLING ME SHAMELESS IS *MORE* SHAMELESS.
IF I GET EMBAR-RASSED, I LOSE.
SHUT UP.

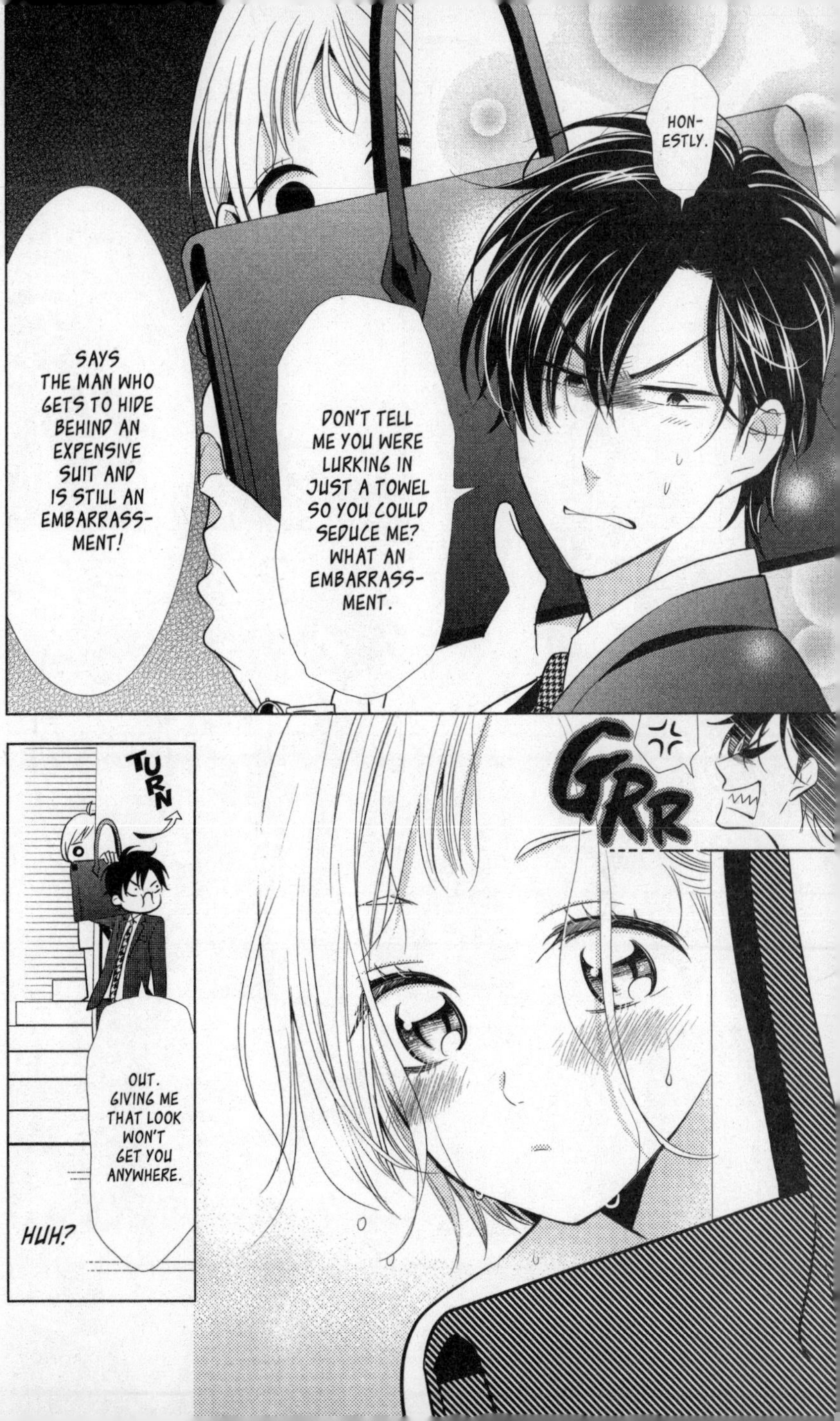
HON-ESTLY.
DON'T TELL ME YOU WERE LURKING IN JUST A TOWEL SO YOU COULD SEDUCE ME? WHAT AN EMBARRASS-MENT.
SAYS THE MAN WHO GETS TO HIDE BEHIND AN EXPENSIVE SUIT AND IS STILL AN EMBARRASS-MENT!
GRR
TURN
OUT. GIVING ME THAT LOOK WON'T GET YOU ANYWHERE.
HUH?

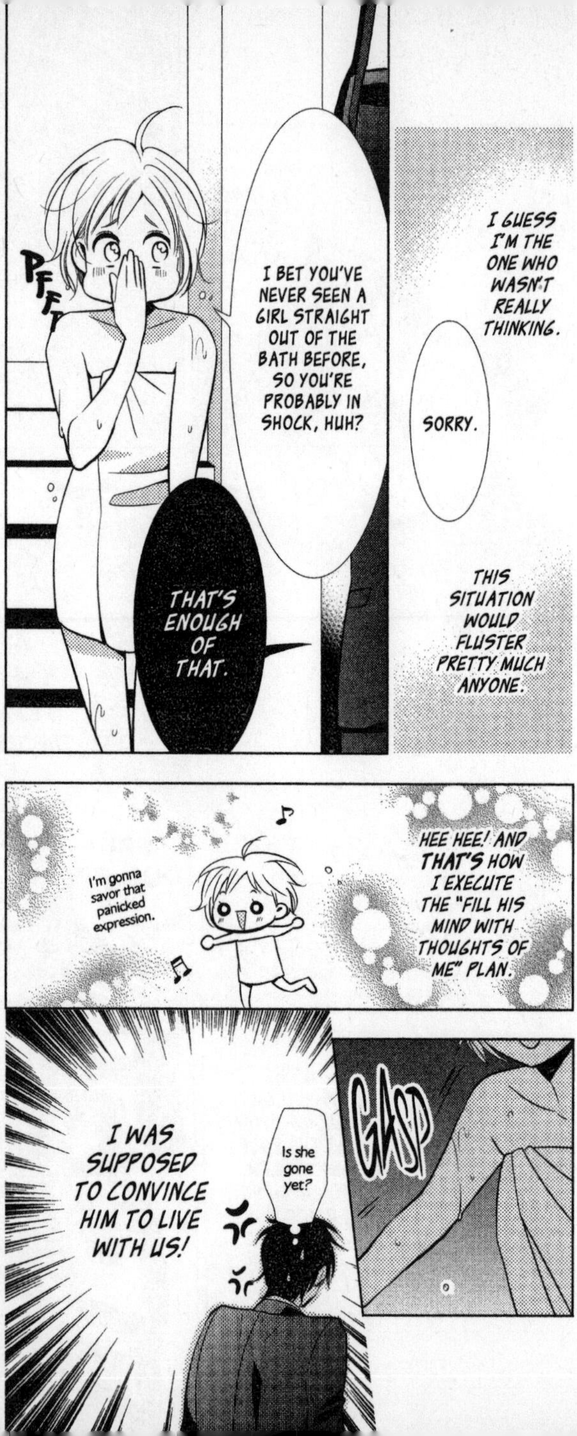
I GUESS I'M THE ONE WHO WASN'T REALLY THINKING.
SORRY.
THIS SITUATION WOULD FLUSTER PRETTY MUCH ANYONE.
I BET YOU'VE NEVER SEEN A GIRL STRAIGHT OUT OF THE BATH BEFORE, SO YOU'RE PROBABLY IN SHOCK, HUH?
PFFT
THAT'S ENOUGH OF THAT.
HEE HEE! AND THAT'S HOW I EXECUTE THE "FILL HIS MIND WITH THOUGHTS OF ME" PLAN.
I'm gonna savor that panicked expression.
GASP
Is she gone yet?
I WAS SUPPOSED TO CONVINCE HIM TO LIVE WITH US!

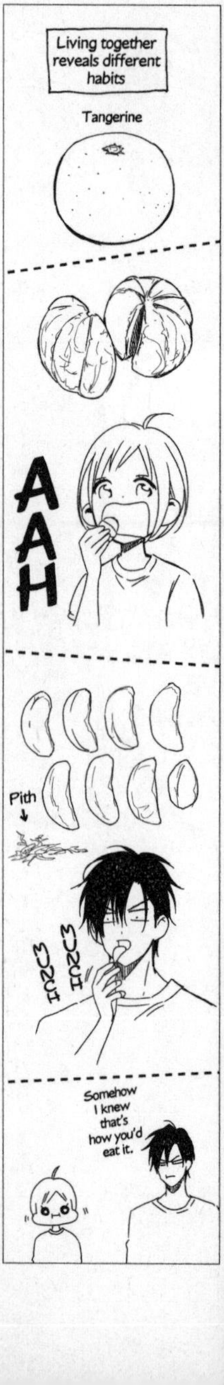
Living together reveals different habits
Tangerine
AAH
Pith
MUNCH MUNCH
Somehow I knew that's how you'd eat it.

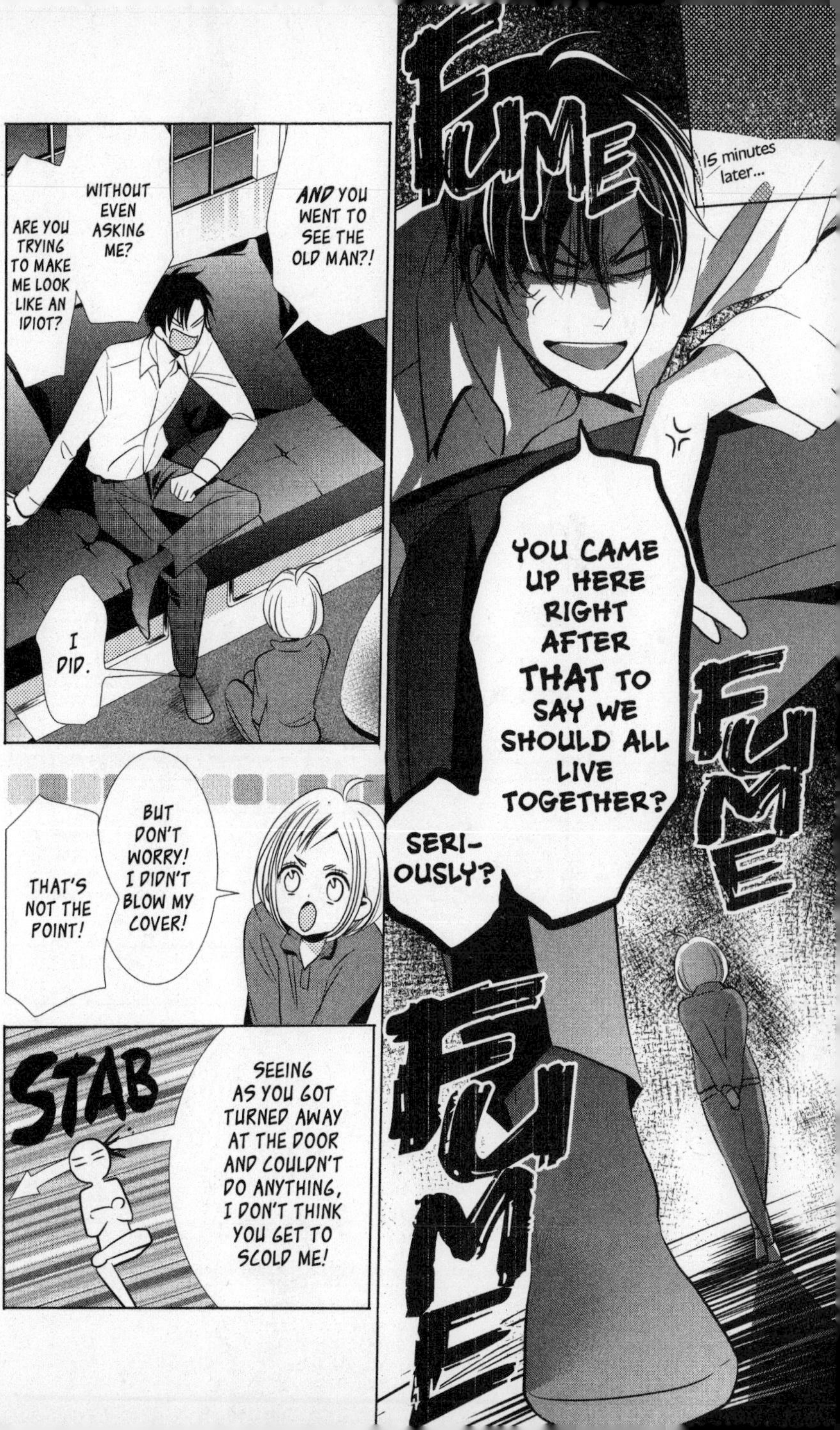
15 minutes later...
FUME
FUME
YOU CAME UP HERE RIGHT AFTER THAT TO SAY WE SHOULD ALL LIVE TOGETHER?
SERI-OUSLY?
FUME
AND YOU WENT TO SEE THE OLD MAN?!
WITHOUT EVEN ASKING ME?
ARE YOU TRYING TO MAKE ME LOOK LIKE AN IDIOT?
I DID.
BUT DON'T WORRY! I DIDN'T BLOW MY COVER!
THAT'S NOT THE POINT!
SEEING AS YOU GOT TURNED AWAY AT THE DOOR AND COULDN'T DO ANYTHING, I DON'T THINK YOU GET TO SCOLD ME!
STAB

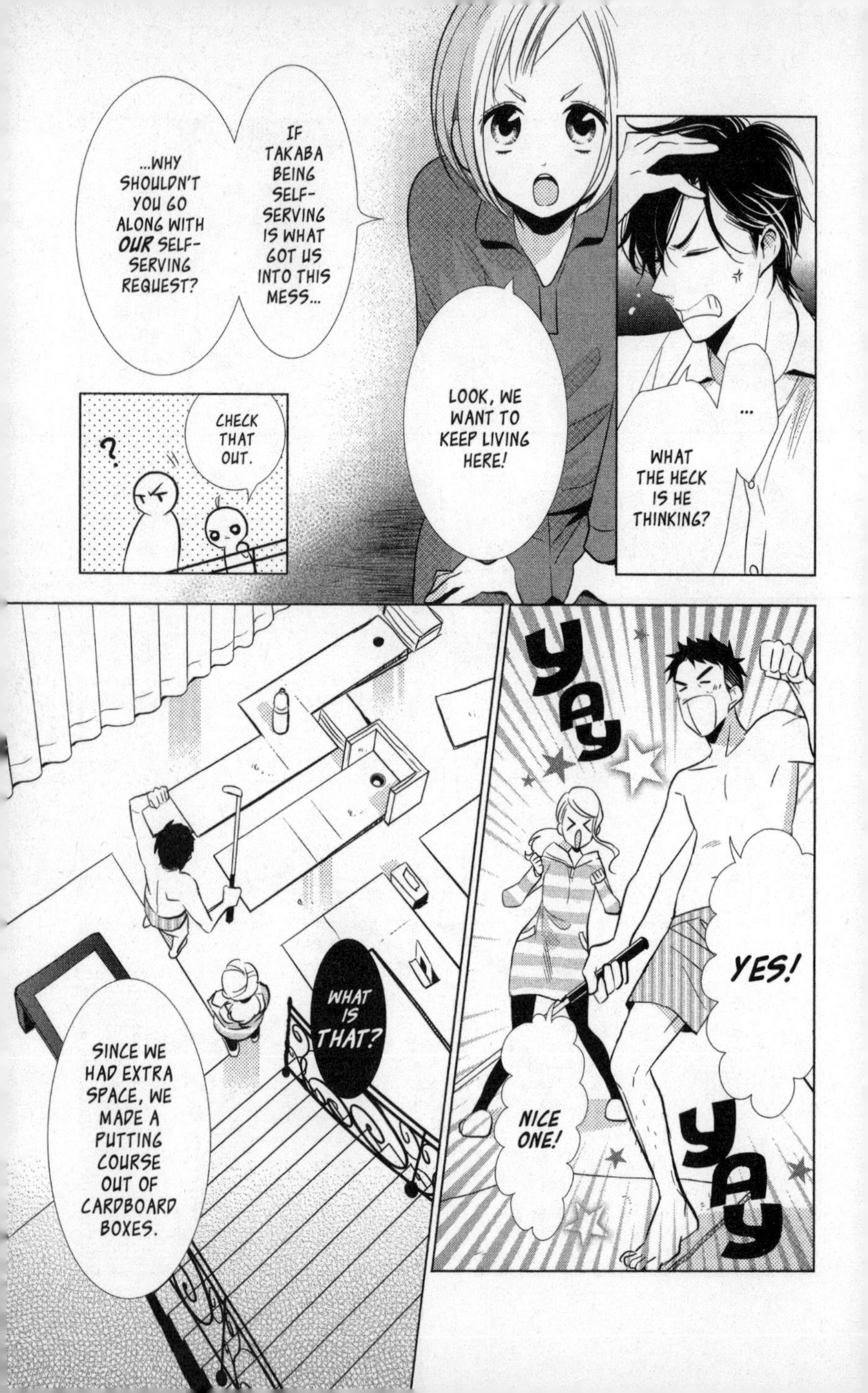
IF TAKABA BEING SELF-SERVING IS WHAT GOT US INTO THIS MESS...
...WHY SHOULDN'T YOU GO ALONG WITH OUR SELF-SERVING REQUEST?
LOOK, WE WANT TO KEEP LIVING HERE!
...
WHAT THE HECK IS HE THINKING?
CHECK THAT OUT.
?
YAY
YES!
NICE ONE!
YAY
WHAT IS THAT?
SINCE WE HAD EXTRA SPACE, WE MADE A PUTTING COURSE OUT OF CARDBOARD BOXES.

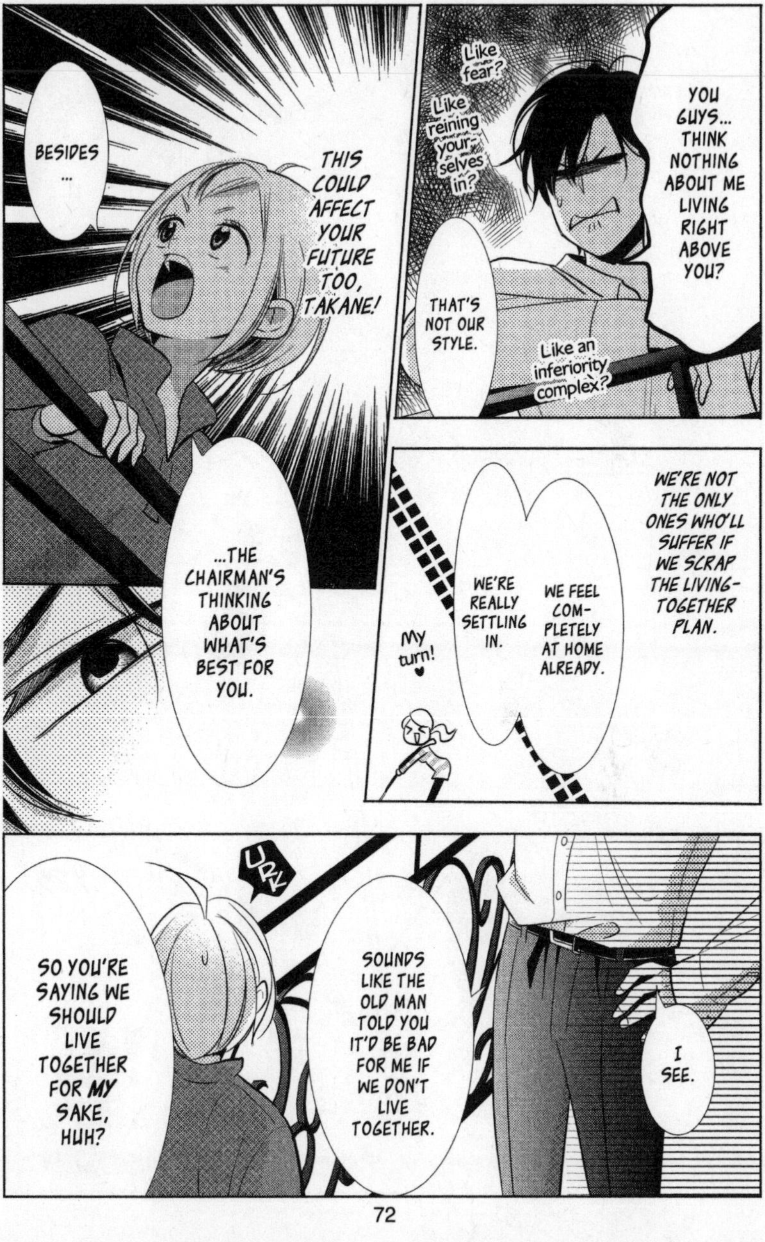
YOU GUYS... THINK NOTHING ABOUT ME LIVING RIGHT ABOVE YOU?
Like fear?
Like reining yourselves in?
THAT'S NOT OUR STYLE.
Like an inferiority complex?
WE'RE NOT THE ONLY ONES WHO'LL SUFFER IF WE SCRAP THE LIVING-TOGETHER PLAN.
WE FEEL COMPLETELY AT HOME ALREADY.
WE'RE REALLY SETTLING IN.
My turn! ♥
THIS COULD AFFECT YOUR FUTURE TOO, TAKANE!
BESIDES...
...THE CHAIRMAN'S THINKING ABOUT WHAT'S BEST FOR YOU.
I SEE.
SOUNDS LIKE THE OLD MAN TOLD YOU IT'D BE BAD FOR ME IF WE DON'T LIVE TOGETHER.
URK
SO YOU'RE SAYING WE SHOULD LIVE TOGETHER FOR *MY* SAKE, HUH?

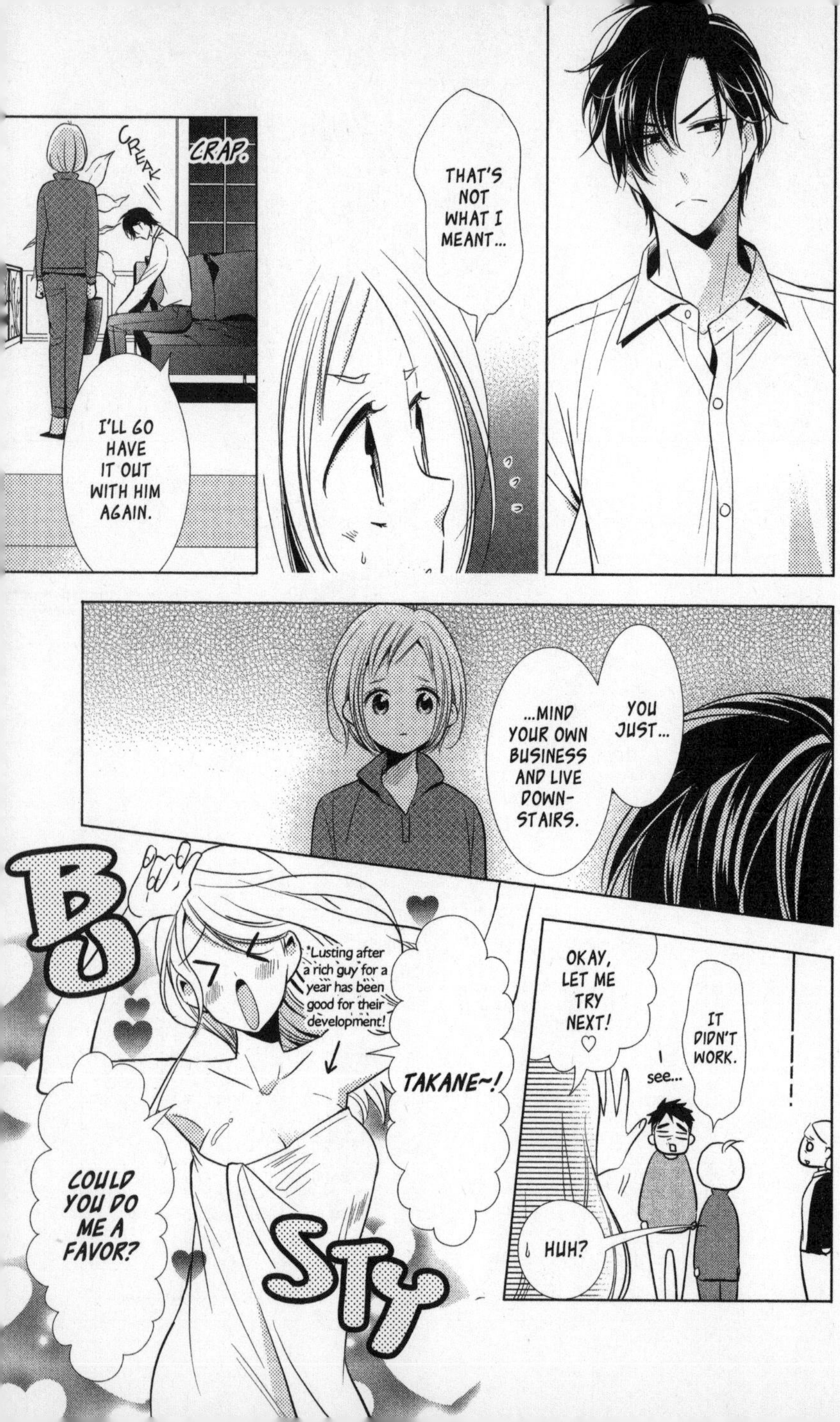
THAT'S NOT WHAT I MEANT...
CREAK
CRAP.
I'LL GO HAVE IT OUT WITH HIM AGAIN.
YOU JUST...
...MIND YOUR OWN BUSINESS AND LIVE DOWN-STAIRS.
IT DIDN'T WORK.
I see...
OKAY, LET ME TRY NEXT! ♡
HUH?
BUSTY
TAKANE~!
*Lusting after a rich guy for a year has been good for their development!
COULD YOU DO ME A FAVOR?

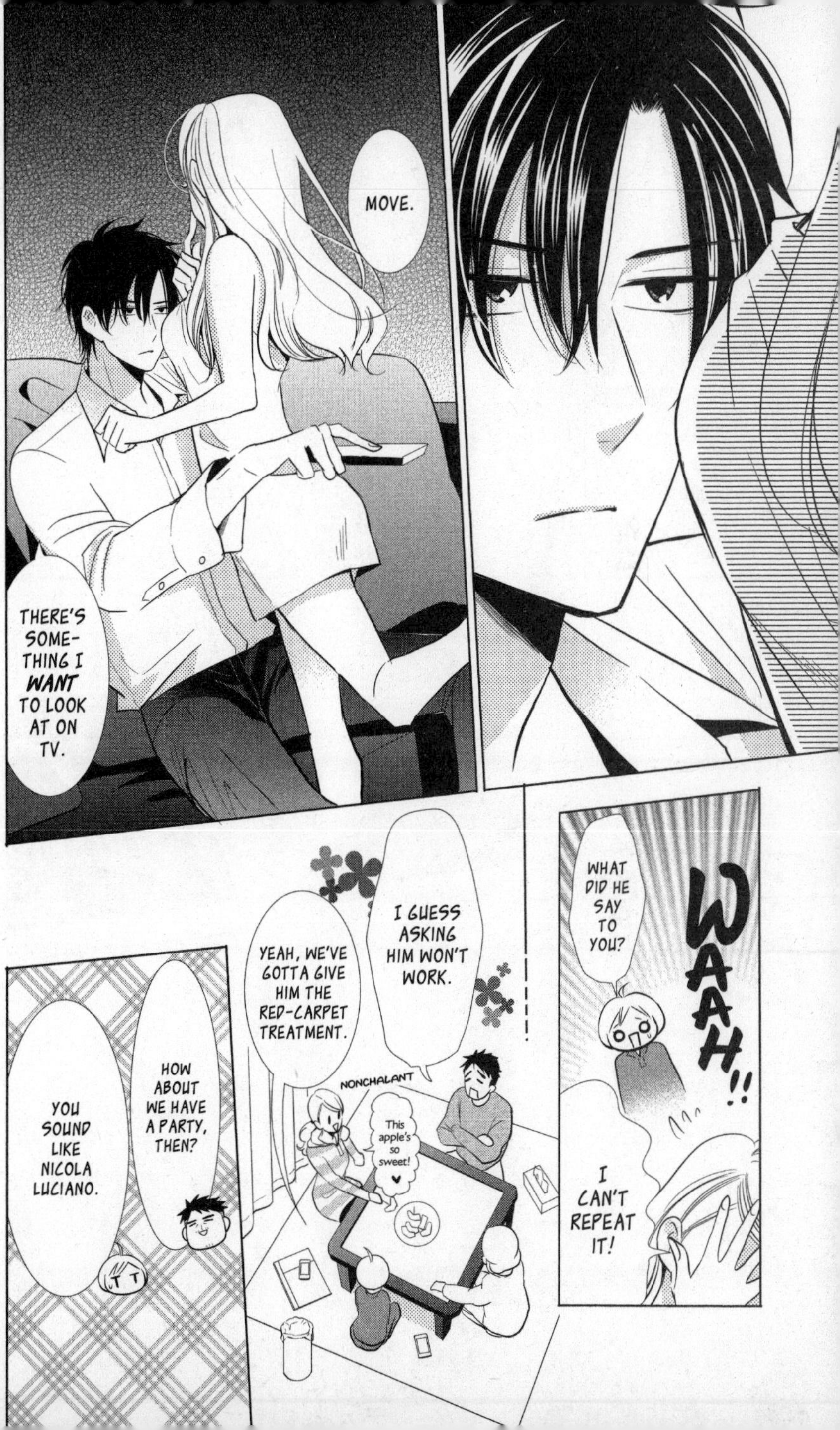
MOVE.
THERE'S SOME-THING I WANT TO LOOK AT ON TV.
WHAT DID HE SAY TO YOU?
WAAH!!
I CAN'T REPEAT IT!
I GUESS ASKING HIM WON'T WORK.
YEAH, WE'VE GOTTA GIVE HIM THE RED-CARPET TREATMENT.
NONCHALANT
This apple's so sweet! ♥
HOW ABOUT WE HAVE A PARTY, THEN?
YOU SOUND LIKE NICOLA LUCIANO.

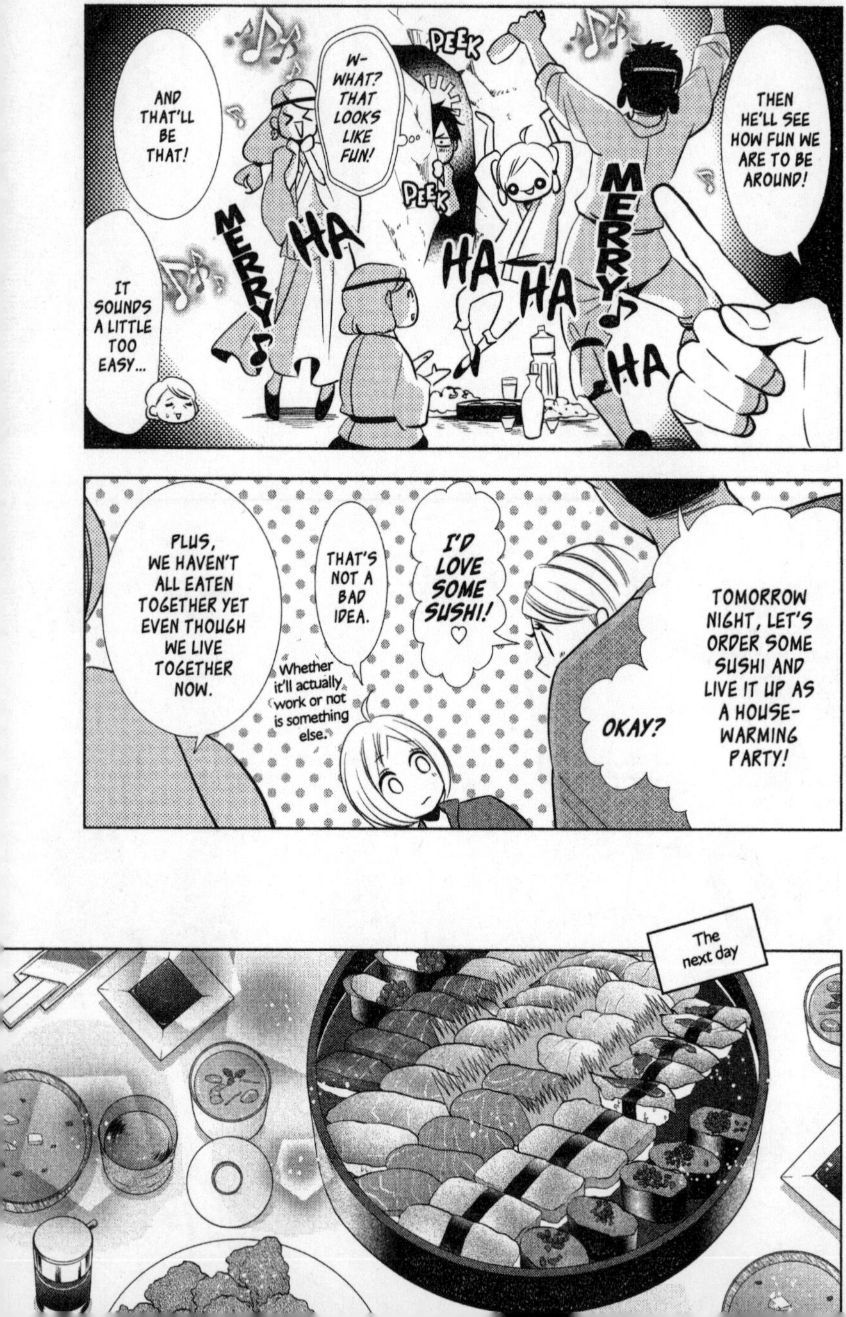
THEN HE'LL SEE HOW FUN WE ARE TO BE AROUND!
PEEK
W-WHAT? THAT LOOKS LIKE FUN!
AND THAT'LL BE THAT!
MERRY♪
HA HA HA HA
PEEK
MERRY♪
IT SOUNDS A LITTLE TOO EASY...
TOMORROW NIGHT, LET'S ORDER SOME SUSHI AND LIVE IT UP AS A HOUSE-WARMING PARTY!
OKAY?
I'D LOVE SOME SUSHI! ♡
THAT'S NOT A BAD IDEA.
Whether it'll actually work or not is something else.
PLUS, WE HAVEN'T ALL EATEN TOGETHER YET EVEN THOUGH WE LIVE TOGETHER NOW.
The next day

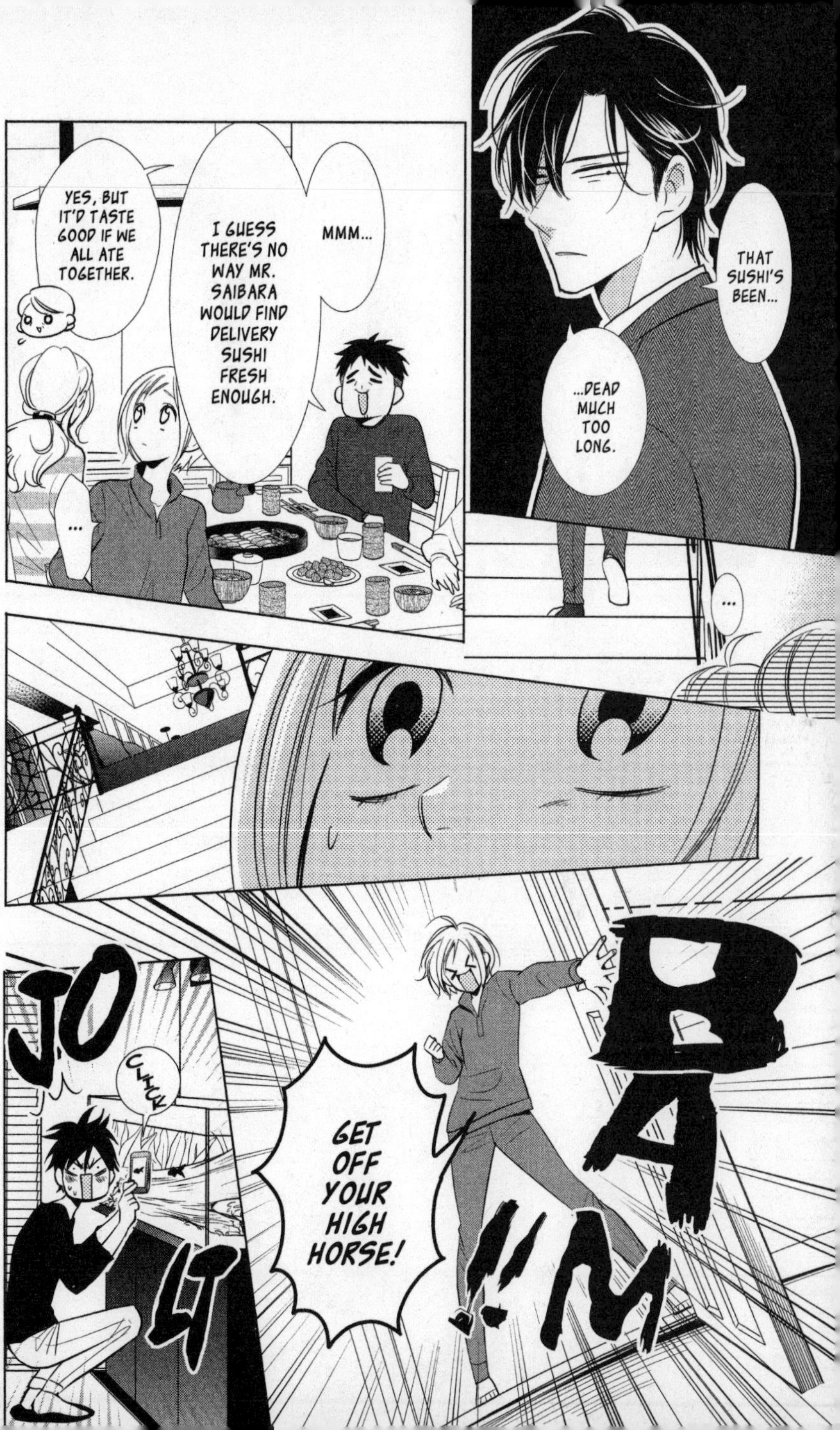
THAT SUSHI'S BEEN...
...DEAD MUCH TOO LONG.
...
MMM...
I GUESS THERE'S NO WAY MR. SAIBARA WOULD FIND DELIVERY SUSHI FRESH ENOUGH.
YES, BUT IT'D TASTE GOOD IF WE ALL ATE TOGETHER.
...
BAM
GET OFF YOUR HIGH HORSE!
JOLT
CLICK

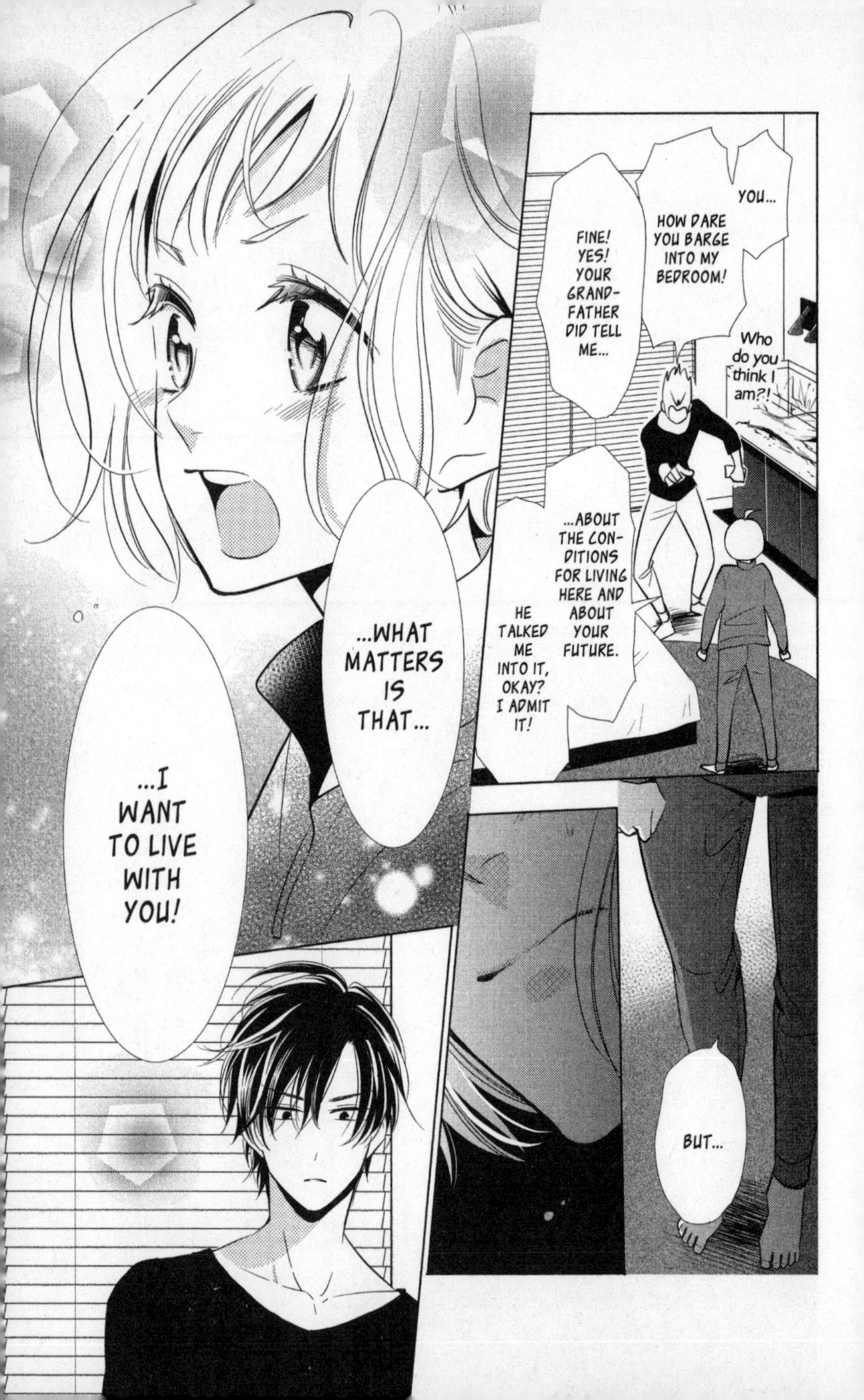
YOU...
HOW DARE YOU BARGE INTO MY BEDROOM!
Who do you think I am?!
FINE! YES! YOUR GRAND-FATHER DID TELL ME...
...ABOUT THE CON-DITIONS FOR LIVING HERE AND ABOUT YOUR FUTURE.
HE TALKED ME INTO IT, OKAY? I ADMIT IT!
BUT...
...WHAT MATTERS IS THAT...
...I WANT TO LIVE WITH YOU!

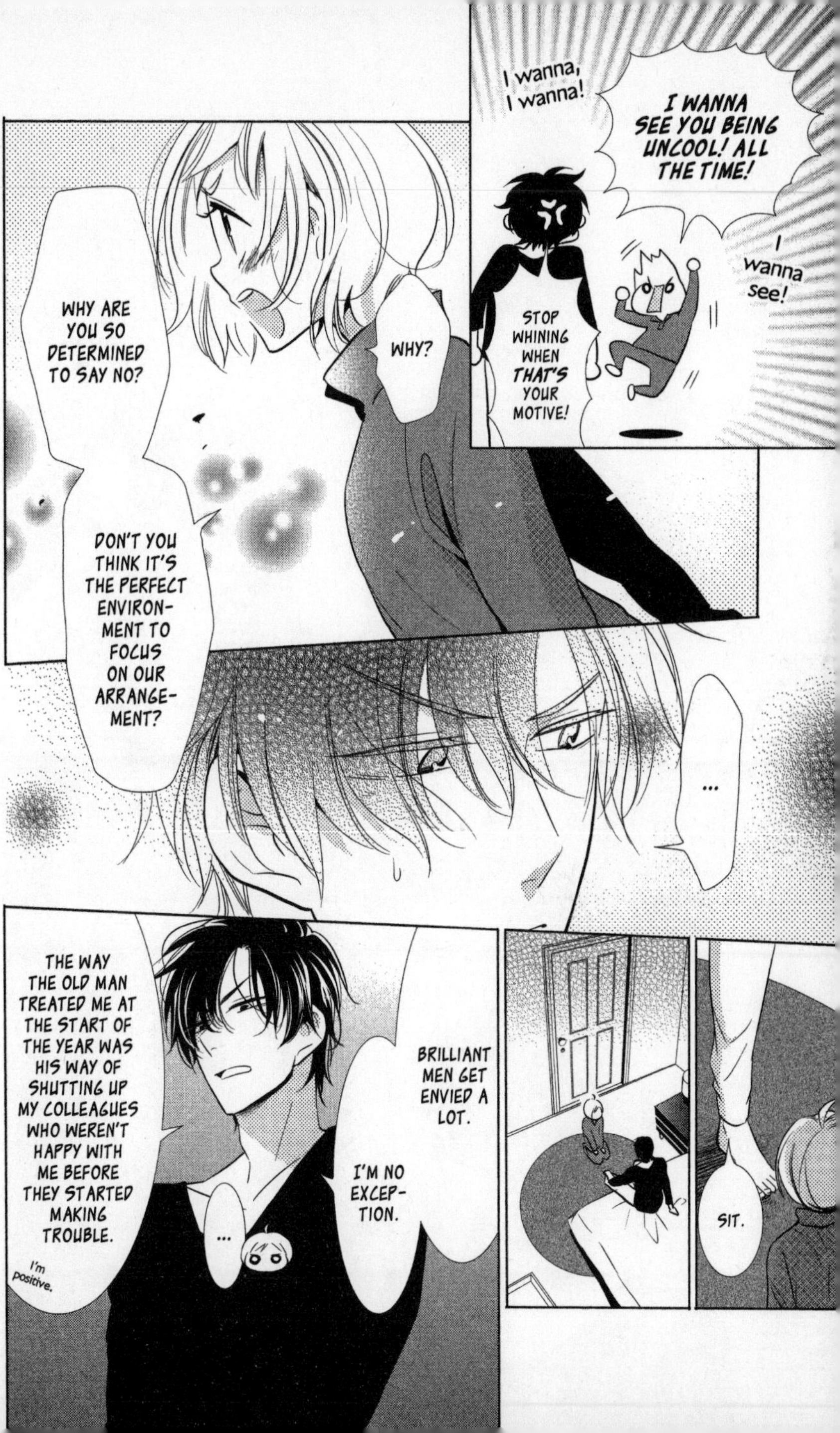
I WANNA SEE YOU BEING UNCOOL! ALL THE TIME!
I wanna, I wanna!
I wanna see!
STOP WHINING WHEN THAT'S YOUR MOTIVE!
WHY?
WHY ARE YOU SO DETERMINED TO SAY NO?
DON'T YOU THINK IT'S THE PERFECT ENVIRONMENT TO FOCUS ON OUR ARRANGEMENT?
...
SIT.
BRILLIANT MEN GET ENVIED A LOT.
I'M NO EXCEPTION.
THE WAY THE OLD MAN TREATED ME AT THE START OF THE YEAR WAS HIS WAY OF SHUTTING UP MY COLLEAGUES WHO WEREN'T HAPPY WITH ME BEFORE THEY STARTED MAKING TROUBLE.
...
I'm positive.

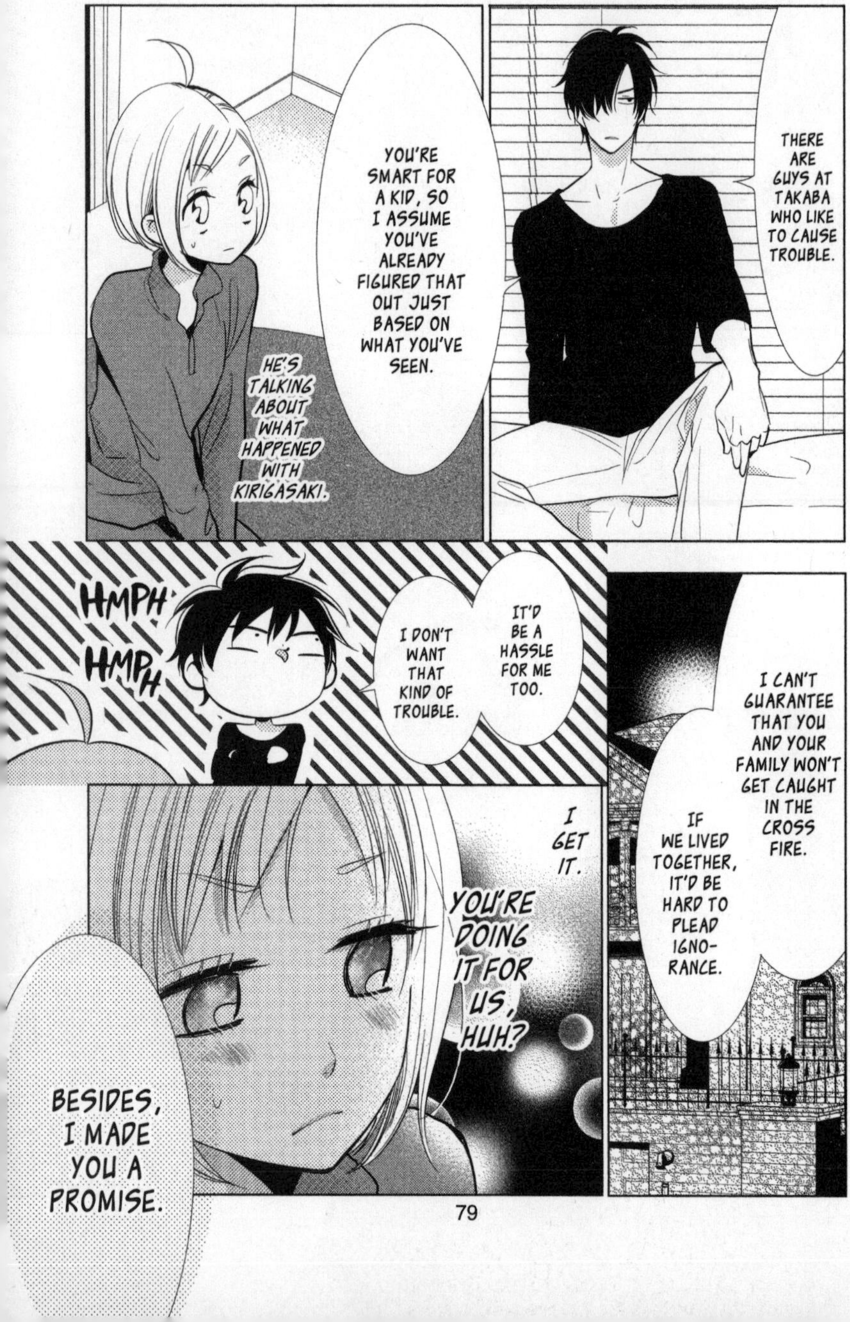
THERE ARE GUYS AT TAKABA WHO LIKE TO CAUSE TROUBLE.
YOU'RE SMART FOR A KID, SO I ASSUME YOU'VE ALREADY FIGURED THAT OUT JUST BASED ON WHAT YOU'VE SEEN.
HE'S TALKING ABOUT WHAT HAPPENED WITH KIRIGASAKI.
I CAN'T GUARANTEE THAT YOU AND YOUR FAMILY WON'T GET CAUGHT IN THE CROSS FIRE.
IF WE LIVED TOGETHER, IT'D BE HARD TO PLEAD IGNO-RANCE.
IT'D BE A HASSLE FOR ME TOO.
I DON'T WANT THAT KIND OF TROUBLE.
HMPH
HMPH
I GET IT.
YOU'RE DOING IT FOR US, HUH?
BESIDES, I MADE YOU A PROMISE.

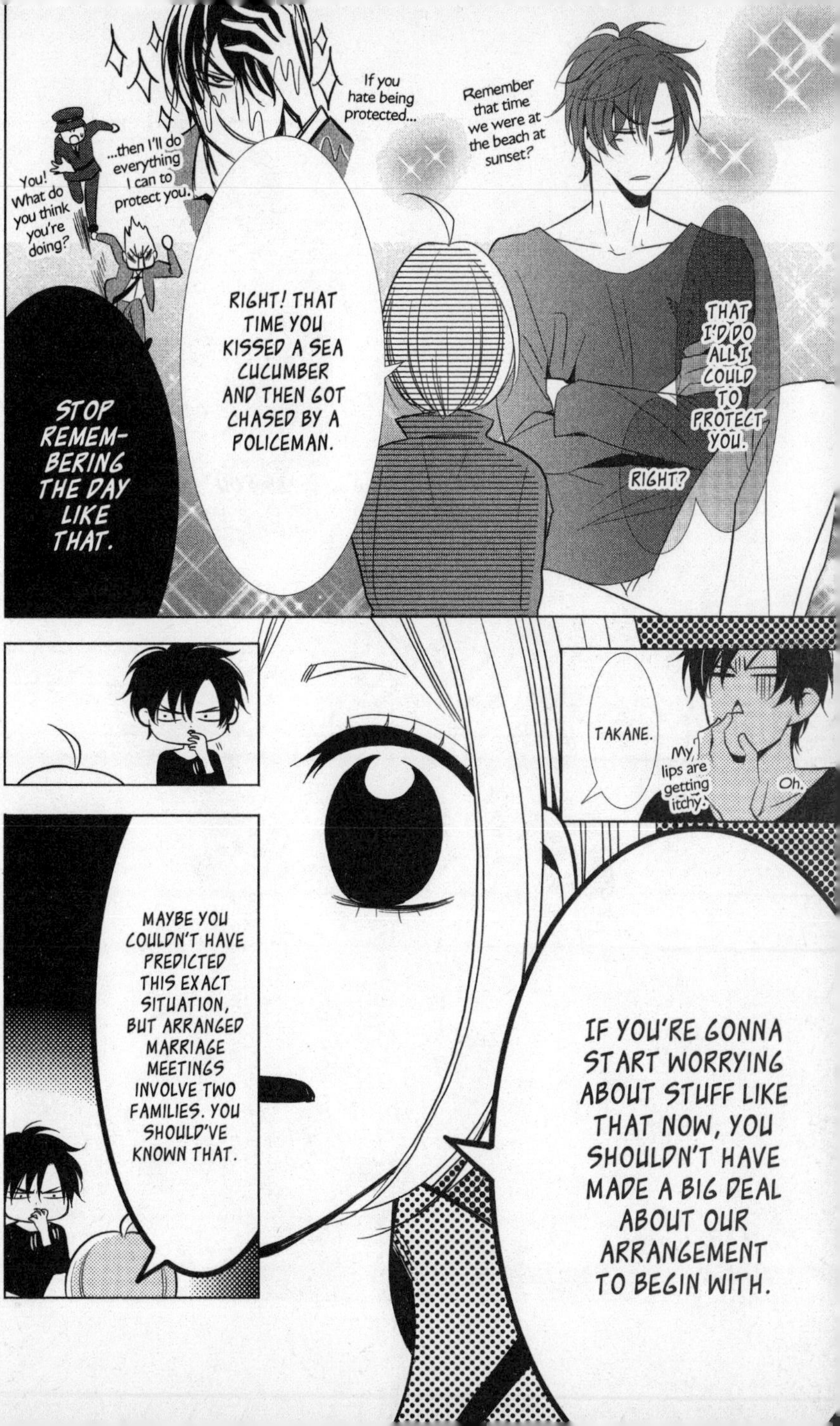
Remember that time we were at the beach at sunset?
THAT I'D DO ALL I COULD TO PROTECT YOU.
RIGHT?
If you hate being protected...
...then I'll do everything I can to protect you.
You! What do you think you're doing?
RIGHT! THAT TIME YOU KISSED A SEA CUCUMBER AND THEN GOT CHASED BY A POLICEMAN.
STOP REMEMBERING THE DAY LIKE THAT.
Oh.
My lips are getting itchy.
TAKANE.
IF YOU'RE GONNA START WORRYING ABOUT STUFF LIKE THAT NOW, YOU SHOULDN'T HAVE MADE A BIG DEAL ABOUT OUR ARRANGEMENT TO BEGIN WITH.
MAYBE YOU COULDN'T HAVE PREDICTED THIS EXACT SITUATION, BUT ARRANGED MARRIAGE MEETINGS INVOLVE TWO FAMILIES. YOU SHOULD'VE KNOWN THAT.

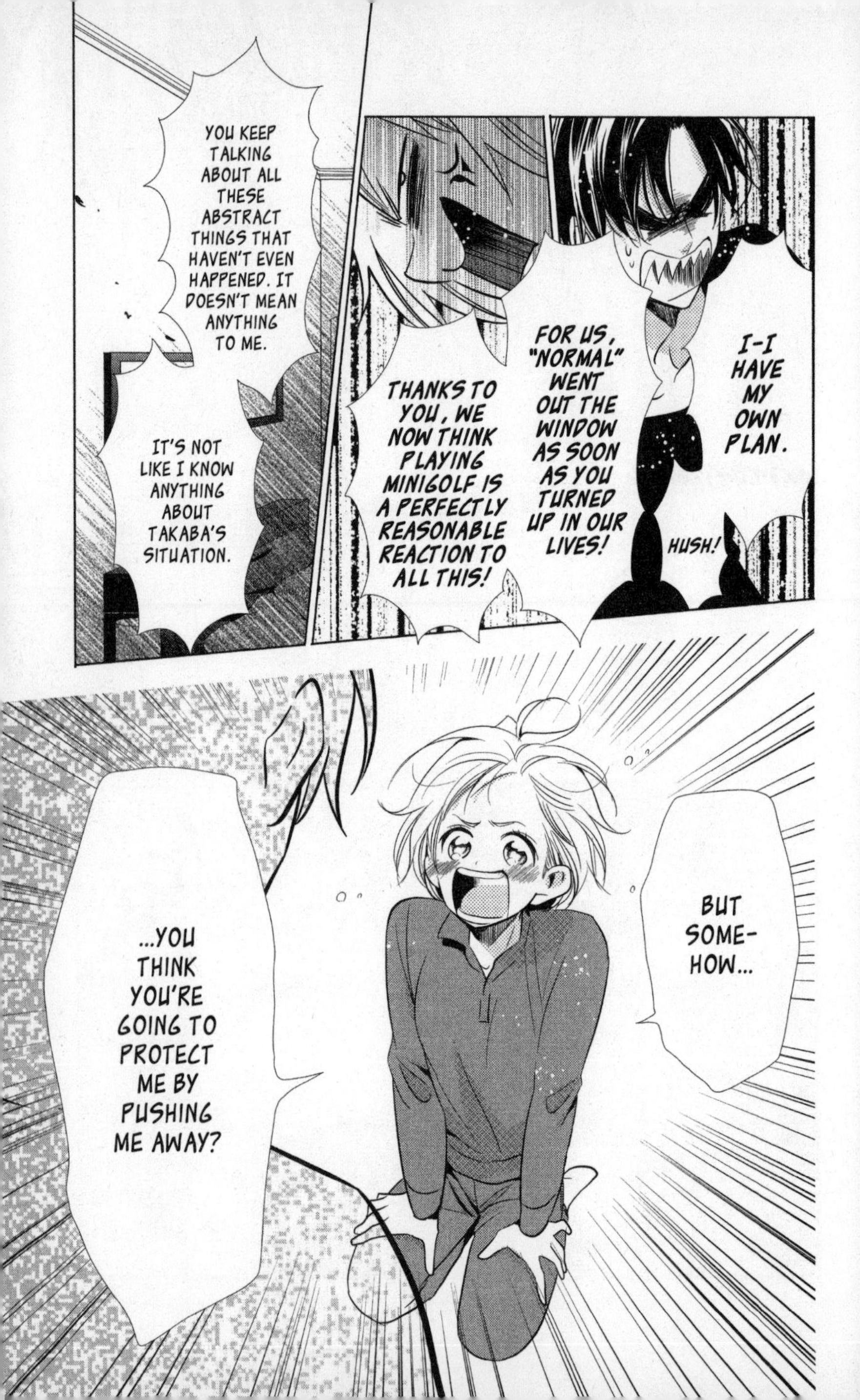
I-I HAVE MY OWN PLAN.
HUSH!
FOR US, "NORMAL" WENT OUT THE WINDOW AS SOON AS YOU TURNED UP IN OUR LIVES!
THANKS TO YOU, WE NOW THINK PLAYING MINIGOLF IS A PERFECTLY REASONABLE REACTION TO ALL THIS!
YOU KEEP TALKING ABOUT ALL THESE ABSTRACT THINGS THAT HAVEN'T EVEN HAPPENED. IT DOESN'T MEAN ANYTHING TO ME.
IT'S NOT LIKE I KNOW ANYTHING ABOUT TAKABA'S SITUATION.
BUT SOME-HOW...
...YOU THINK YOU'RE GOING TO PROTECT ME BY PUSHING ME AWAY?

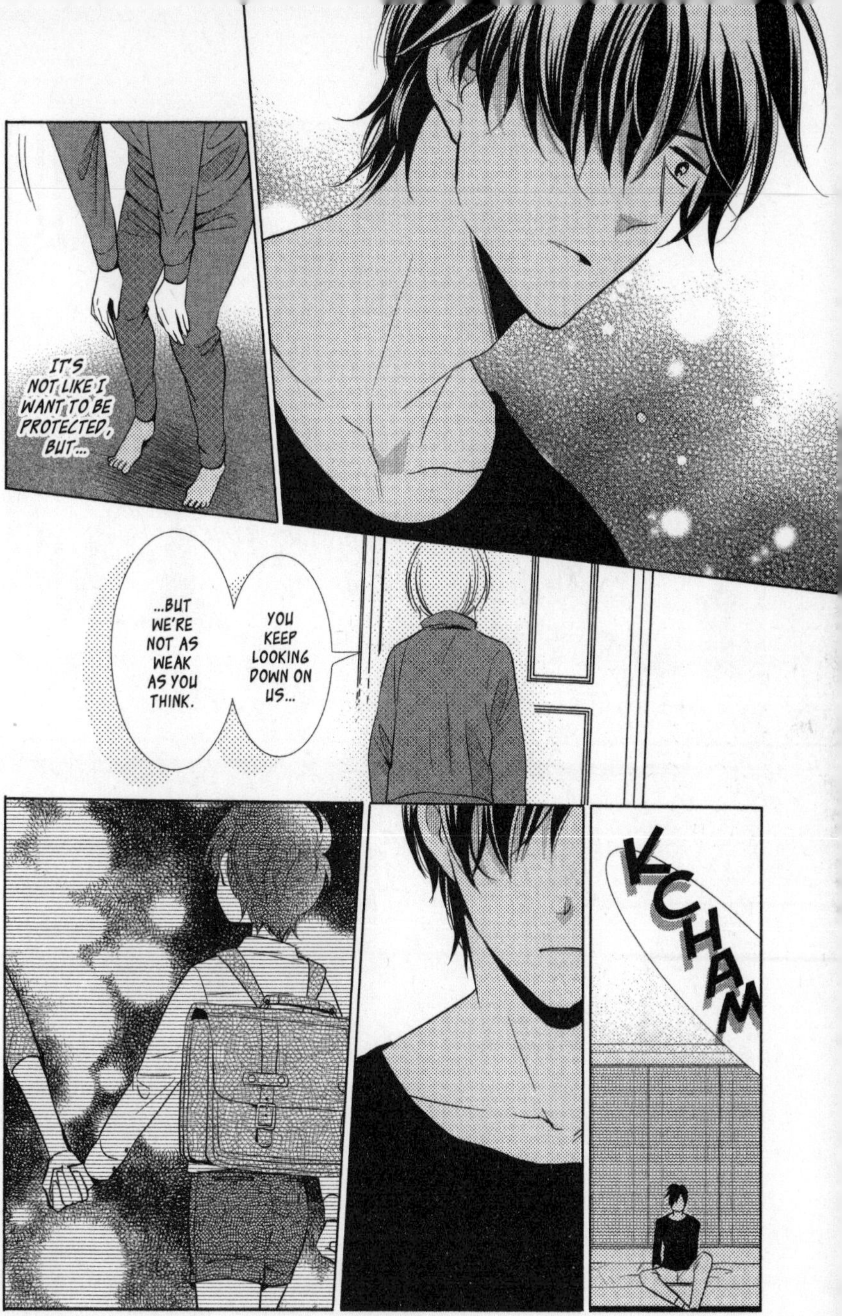
IT'S NOT LIKE I WANT TO BE PROTECTED, BUT...
YOU KEEP LOOKING DOWN ON US...
...BUT WE'RE NOT AS WEAK AS YOU THINK.
VCHAM

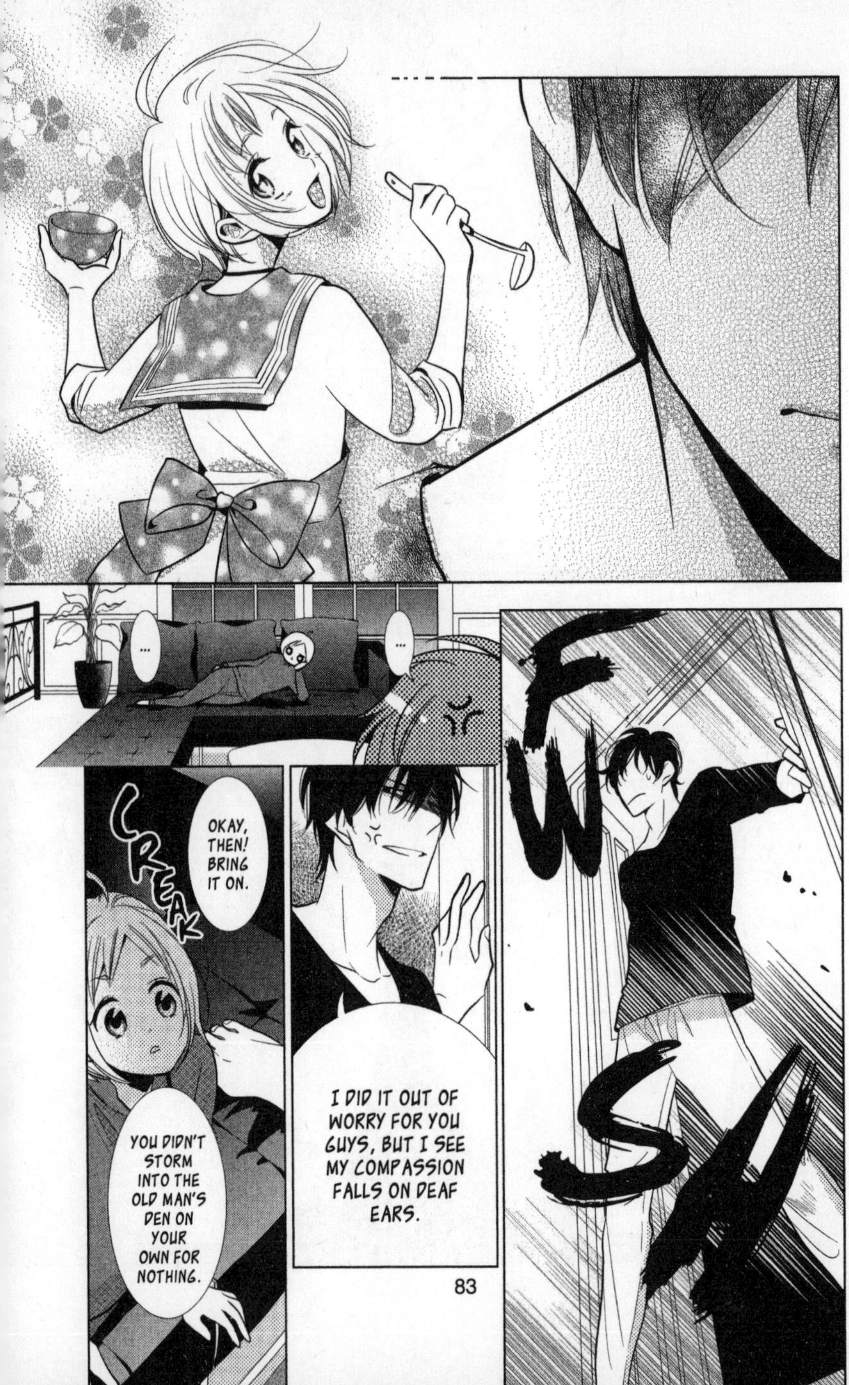
FWSH
...
...
...
I DID IT OUT OF WORRY FOR YOU GUYS, BUT I SEE MY COMPASSION FALLS ON DEAF EARS.
OKAY, THEN! BRING IT ON.
CREAK
YOU DIDN'T STORM INTO THE OLD MAN'S DEN ON YOUR OWN FOR NOTHING.

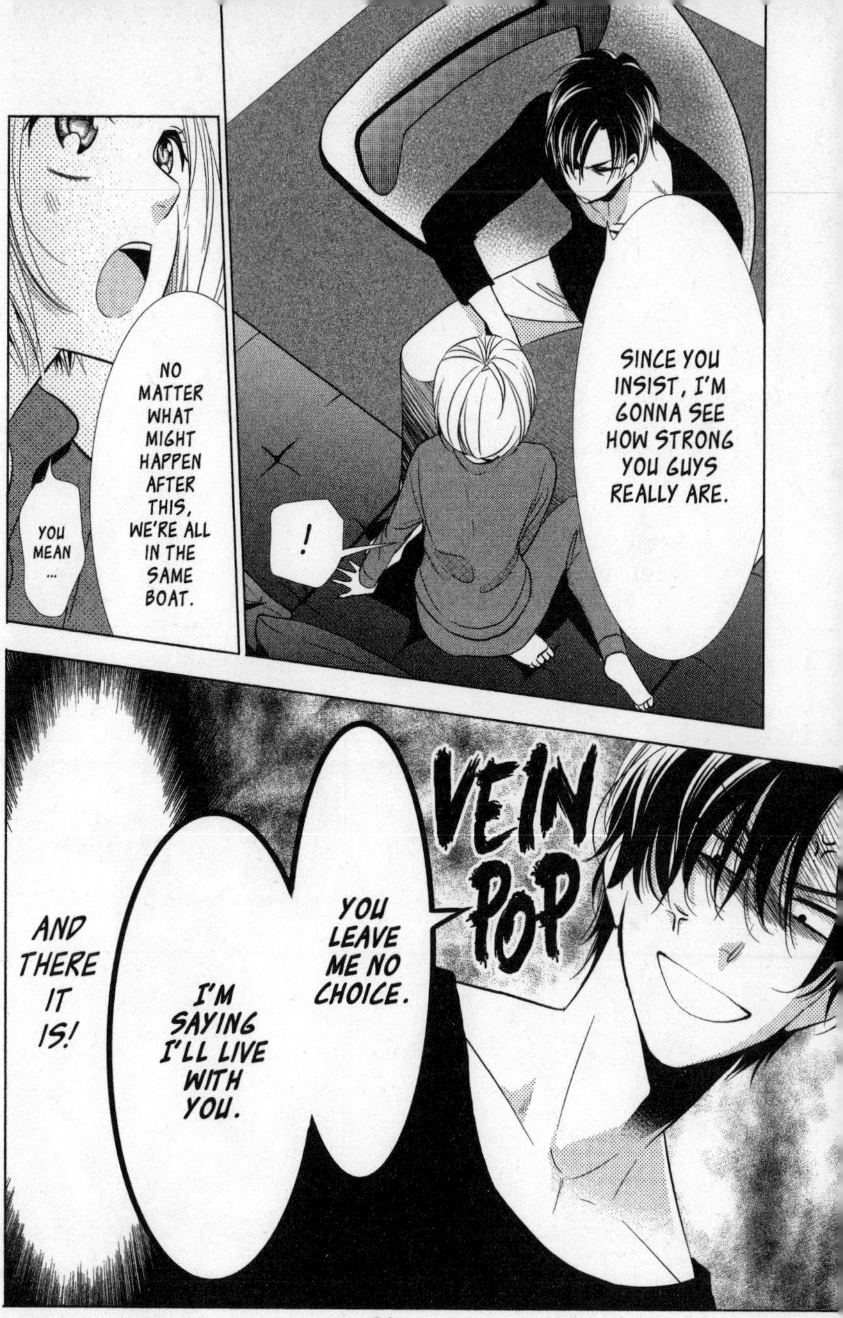
SINCE YOU INSIST, I'M GONNA SEE HOW STRONG YOU GUYS REALLY ARE.
!
NO MATTER WHAT MIGHT HAPPEN AFTER THIS, WE'RE ALL IN THE SAME BOAT.
YOU MEAN ...
VEIN POP
YOU LEAVE ME NO CHOICE.
I'M SAYING I'LL LIVE WITH YOU.
AND THERE IT IS!

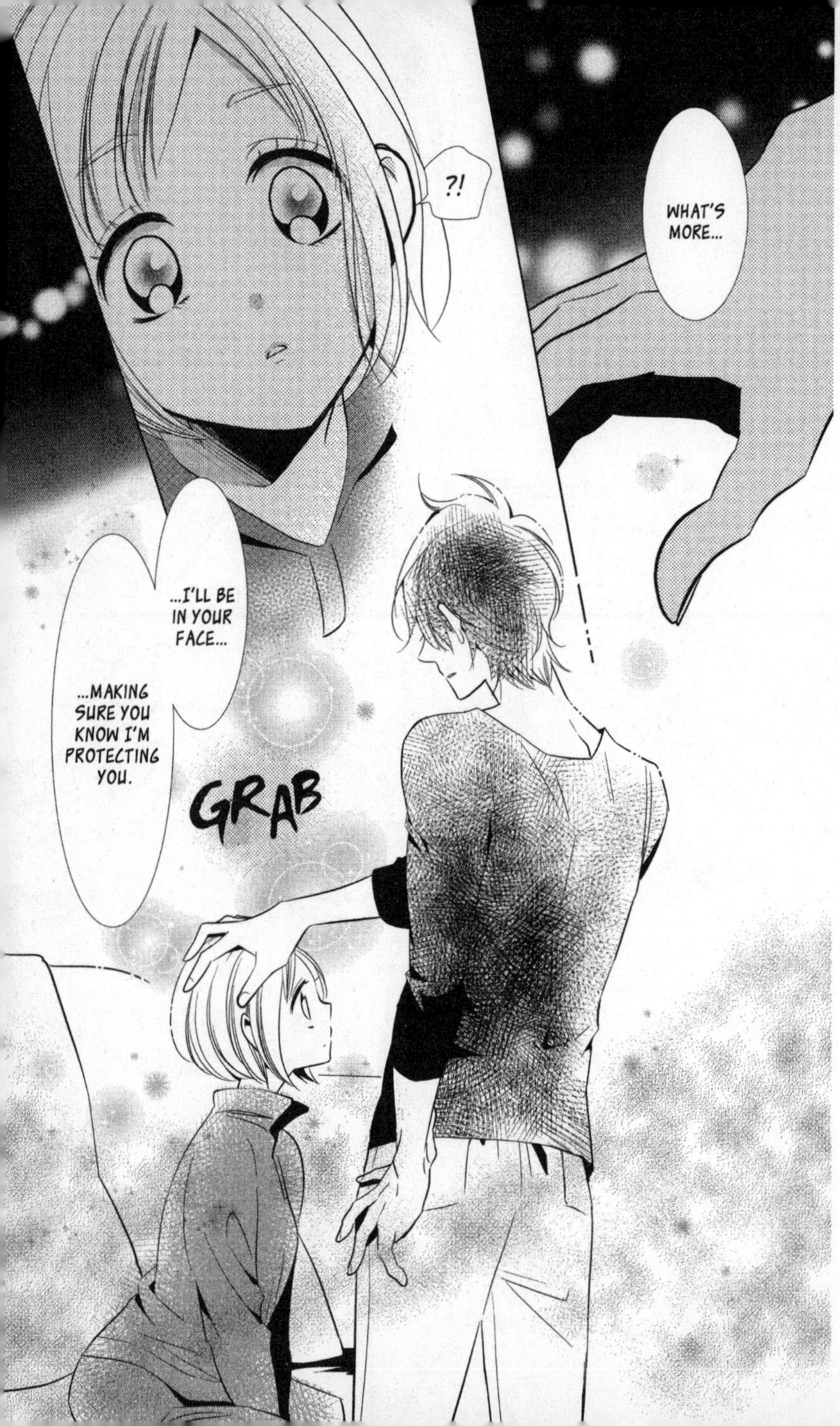
WHAT'S MORE...
?!
...I'LL BE IN YOUR FACE...
...MAKING SURE YOU KNOW I'M PROTECTING YOU.
GRAB

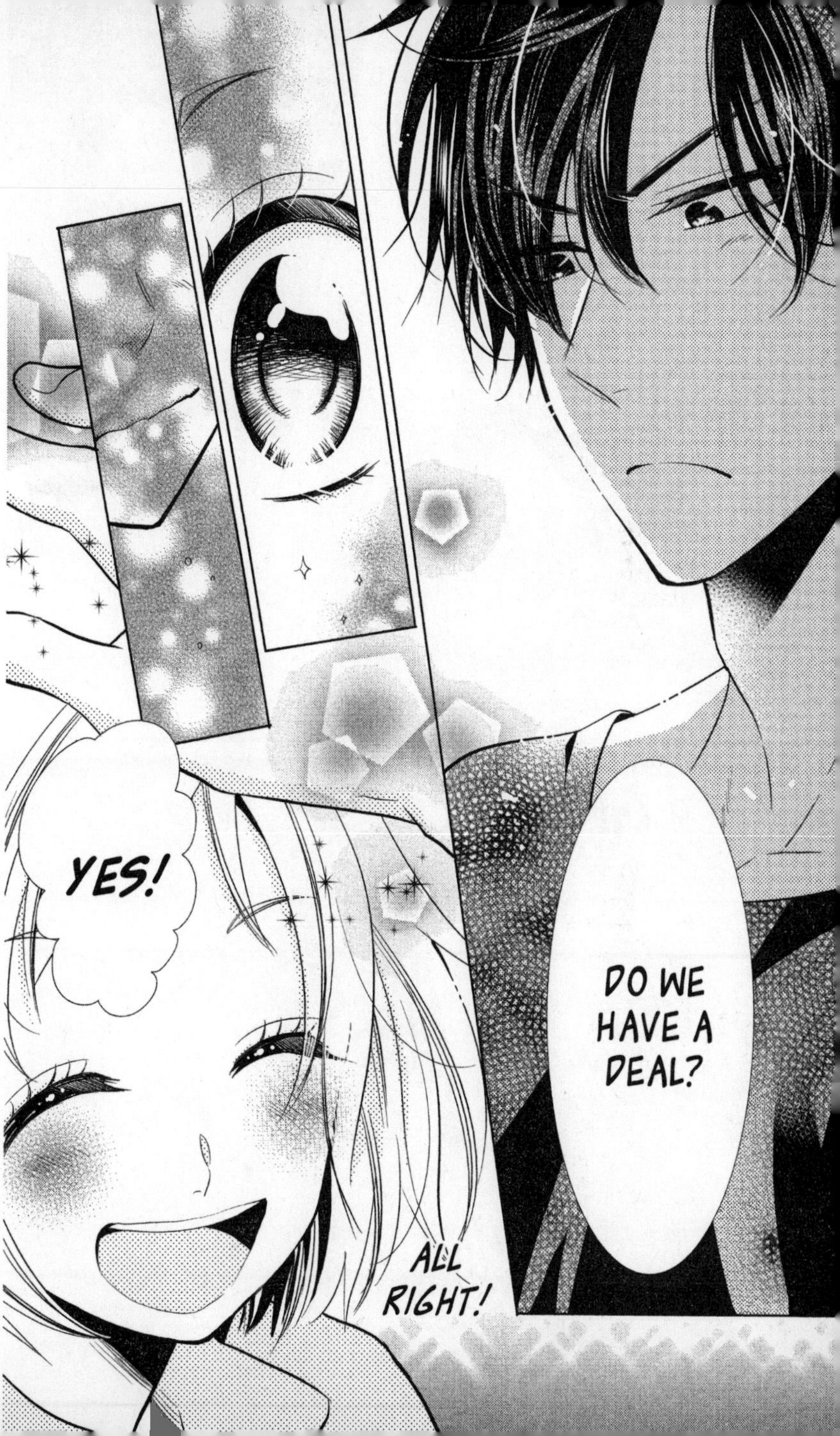
DO WE HAVE A DEAL?
YES!
ALL RIGHT!

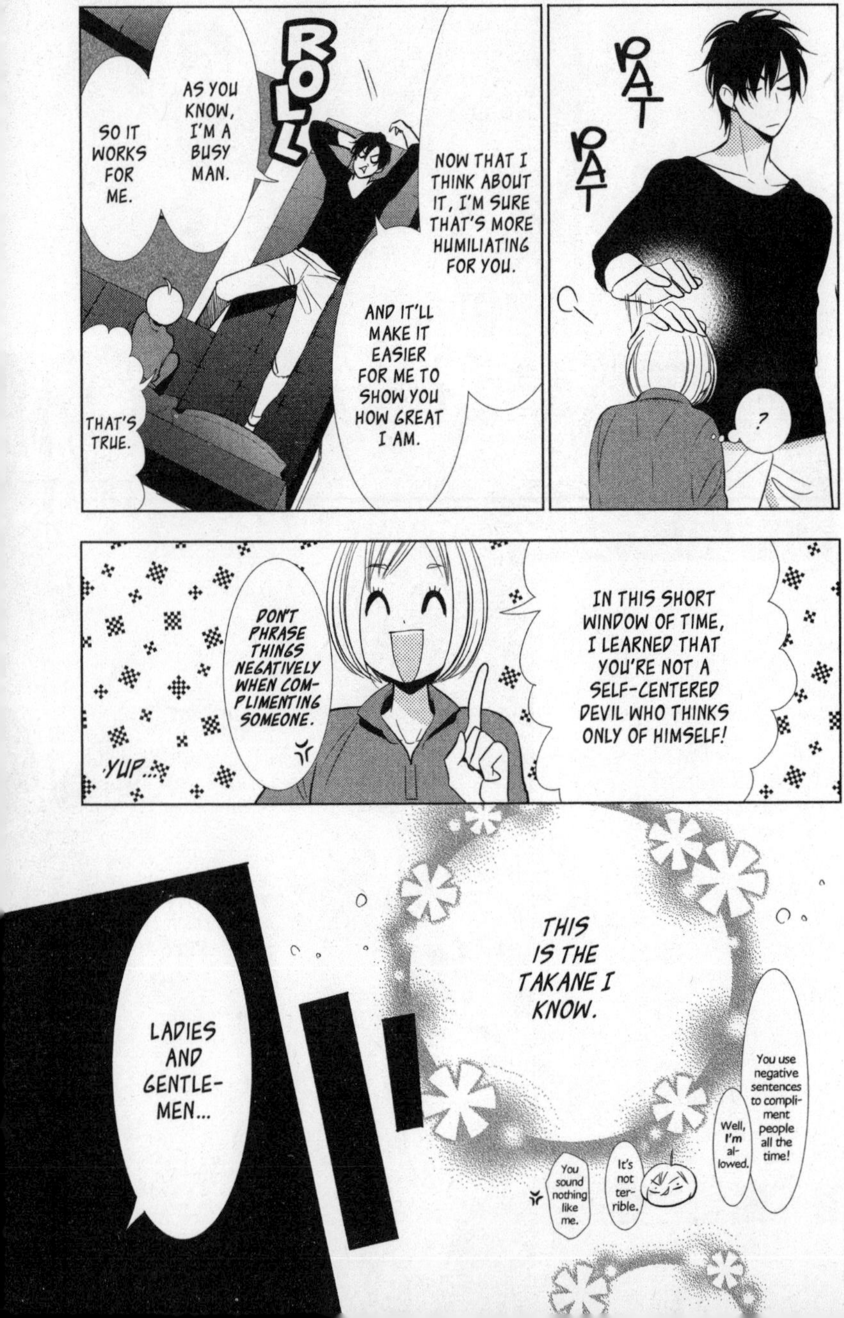
PAT
PAT
?
NOW THAT I THINK ABOUT IT, I'M SURE THAT'S MORE HUMILIATING FOR YOU.
AND IT'LL MAKE IT EASIER FOR ME TO SHOW YOU HOW GREAT I AM.
ROLL
AS YOU KNOW, I'M A BUSY MAN.
SO IT WORKS FOR ME.
THAT'S TRUE.
IN THIS SHORT WINDOW OF TIME, I LEARNED THAT YOU'RE NOT A SELF-CENTERED DEVIL WHO THINKS ONLY OF HIMSELF!
DON'T PHRASE THINGS NEGATIVELY WHEN COM-PLIMENTING SOMEONE.
YUP...
THIS IS THE TAKANE I KNOW.
You use negative sentences to compli-ment people all the time!
Well, I'm al-lowed.
It's not ter-rible.
You sound nothing like me.
LADIES AND GENTLE-MEN...

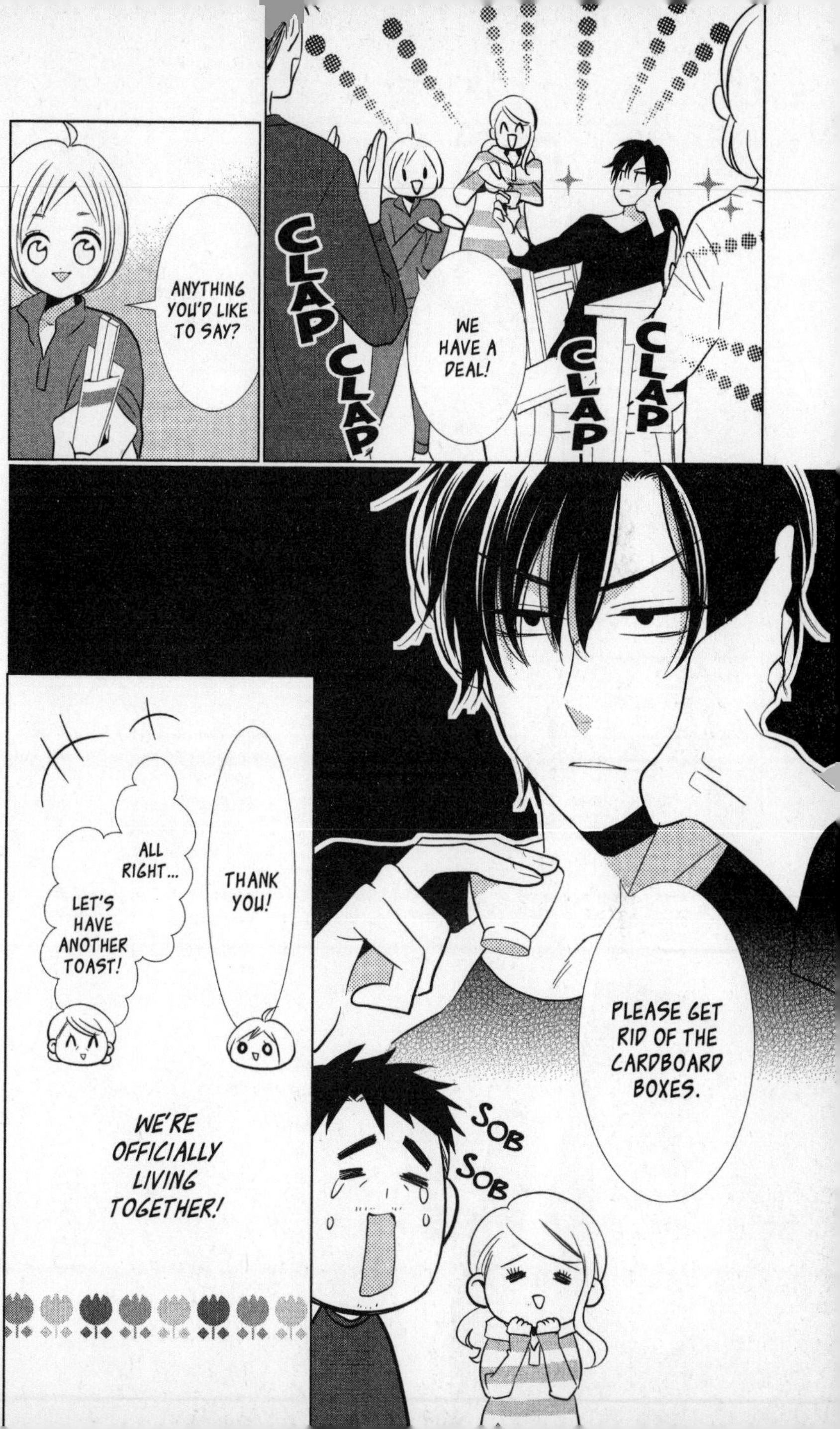
CLAP
CLAP
CLAP
CLAP
WE HAVE A DEAL!
ANYTHING YOU'D LIKE TO SAY?
PLEASE GET RID OF THE CARDBOARD BOXES.
SOB
SOB
THANK YOU!
ALL RIGHT...
LET'S HAVE ANOTHER TOAST!
WE'RE OFFICIALLY LIVING TOGETHER!

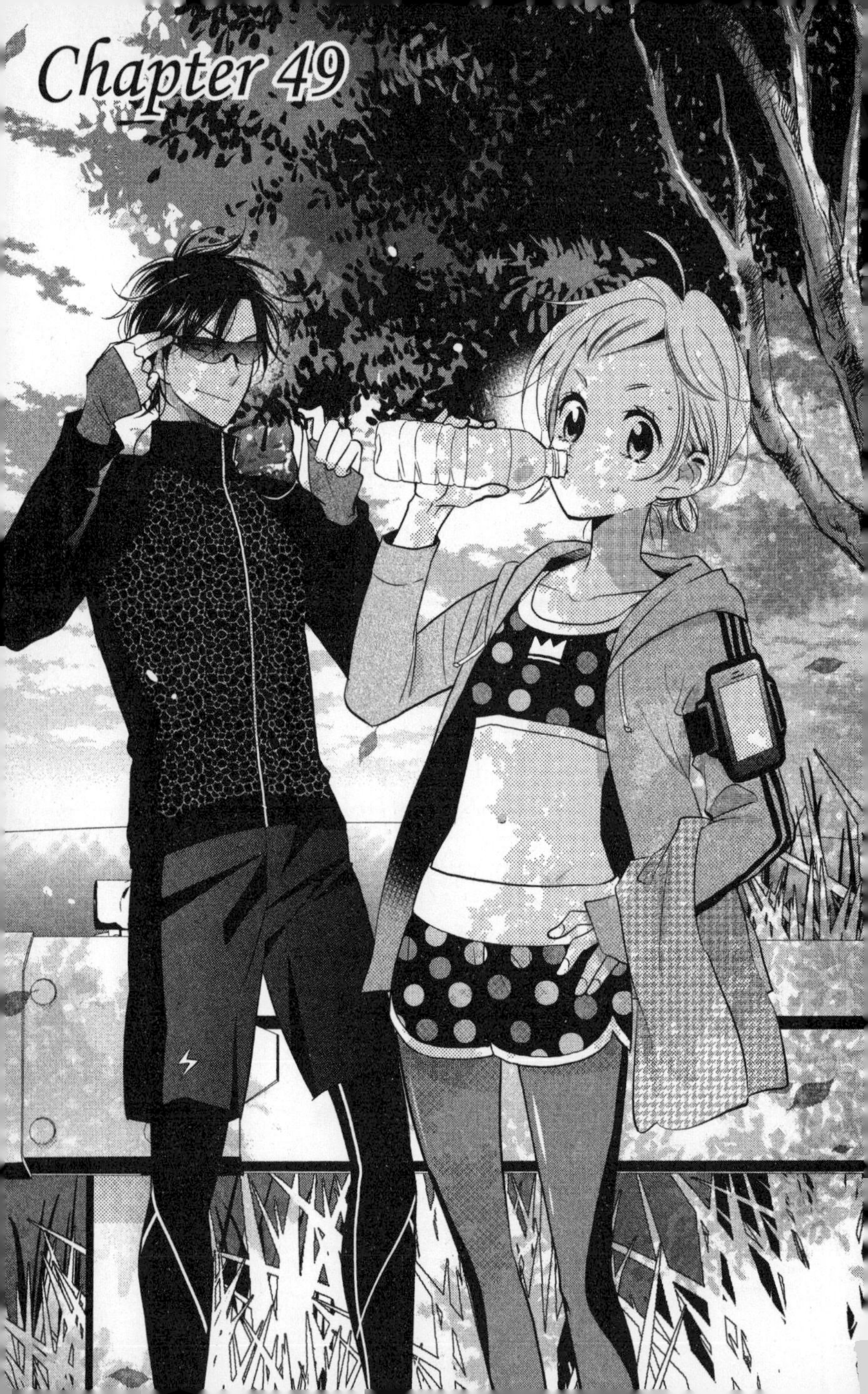
Chapter 49

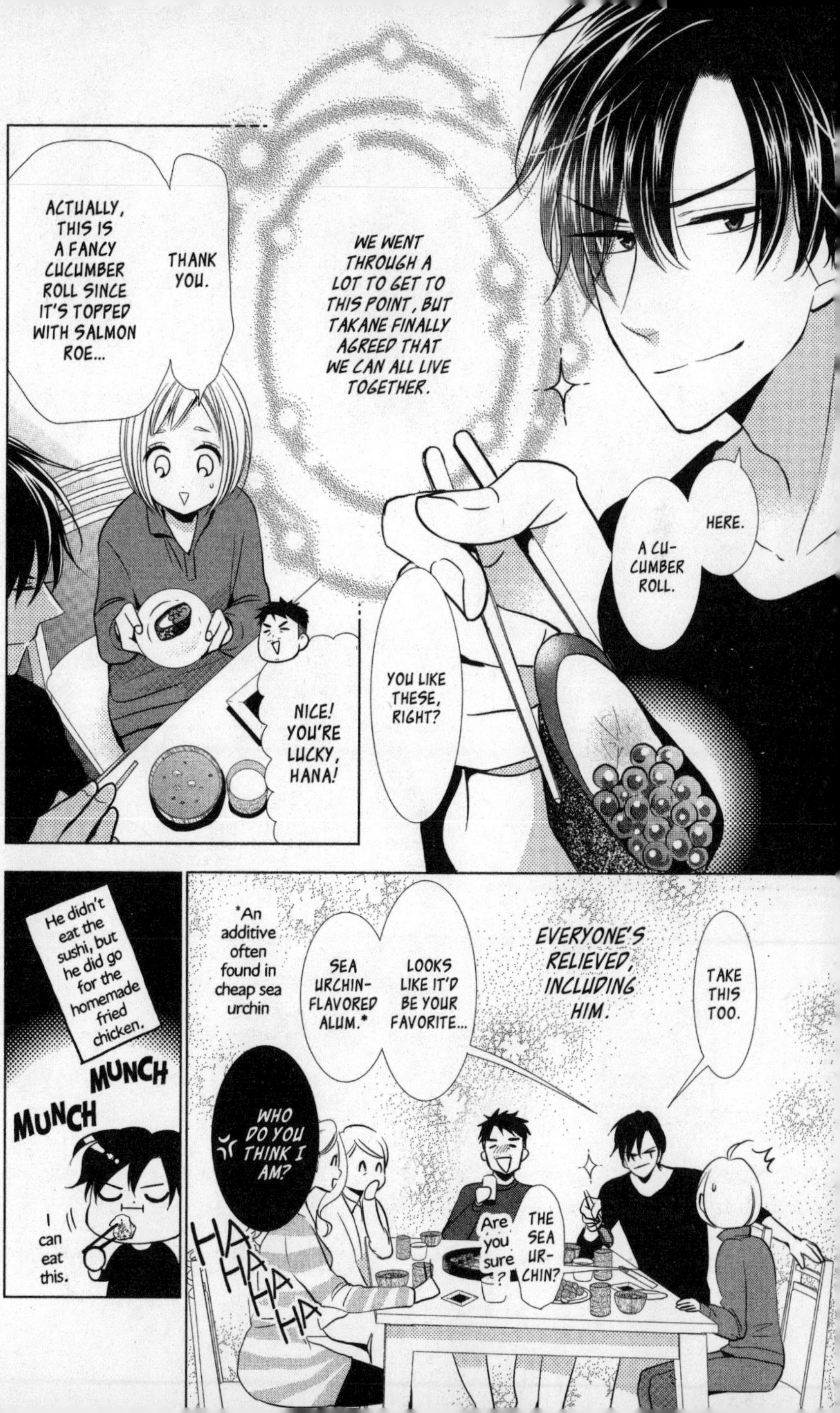
WE WENT THROUGH A LOT TO GET TO THIS POINT, BUT TAKANE FINALLY AGREED THAT WE CAN ALL LIVE TOGETHER.
HERE.
A CUCUMBER ROLL.
YOU LIKE THESE, RIGHT?
THANK YOU.
ACTUALLY, THIS IS A FANCY CUCUMBER ROLL SINCE IT'S TOPPED WITH SALMON ROE...
NICE! YOU'RE LUCKY, HANA!
EVERYONE'S RELIEVED, INCLUDING HIM.
TAKE THIS TOO.
LOOKS LIKE IT'D BE YOUR FAVORITE...
SEA URCHIN-FLAVORED ALUM.*
*An additive often found in cheap sea urchin
THE SEA URCHIN?
Are you sure?
WHO DO YOU THINK I AM?
HA HA HA HA
He didn't eat the sushi, but he did go for the homemade fried chicken.
MUNCH
MUNCH
I can eat this.

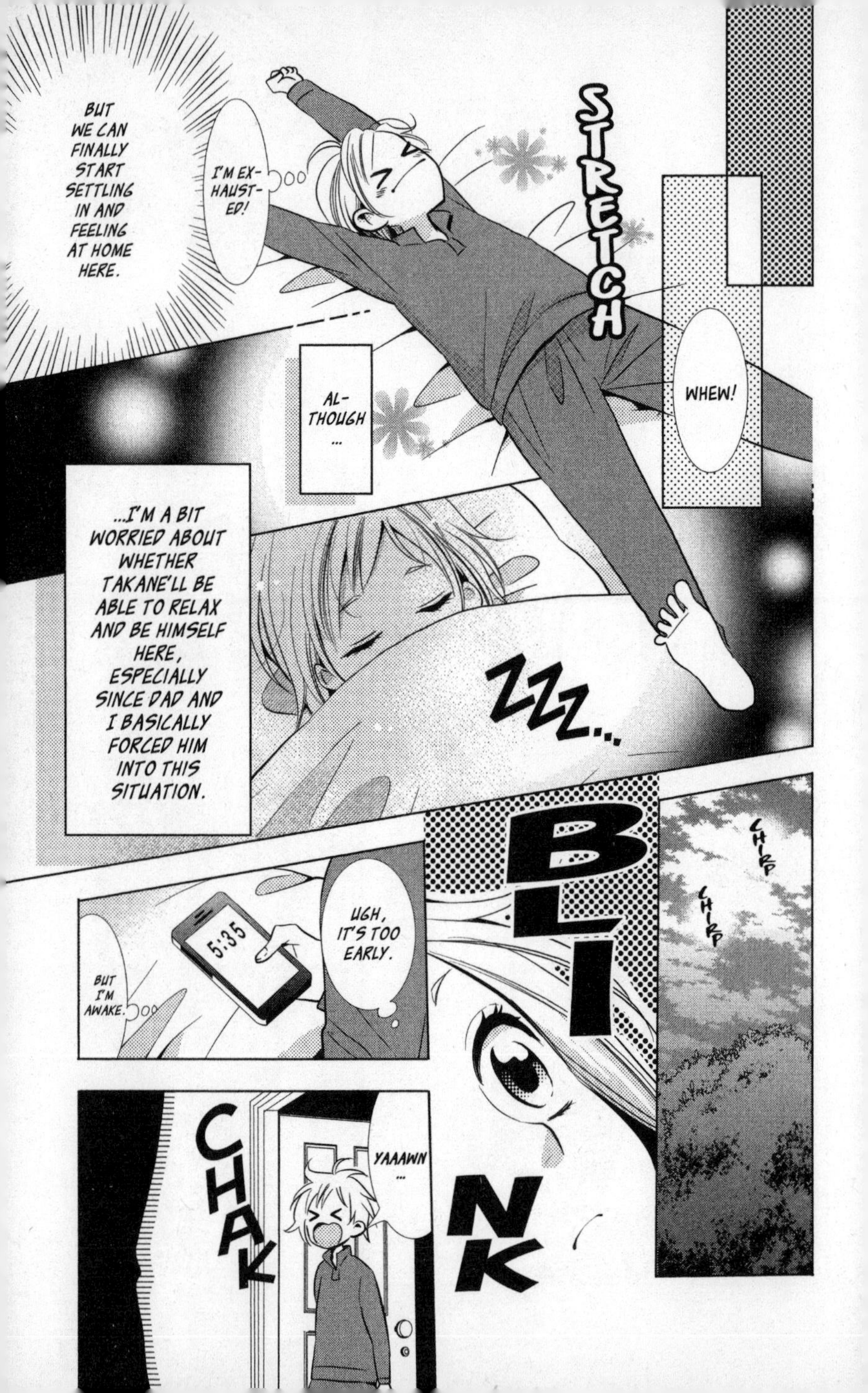
STRETCH
WHEW!
I'M EX-HAUST-ED!
BUT WE CAN FINALLY START SETTLING IN AND FEELING AT HOME HERE.
AL-THOUGH ...
...I'M A BIT WORRIED ABOUT WHETHER TAKANE'LL BE ABLE TO RELAX AND BE HIMSELF HERE, ESPECIALLY SINCE DAD AND I BASICALLY FORCED HIM INTO THIS SITUATION.
ZZZ...
CHIRP
CHIRP
BLI
UGH, IT'S TOO EARLY.
5:35
BUT I'M AWAKE.
YAAAWN ...
CHAK
NK

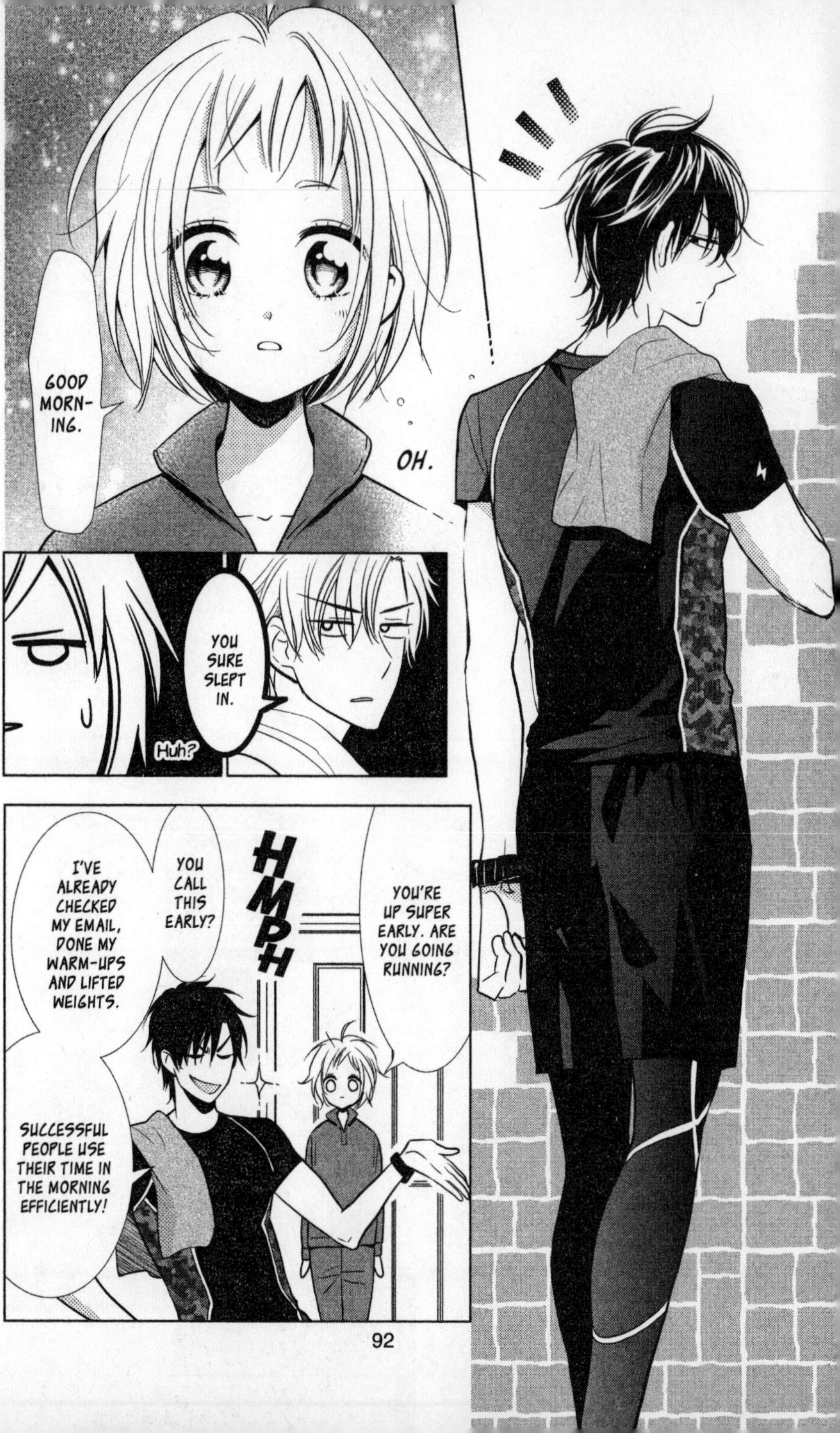
OH.
GOOD MORNING.
YOU SURE SLEPT IN.
Huh?
YOU'RE UP SUPER EARLY. ARE YOU GOING RUNNING?
HMPH
YOU CALL THIS EARLY?
I'VE ALREADY CHECKED MY EMAIL, DONE MY WARM-UPS AND LIFTED WEIGHTS.
SUCCESSFUL PEOPLE USE THEIR TIME IN THE MORNING EFFICIENTLY!

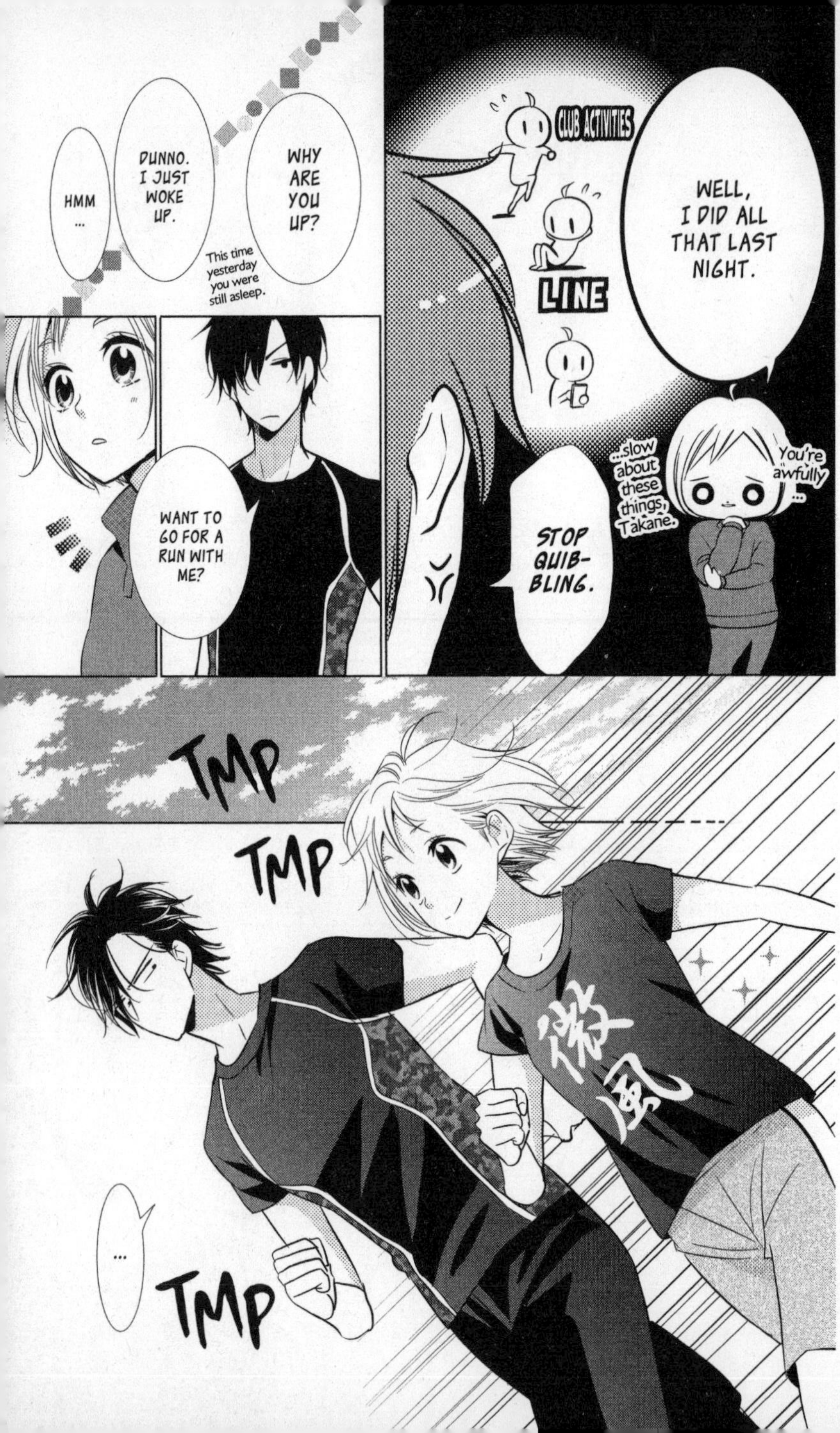
CLUB ACTIVITIES
LINE
WELL, I DID ALL THAT LAST NIGHT.
You're awfully ...
...slow about these things, Takane.
STOP QUIB-BLING.
WHY ARE YOU UP?
This time yesterday you were still asleep.
DUNNO. I JUST WOKE UP.
HMM ...
WANT TO GO FOR A RUN WITH ME?
TMP
TMP
TMP
...

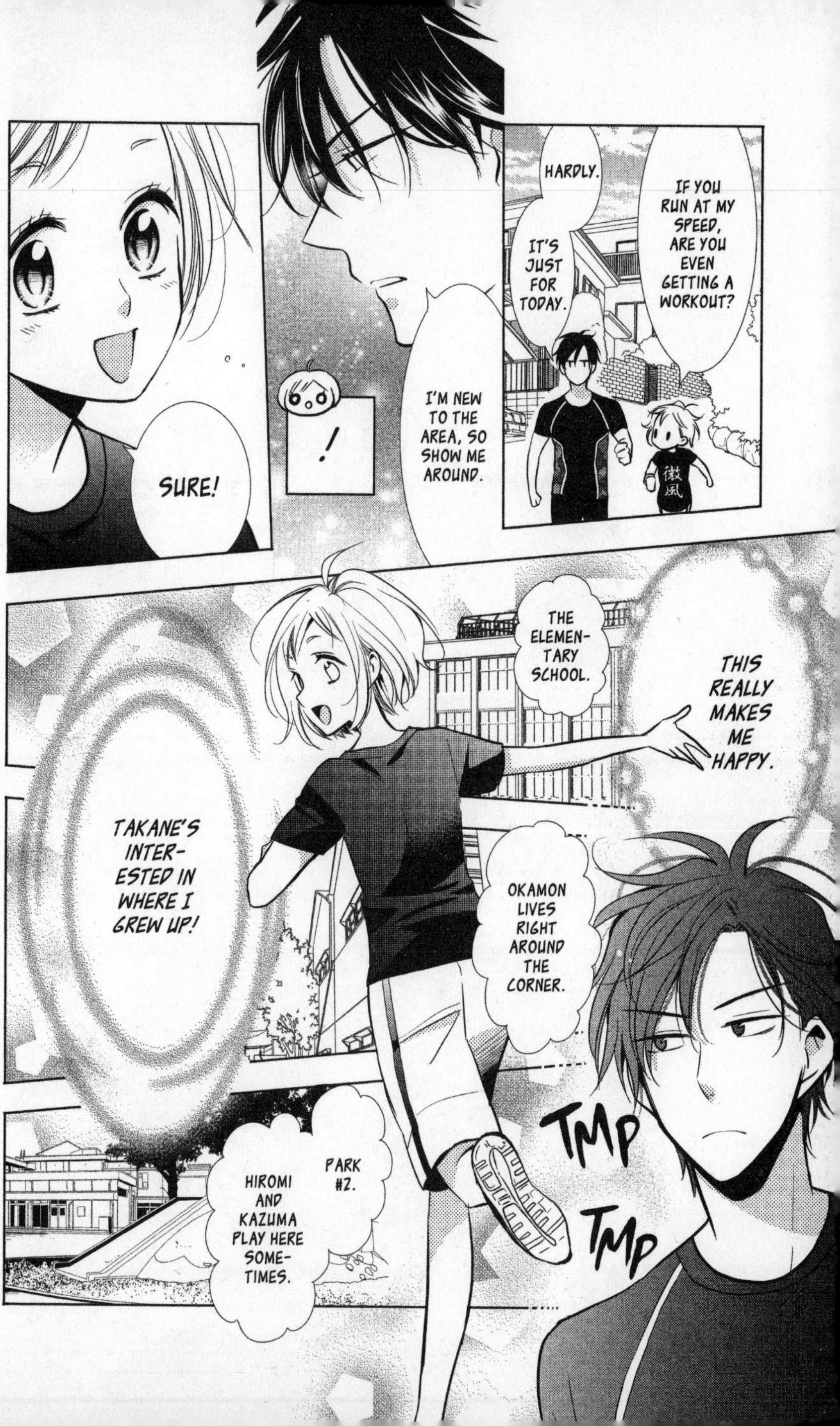
IF YOU RUN AT MY SPEED, ARE YOU EVEN GETTING A WORKOUT?
HARDLY.
IT'S JUST FOR TODAY.
徹風
I'M NEW TO THE AREA, SO SHOW ME AROUND.
!
SURE!
THIS REALLY MAKES ME HAPPY.
THE ELEMENTARY SCHOOL.
TAKANE'S INTERESTED IN WHERE I GREW UP!
OKAMON LIVES RIGHT AROUND THE CORNER.
TMP
TMP
PARK #2.
HIROMI AND KAZUMA PLAY HERE SOMETIMES.

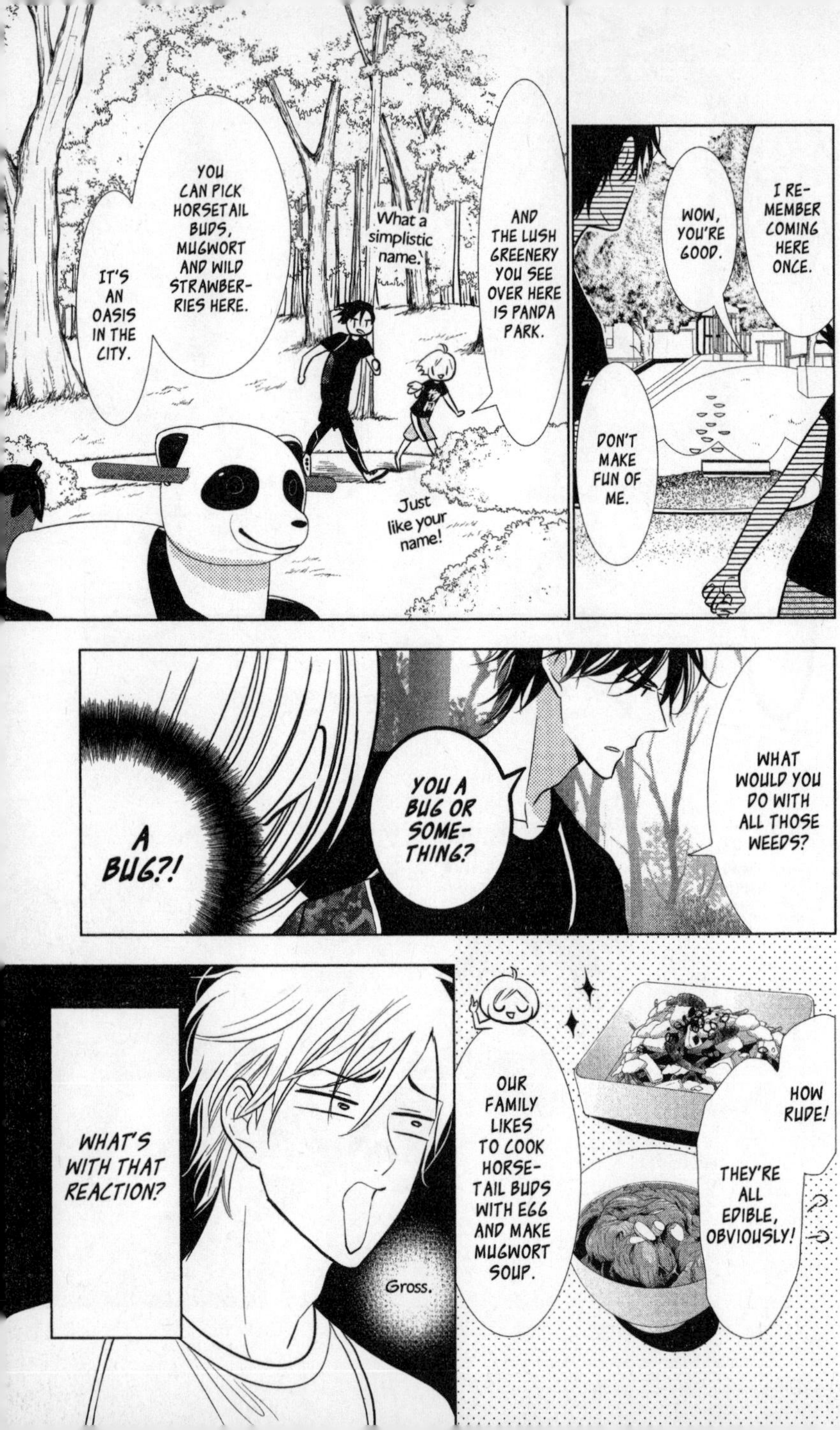
I REMEMBER COMING HERE ONCE.
WOW, YOU'RE GOOD.
DON'T MAKE FUN OF ME.
AND THE LUSH GREENERY YOU SEE OVER HERE IS PANDA PARK.
What a simplistic name.
YOU CAN PICK HORSETAIL BUDS, MUGWORT AND WILD STRAWBERRIES HERE.
IT'S AN OASIS IN THE CITY.
Just like your name!
WHAT WOULD YOU DO WITH ALL THOSE WEEDS?
YOU A BUG OR SOMETHING?
A BUG?!
HOW RUDE!
THEY'RE ALL EDIBLE, OBVIOUSLY!
OUR FAMILY LIKES TO COOK HORSETAIL BUDS WITH EGG AND MAKE MUGWORT SOUP.
Gross.
WHAT'S WITH THAT REACTION?

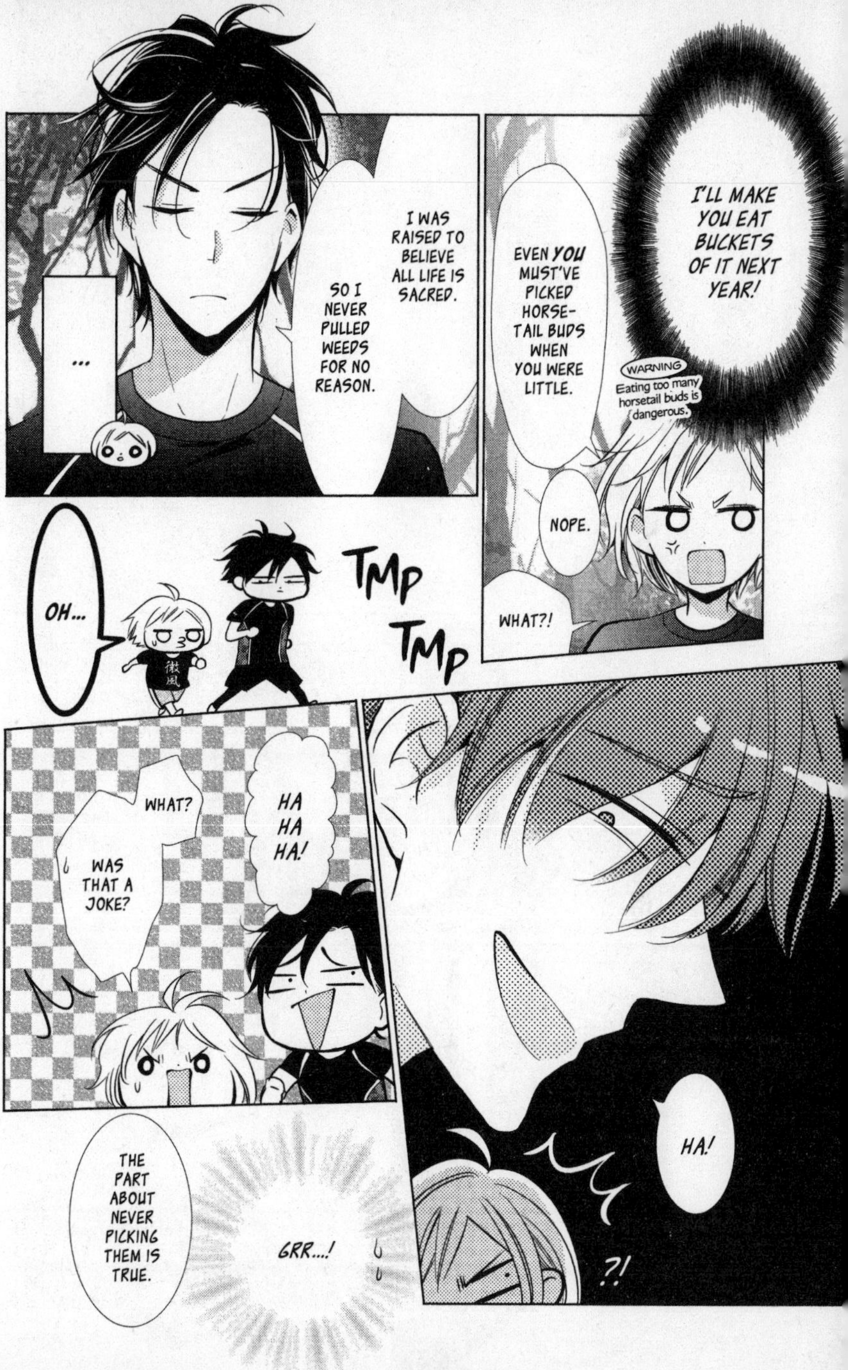

I'LL MAKE YOU EAT BUCKETS OF IT NEXT YEAR!
EVEN YOU MUST'VE PICKED HORSE-TAIL BUDS WHEN YOU WERE LITTLE.
WARNING
Eating too many horsetail buds is dangerous.
NOPE.
WHAT?!
I WAS RAISED TO BELIEVE ALL LIFE IS SACRED.
SO I NEVER PULLED WEEDS FOR NO REASON.
...
TMP
TMP
OH...
HA!
?!
HA HA HA!
WHAT?
WAS THAT A JOKE?
THE PART ABOUT NEVER PICKING THEM IS TRUE.
GRR...!

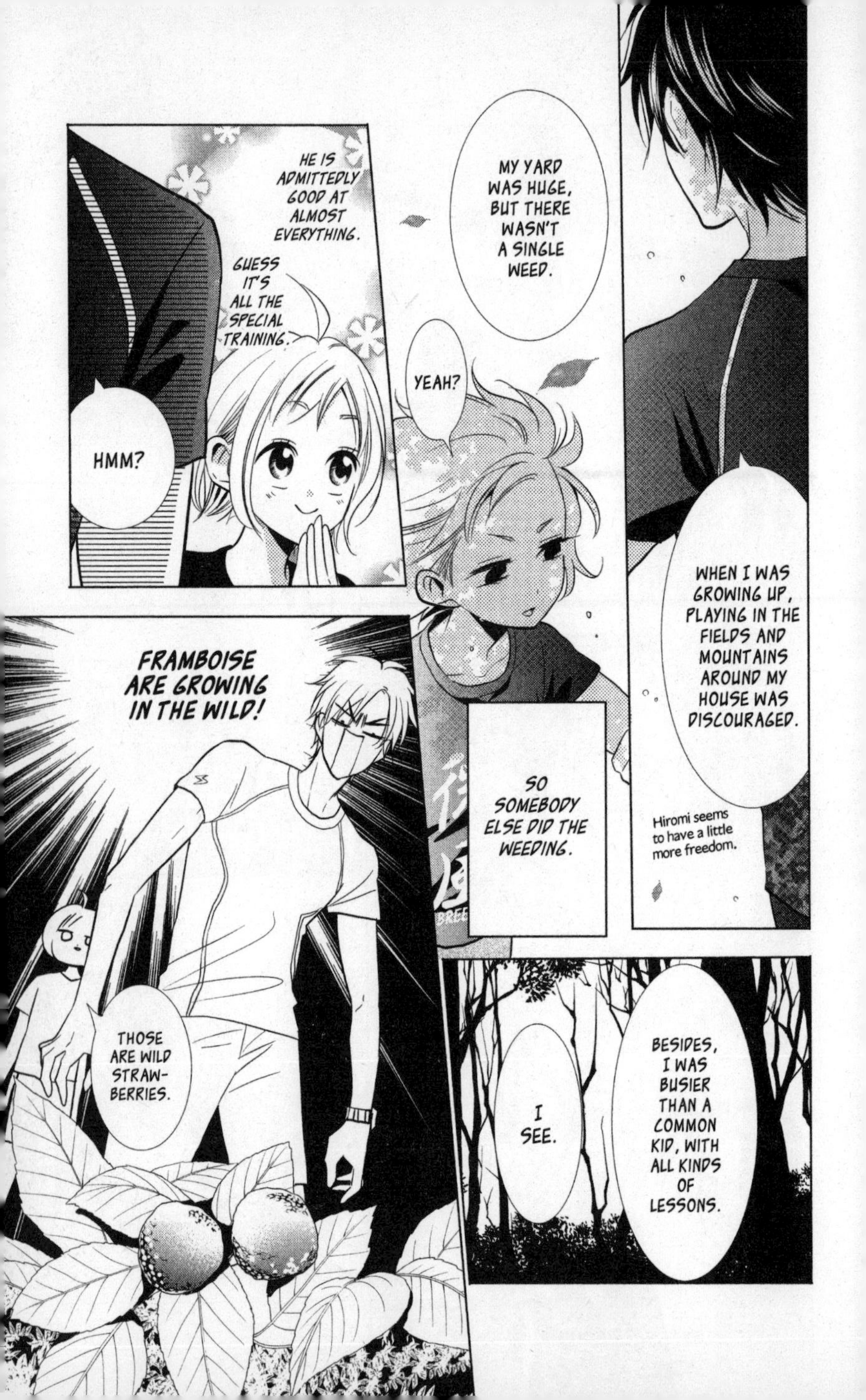
WHEN I WAS GROWING UP, PLAYING IN THE FIELDS AND MOUNTAINS AROUND MY HOUSE WAS DISCOURAGED.
Hiromi seems to have a little more freedom.
MY YARD WAS HUGE, BUT THERE WASN'T A SINGLE WEED.
YEAH?
SO SOMEBODY ELSE DID THE WEEDING.
HE IS ADMITTEDLY GOOD AT ALMOST EVERYTHING.
GUESS IT'S ALL THE SPECIAL TRAINING.
HMM?
BESIDES, I WAS BUSIER THAN A COMMON KID, WITH ALL KINDS OF LESSONS.
I SEE.
FRAMBOISE ARE GROWING IN THE WILD!
THOSE ARE WILD STRAW-BERRIES.

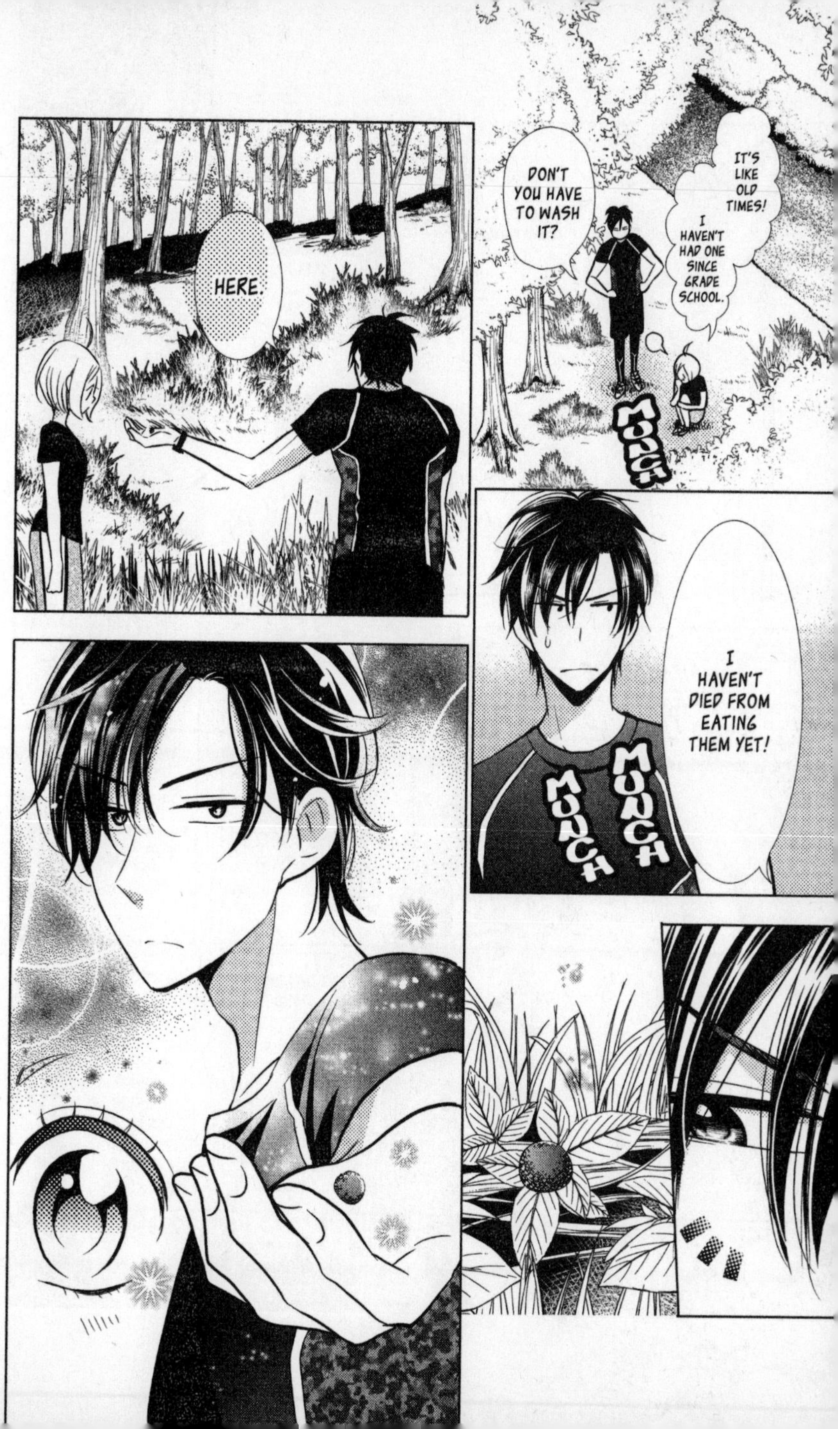
IT'S LIKE OLD TIMES!
I HAVEN'T HAD ONE SINCE GRADE SCHOOL.
DON'T YOU HAVE TO WASH IT?
MUNCH
HERE.
I HAVEN'T DIED FROM EATING THEM YET!
MUNCH MUNCH

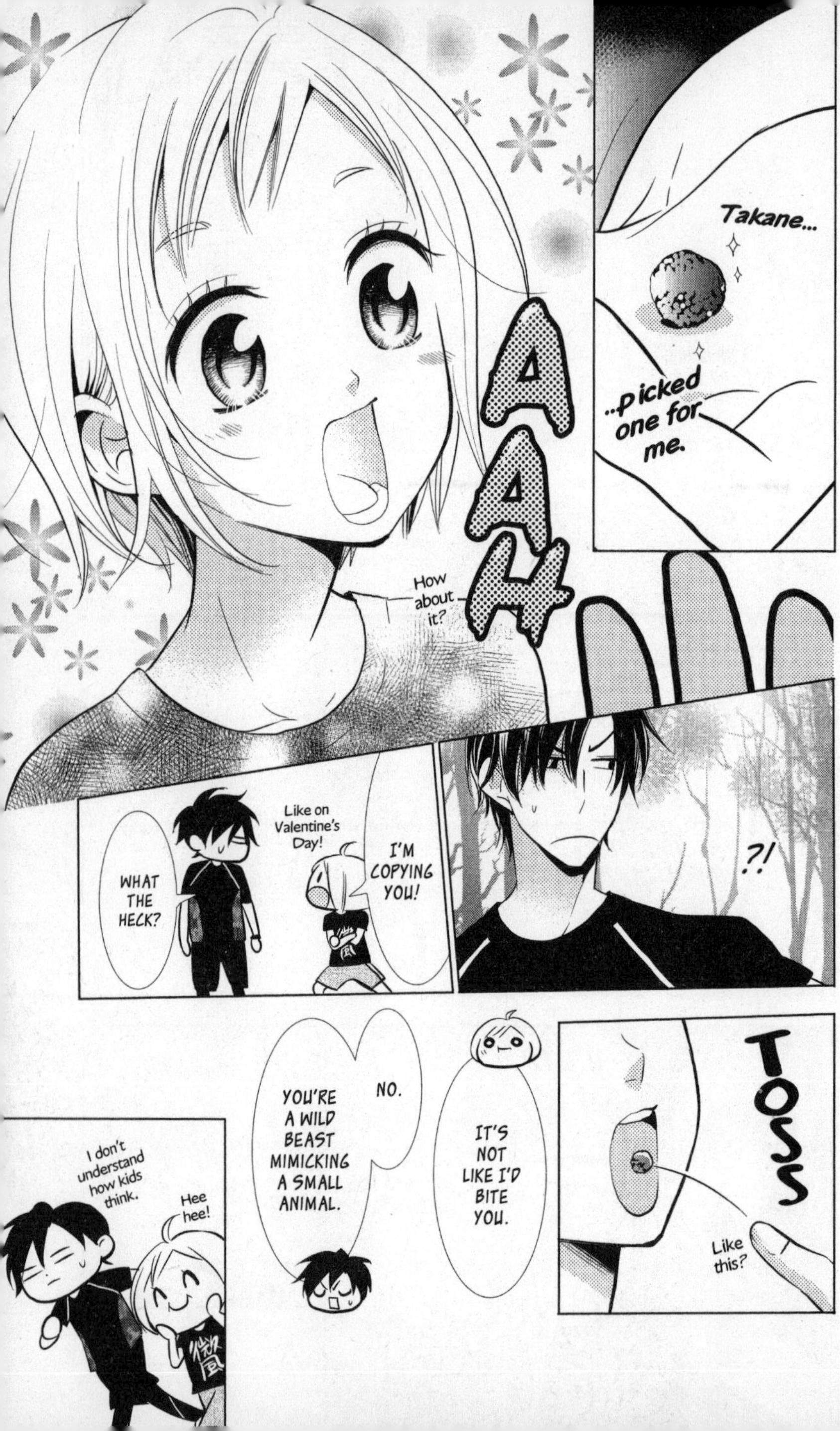
Takane...
...picked one for me.
AAH
How about it?
?!
I'M COPYING YOU!
Like on Valentine's Day!
WHAT THE HECK?
TOSS
Like this?
IT'S NOT LIKE I'D BITE YOU.
NO.
YOU'RE A WILD BEAST MIMICKING A SMALL ANIMAL.
I don't understand how kids think.
Hee hee!

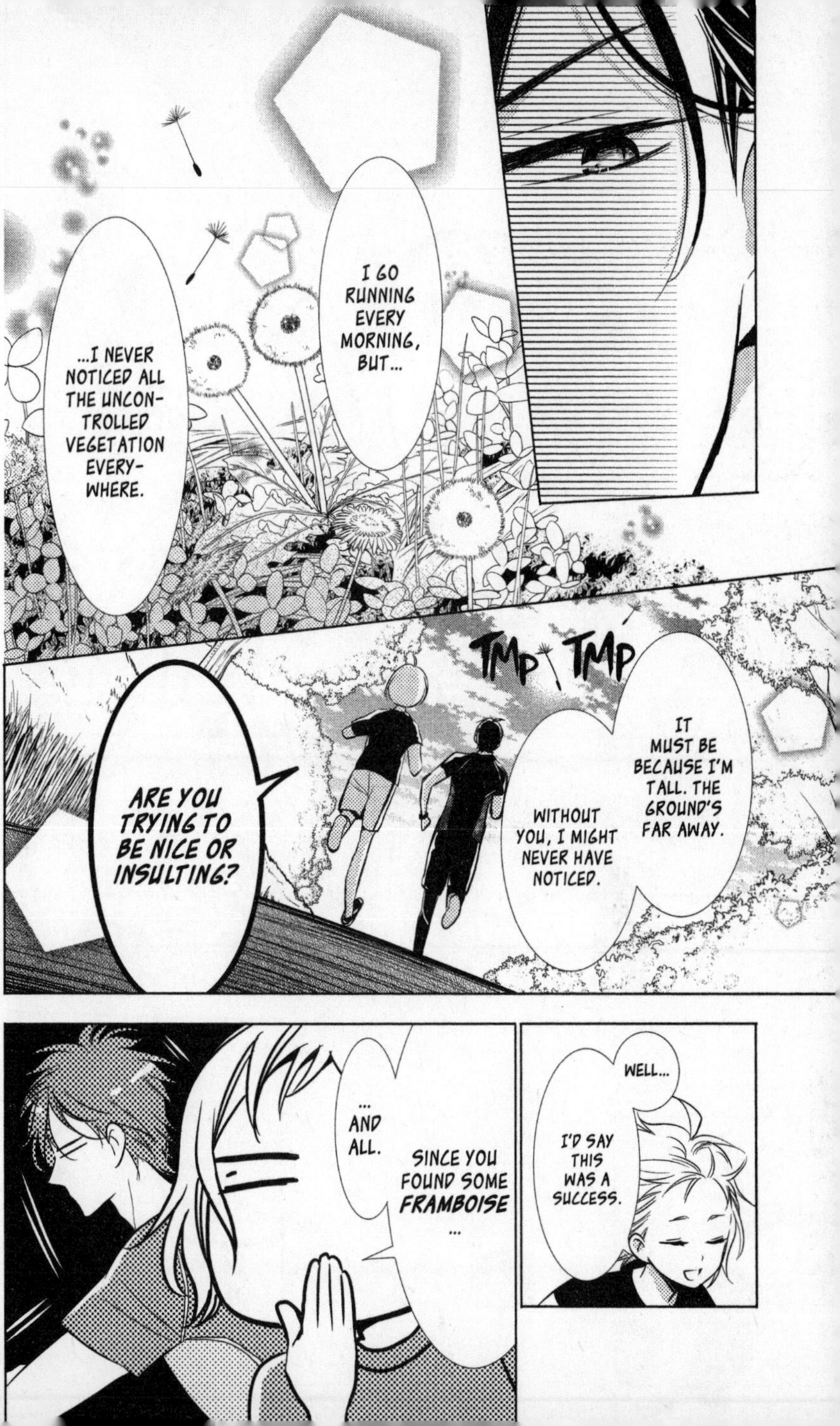
I GO RUNNING EVERY MORNING, BUT...
...I NEVER NOTICED ALL THE UNCON-TROLLED VEGETATION EVERY-WHERE.
IT MUST BE BECAUSE I'M TALL. THE GROUND'S FAR AWAY.
WITHOUT YOU, I MIGHT NEVER HAVE NOTICED.
TMP TMP
ARE YOU TRYING TO BE NICE OR INSULTING?
WELL...
I'D SAY THIS WAS A SUCCESS.
SINCE YOU FOUND SOME *FRAMBOISE* ...
... AND ALL.

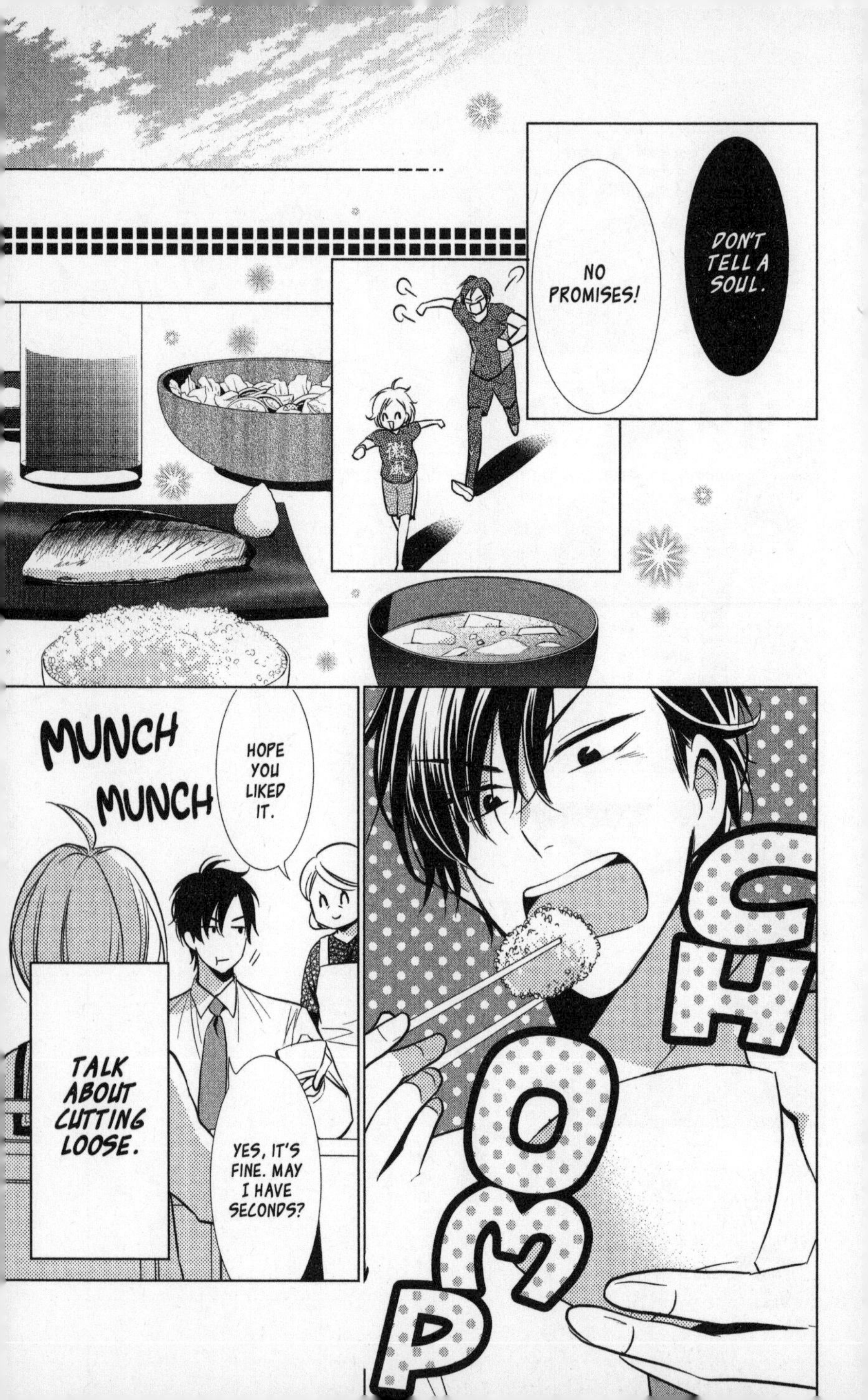
DON'T TELL A SOUL.
NO PROMISES!
CHOMP
HOPE YOU LIKED IT.
MUNCH MUNCH
YES, IT'S FINE. MAY I HAVE SECONDS?
TALK ABOUT CUTTING LOOSE.

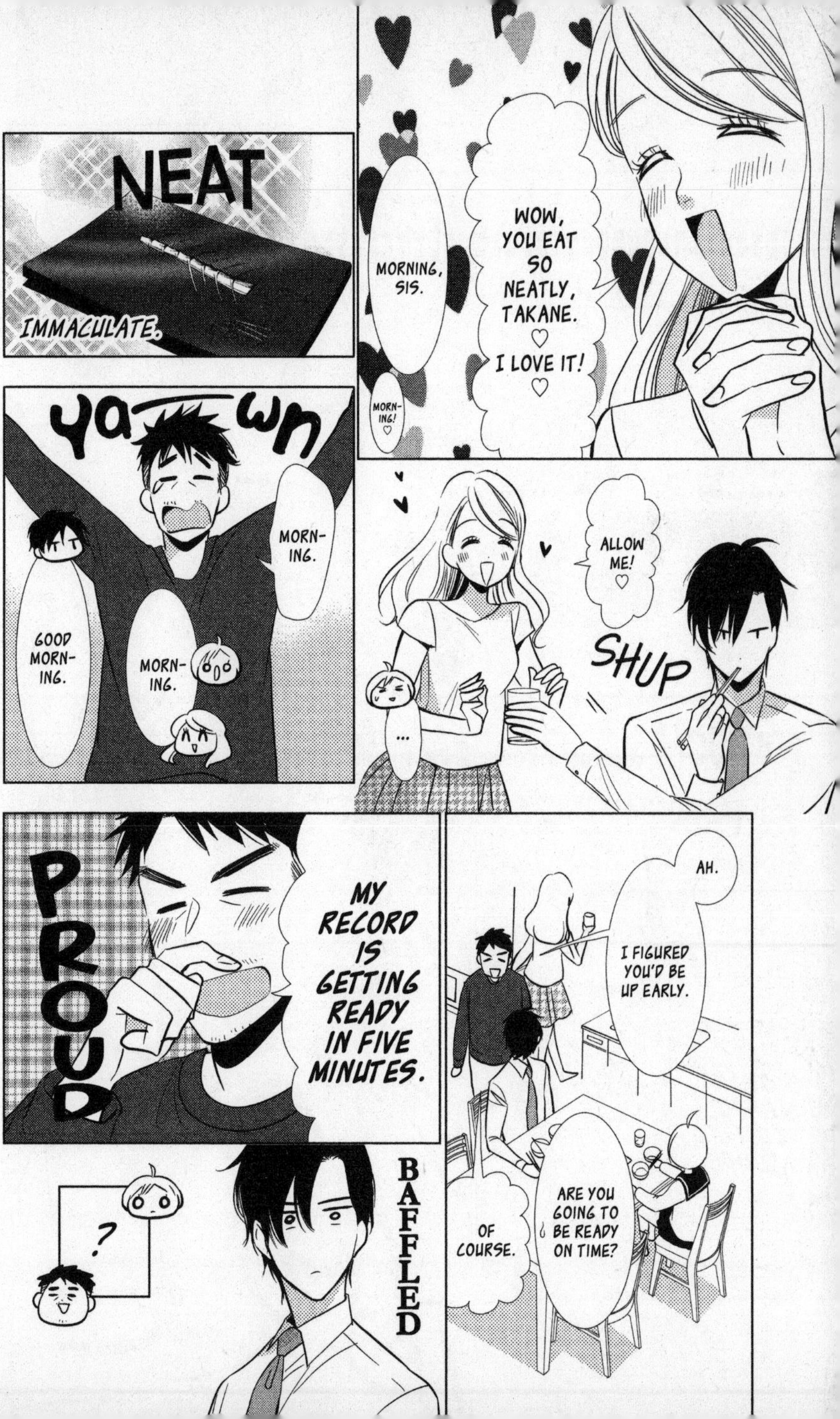
WOW, YOU EAT SO NEATLY, TAKANE. ♡ I LOVE IT! ♡
MORNING, SIS.
MORN-ING! ♡
NEAT
IMMACULATE.
ALLOW ME! ♡
SHUP
...
YA—WN
MORN-ING.
MORN-ING.
GOOD MORN-ING.
AH.
I FIGURED YOU'D BE UP EARLY.
ARE YOU GOING TO BE READY ON TIME?
OF COURSE.
MY RECORD IS GETTING READY IN FIVE MINUTES.
PROUD
BAFFLED
?

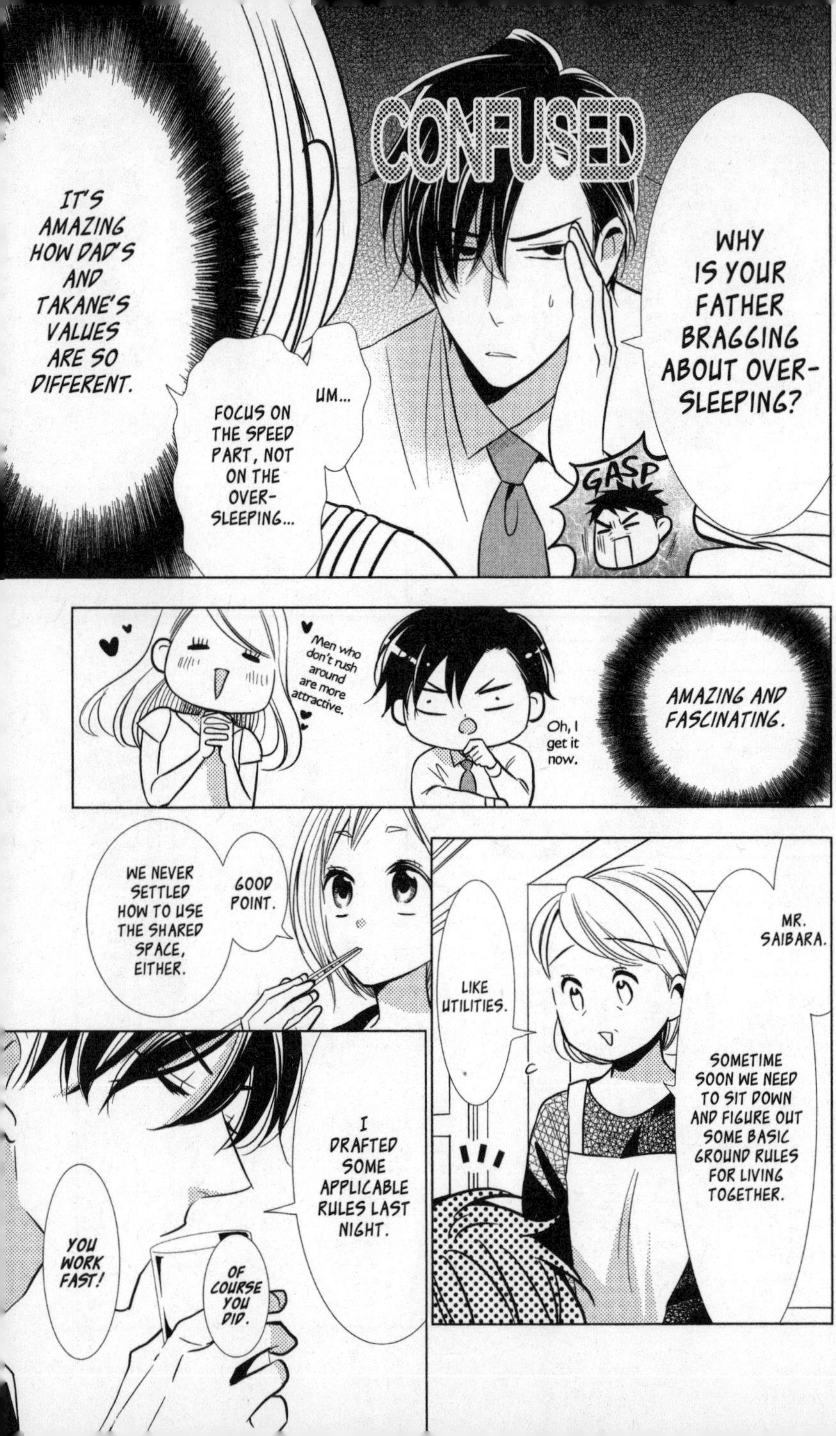
CONFUSED
WHY IS YOUR FATHER BRAGGING ABOUT OVER-SLEEPING?
GASP
UM...
FOCUS ON THE SPEED PART, NOT ON THE OVER-SLEEPING...
IT'S AMAZING HOW DAD'S AND TAKANE'S VALUES ARE SO DIFFERENT.
AMAZING AND FASCINATING.
Oh, I get it now.
Men who don't rush around are more attractive.
MR. SAIBARA.
SOMETIME SOON WE NEED TO SIT DOWN AND FIGURE OUT SOME BASIC GROUND RULES FOR LIVING TOGETHER.
LIKE UTILITIES.
GOOD POINT.
WE NEVER SETTLED HOW TO USE THE SHARED SPACE, EITHER.
I DRAFTED SOME APPLICABLE RULES LAST NIGHT.
YOU WORK FAST!
OF COURSE YOU DID.

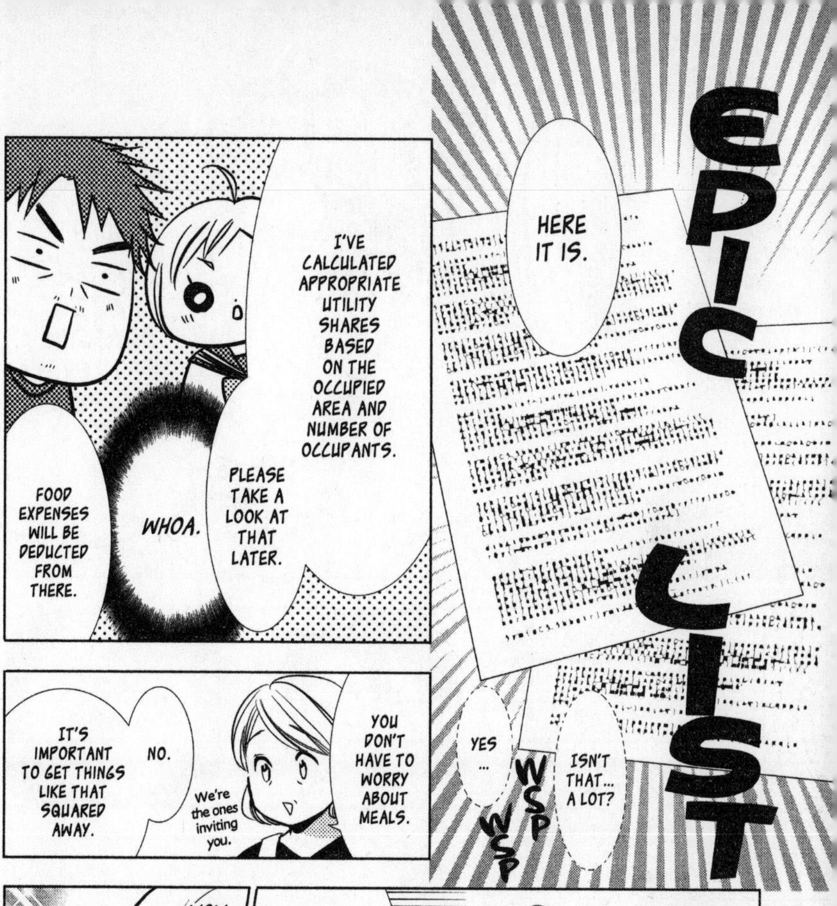
EPIC LIST
HERE IT IS.
ISN'T THAT... A LOT?
WSP WSP
YES...
I'VE CALCULATED APPROPRIATE UTILITY SHARES BASED ON THE OCCUPIED AREA AND NUMBER OF OCCUPANTS.
PLEASE TAKE A LOOK AT THAT LATER.
WHOA.
FOOD EXPENSES WILL BE DEDUCTED FROM THERE.
YOU DON'T HAVE TO WORRY ABOUT MEALS.
We're the ones inviting you.
NO.
IT'S IMPORTANT TO GET THINGS LIKE THAT SQUARED AWAY.
AS FAR AS THE SHARED SPACE IS CONCERNED...
...DON'T PUT ANYTHING IN THERE, AND WEAR INDOOR SLIPPERS WHEN ENTERING.
I HAVE A HOUSEKEEPER COMING EVERY THREE DAYS TO CLEAN MY AREA, SO I'LL HAVE HER CLEAN THE SHARED SPACE AS WELL.
So much trouble!
...
I appreciate that.
WOW.
HE'S LIKE A DEPENDABLE GROWN-UP.
NOW, SOME OTHER GENERAL RULES.

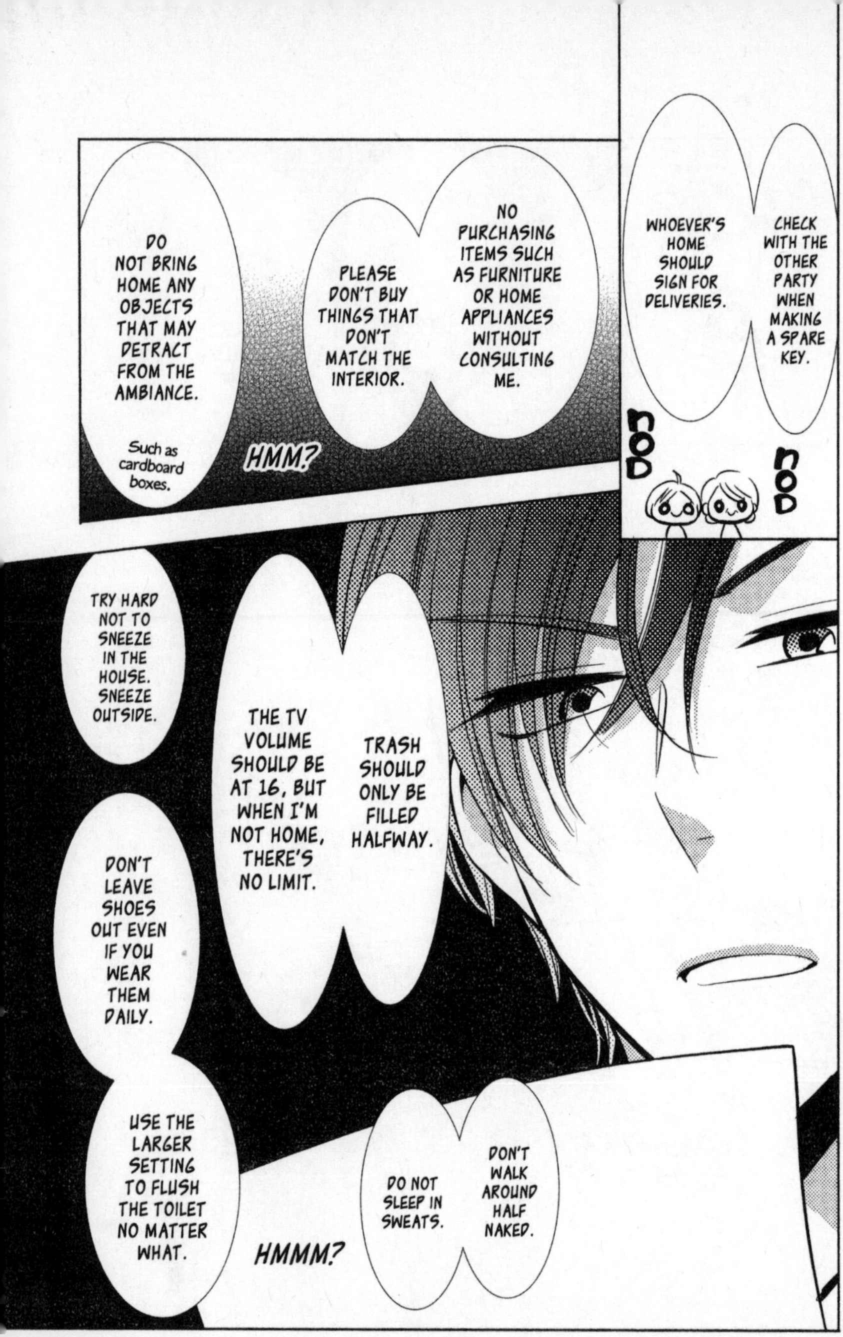
CHECK WITH THE OTHER PARTY WHEN MAKING A SPARE KEY.
WHOEVER'S HOME SHOULD SIGN FOR DELIVERIES.
NOD
NOD
NO PURCHASING ITEMS SUCH AS FURNITURE OR HOME APPLIANCES WITHOUT CONSULTING ME.
PLEASE DON'T BUY THINGS THAT DON'T MATCH THE INTERIOR.
DO NOT BRING HOME ANY OBJECTS THAT MAY DETRACT FROM THE AMBIANCE.
Such as cardboard boxes.
HMM?
TRASH SHOULD ONLY BE FILLED HALFWAY.
THE TV VOLUME SHOULD BE AT 16, BUT WHEN I'M NOT HOME, THERE'S NO LIMIT.
TRY HARD NOT TO SNEEZE IN THE HOUSE. SNEEZE OUTSIDE.
DON'T LEAVE SHOES OUT EVEN IF YOU WEAR THEM DAILY.
DON'T WALK AROUND HALF NAKED.
DO NOT SLEEP IN SWEATS.
USE THE LARGER SETTING TO FLUSH THE TOILET NO MATTER WHAT.
HMMM?

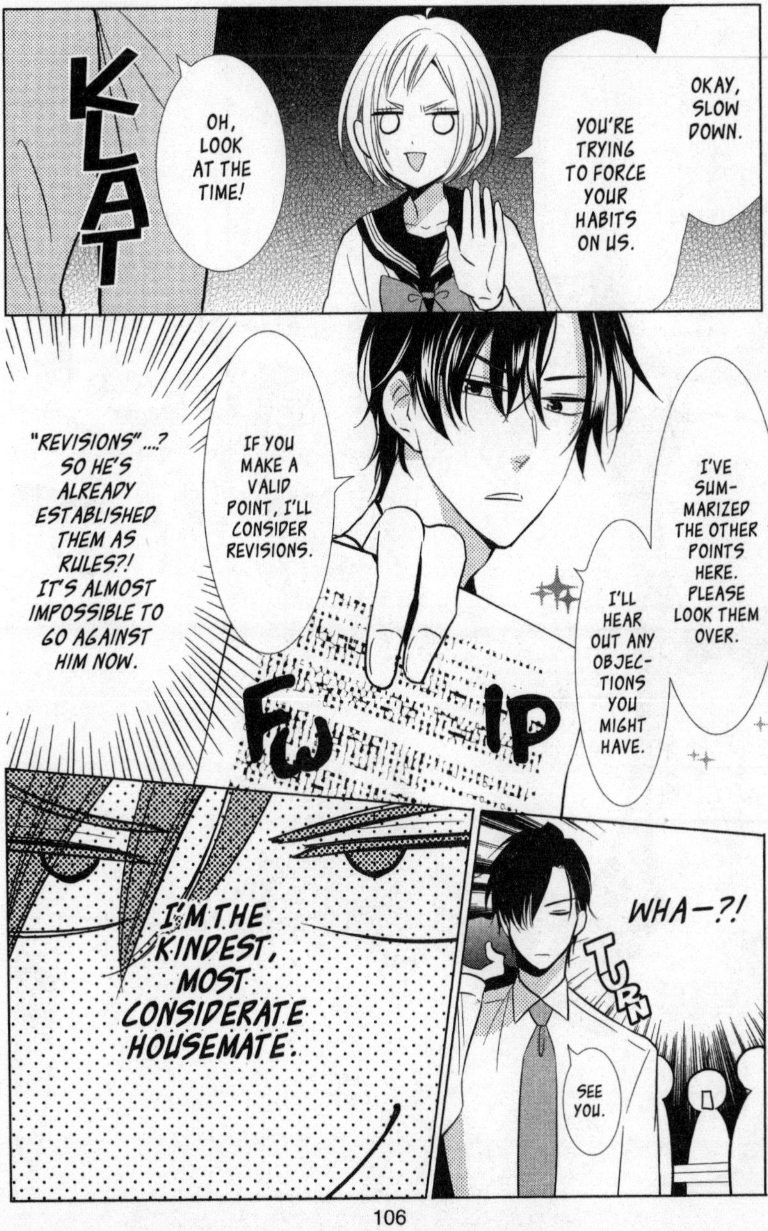
OKAY, SLOW DOWN.
YOU'RE TRYING TO FORCE YOUR HABITS ON US.
OH, LOOK AT THE TIME!
KLAT
I'VE SUM-MARIZED THE OTHER POINTS HERE. PLEASE LOOK THEM OVER.
I'LL HEAR OUT ANY OBJEC-TIONS YOU MIGHT HAVE.
FWIP
IF YOU MAKE A VALID POINT, I'LL CONSIDER REVISIONS.
"REVISIONS"...? SO HE'S ALREADY ESTABLISHED THEM AS RULES?! IT'S ALMOST IMPOSSIBLE TO GO AGAINST HIM NOW.
WHA-?!
TURN
SEE YOU.
I'M THE KINDEST, MOST CONSIDERATE HOUSEMATE.

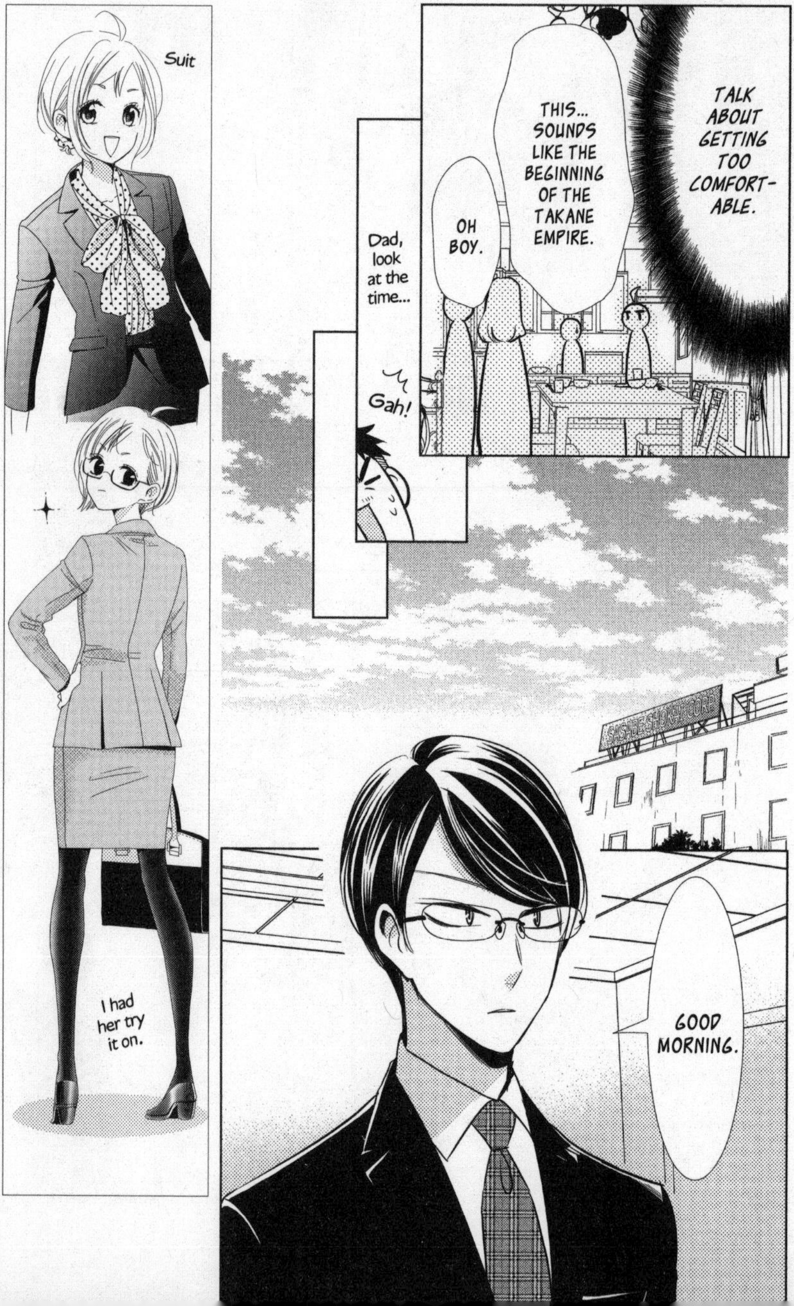
TALK ABOUT GETTING TOO COMFORT-ABLE.
THIS... SOUNDS LIKE THE BEGINNING OF THE TAKANE EMPIRE.
OH BOY.
Dad, look at the time...
Gah!
SASABE SHOKAI CORP.
GOOD MORNING.
Suit
I had her try it on.

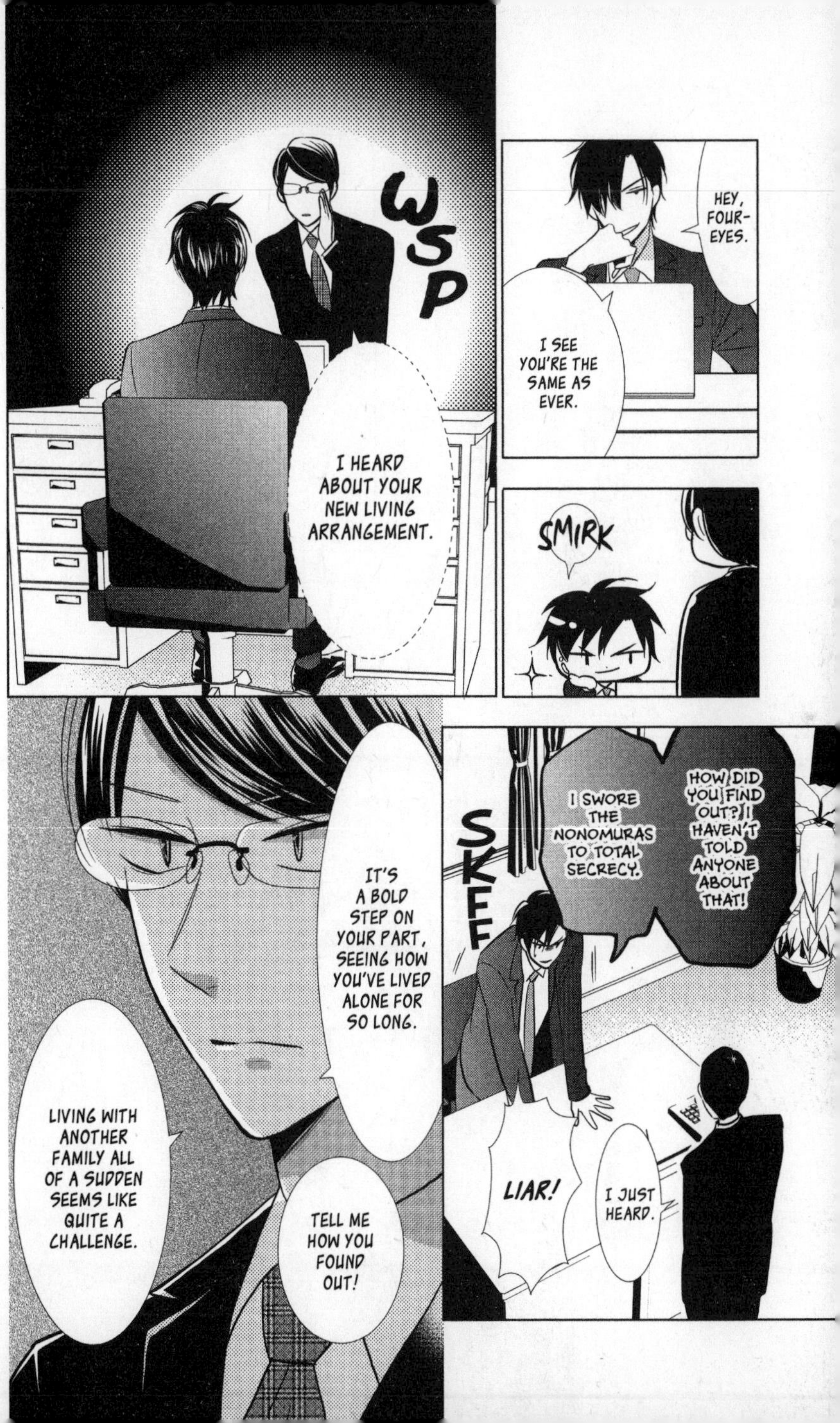
HEY, FOUR-EYES.
I SEE YOU'RE THE SAME AS EVER.
SMIRK
WSP
I HEARD ABOUT YOUR NEW LIVING ARRANGEMENT.
HOW DID YOU FIND OUT? I HAVEN'T TOLD ANYONE ABOUT THAT!
I SWORE THE NONOMURAS TO TOTAL SECRECY.
SKFF
I JUST HEARD.
LIAR!
IT'S A BOLD STEP ON YOUR PART, SEEING HOW YOU'VE LIVED ALONE FOR SO LONG.
LIVING WITH ANOTHER FAMILY ALL OF A SUDDEN SEEMS LIKE QUITE A CHALLENGE.
TELL ME HOW YOU FOUND OUT!

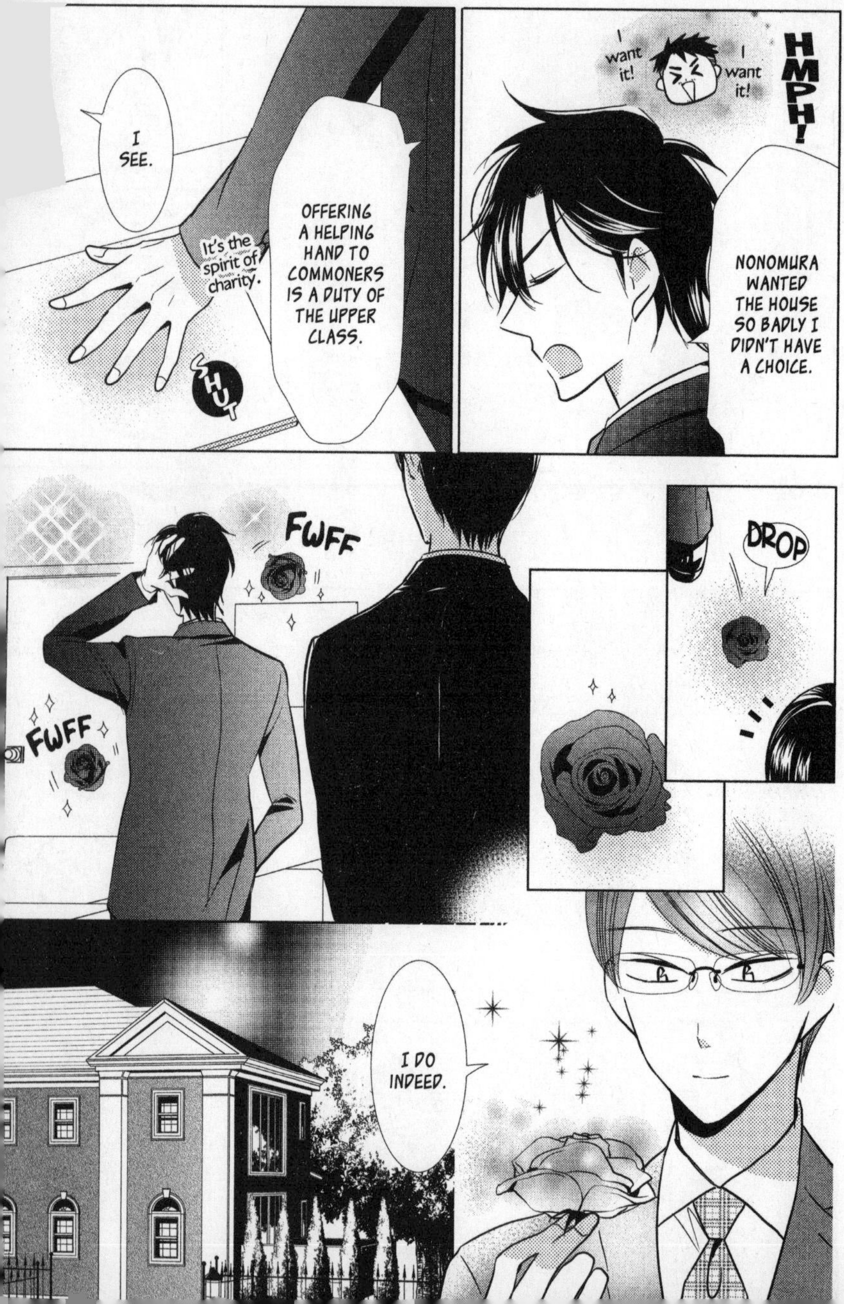
HMPH!
I want it!
I want it!
NONOMURA WANTED THE HOUSE SO BADLY I DIDN'T HAVE A CHOICE.
OFFERING A HELPING HAND TO COMMONERS IS A DUTY OF THE UPPER CLASS.
It's the spirit of charity.
I SEE.
SHUT
DROP
FWFF
FWFF
I DO INDEED.

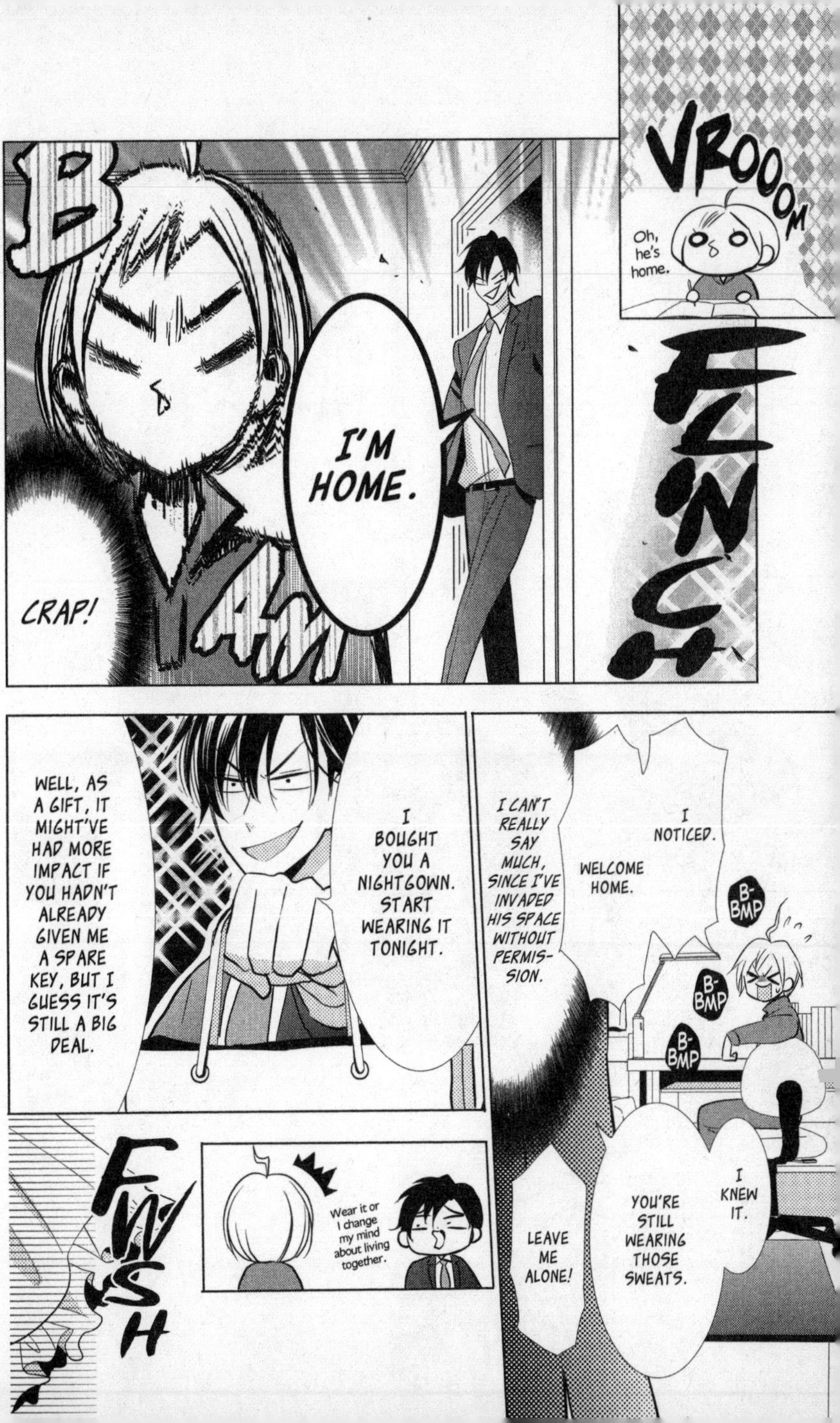
VROOOM
Oh, he's home.
FLING
B
I'M HOME.
CRAP!
I NOTICED.
WELCOME HOME.
I CAN'T REALLY SAY MUCH, SINCE I'VE INVADED HIS SPACE WITHOUT PERMIS-SION.
B-BMP
B-BMP
B-BMP
I KNEW IT.
YOU'RE STILL WEARING THOSE SWEATS.
LEAVE ME ALONE!
I BOUGHT YOU A NIGHTGOWN. START WEARING IT TONIGHT.
WELL, AS A GIFT, IT MIGHT'VE HAD MORE IMPACT IF YOU HADN'T ALREADY GIVEN ME A SPARE KEY, BUT I GUESS IT'S STILL A BIG DEAL.
Wear it or I change my mind about living together.
FWISH

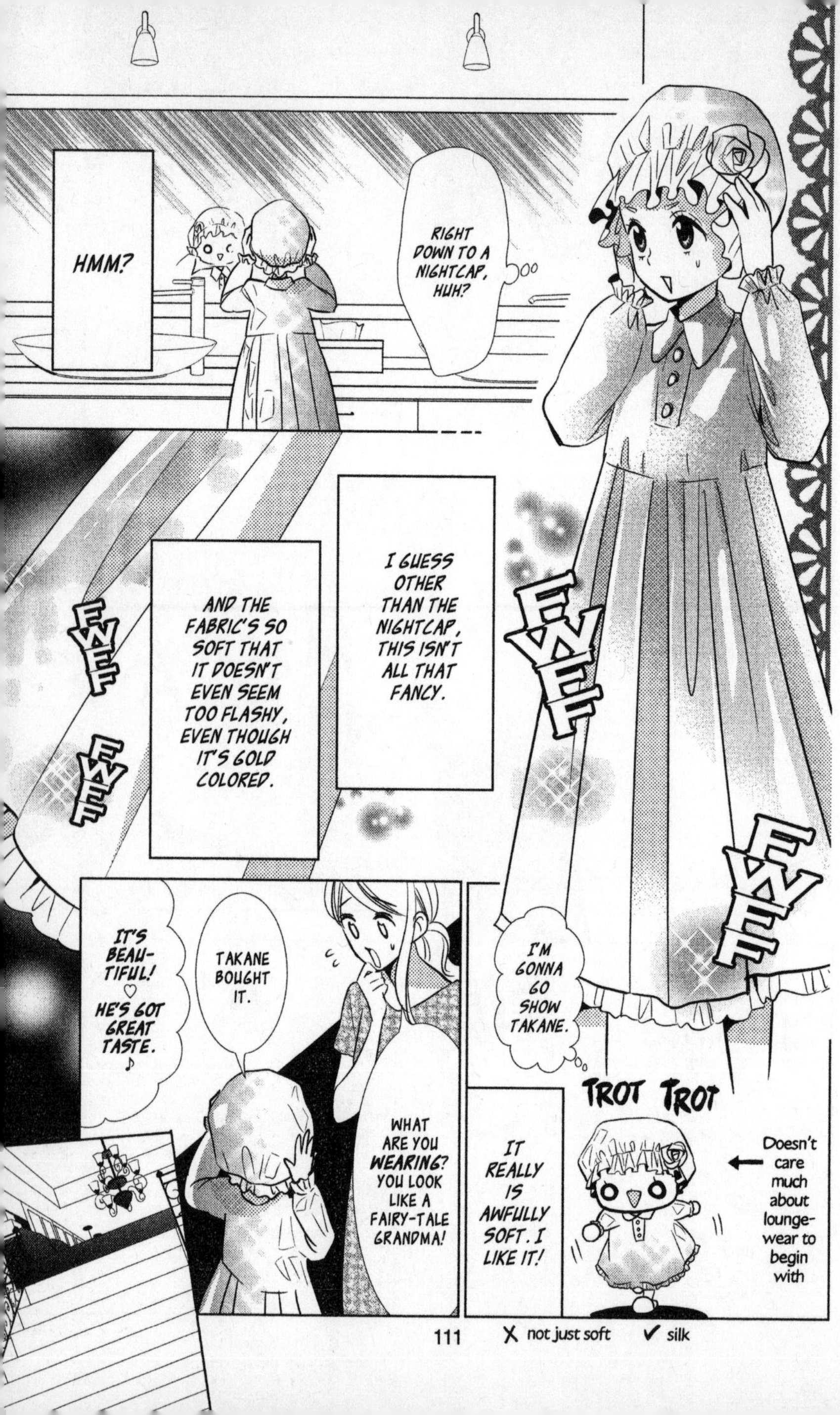
RIGHT DOWN TO A NIGHTCAP, HUH?
HMM?
I GUESS OTHER THAN THE NIGHTCAP, THIS ISN'T ALL THAT FANCY.
AND THE FABRIC'S SO SOFT THAT IT DOESN'T EVEN SEEM TOO FLASHY, EVEN THOUGH IT'S GOLD COLORED.
FWEF
FWEF
FWEF
FWEF
I'M GONNA GO SHOW TAKANE.
TROT TROT
Doesn't care much about lounge-wear to begin with
IT REALLY IS AWFULLY SOFT. I LIKE IT!
WHAT ARE YOU WEARING? YOU LOOK LIKE A FAIRY-TALE GRANDMA!
TAKANE BOUGHT IT.
IT'S BEAUTIFUL! ♡ HE'S GOT GREAT TASTE. ♪

X not just soft ✓ silk

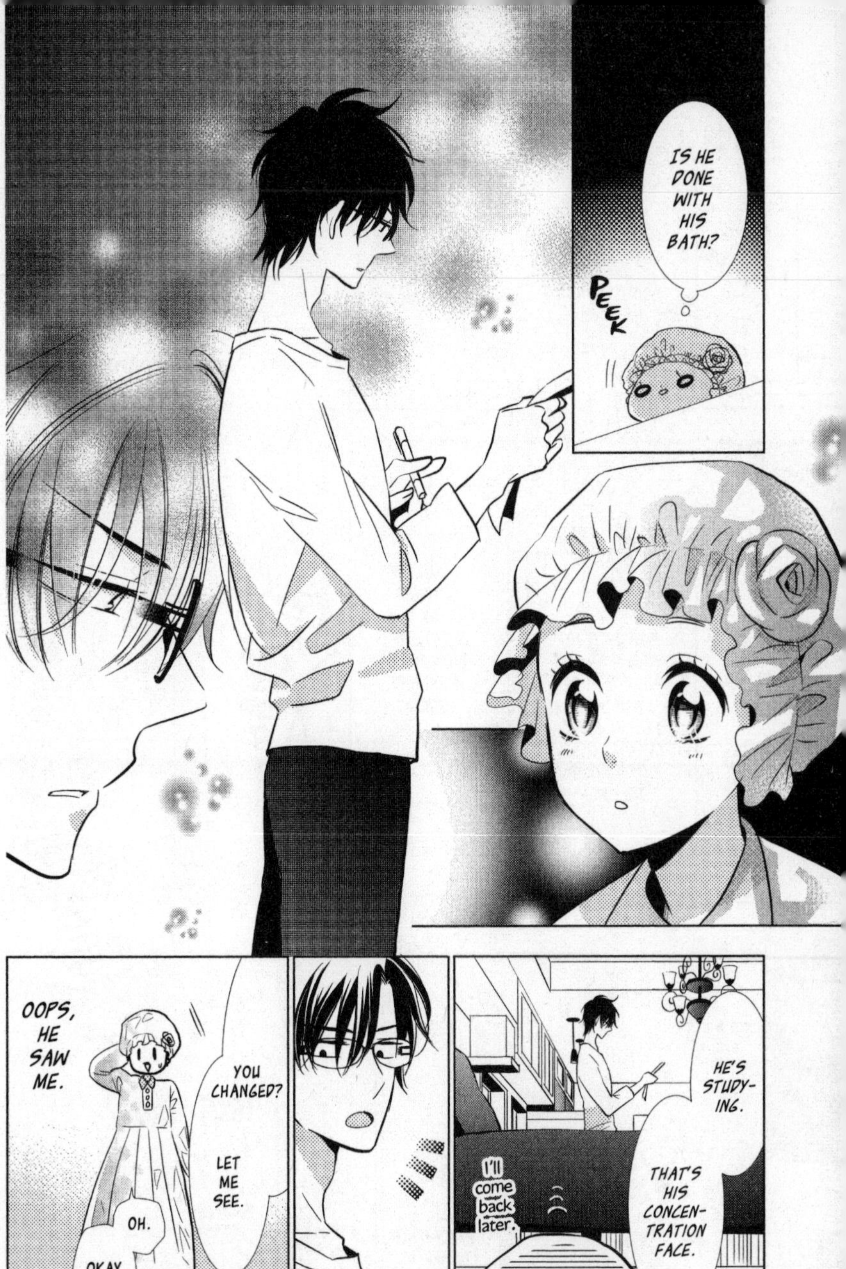
IS HE DONE WITH HIS BATH?
PEEK
HE'S STUDYING.
THAT'S HIS CONCENTRATION FACE.
I'll come back later.
YOU CHANGED?
LET ME SEE.
OOPS, HE SAW ME.
OH.
OKAY.

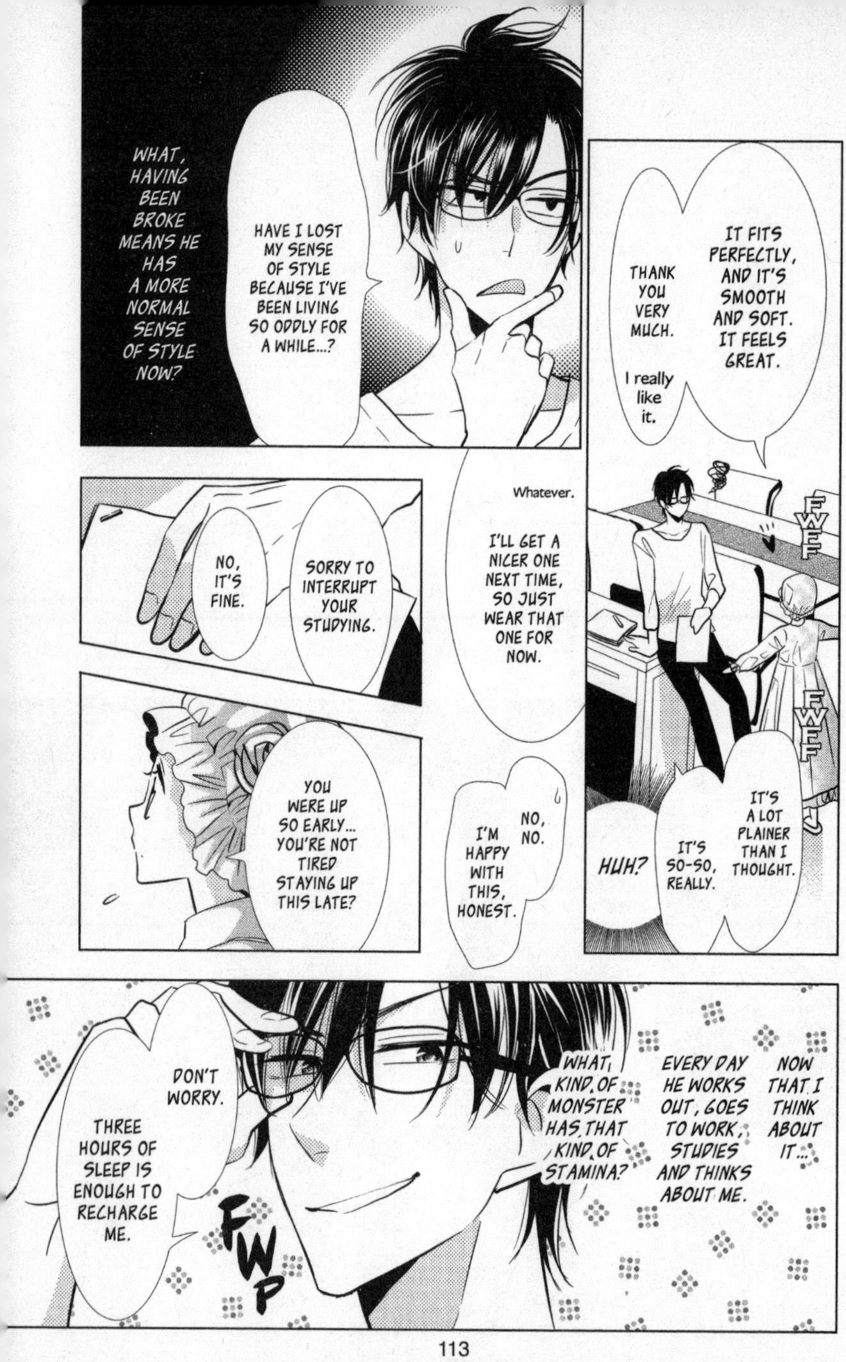
IT FITS PERFECTLY, AND IT'S SMOOTH AND SOFT. IT FEELS GREAT.
THANK YOU VERY MUCH.
I really like it.
FWF
FWF
IT'S A LOT PLAINER THAN I THOUGHT.
IT'S SO-SO, REALLY.
HUH?
WHAT, HAVING BEEN BROKE MEANS HE HAS A MORE NORMAL SENSE OF STYLE NOW?
HAVE I LOST MY SENSE OF STYLE BECAUSE I'VE BEEN LIVING SO ODDLY FOR A WHILE...?
Whatever.
I'LL GET A NICER ONE NEXT TIME, SO JUST WEAR THAT ONE FOR NOW.
NO, NO.
I'M HAPPY WITH THIS, HONEST.
SORRY TO INTERRUPT YOUR STUDYING.
NO, IT'S FINE.
YOU WERE UP SO EARLY... YOU'RE NOT TIRED STAYING UP THIS LATE?
NOW THAT I THINK ABOUT IT...
EVERY DAY HE WORKS OUT, GOES TO WORK, STUDIES AND THINKS ABOUT ME.
WHAT KIND OF MONSTER HAS THAT KIND OF STAMINA?
DON'T WORRY.
THREE HOURS OF SLEEP IS ENOUGH TO RECHARGE ME.
FWP

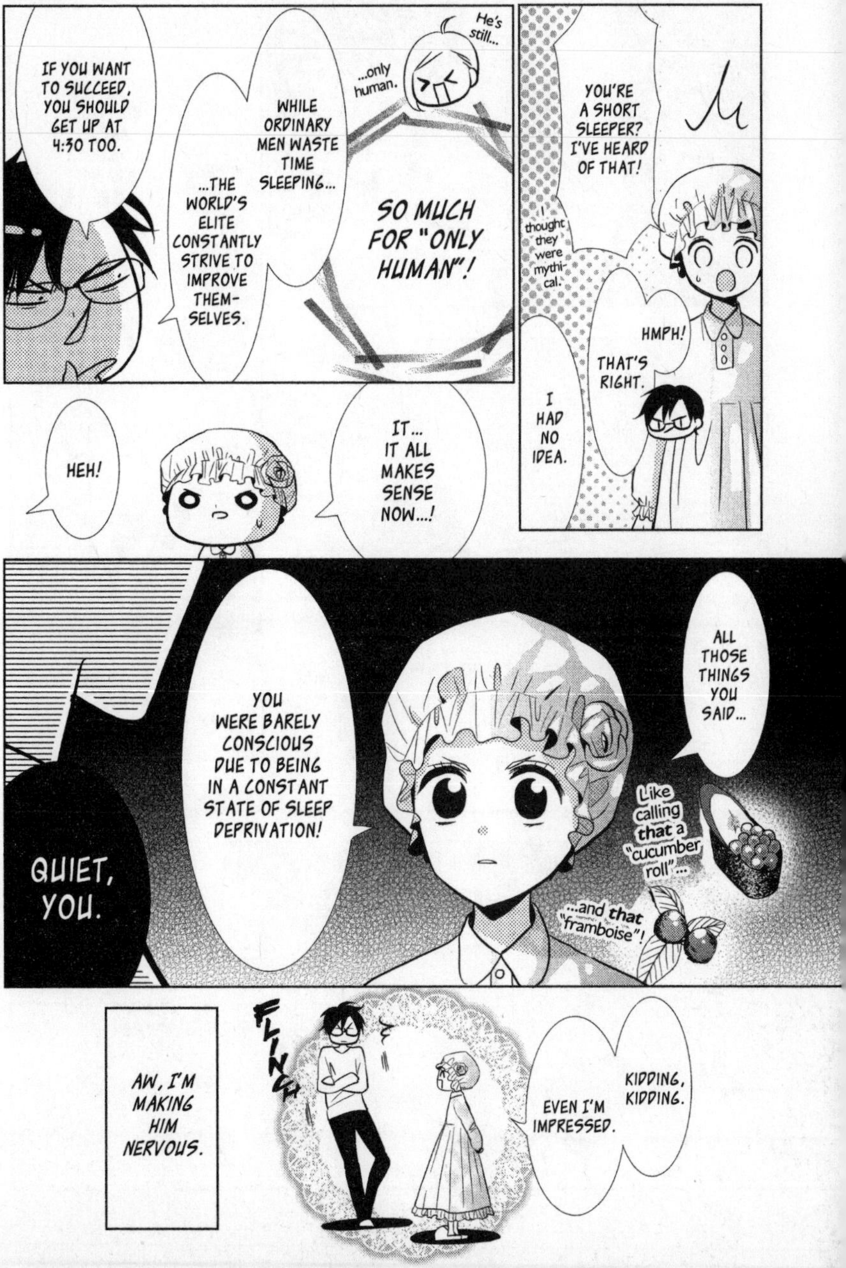
YOU'RE A SHORT SLEEPER? I'VE HEARD OF THAT!
I thought they were mythical.
HMPH! THAT'S RIGHT.
I HAD NO IDEA.
He's still...
...only human.
WHILE ORDINARY MEN WASTE TIME SLEEPING...
...THE WORLD'S ELITE CONSTANTLY STRIVE TO IMPROVE THEMSELVES.
IF YOU WANT TO SUCCEED, YOU SHOULD GET UP AT 4:30 TOO.
SO MUCH FOR "ONLY HUMAN"!
IT... IT ALL MAKES SENSE NOW...!
HEH!
ALL THOSE THINGS YOU SAID...
Like calling that a "cucumber roll"...
...and that "framboise"!
YOU WERE BARELY CONSCIOUS DUE TO BEING IN A CONSTANT STATE OF SLEEP DEPRIVATION!
QUIET, YOU.
KIDDING, KIDDING.
EVEN I'M IMPRESSED.
FLINCH
AW, I'M MAKING HIM NERVOUS.

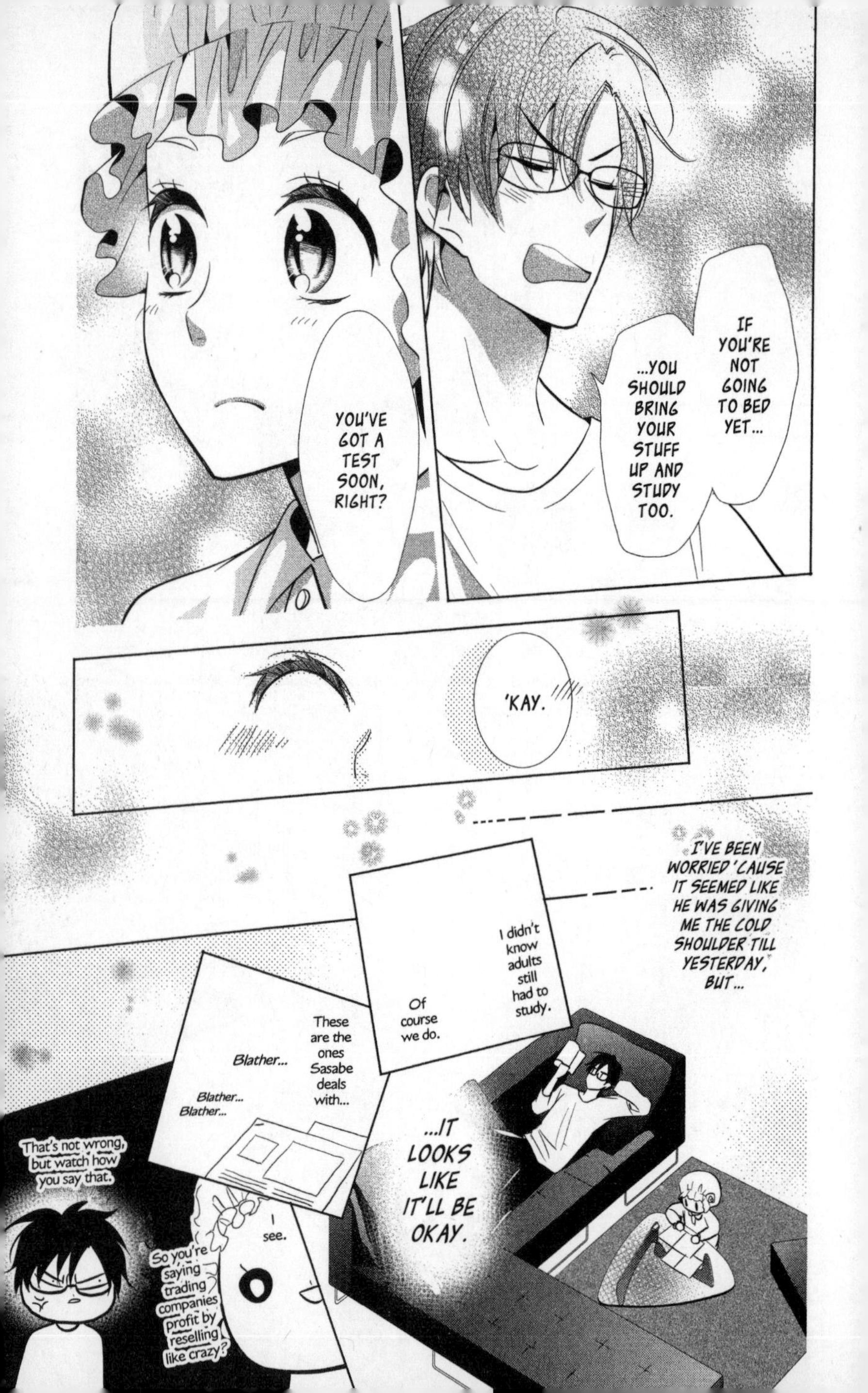
IF YOU'RE NOT GOING TO BED YET...
...YOU SHOULD BRING YOUR STUFF UP AND STUDY TOO.
YOU'VE GOT A TEST SOON, RIGHT?
'KAY.
I'VE BEEN WORRIED 'CAUSE IT SEEMED LIKE HE WAS GIVING ME THE COLD SHOULDER TILL YESTERDAY, BUT...
I didn't know adults still had to study.
Of course we do.
These are the ones Sasabe deals with...
Blather...
Blather... Blather...
...IT LOOKS LIKE IT'LL BE OKAY.
I see.
So you're saying trading companies profit by reselling like crazy?
That's not wrong, but watch how you say that.

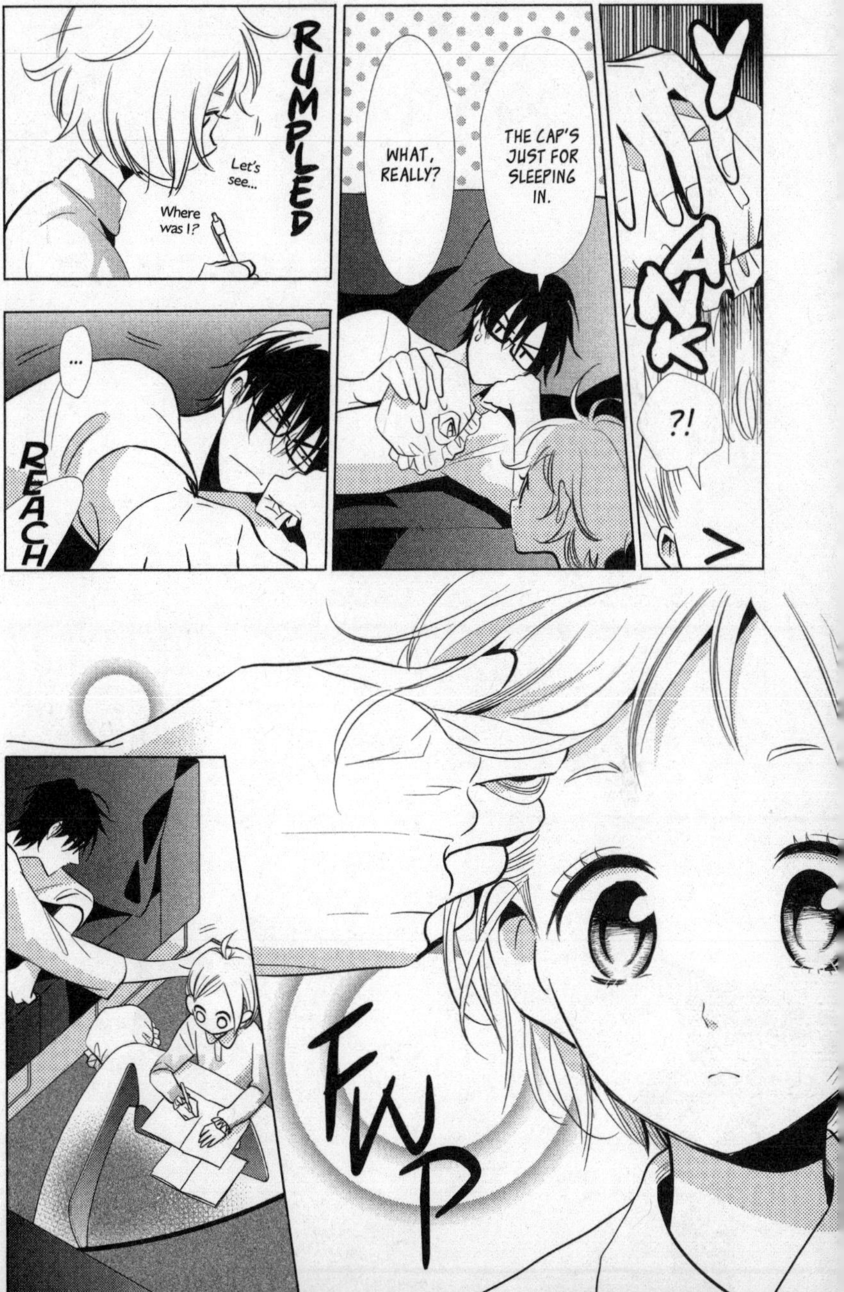
YANK
?!
THE CAP'S JUST FOR SLEEPING IN.
WHAT, REALLY?
RUMPLED
Let's see...
Where was I?
...
REACH
FWP

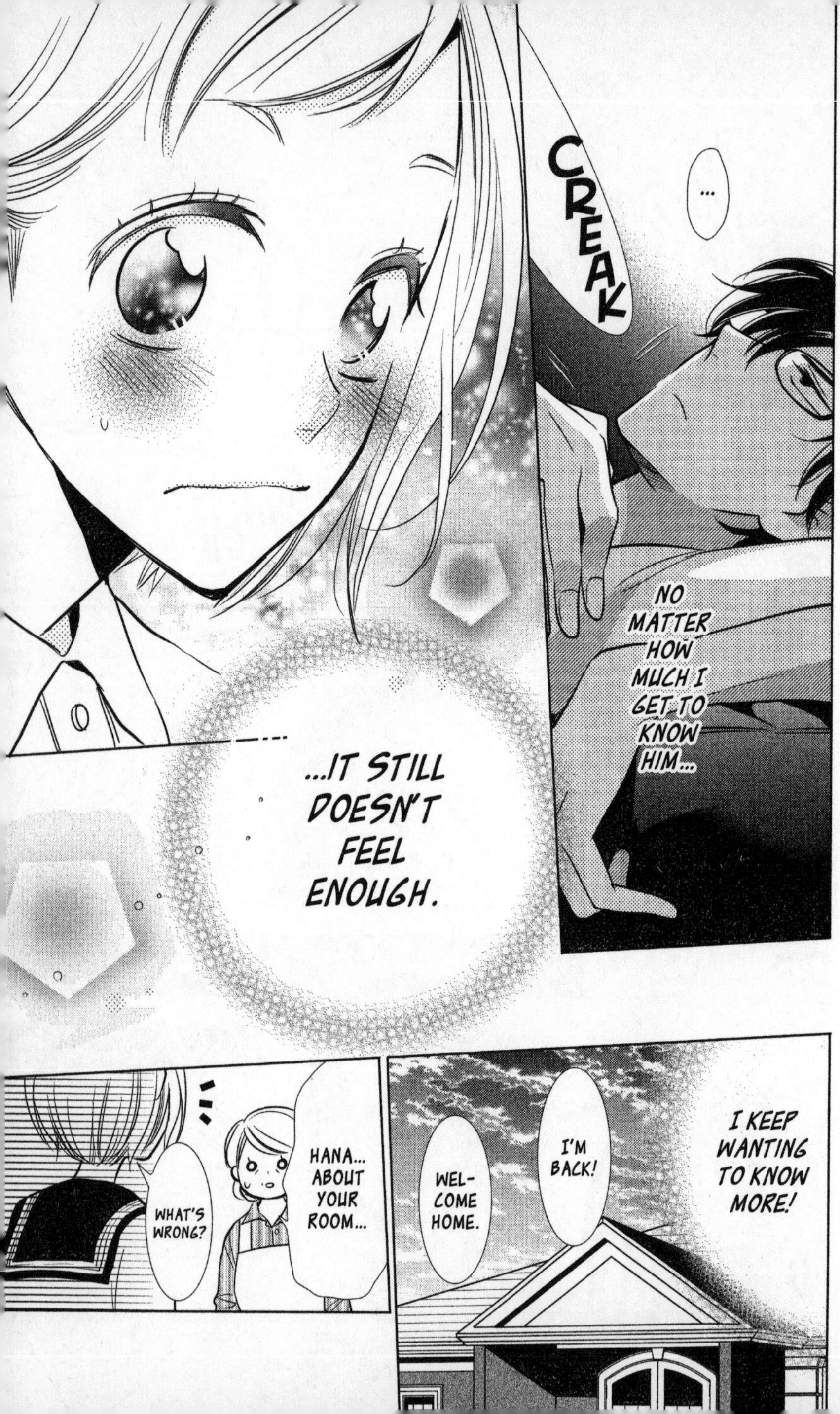
...
CREAK
NO MATTER HOW MUCH I GET TO KNOW HIM...
...IT STILL DOESN'T FEEL ENOUGH.
I KEEP WANTING TO KNOW MORE!
I'M BACK!
WEL-COME HOME.
HANA... ABOUT YOUR ROOM...
WHAT'S WRONG?

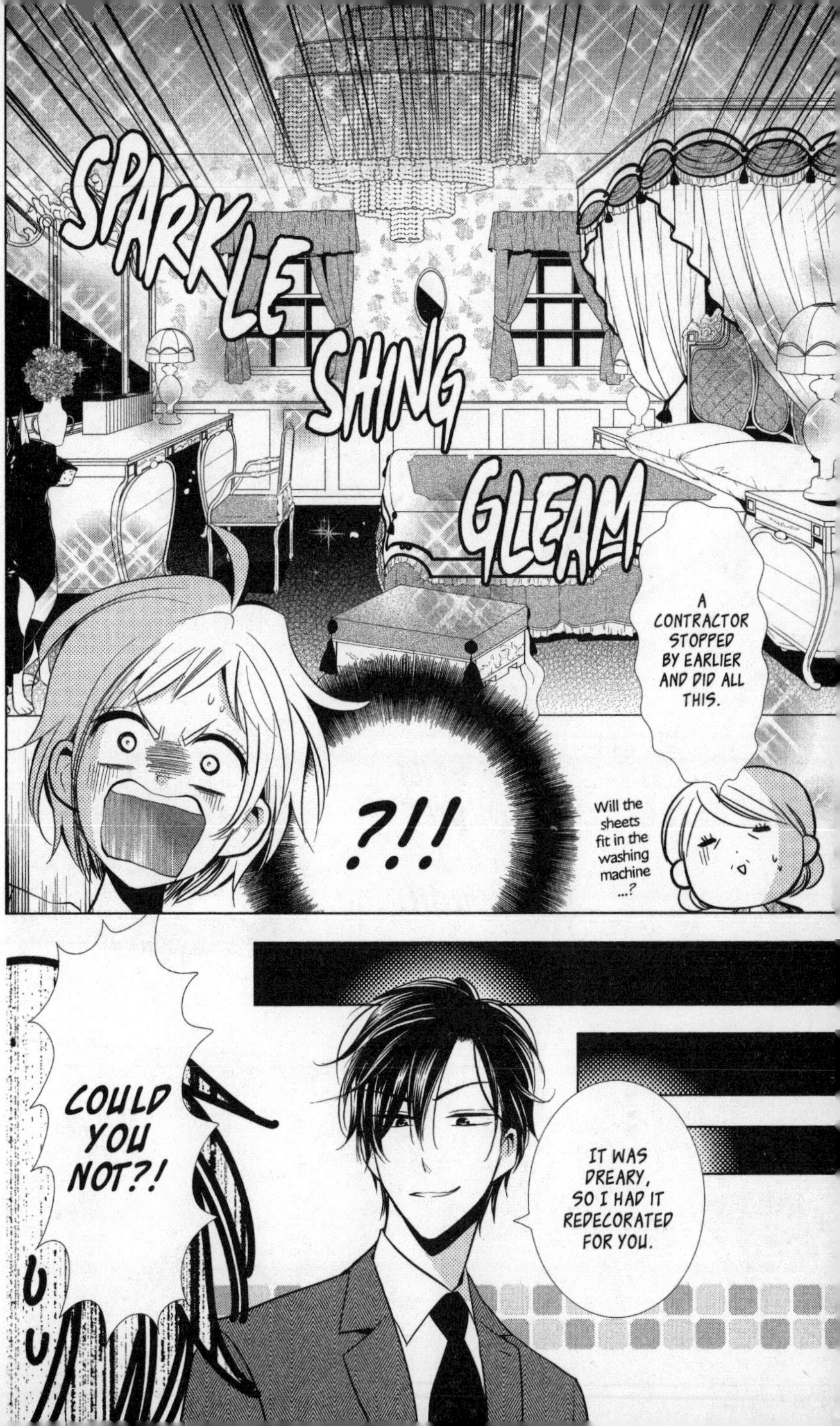
SPARKLE
SHING
GLEAM
A CONTRACTOR STOPPED BY EARLIER AND DID ALL THIS.
Will the sheets fit in the washing machine ...?
?!!
IT WAS DREARY, SO I HAD IT REDECORATED FOR YOU.
COULD YOU NOT?!
UU

Chapter 50

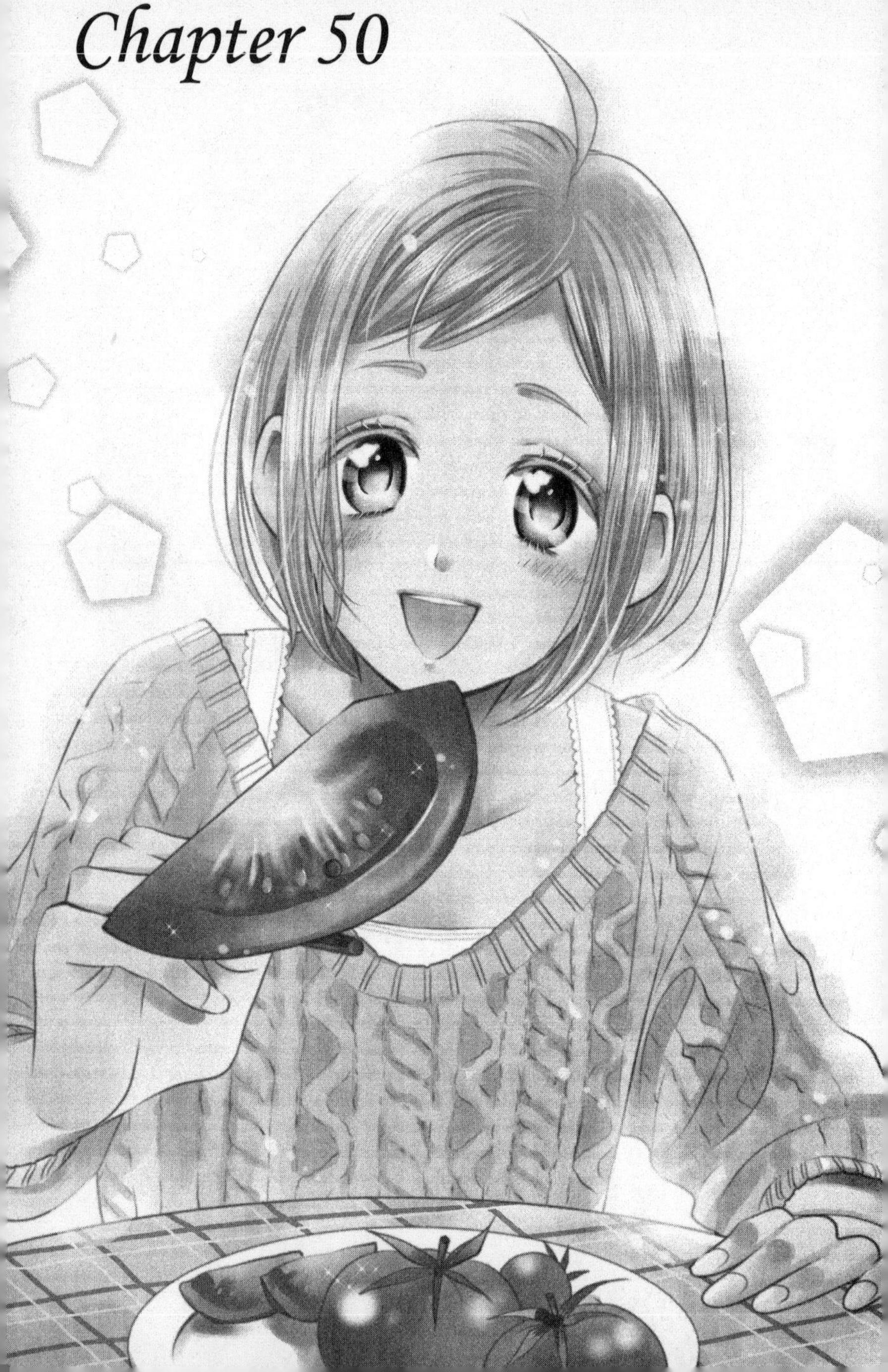

Payback

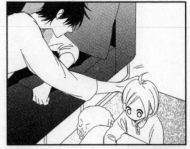

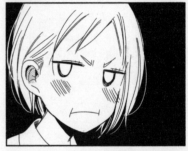

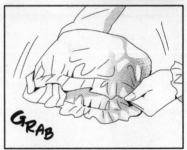

GRAB

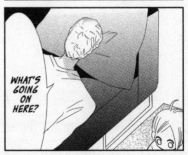

WHAT'S GOING ON HERE?

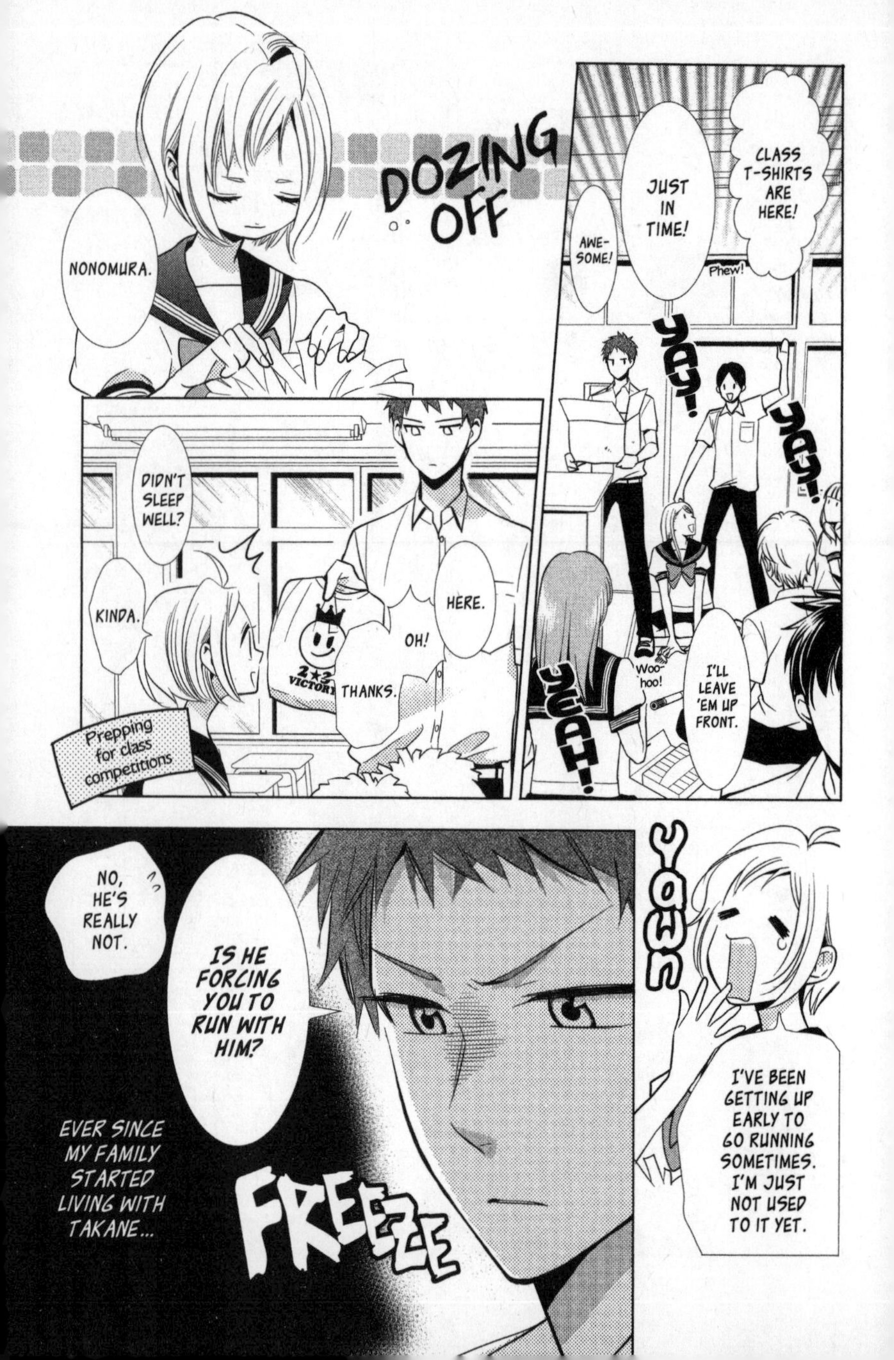
CLASS T-SHIRTS ARE HERE!
JUST IN TIME!
AWESOME!
Phew!
YAY!
YAY!
I'LL LEAVE 'EM UP FRONT.
Woo-hoo!
YEAH!
DOZING OFF
NONOMURA.
HERE.
OH!
THANKS.
2★3 VICTORY
DIDN'T SLEEP WELL?
KINDA.
Prepping for class competitions
YAWN
I'VE BEEN GETTING UP EARLY TO GO RUNNING SOMETIMES. I'M JUST NOT USED TO IT YET.
IS HE FORCING YOU TO RUN WITH HIM?
NO, HE'S REALLY NOT.
FREEZE
EVER SINCE MY FAMILY STARTED LIVING WITH TAKANE...

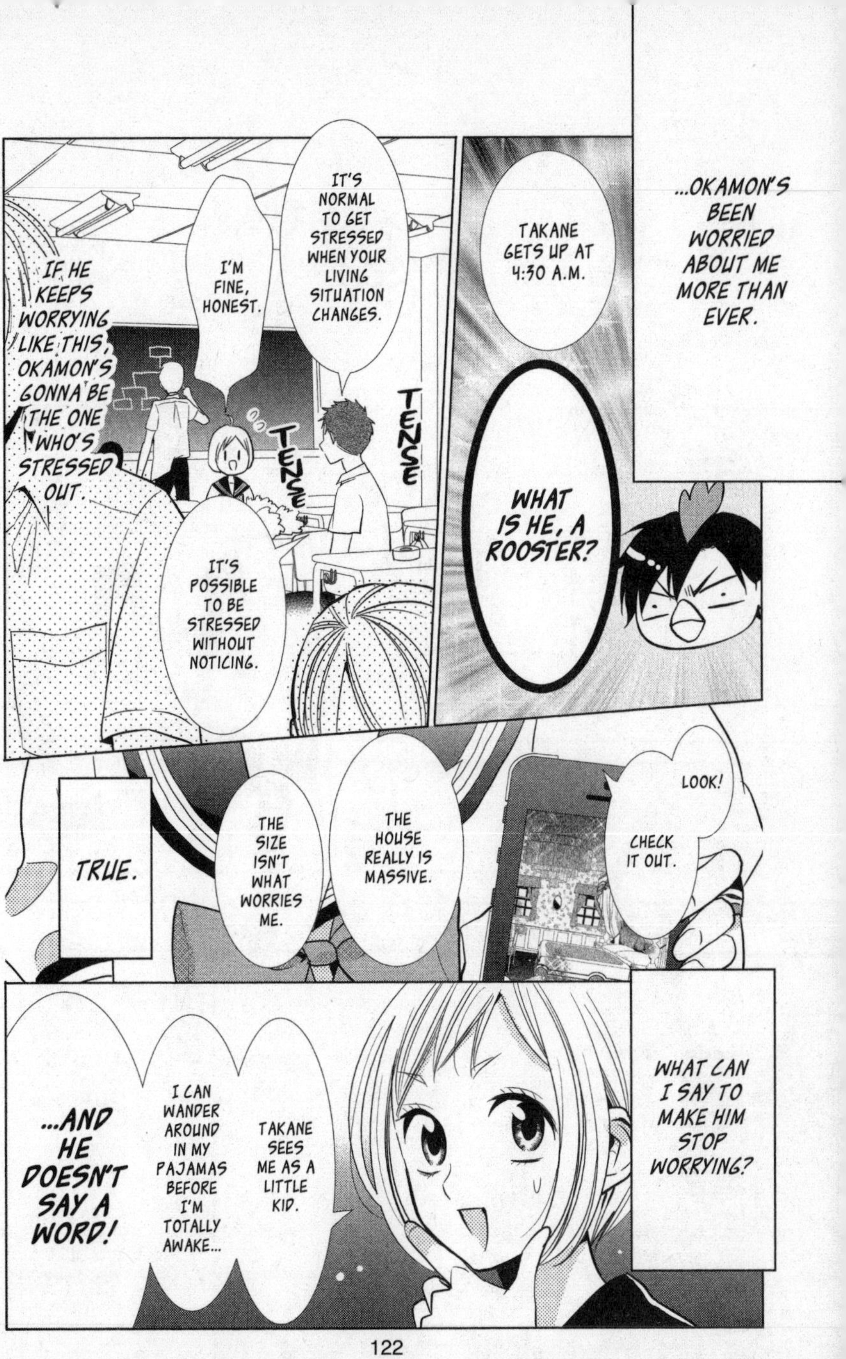
...OKAMON'S BEEN WORRIED ABOUT ME MORE THAN EVER.
TAKANE GETS UP AT 4:30 A.M.
WHAT IS HE, A ROOSTER?
IT'S NORMAL TO GET STRESSED WHEN YOUR LIVING SITUATION CHANGES.
I'M FINE, HONEST.
TENSE
TENSE
IT'S POSSIBLE TO BE STRESSED WITHOUT NOTICING.
IF HE KEEPS WORRYING LIKE THIS, OKAMON'S GONNA BE THE ONE WHO'S STRESSED OUT.
LOOK!
CHECK IT OUT.
THE HOUSE REALLY IS MASSIVE.
THE SIZE ISN'T WHAT WORRIES ME.
TRUE.
WHAT CAN I SAY TO MAKE HIM STOP WORRYING?
TAKANE SEES ME AS A LITTLE KID.
I CAN WANDER AROUND IN MY PAJAMAS BEFORE I'M TOTALLY AWAKE...
...AND HE DOESN'T SAY A WORD!

Daruma
• Commemorating the Series' 50th Consecutive Installment! •

When chapter 50 was published in *Hana to Yume* magazine, to commemorate the occasion we ran a special promotion to give away some daruma.

Ta-da!

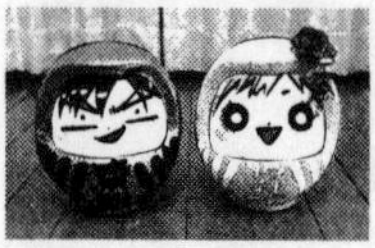

We asked craftsmen from Takasaki, a location famous for producing daruma, to make ten of each of these for a total of 20 daruma.

I drew the faces. On the Takane daruma, I had them write *"Yuiga dokuson"* (self-righteousness) on the back, and on the back of the Hana daruma, *"Futoh fukutsu"* (dauntless).

Each one was unique with lots of character.

We hope they'll bring good fortune to whoever wins them!

The Takane daruma is an opulent gold, while the Hana daruma is an adorable pink. ✧

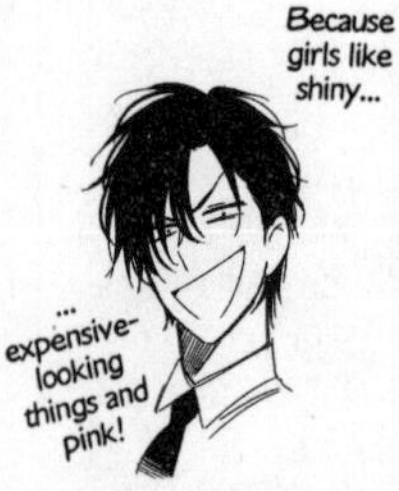
Because girls like shiny...
...expensive-looking things and pink!

According to Takane

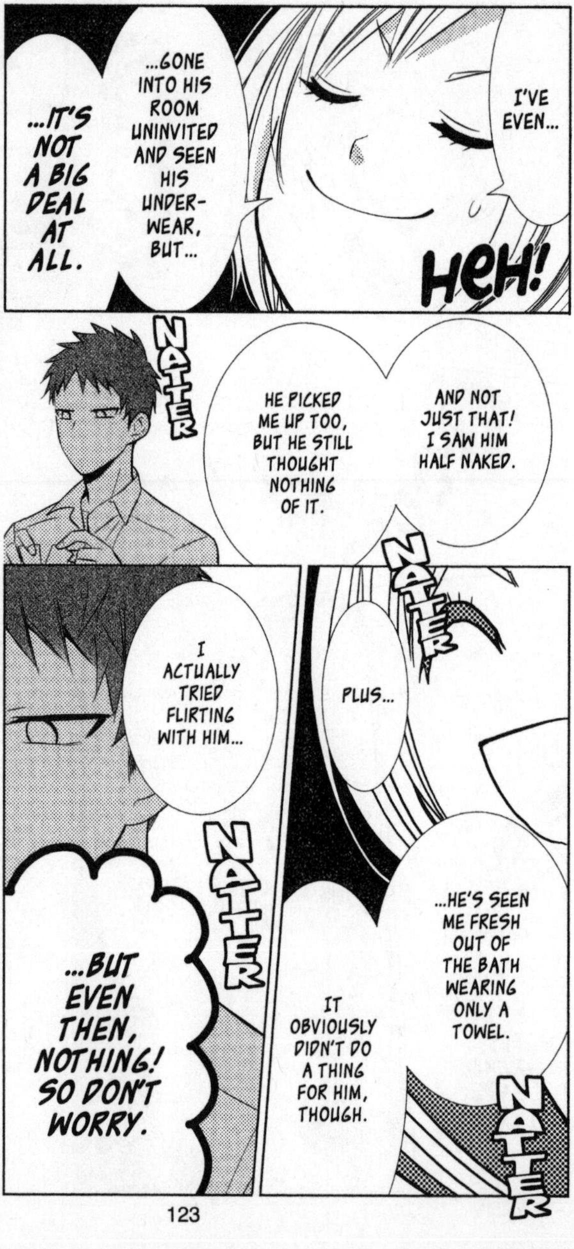
I'VE EVEN...
...GONE INTO HIS ROOM UNINVITED AND SEEN HIS UNDERWEAR, BUT...
...IT'S NOT A BIG DEAL AT ALL.
HEH!
AND NOT JUST THAT! I SAW HIM HALF NAKED.
HE PICKED ME UP TOO, BUT HE STILL THOUGHT NOTHING OF IT.
NATTER
NATTER
PLUS...
...HE'S SEEN ME FRESH OUT OF THE BATH WEARING ONLY A TOWEL.
IT OBVIOUSLY DIDN'T DO A THING FOR HIM, THOUGH.
NATTER
I ACTUALLY TRIED FLIRTING WITH HIM...
...BUT EVEN THEN, NOTHING! SO DON'T WORRY.
NATTER

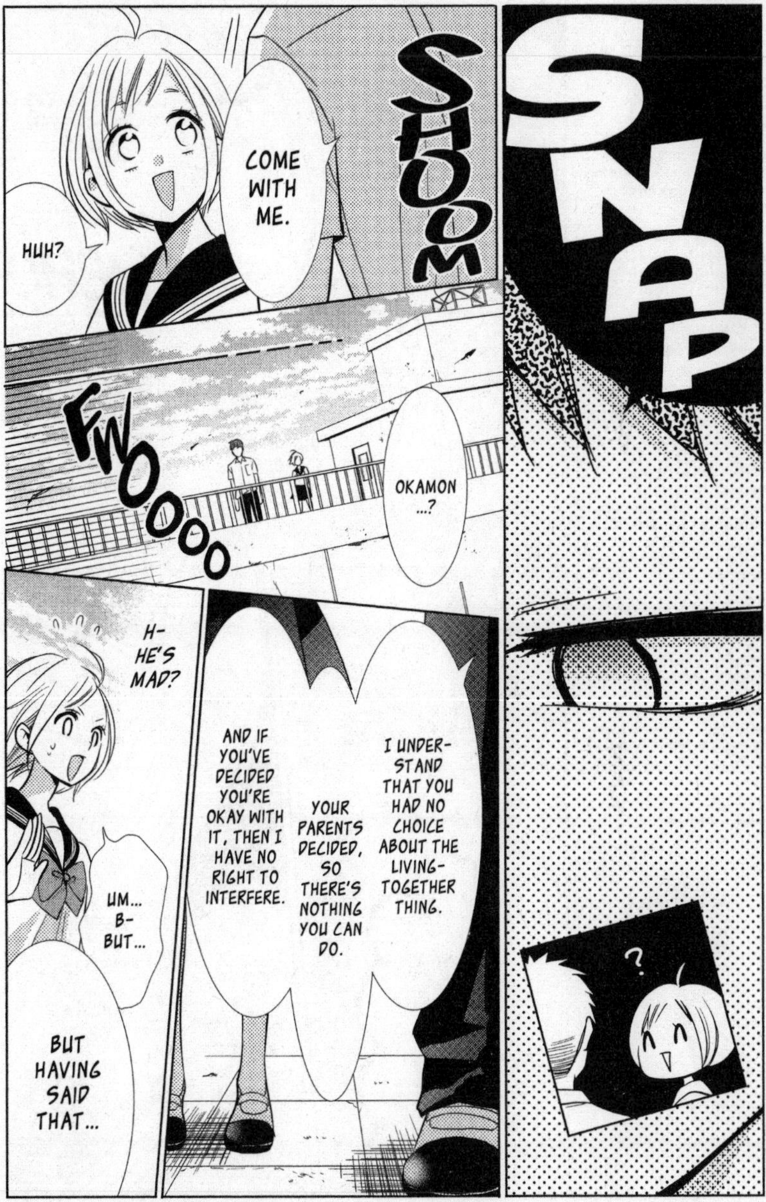
SNAP
?
SHOOM
COME WITH ME.
HUH?
FWOOOO
OKAMON ...?
I UNDER-STAND THAT YOU HAD NO CHOICE ABOUT THE LIVING-TOGETHER THING.
YOUR PARENTS DECIDED, SO THERE'S NOTHING YOU CAN DO.
AND IF YOU'VE DECIDED YOU'RE OKAY WITH IT, THEN I HAVE NO RIGHT TO INTERFERE.
H-HE'S MAD?
UM... B-BUT...
BUT HAVING SAID THAT...

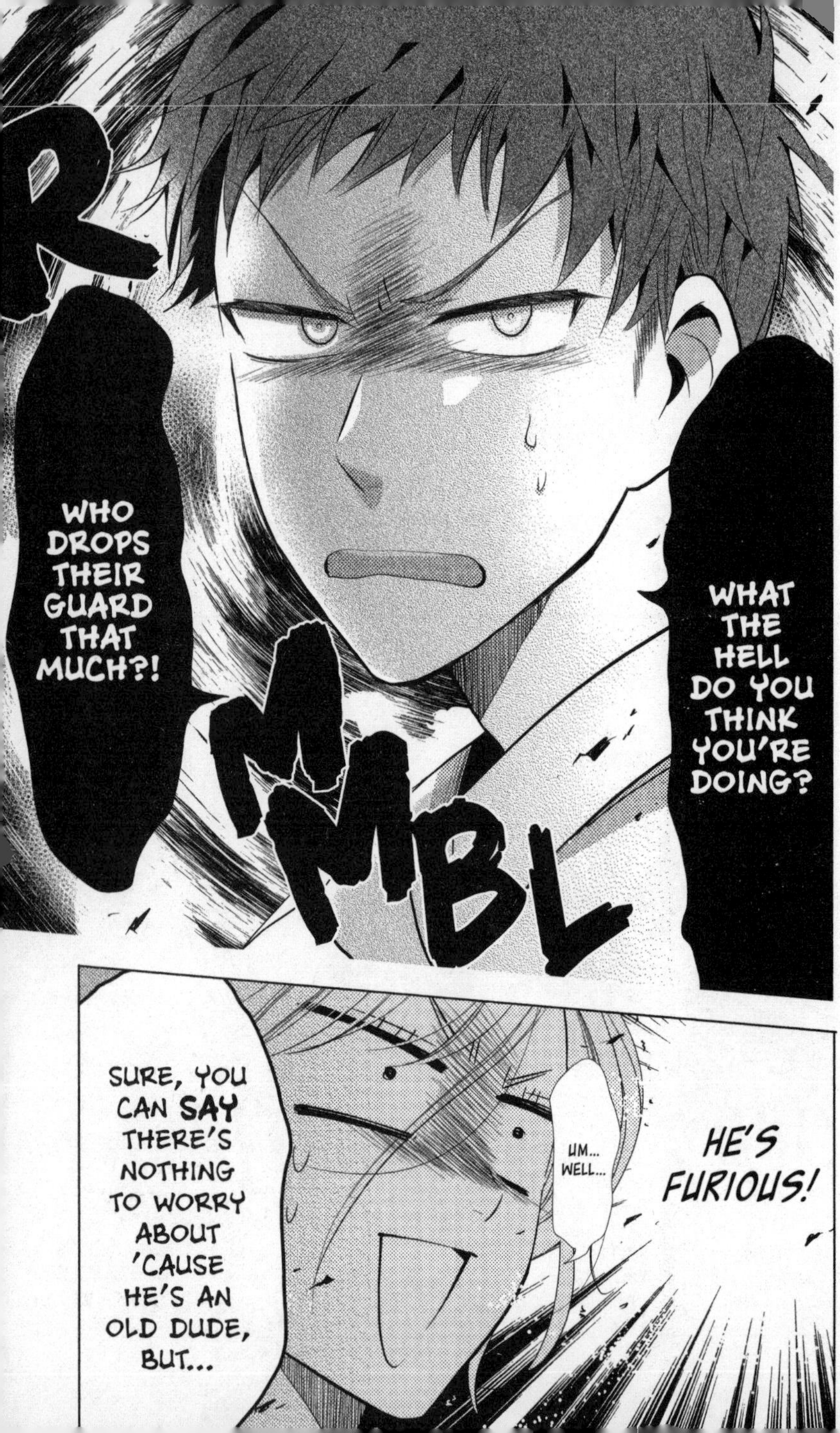
WHAT THE HELL DO YOU THINK YOU'RE DOING?
WHO DROPS THEIR GUARD THAT MUCH?!
RMMBL
HE'S FURIOUS!
UM... WELL...
SURE, YOU CAN **SAY** THERE'S NOTHING TO WORRY ABOUT 'CAUSE HE'S AN OLD DUDE, BUT...

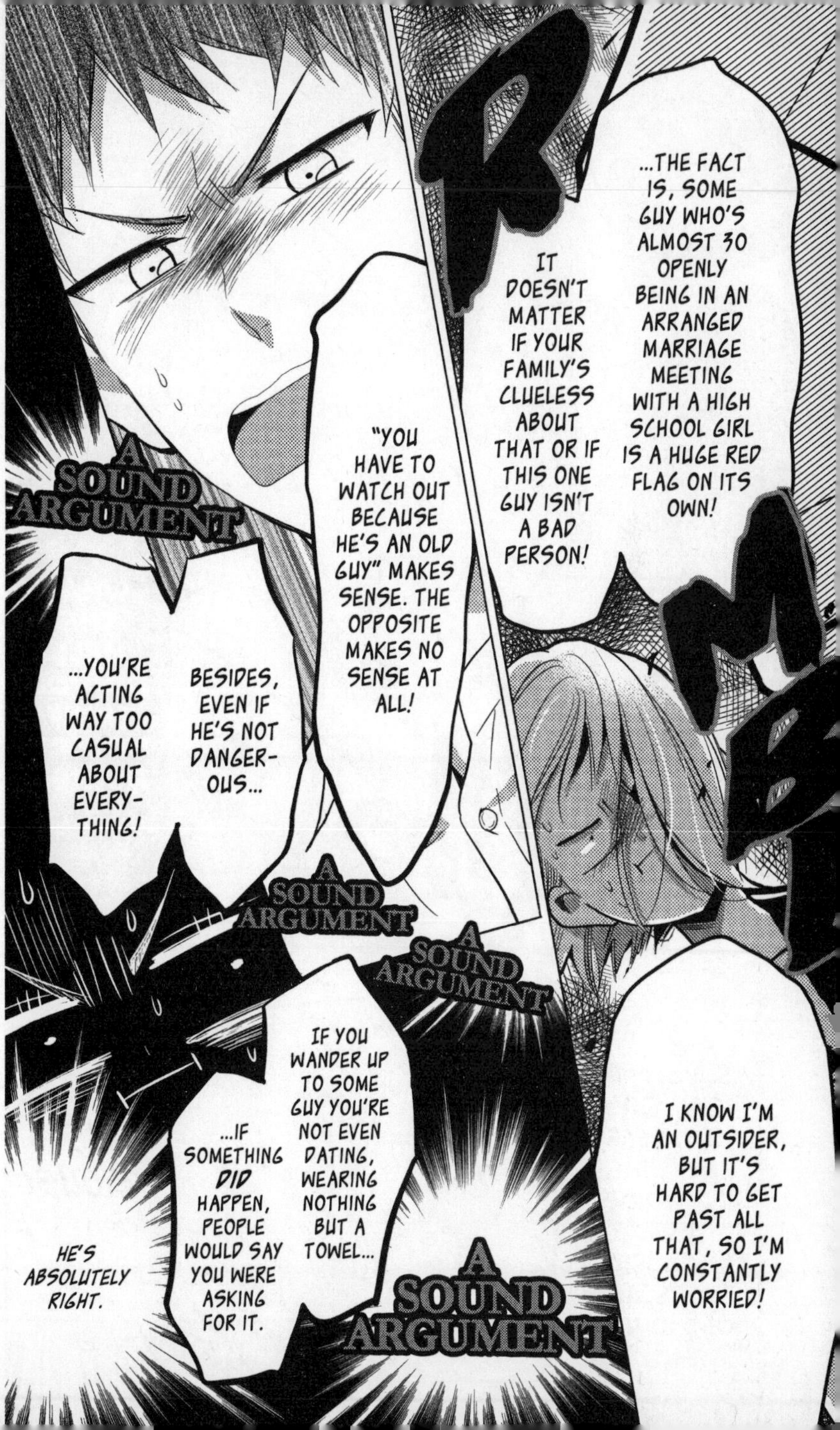
...THE FACT IS, SOME GUY WHO'S ALMOST 30 OPENLY BEING IN AN ARRANGED MARRIAGE MEETING WITH A HIGH SCHOOL GIRL IS A HUGE RED FLAG ON ITS OWN!
IT DOESN'T MATTER IF YOUR FAMILY'S CLUELESS ABOUT THAT OR IF THIS ONE GUY ISN'T A BAD PERSON!
"YOU HAVE TO WATCH OUT BECAUSE HE'S AN OLD GUY" MAKES SENSE. THE OPPOSITE MAKES NO SENSE AT ALL!
A SOUND ARGUMENT
BESIDES, EVEN IF HE'S NOT DANGER-OUS...
...YOU'RE ACTING WAY TOO CASUAL ABOUT EVERY-THING!
I KNOW I'M AN OUTSIDER, BUT IT'S HARD TO GET PAST ALL THAT, SO I'M CONSTANTLY WORRIED!
A SOUND ARGUMENT
A SOUND ARGUMENT
IF YOU WANDER UP TO SOME GUY YOU'RE NOT EVEN DATING, WEARING NOTHING BUT A TOWEL...
...IF SOMETHING *DID* HAPPEN, PEOPLE WOULD SAY YOU WERE ASKING FOR IT.
A SOUND ARGUMENT
HE'S ABSOLUTELY RIGHT.

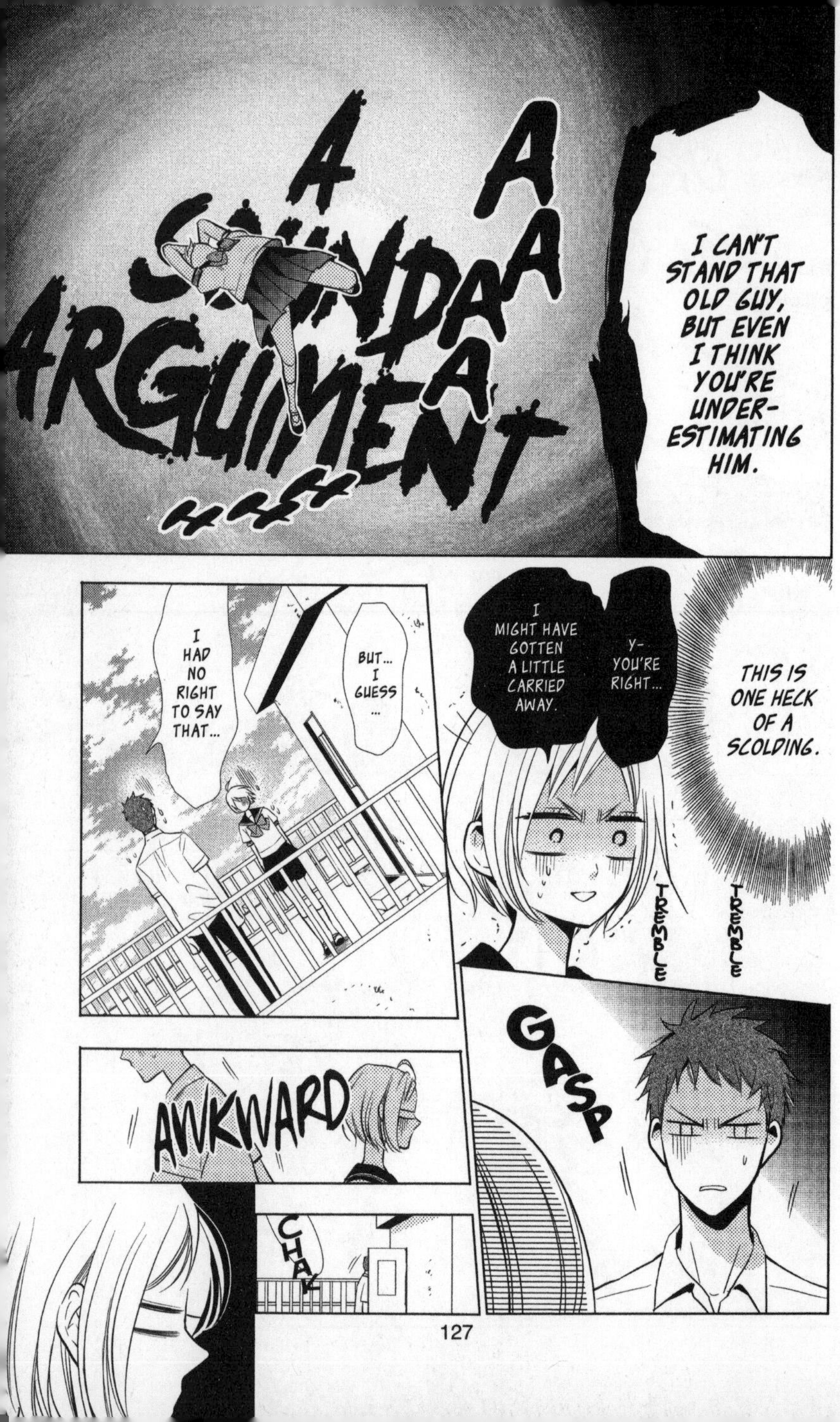
I CAN'T STAND THAT OLD GUY, BUT EVEN I THINK YOU'RE UNDER-ESTIMATING HIM.
ARGUMENT
THIS IS ONE HECK OF A SCOLDING.
Y- YOU'RE RIGHT...
I MIGHT HAVE GOTTEN A LITTLE CARRIED AWAY.
TREMBLE
TREMBLE
BUT... I GUESS ...
I HAD NO RIGHT TO SAY THAT...
GASP
AWKWARD
CHAK

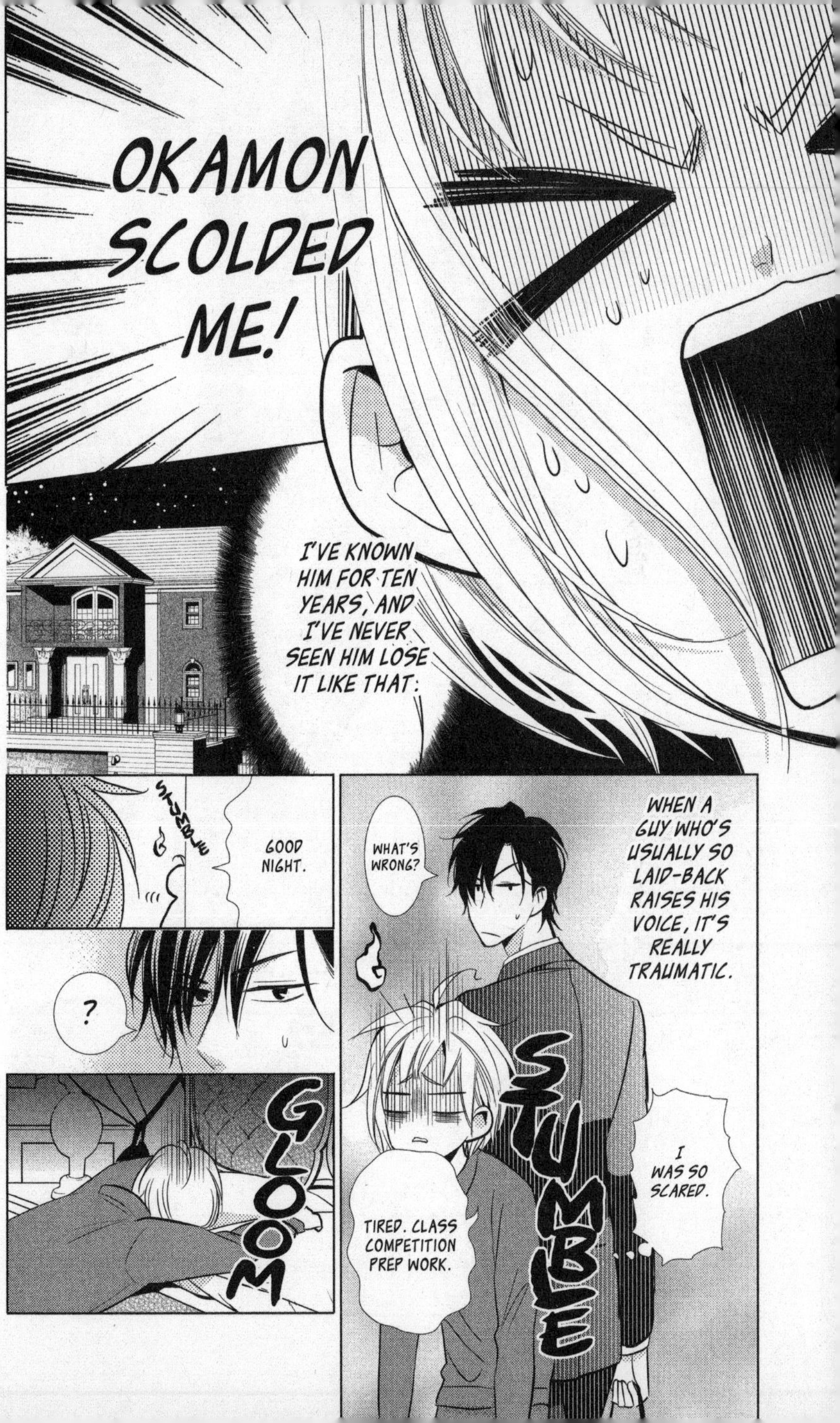

OKAMON SCOLDED ME!
I'VE KNOWN HIM FOR TEN YEARS, AND I'VE NEVER SEEN HIM LOSE IT LIKE THAT.
WHEN A GUY WHO'S USUALLY SO LAID-BACK RAISES HIS VOICE, IT'S REALLY TRAUMATIC.
WHAT'S WRONG?
STUMBLE
I WAS SO SCARED.
TIRED. CLASS COMPETITION PREP WORK.
STUMBLE
GOOD NIGHT.
?
GLOOM

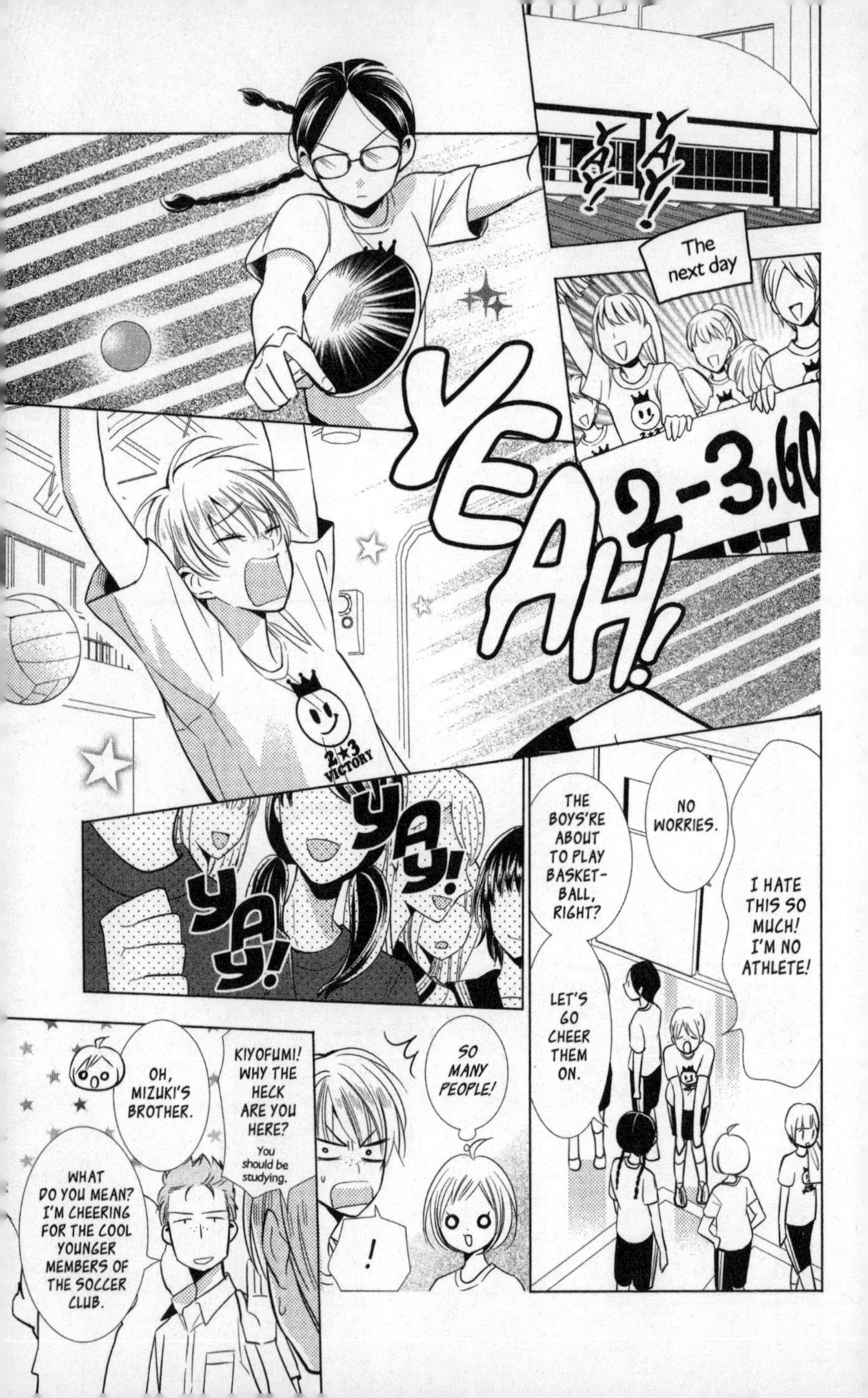

YAY! YAY!
The next day
2-3,GO
YEAH!
I HATE THIS SO MUCH! I'M NO ATHLETE!
NO WORRIES.
THE BOYS'RE ABOUT TO PLAY BASKET-BALL, RIGHT?
LET'S GO CHEER THEM ON.
YAY! YAY!
SO MANY PEOPLE!
!
KIYOFUMI! WHY THE HECK ARE YOU HERE?
You should be studying.
OH, MIZUKI'S BROTHER.
WHAT DO YOU MEAN? I'M CHEERING FOR THE COOL YOUNGER MEMBERS OF THE SOCCER CLUB.

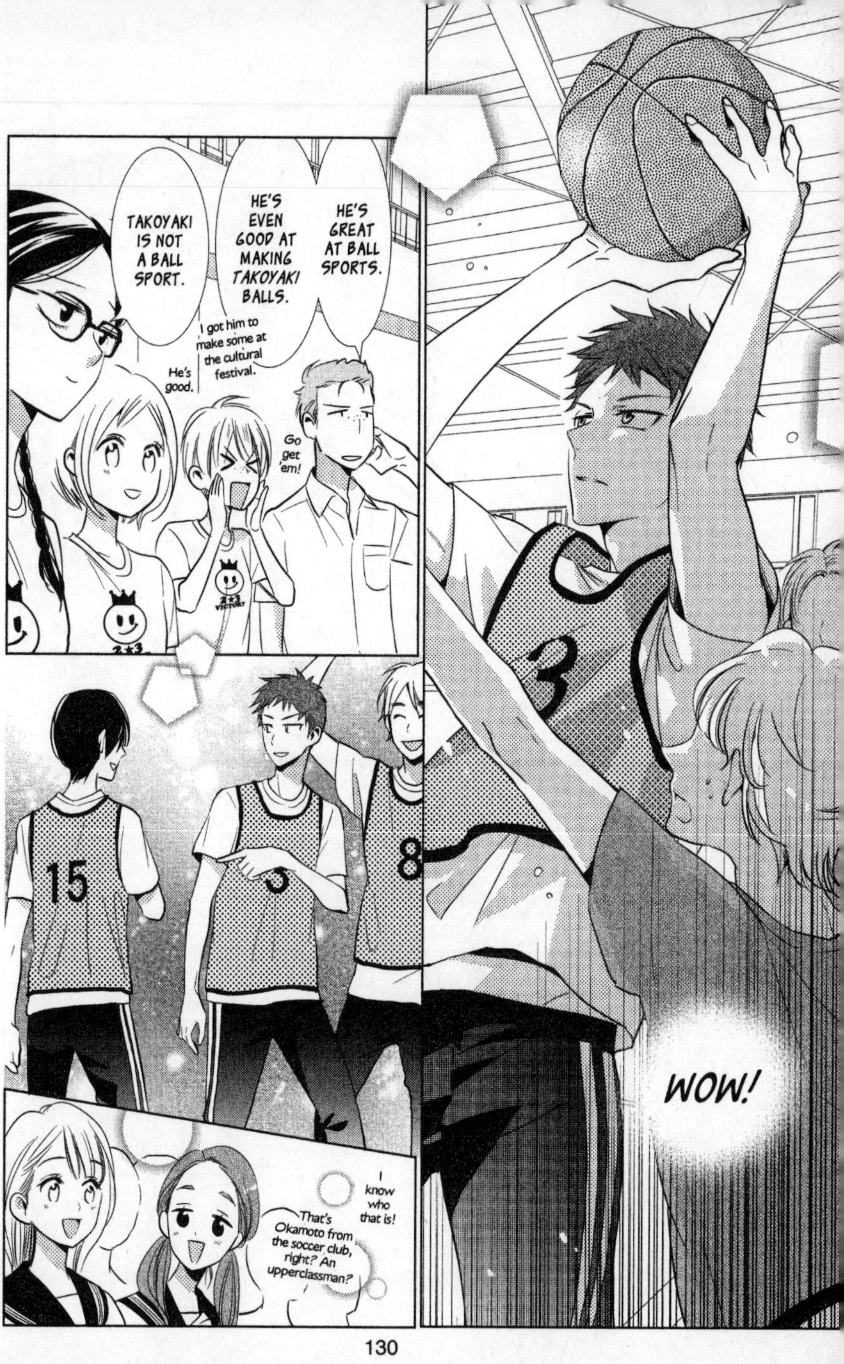
WOW!
HE'S GREAT AT BALL SPORTS.
Go get 'em!
HE'S EVEN GOOD AT MAKING TAKOYAKI BALLS.
I got him to make some at the cultural festival.
TAKOYAKI IS NOT A BALL SPORT.
He's good.
I know who that is!
That's Okamoto from the soccer club, right? An upperclassman?

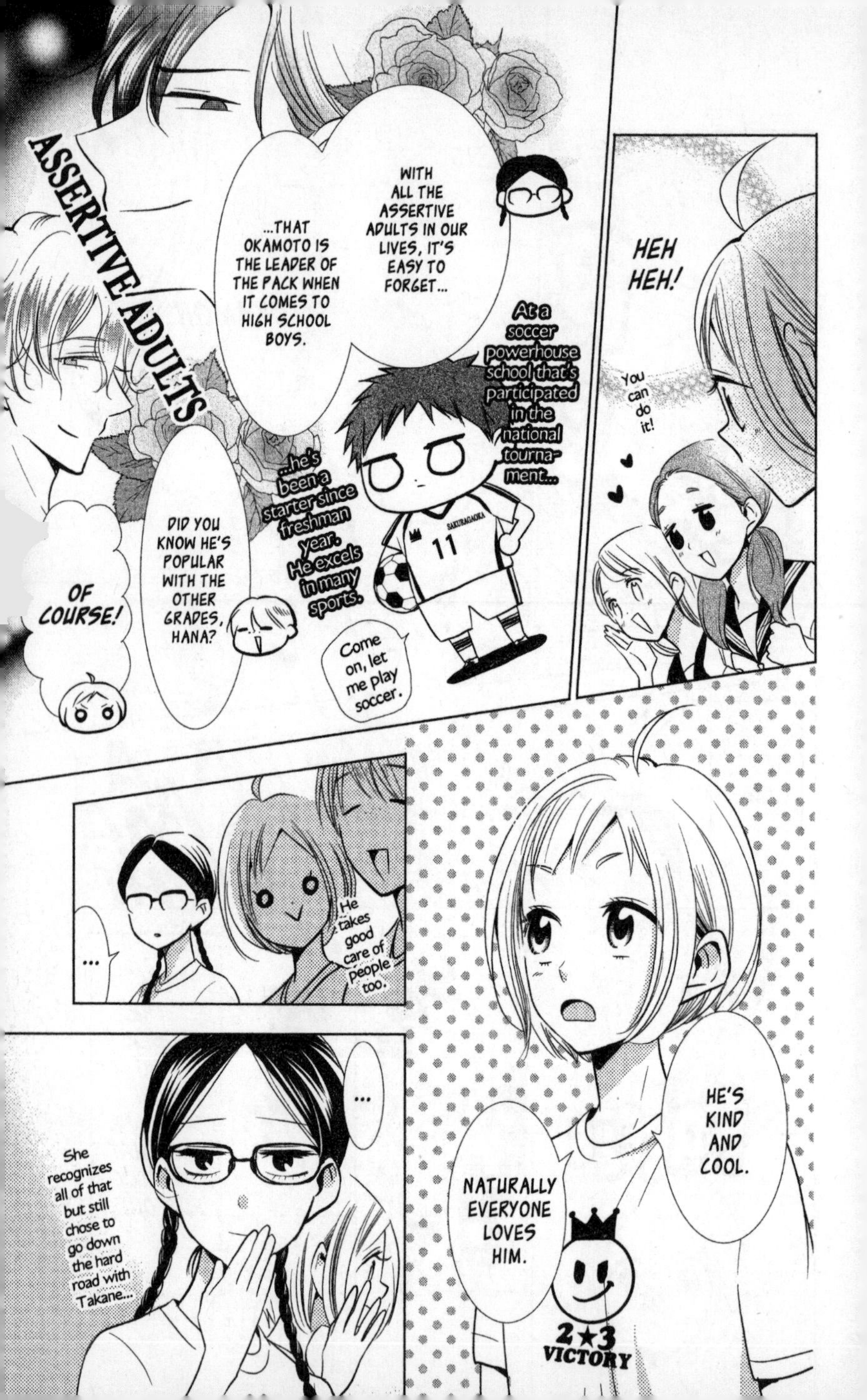
HEH HEH!
You can do it!
WITH ALL THE ASSERTIVE ADULTS IN OUR LIVES, IT'S EASY TO FORGET...
...THAT OKAMOTO IS THE LEADER OF THE PACK WHEN IT COMES TO HIGH SCHOOL BOYS.
ASSERTIVE ADULTS
At a soccer powerhouse school that's participated in the national tournament...
...he's been a starter since freshman year. He excels in many sports.
SAKURAGAOKA
11
DID YOU KNOW HE'S POPULAR WITH THE OTHER GRADES, HANA?
OF COURSE!
Come on, let me play soccer.
HE'S KIND AND COOL.
NATURALLY EVERYONE LOVES HIM.
2★3 VICTORY
He takes good care of people too.
...
...
She recognizes all of that but still chose to go down the hard road with Takane...

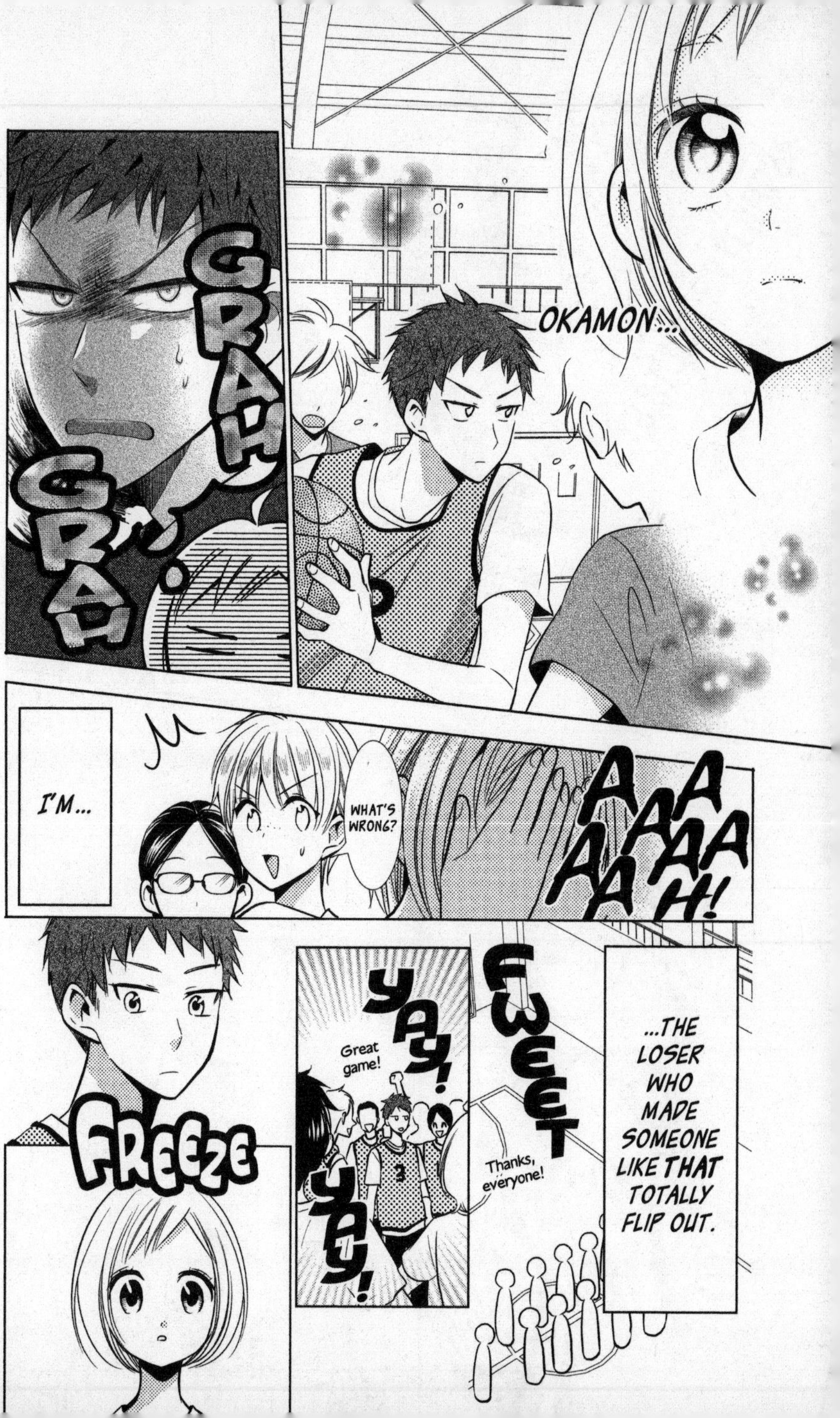
OKAMON...
GRAH
GRAH
AAAAAAH!
WHAT'S WRONG?
I'M...
...THE LOSER WHO MADE SOMEONE LIKE THAT TOTALLY FLIP OUT.
FWEET
Thanks, everyone!
YAY!
Great game!
YAY!
FREEZE

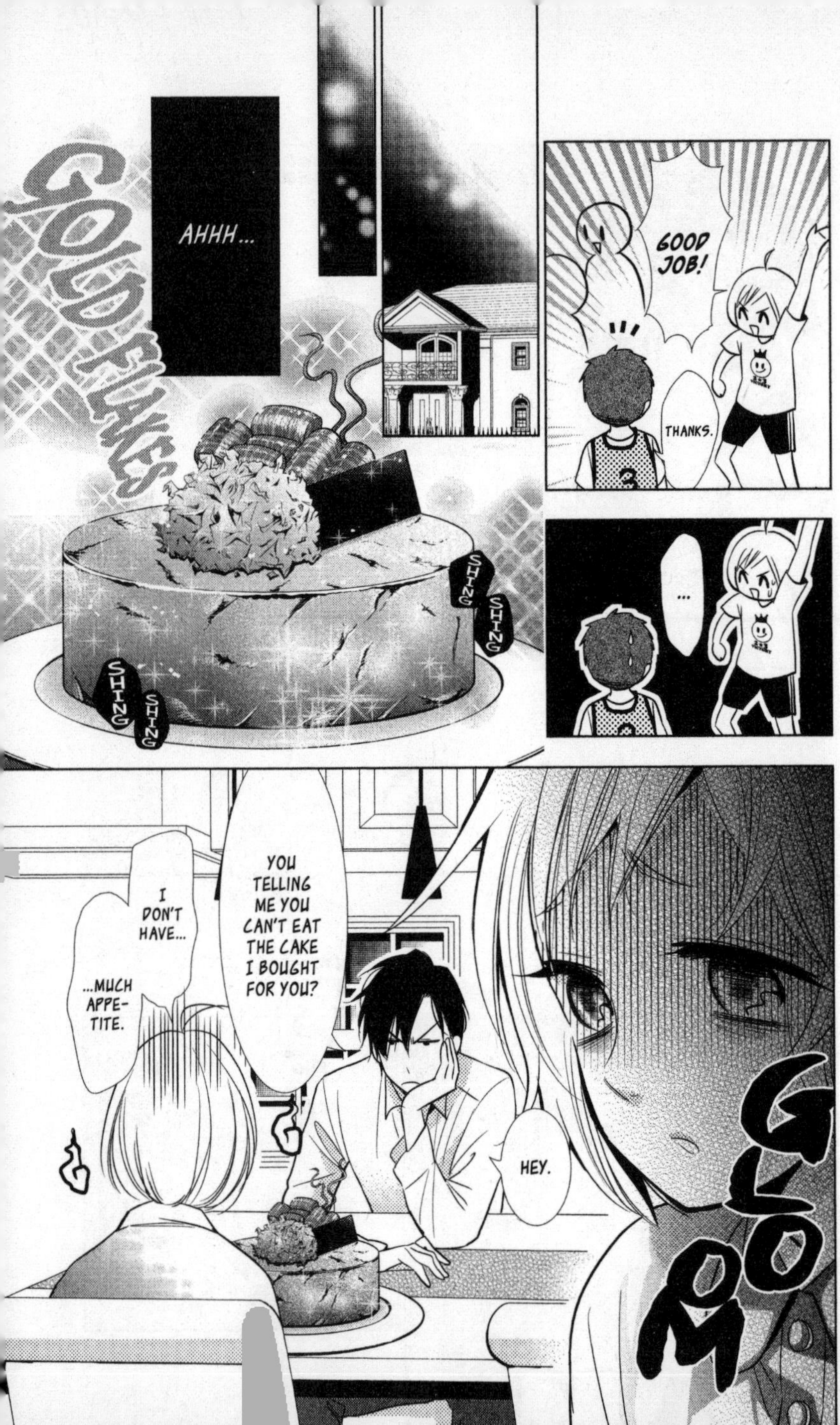
GOOD JOB!
THANKS.
...
AHHH...
GOLD FLAKES
SHING SHING
SHING SHING
HEY.
GLOOM
YOU TELLING ME YOU CAN'T EAT THE CAKE I BOUGHT FOR YOU?
I DON'T HAVE...
...MUCH APPE-TITE.

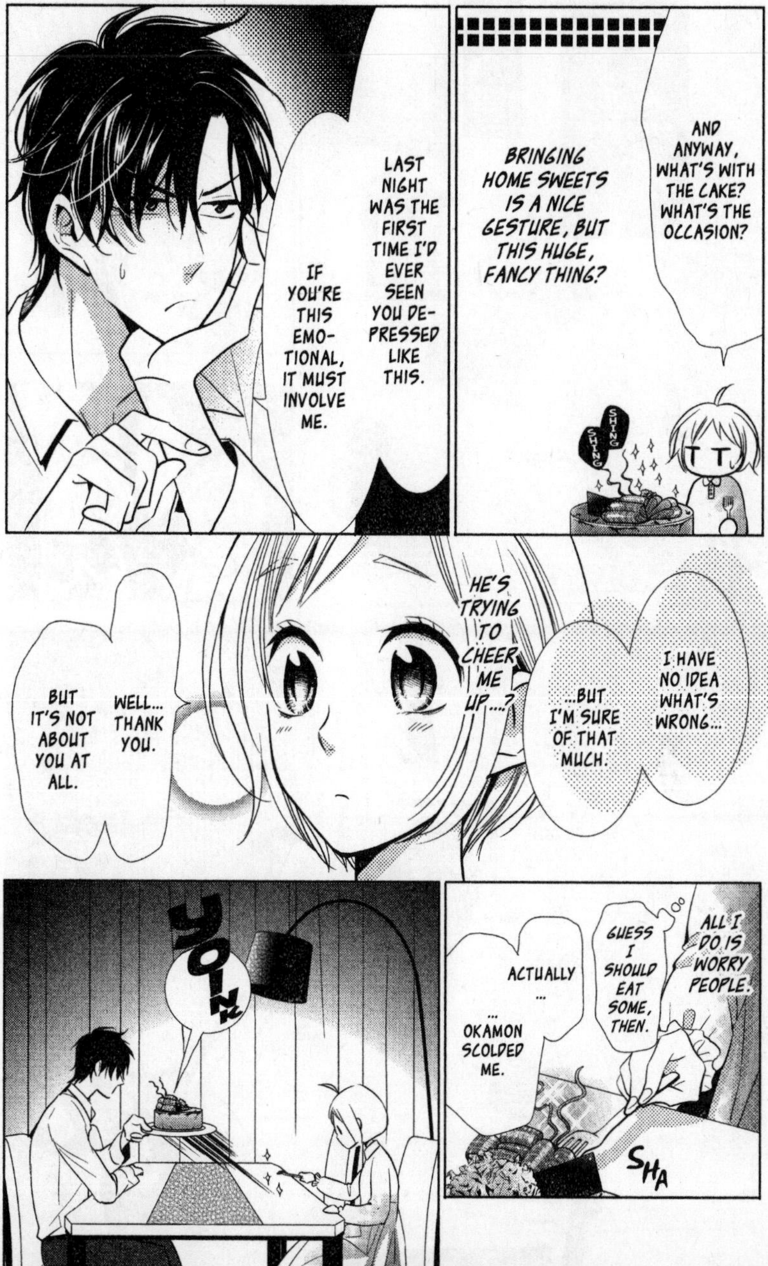
AND ANYWAY, WHAT'S WITH THE CAKE? WHAT'S THE OCCASION?
BRINGING HOME SWEETS IS A NICE GESTURE, BUT THIS HUGE, FANCY THING?
SHING SHING
LAST NIGHT WAS THE FIRST TIME I'D EVER SEEN YOU DE-PRESSED LIKE THIS.
IF YOU'RE THIS EMO-TIONAL, IT MUST INVOLVE ME.
I HAVE NO IDEA WHAT'S WRONG...
...BUT I'M SURE OF THAT MUCH.
HE'S TRYING TO CHEER ME UP...?
WELL... THANK YOU.
BUT IT'S NOT ABOUT YOU AT ALL.
ALL I DO IS WORRY PEOPLE.
GUESS I SHOULD EAT SOME, THEN.
ACTUALLY ...
... OKAMON SCOLDED ME.
SHA
YOINK

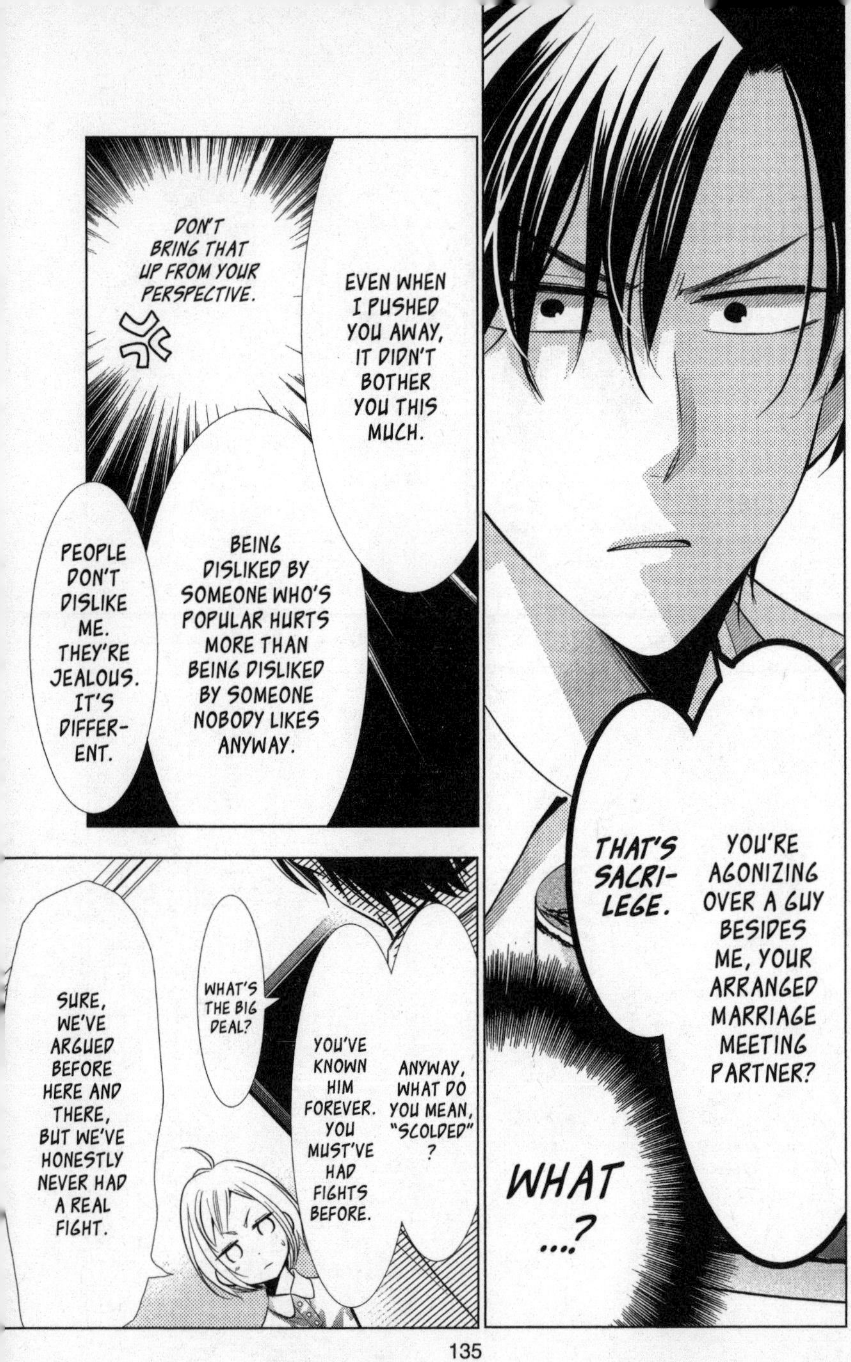
YOU'RE AGONIZING OVER A GUY BESIDES ME, YOUR ARRANGED MARRIAGE MEETING PARTNER?
THAT'S SACRI-LEGE.
WHAT ...?
EVEN WHEN I PUSHED YOU AWAY, IT DIDN'T BOTHER YOU THIS MUCH.
DON'T BRING THAT UP FROM YOUR PERSPECTIVE.
BEING DISLIKED BY SOMEONE WHO'S POPULAR HURTS MORE THAN BEING DISLIKED BY SOMEONE NOBODY LIKES ANYWAY.
PEOPLE DON'T DISLIKE ME. THEY'RE JEALOUS. IT'S DIFFER-ENT.
ANYWAY, WHAT DO YOU MEAN, "SCOLDED" ?
YOU'VE KNOWN HIM FOREVER. YOU MUST'VE HAD FIGHTS BEFORE.
WHAT'S THE BIG DEAL?
SURE, WE'VE ARGUED BEFORE HERE AND THERE, BUT WE'VE HONESTLY NEVER HAD A REAL FIGHT.

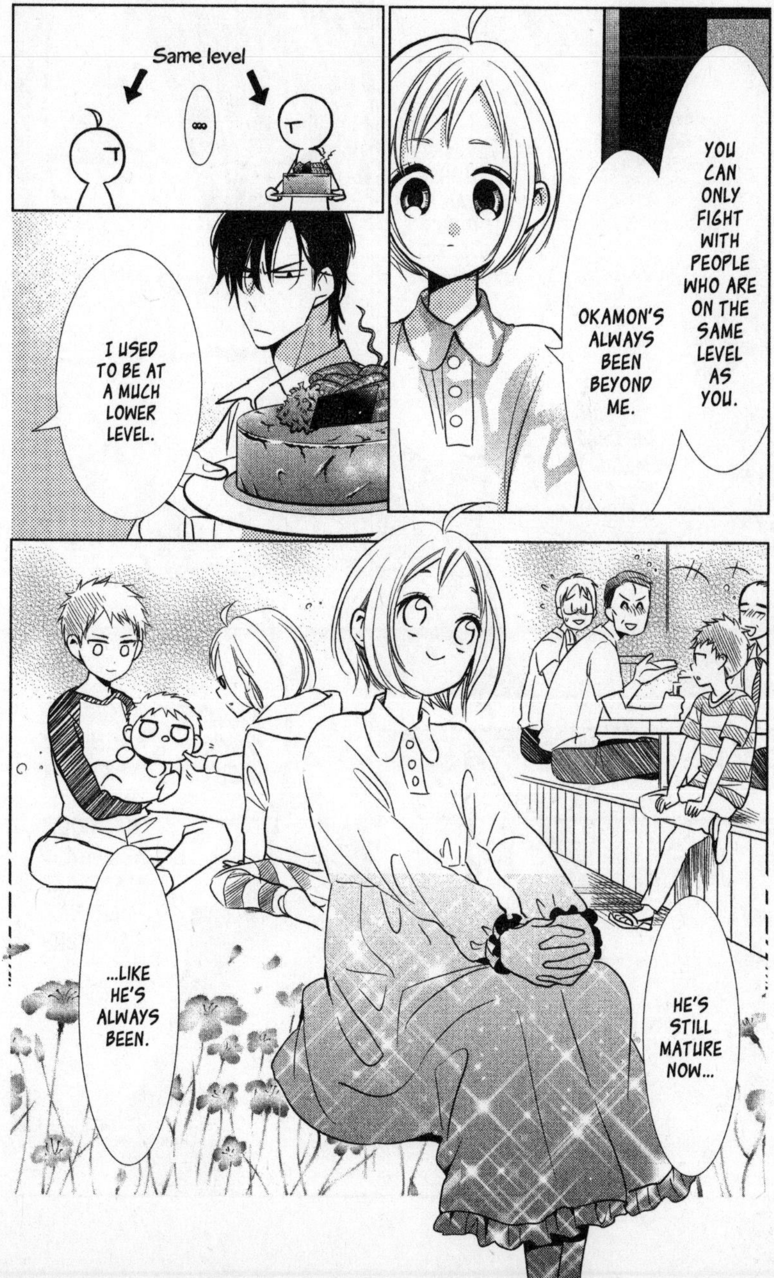
YOU CAN ONLY FIGHT WITH PEOPLE WHO ARE ON THE SAME LEVEL AS YOU.
OKAMON'S ALWAYS BEEN BEYOND ME.
Same level
...
I USED TO BE AT A MUCH LOWER LEVEL.
HE'S STILL MATURE NOW...
...LIKE HE'S ALWAYS BEEN.

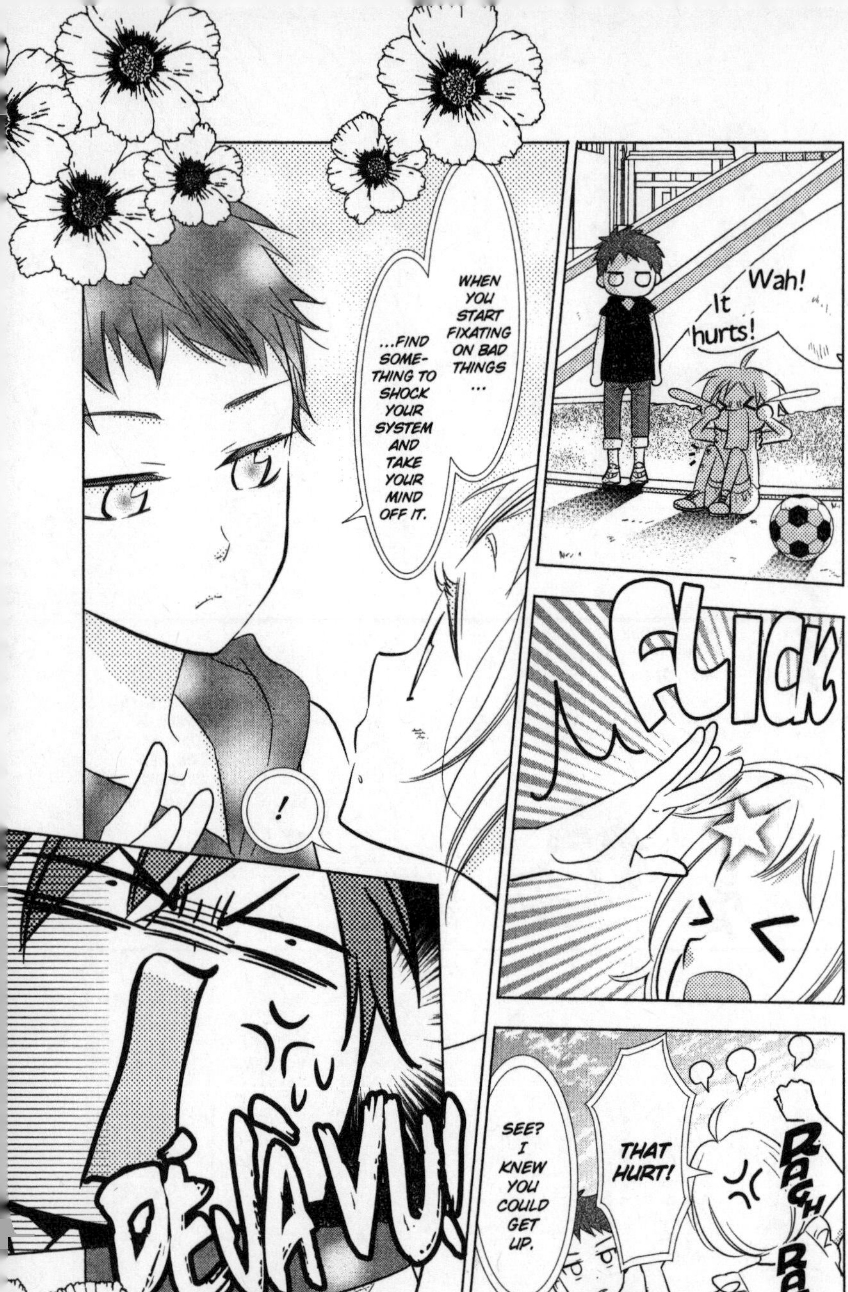
Wah!
It hurts!
FLICK
RAGH RAGH
THAT HURT!
SEE? I KNEW YOU COULD GET UP.
WHEN YOU START FIXATING ON BAD THINGS...
...FIND SOMETHING TO SHOCK YOUR SYSTEM AND TAKE YOUR MIND OFF IT.
!
DÉJÀ VU!
See chapter 1!

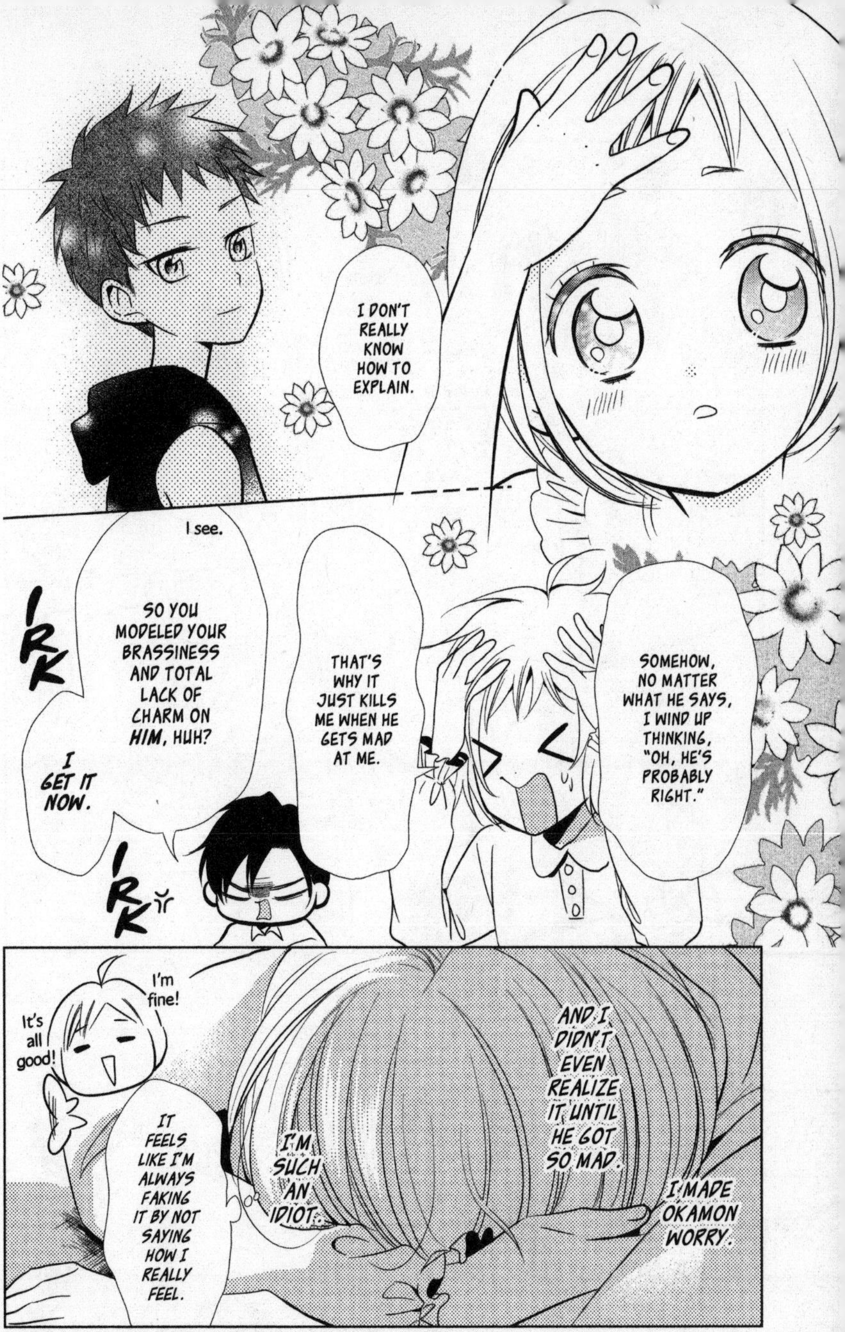

I DON'T REALLY KNOW HOW TO EXPLAIN.
SOMEHOW, NO MATTER WHAT HE SAYS, I WIND UP THINKING, "OH, HE'S PROBABLY RIGHT."
THAT'S WHY IT JUST KILLS ME WHEN HE GETS MAD AT ME.
I see.
SO YOU MODELED YOUR BRASSINESS AND TOTAL LACK OF CHARM ON HIM, HUH?
I GET IT NOW.
IRK
IRK
I MADE OKAMON WORRY.
AND I DIDN'T EVEN REALIZE IT UNTIL HE GOT SO MAD.
I'M SUCH AN IDIOT.
IT FEELS LIKE I'M ALWAYS FAKING IT BY NOT SAYING HOW I REALLY FEEL.
I'm fine!
It's all good!

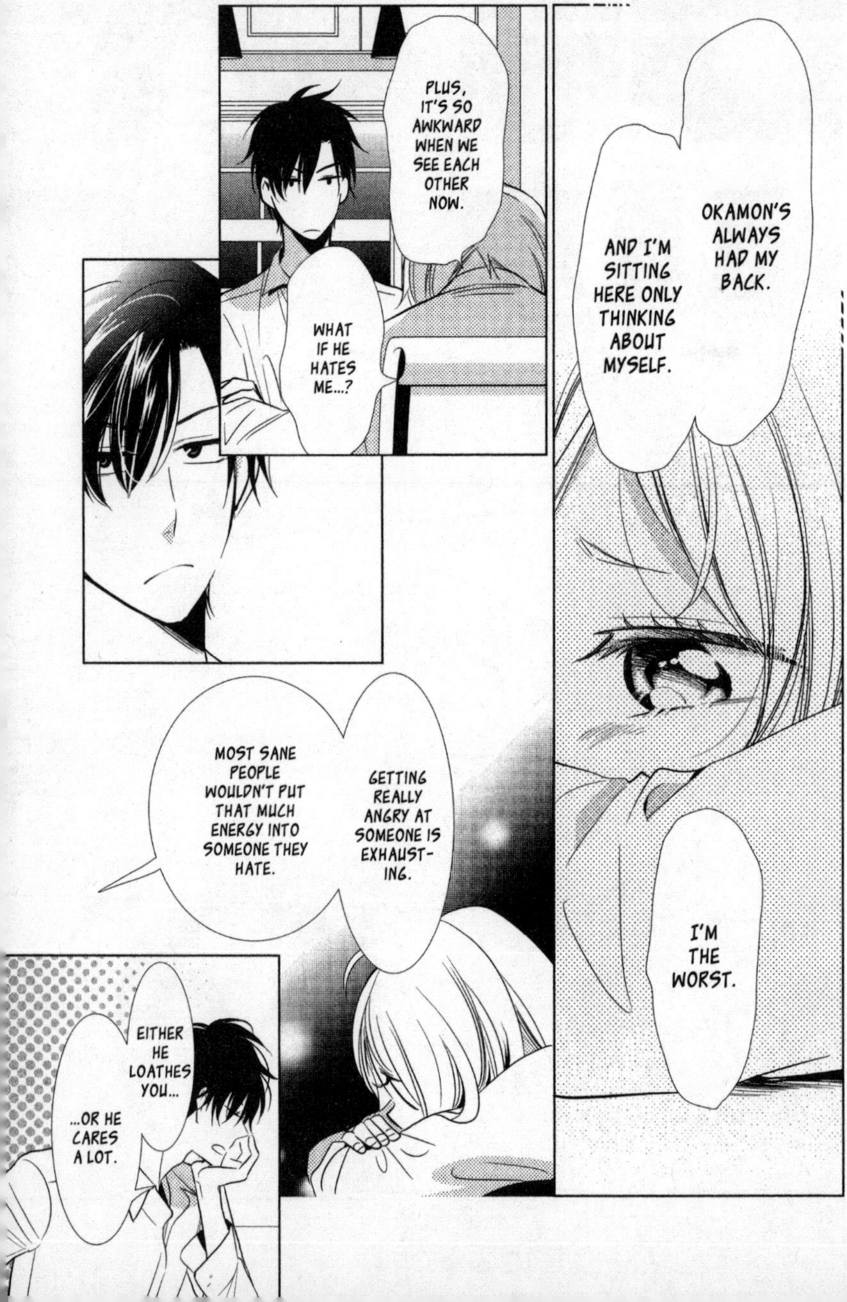
OKAMON'S ALWAYS HAD MY BACK.
AND I'M SITTING HERE ONLY THINKING ABOUT MYSELF.
I'M THE WORST.
PLUS, IT'S SO AWKWARD WHEN WE SEE EACH OTHER NOW.
WHAT IF HE HATES ME...?
GETTING REALLY ANGRY AT SOMEONE IS EXHAUST-ING.
MOST SANE PEOPLE WOULDN'T PUT THAT MUCH ENERGY INTO SOMEONE THEY HATE.
EITHER HE LOATHES YOU...
...OR HE CARES A LOT.

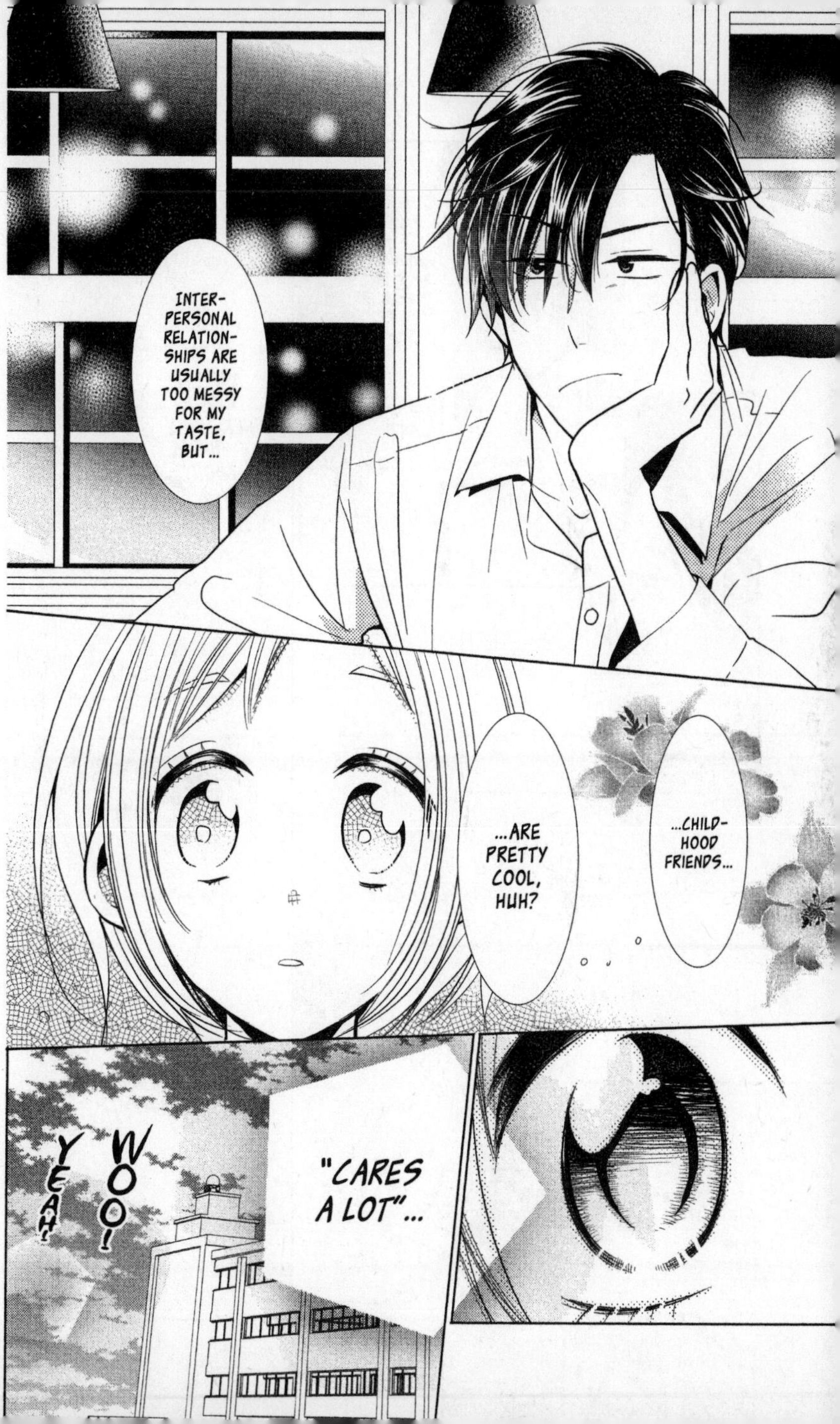
INTER-PERSONAL RELATION-SHIPS ARE USUALLY TOO MESSY FOR MY TASTE, BUT...
...CHILD-HOOD FRIENDS...
...ARE PRETTY COOL, HUH?
"CARES A LOT"...
WOO!
YEAH!

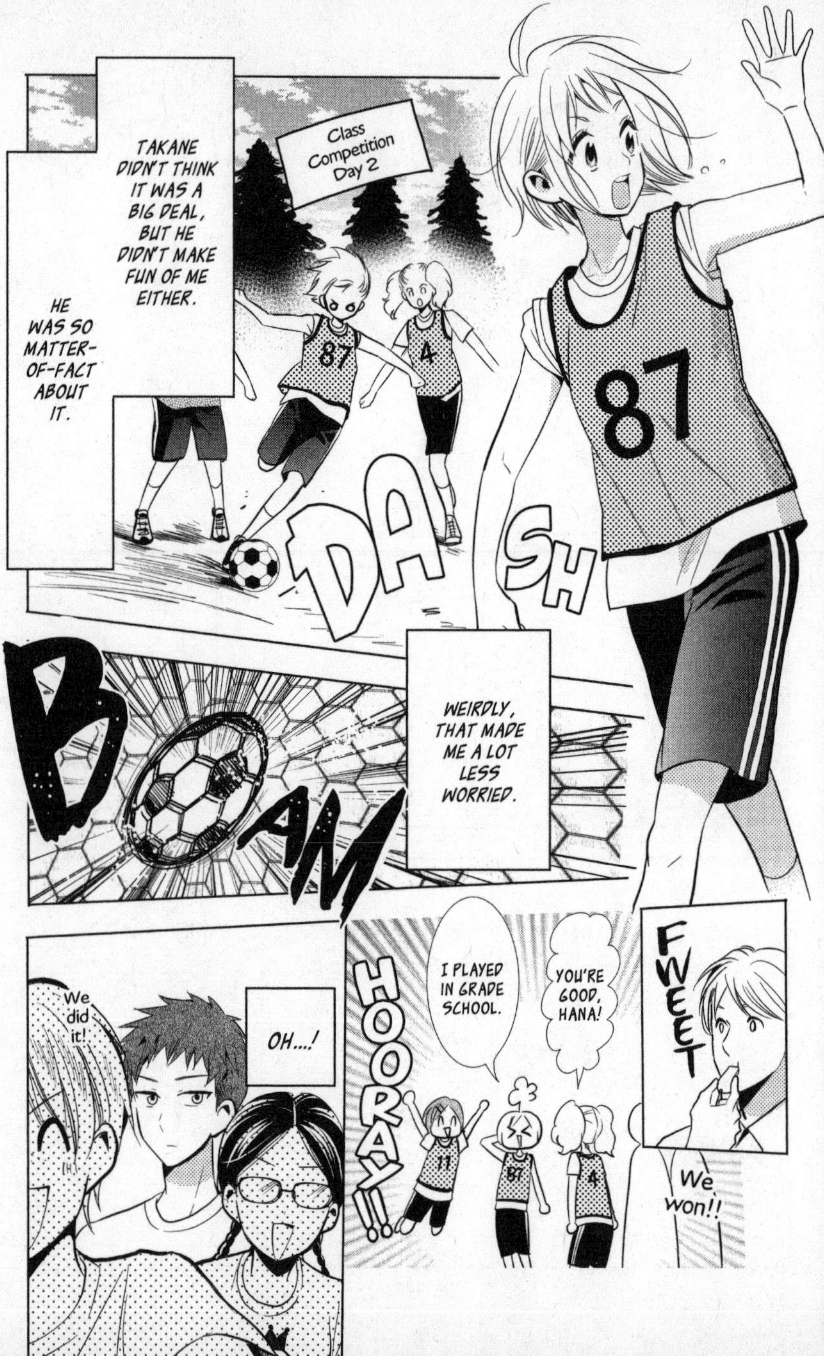
Class Competition Day 2
TAKANE DIDN'T THINK IT WAS A BIG DEAL, BUT HE DIDN'T MAKE FUN OF ME EITHER.
HE WAS SO MATTER-OF-FACT ABOUT IT.
DASH
WEIRDLY, THAT MADE ME A LOT LESS WORRIED.
BAM
FWEET
YOU'RE GOOD, HANA!
I PLAYED IN GRADE SCHOOL.
We won!!
HOORAY!!
OH...!
We did it!

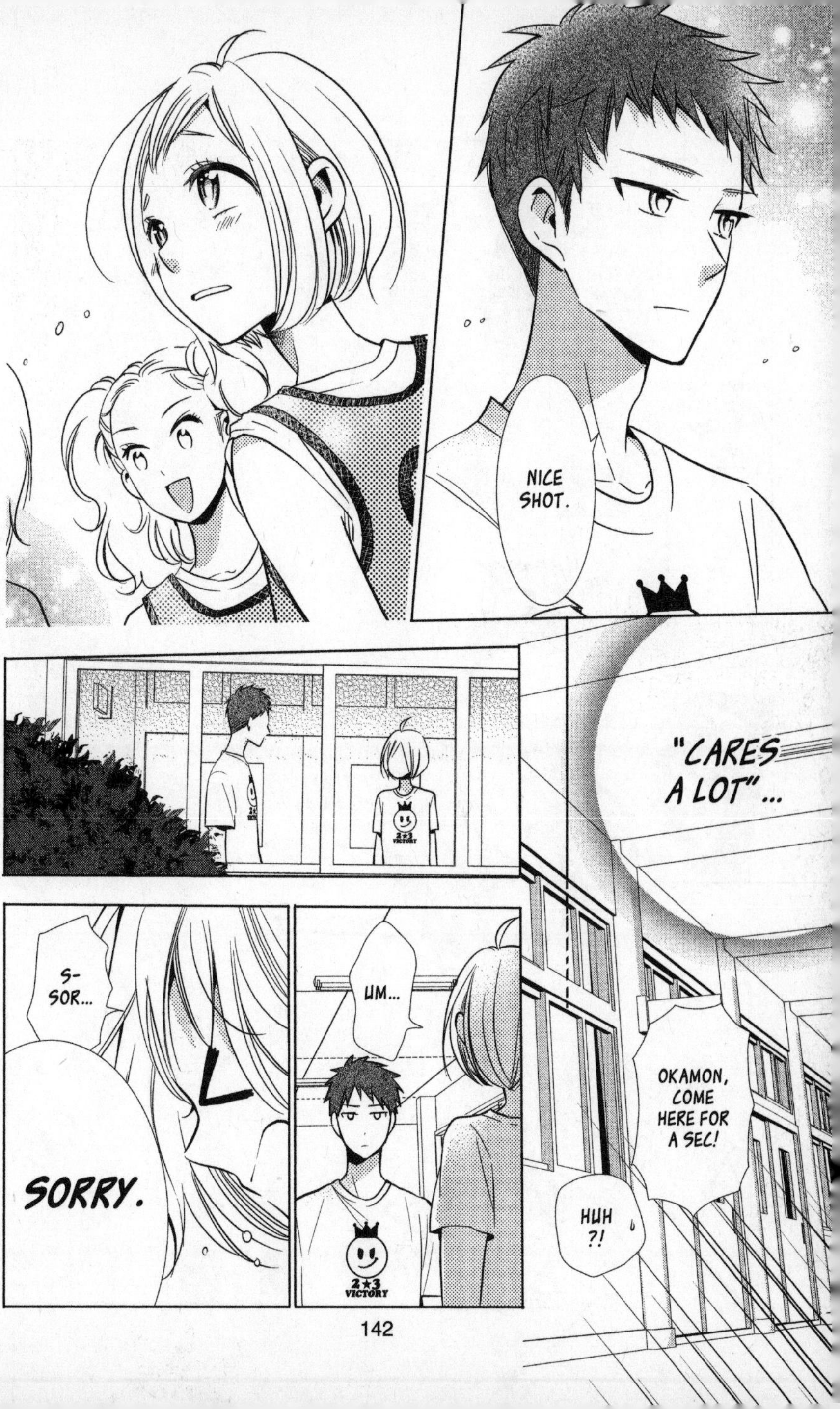
NICE SHOT.
"CARES A LOT"...
OKAMON, COME HERE FOR A SEC!
HUH ?!
UM...
S- SOR...
SORRY.

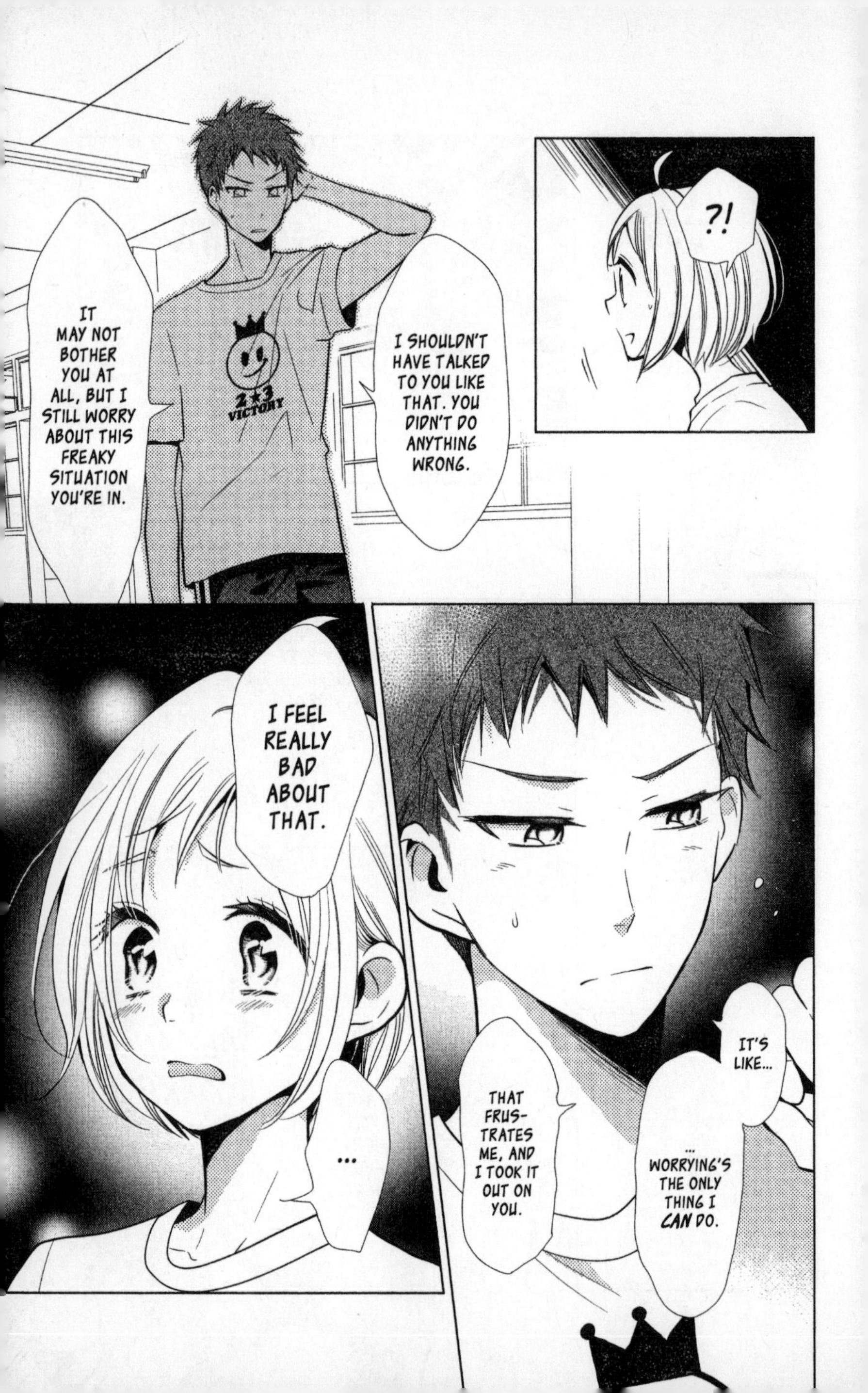
?!
I SHOULDN'T HAVE TALKED TO YOU LIKE THAT. YOU DIDN'T DO ANYTHING WRONG.
IT MAY NOT BOTHER YOU AT ALL, BUT I STILL WORRY ABOUT THIS FREAKY SITUATION YOU'RE IN.
2★3 VICTORY
IT'S LIKE...
... WORRYING'S THE ONLY THING I *CAN* DO.
THAT FRUS-TRATES ME, AND I TOOK IT OUT ON YOU.
I FEEL REALLY BAD ABOUT THAT.
...

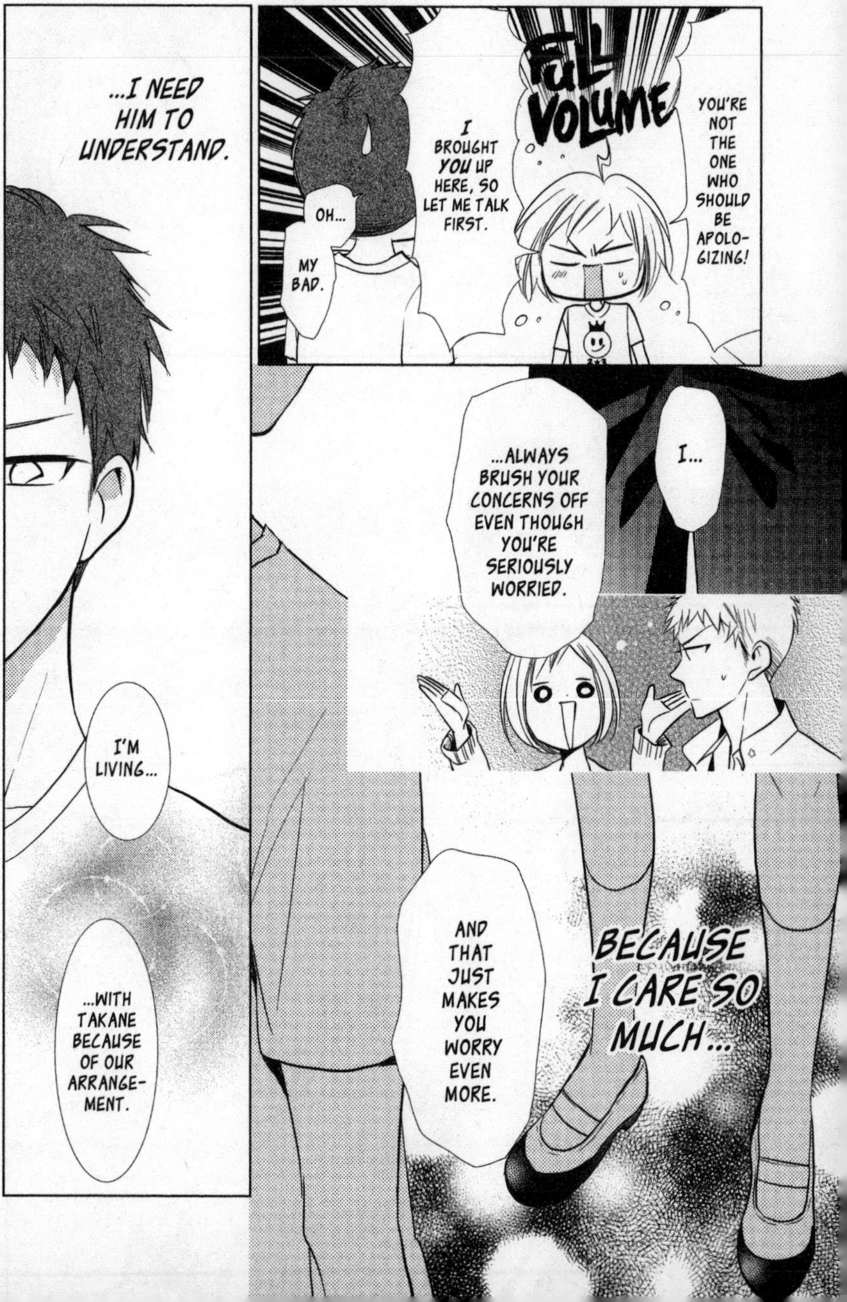
YOU'RE NOT THE ONE WHO SHOULD BE APOLOGIZING!
FULL VOLUME
I BROUGHT YOU UP HERE, SO LET ME TALK FIRST.
OH...
MY BAD.
I...
...ALWAYS BRUSH YOUR CONCERNS OFF EVEN THOUGH YOU'RE SERIOUSLY WORRIED.
AND THAT JUST MAKES YOU WORRY EVEN MORE.
BECAUSE I CARE SO MUCH...
...I NEED HIM TO UNDERSTAND.
I'M LIVING...
...WITH TAKANE BECAUSE OF OUR ARRANGEMENT.

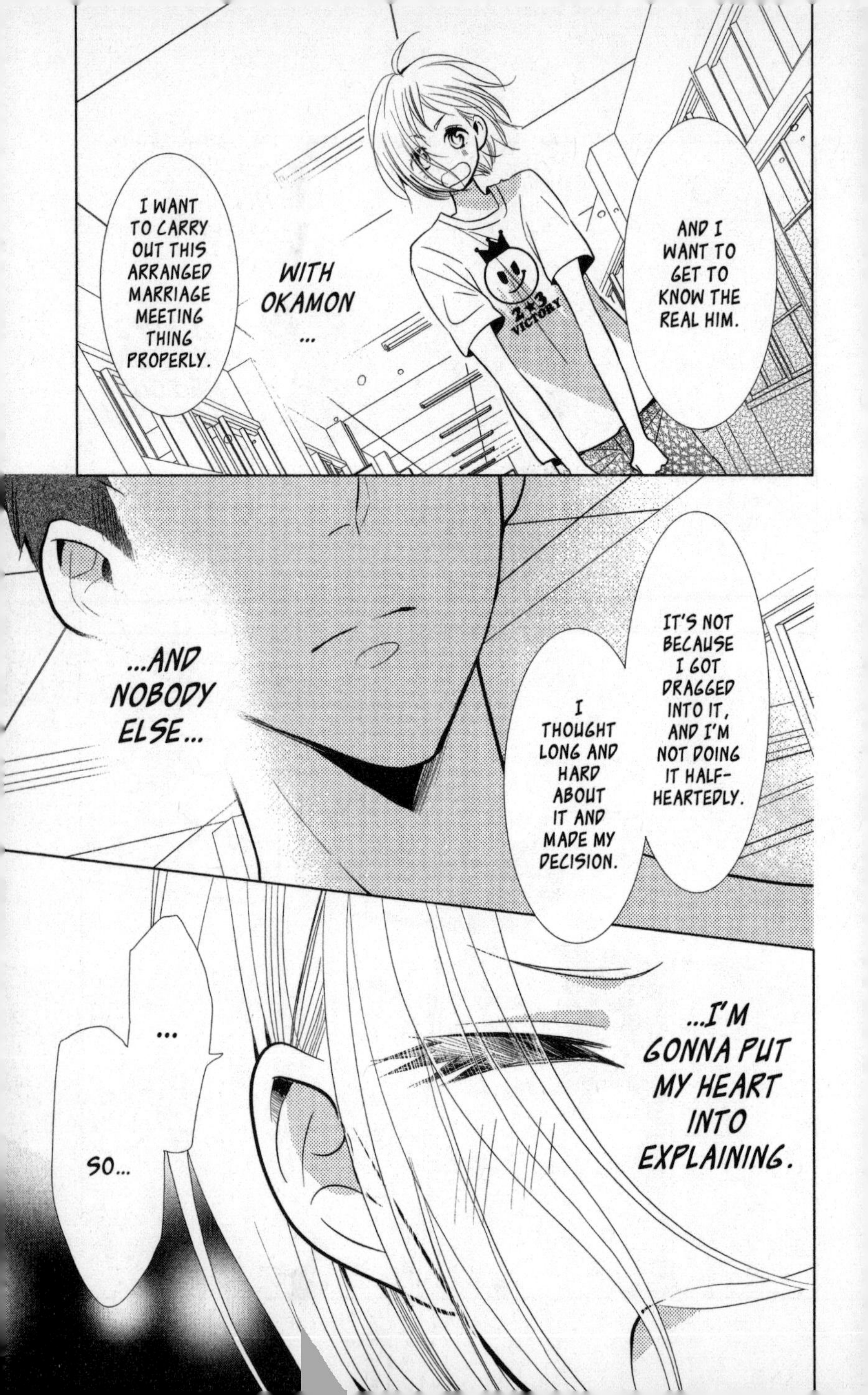
AND I WANT TO GET TO KNOW THE REAL HIM.
WITH OKAMON...
I WANT TO CARRY OUT THIS ARRANGED MARRIAGE MEETING THING PROPERLY.
IT'S NOT BECAUSE I GOT DRAGGED INTO IT, AND I'M NOT DOING IT HALF-HEARTEDLY.
I THOUGHT LONG AND HARD ABOUT IT AND MADE MY DECISION.
...AND NOBODY ELSE...
...I'M GONNA PUT MY HEART INTO EXPLAINING.
...
SO...

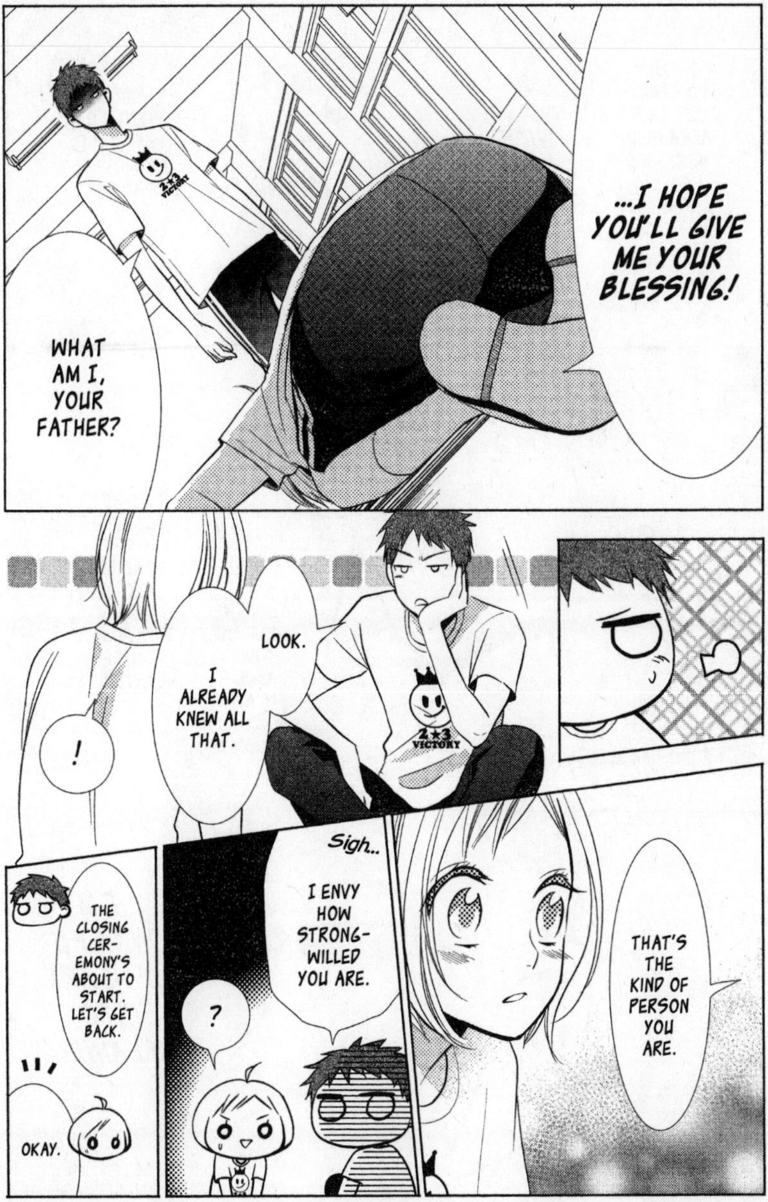
...I HOPE YOU'LL GIVE ME YOUR BLESSING!
WHAT AM I, YOUR FATHER?
LOOK.
I ALREADY KNEW ALL THAT.
!
THAT'S THE KIND OF PERSON YOU ARE.
Sigh...
I ENVY HOW STRONG-WILLED YOU ARE.
?
THE CLOSING CER-EMONY'S ABOUT TO START. LET'S GET BACK.
OKAY.

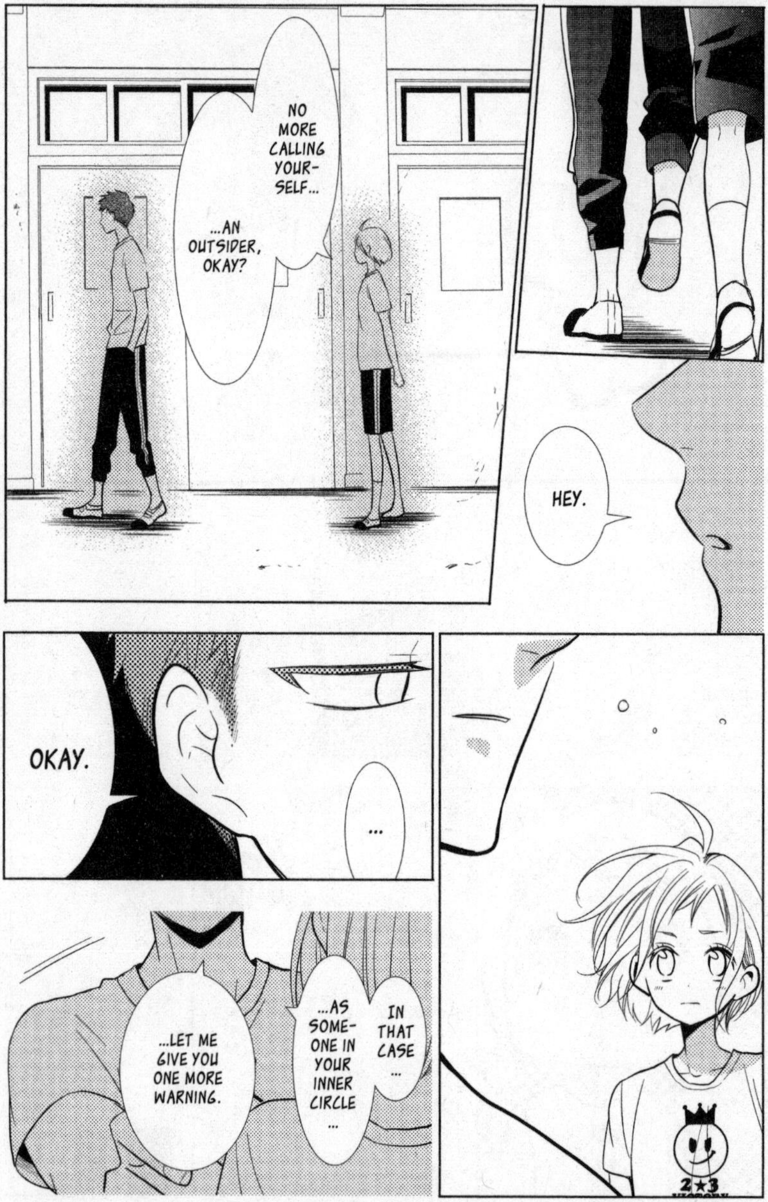
NO MORE CALLING YOUR-SELF...
...AN OUTSIDER, OKAY?
HEY.
...
OKAY.
IN THAT CASE...
...AS SOME-ONE IN YOUR INNER CIRCLE...
...LET ME GIVE YOU ONE MORE WARNING.

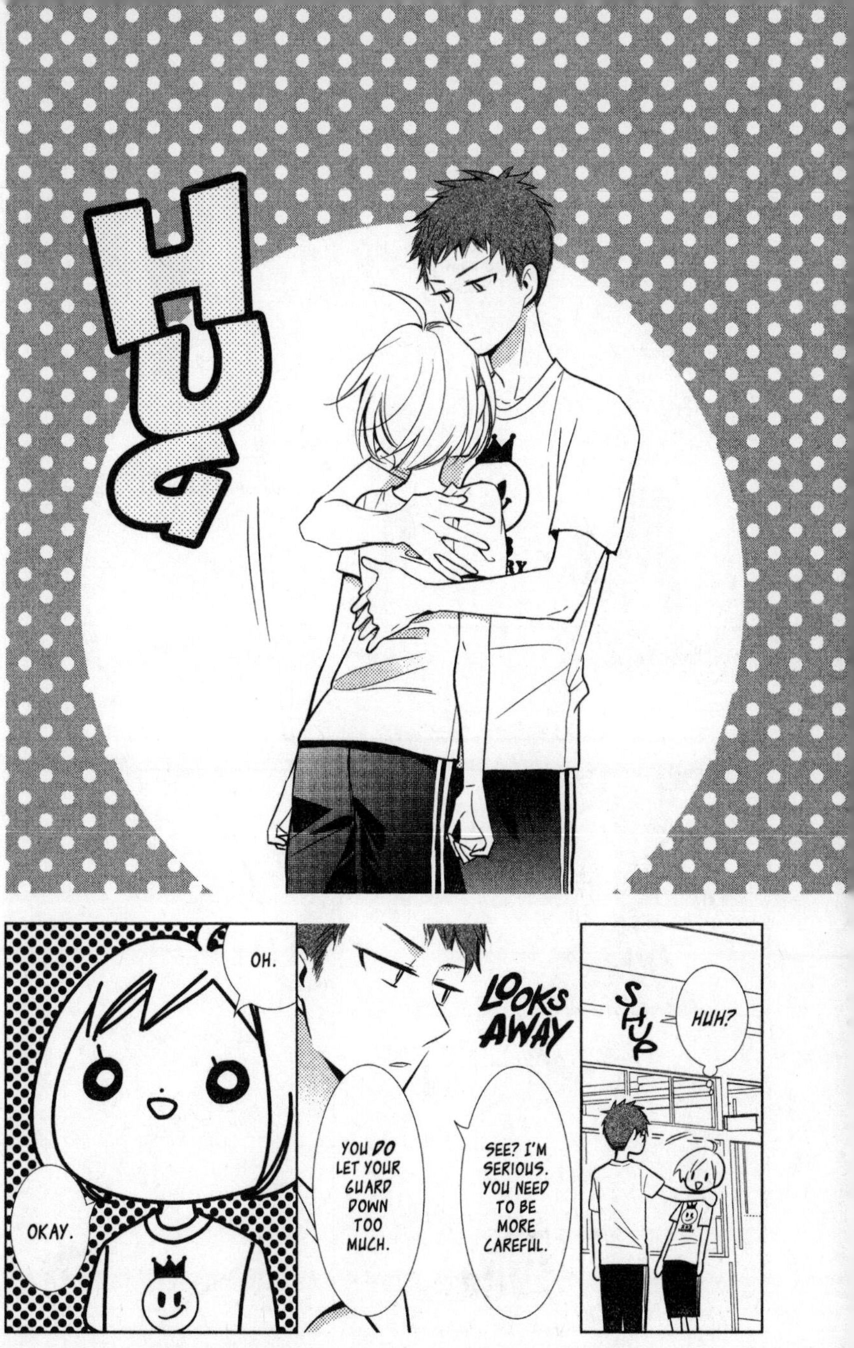
HUG
SHUP
HUH?
LOOKS AWAY
SEE? I'M SERIOUS. YOU NEED TO BE MORE CAREFUL.
YOU *DO* LET YOUR GUARD DOWN TOO MUCH.
OH.
OKAY.

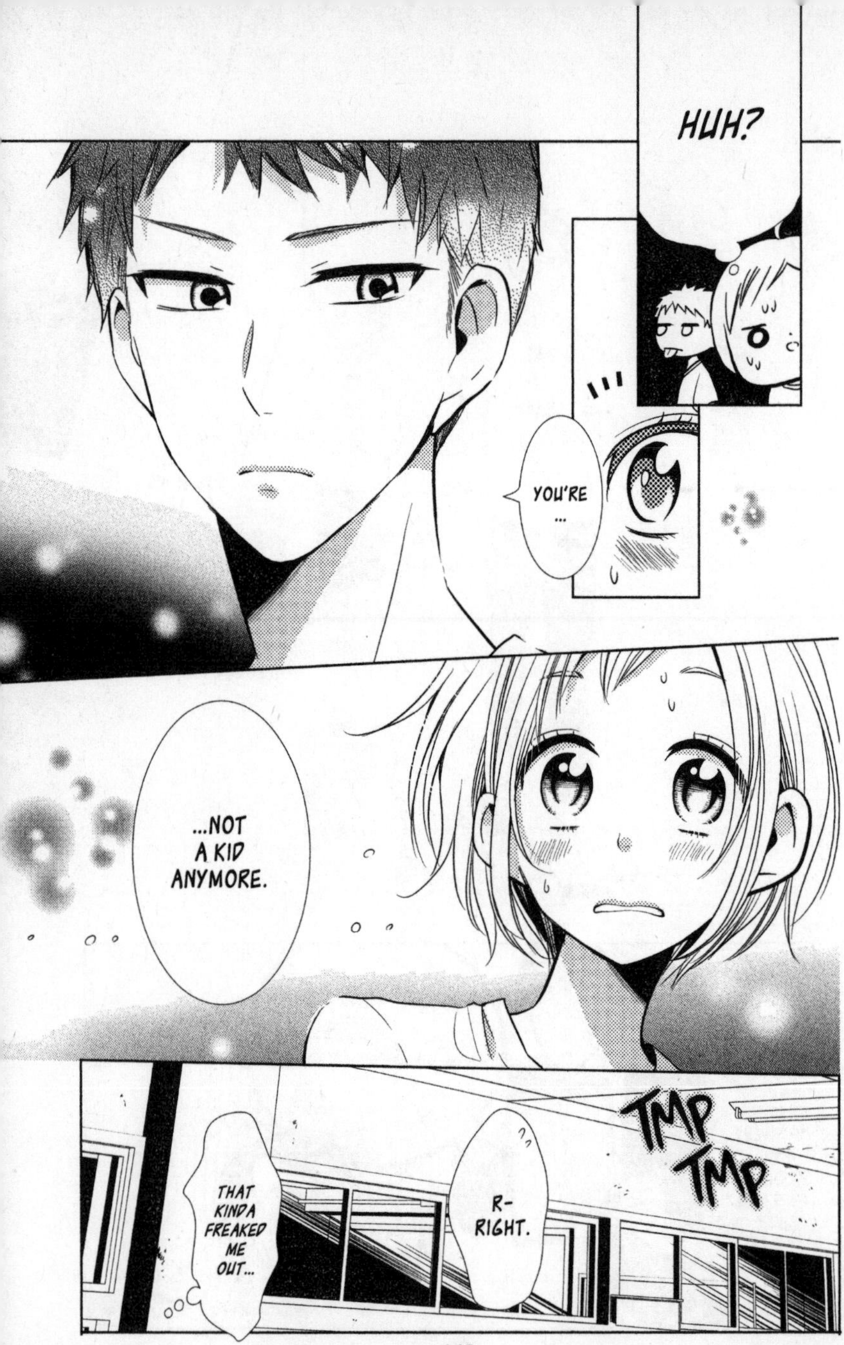
HUH?
YOU'RE ...
...NOT A KID ANYMORE.
TMP TMP
R-RIGHT.
THAT KINDA FREAKED ME OUT...

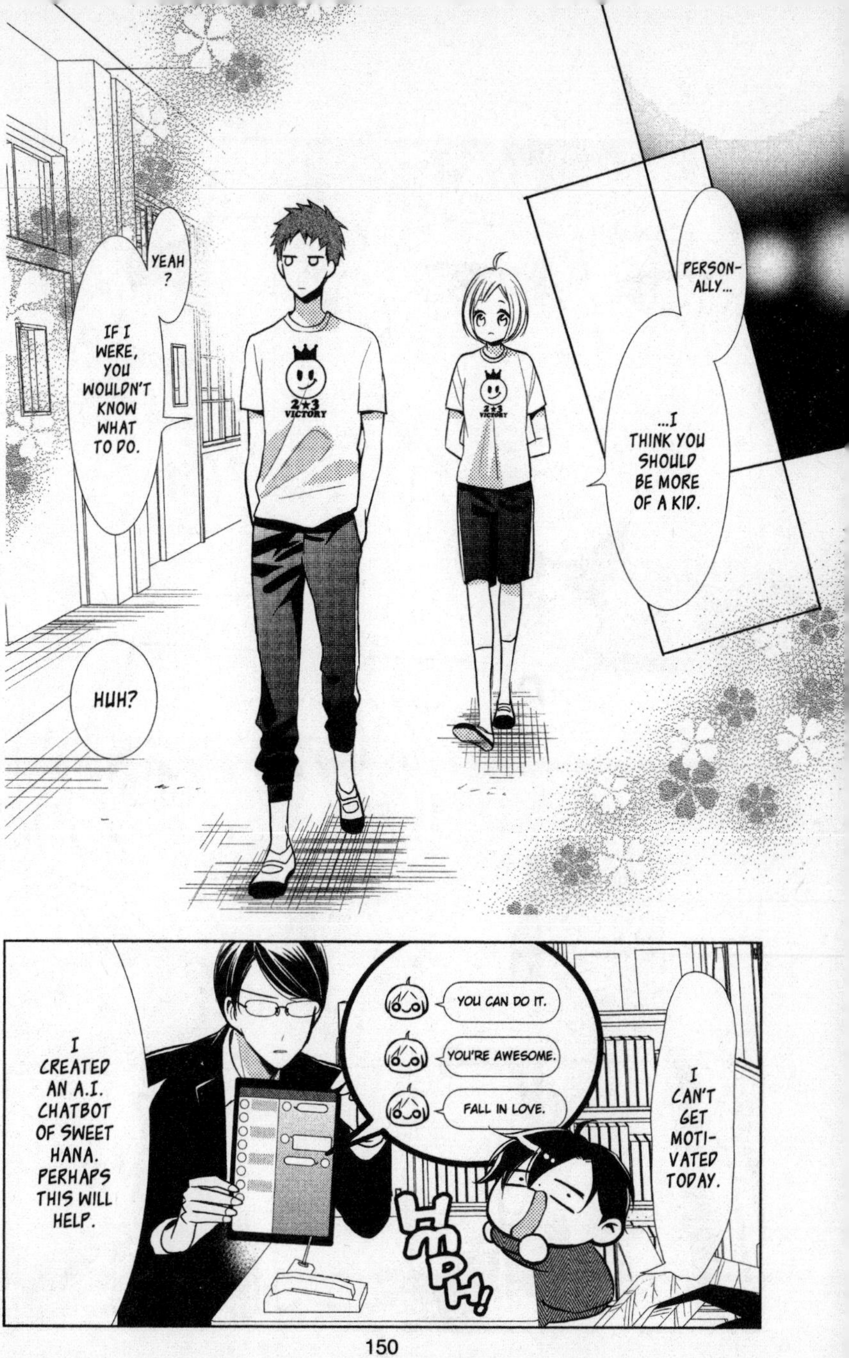
PERSON-ALLY...
...I THINK YOU SHOULD BE MORE OF A KID.
YEAH?
IF I WERE, YOU WOULDN'T KNOW WHAT TO DO.
HUH?
I CAN'T GET MOTI-VATED TODAY.
YOU CAN DO IT.
YOU'RE AWESOME.
FALL IN LOVE.
HMPH!
I CREATED AN A.I. CHATBOT OF SWEET HANA. PERHAPS THIS WILL HELP.

Nakane *

HE NARROWLY ESCAPED TURNING INTO HIKUNE AND IS TRYING TO CLING TO HIS REGULAR SELF.

HE DOESN'T HAVE HIS USUAL ENERGY AND IS LYING AROUND LISTLESSLY.

FLOP

FLOP

SOFA

DIRECTOR?

WHAT'S WRONG?

NOTHING.

HMPH.

"CHILDHOOD FRIENDS ARE PRETTY COOL"? WHAT THE HECK?

*Naka means "medium."

Nakane ②

I'M HOME.
TMP
TMP
HE'S SMALL.
TOUGH TIME TODAY, HUH?
PET PET
Agh!
BOOF
YOU MAKING FUN OF ME?
WHAT ON EARTH ARE YOU?

Chapter 51

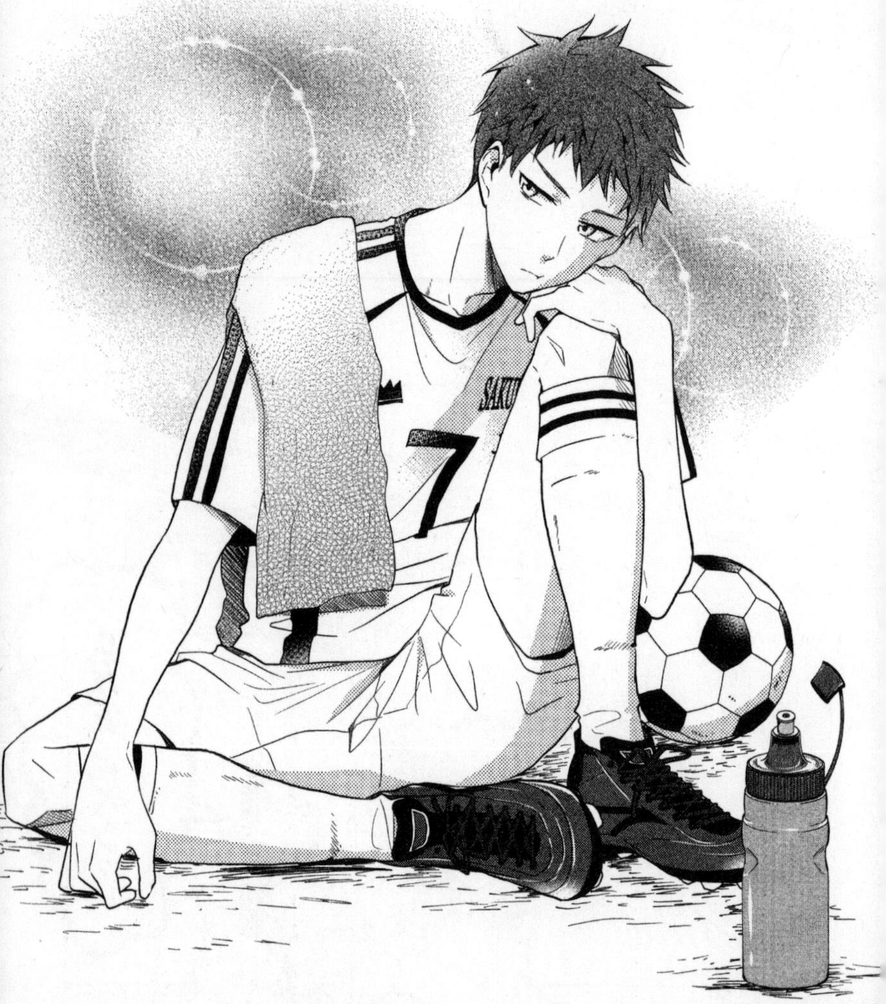

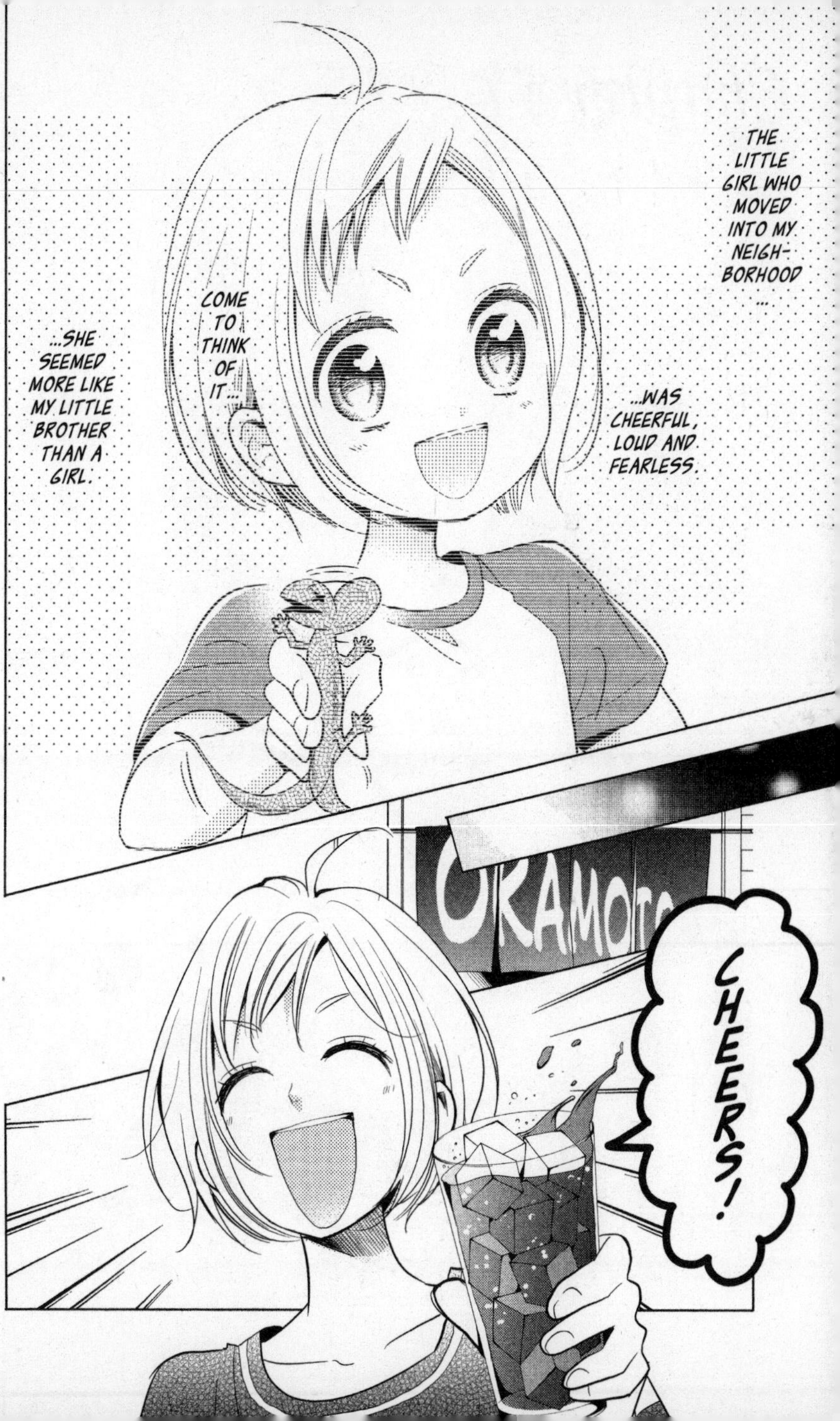
THE LITTLE GIRL WHO MOVED INTO MY NEIGH-BORHOOD...
...WAS CHEERFUL, LOUD AND FEARLESS.
COME TO THINK OF IT...
...SHE SEEMED MORE LIKE MY LITTLE BROTHER THAN A GIRL.
OKAMOTO
CHEERS!

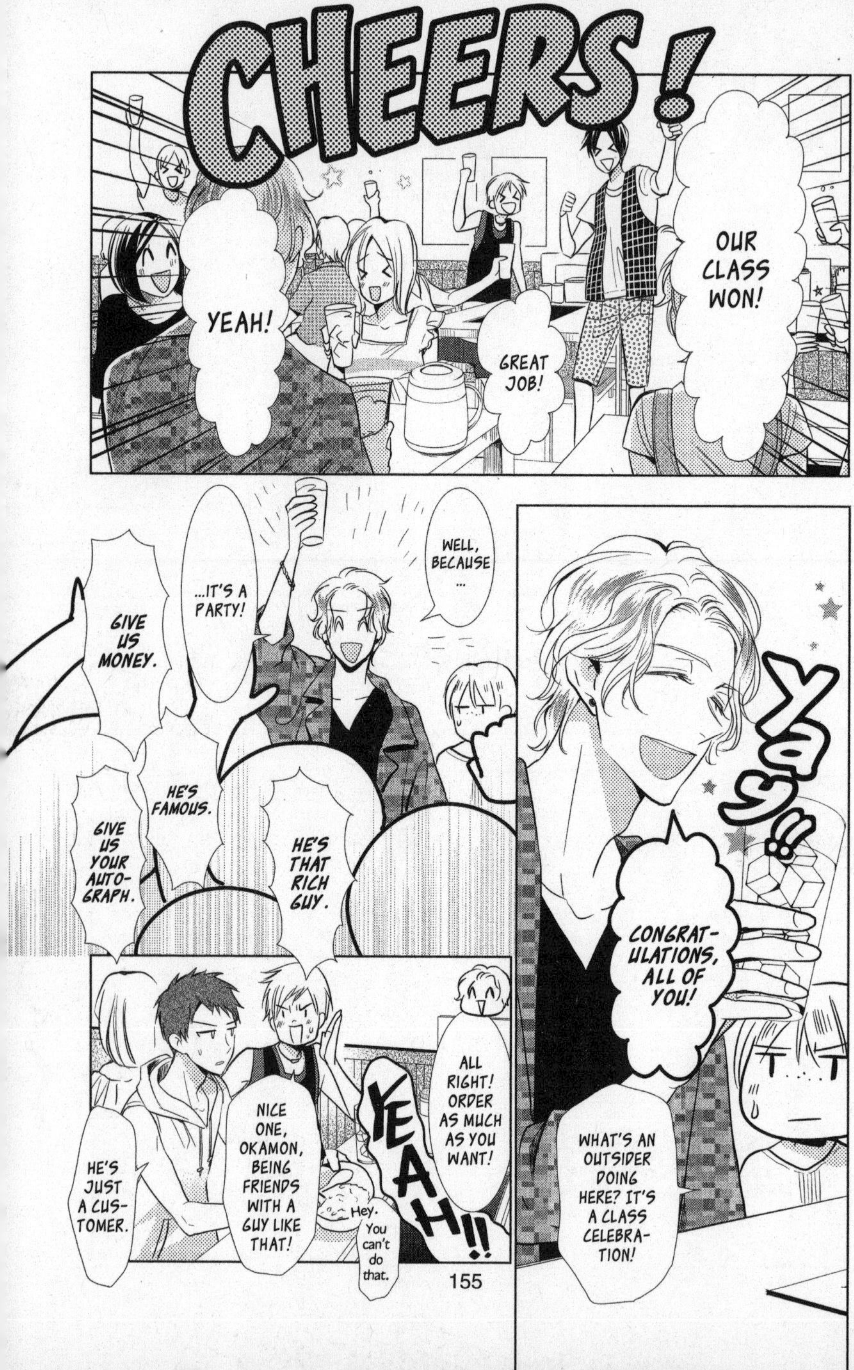
CHEERS!
OUR CLASS WON!
GREAT JOB!
YEAH!
Yay!!
CONGRATULATIONS, ALL OF YOU!
WHAT'S AN OUTSIDER DOING HERE? IT'S A CLASS CELEBRATION!
WELL, BECAUSE ...
...IT'S A PARTY!
GIVE US MONEY.
HE'S THAT RICH GUY.
HE'S FAMOUS.
GIVE US YOUR AUTOGRAPH.
ALL RIGHT! ORDER AS MUCH AS YOU WANT!
YEAH!!
Hey. You can't do that.
NICE ONE, OKAMON, BEING FRIENDS WITH A GUY LIKE THAT!
HE'S JUST A CUSTOMER.

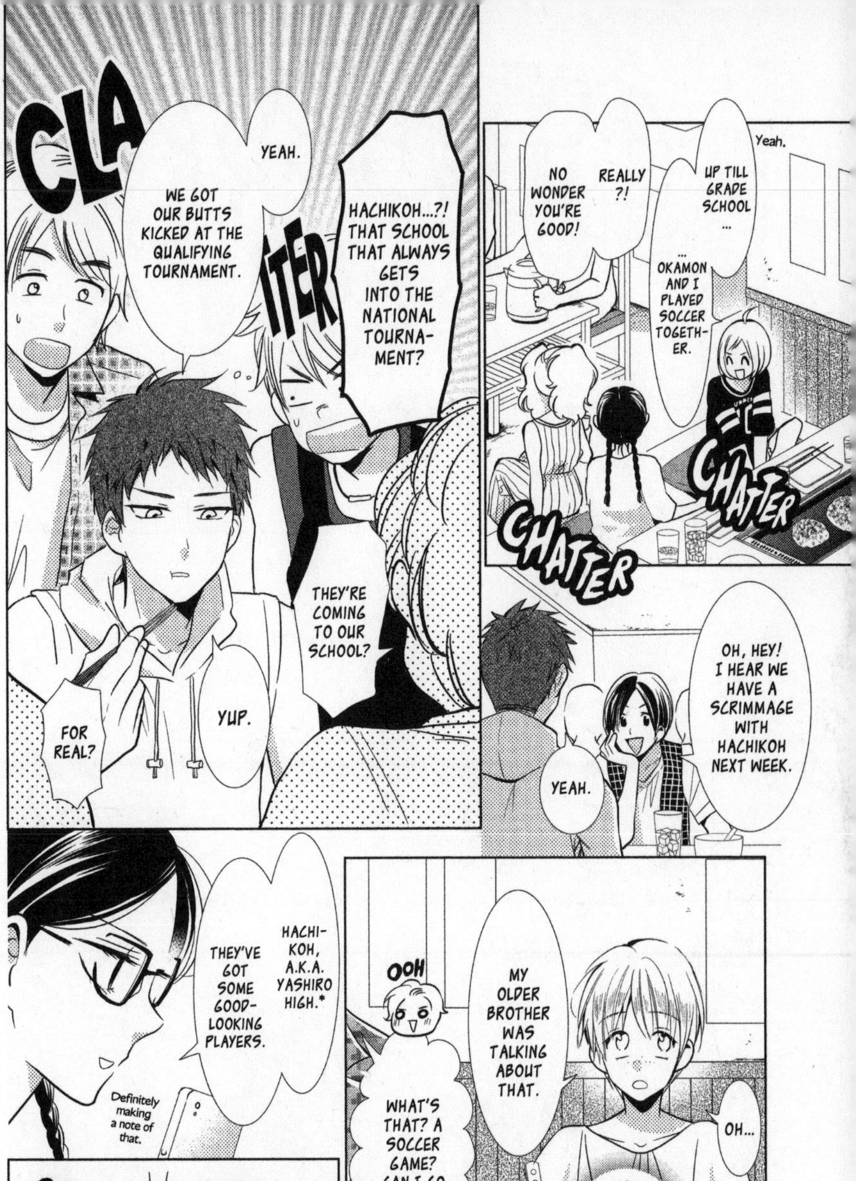
Yeah.
UP TILL GRADE SCHOOL ...
... OKAMON AND I PLAYED SOCCER TOGETHER.
REALLY?!
NO WONDER YOU'RE GOOD!
CHATTER
CHATTER
OH, HEY! I HEAR WE HAVE A SCRIMMAGE WITH HACHIKOH NEXT WEEK.
YEAH.
CLA TTER
HACHIKOH...?! THAT SCHOOL THAT ALWAYS GETS INTO THE NATIONAL TOURNAMENT?
YEAH.
WE GOT OUR BUTTS KICKED AT THE QUALIFYING TOURNAMENT.
THEY'RE COMING TO OUR SCHOOL?
YUP.
FOR REAL?
MY OLDER BROTHER WAS TALKING ABOUT THAT.
OH...
OOH
WHAT'S THAT? A SOCCER GAME? CAN I GO WATCH TOO?
Older brother Kiyofumi
Soccer Club
High school third-year
HACHIKOH, A.K.A. YASHIRO HIGH.*
THEY'VE GOT SOME GOOD-LOOKING PLAYERS.
Definitely making a note of that.
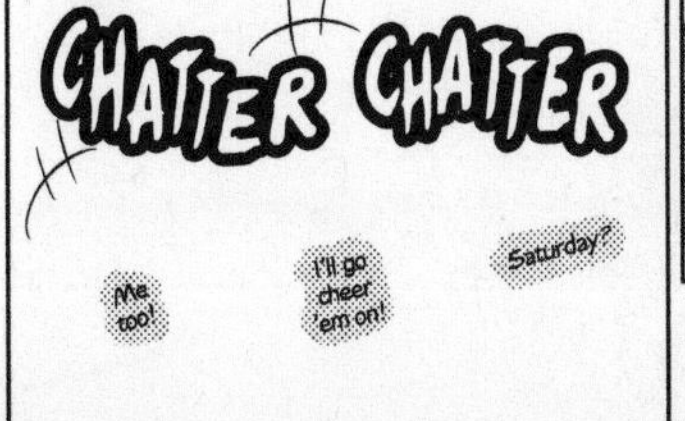
CHATTER CHATTER
Saturday?
I'll go cheer 'em on!
Me too!

*The *ya* character in Yashiro can also be read as *hachi*. *Koh* is short for "high school."

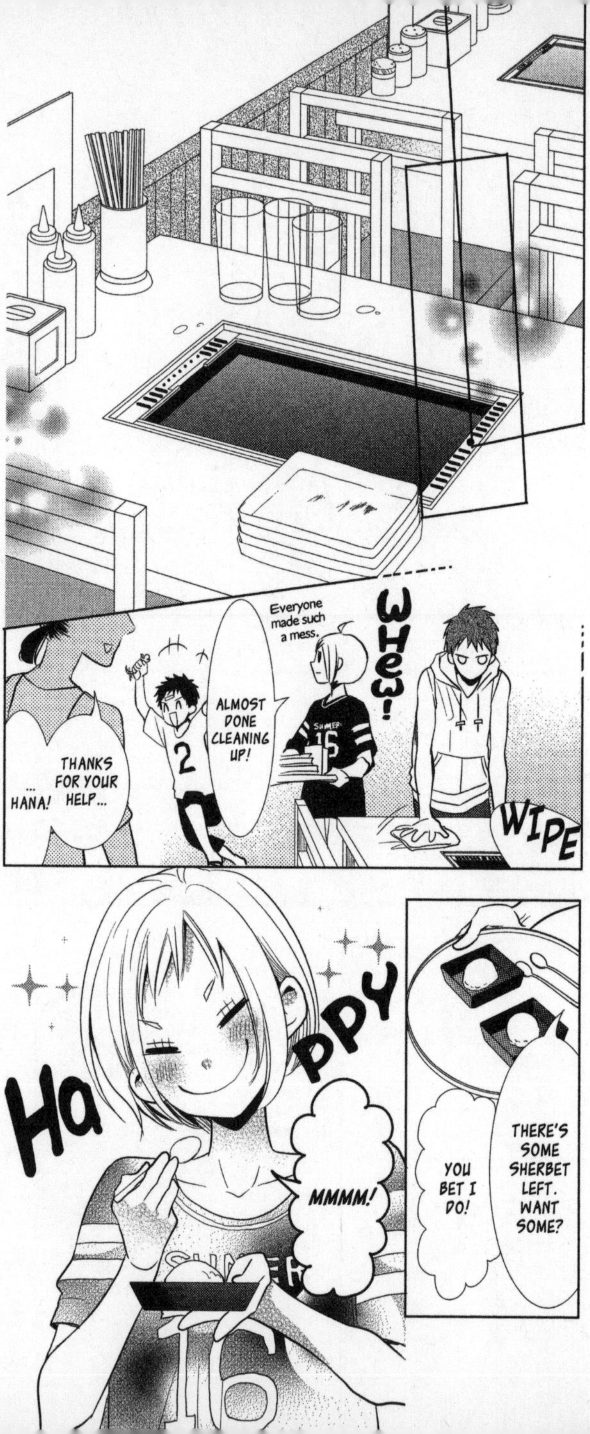
WHEW!
WIPE
Everyone made such a mess.
ALMOST DONE CLEANING UP!
THANKS FOR YOUR HELP...
...HANA!
THERE'S SOME SHERBET LEFT. WANT SOME?
YOU BET I DO!
HAPPY
MMMM!

● Soccer ●

I was finally able to draw him! Okamon in all his soccer-playing glory!

I managed to get through it with the help of my head editor, who used to be on a soccer team.

And the hero from *Wan Tail* makes a surprise appearance! (*Ha ha.*) But actually, this isn't the first time. I drew both Kaguya and Yukichika really small as background characters in chapter 2.

For those of you who're interested, please read *Wan Tail* too!

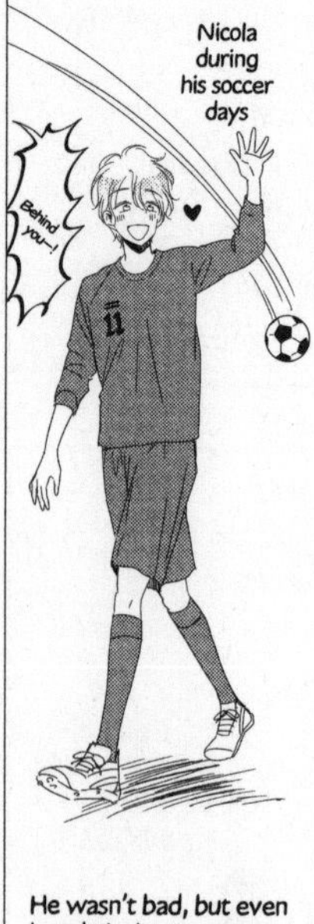
Nicola during his soccer days
Behind you~!

He wasn't bad, but even he admits he was more into girls than goals.

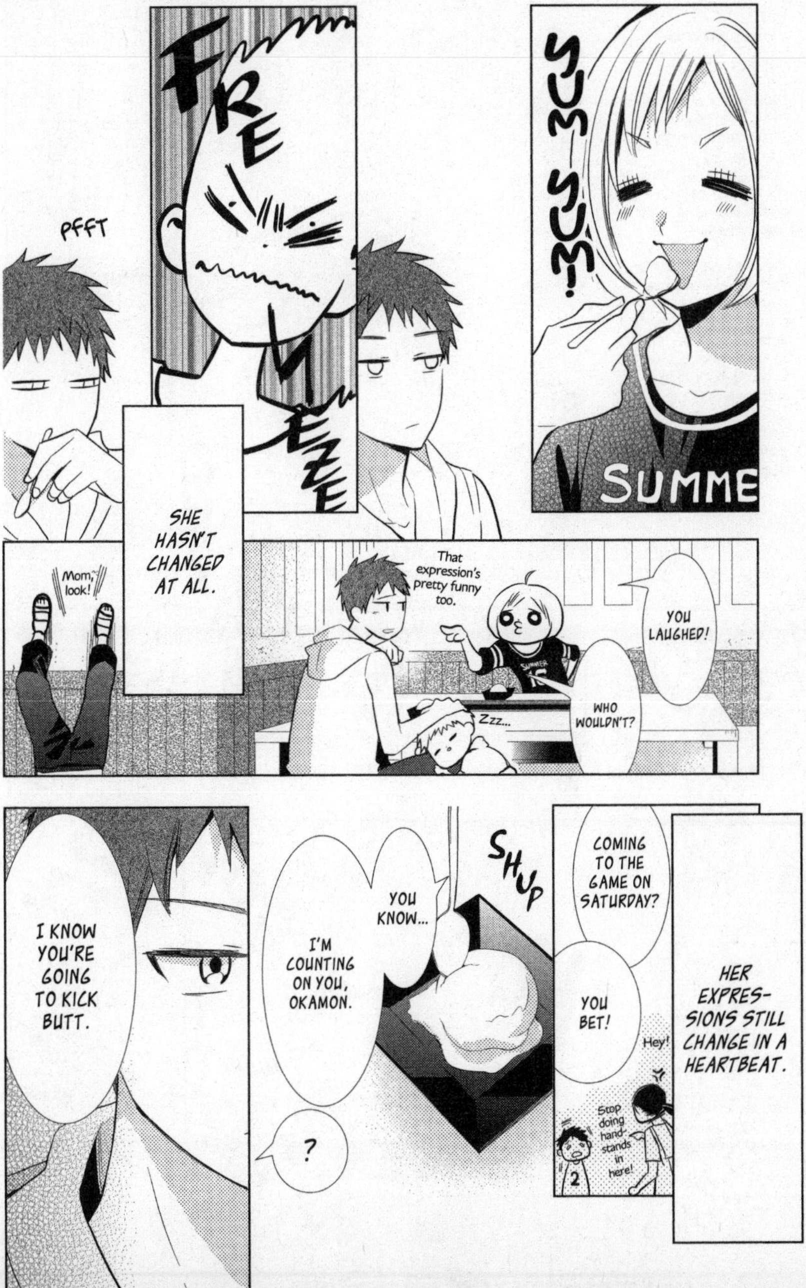
YUM YUM!
SUMME
FREEZE
PFFT
SHE HASN'T CHANGED AT ALL.
YOU LAUGHED!
WHO WOULDN'T?
That expression's pretty funny too.
Zzz...
Mom, look!
HER EXPRES-SIONS STILL CHANGE IN A HEARTBEAT.
COMING TO THE GAME ON SATURDAY?
YOU BET!
Hey!
Stop doing hand-stands in here!
2
SHUP
YOU KNOW...
I'M COUNTING ON YOU, OKAMON.
?
I KNOW YOU'RE GOING TO KICK BUTT.

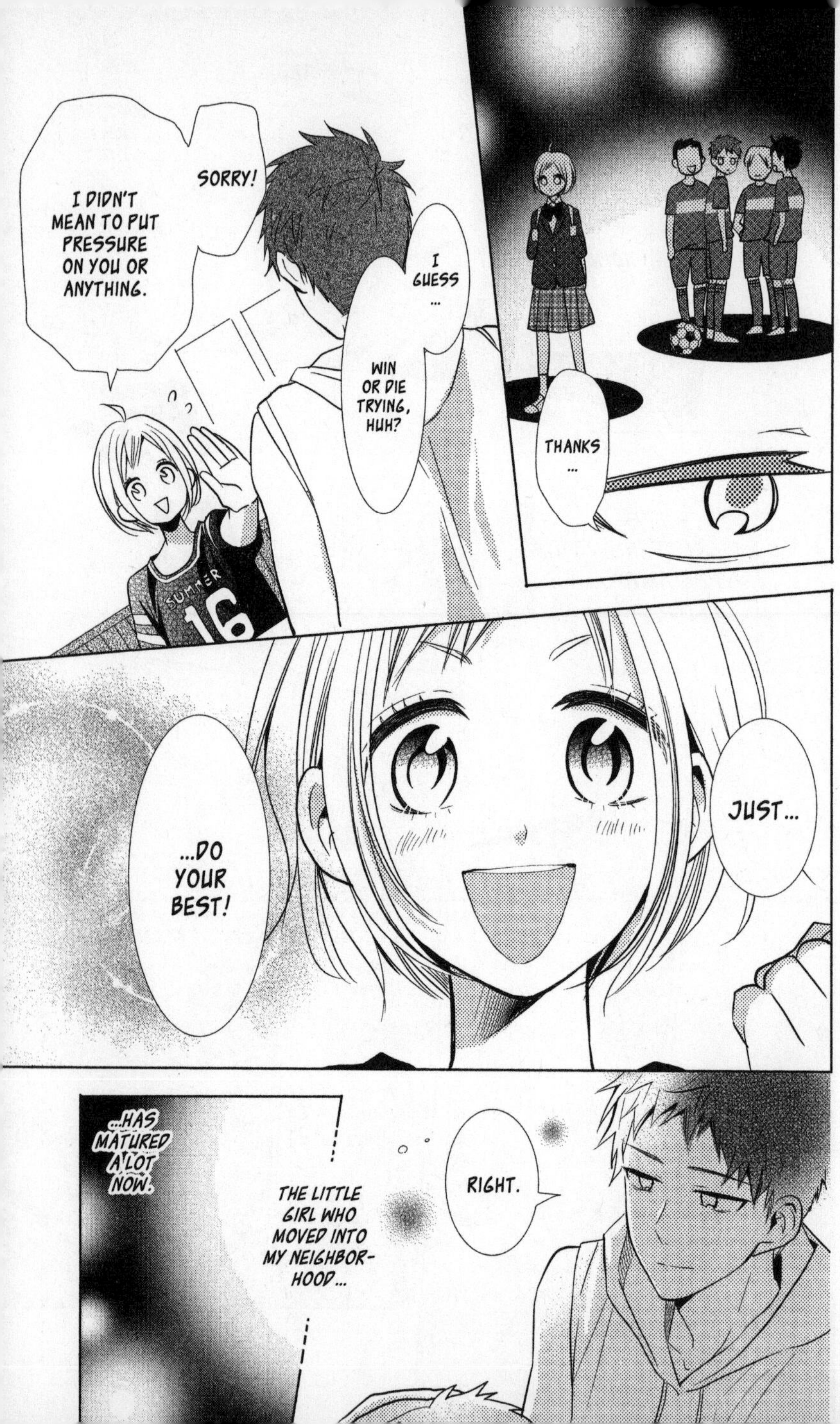
THANKS...
I GUESS...
WIN OR DIE TRYING, HUH?
SORRY!
I DIDN'T MEAN TO PUT PRESSURE ON YOU OR ANYTHING.
SUMMER 16
JUST...
...DO YOUR BEST!
RIGHT.
THE LITTLE GIRL WHO MOVED INTO MY NEIGHBOR-HOOD...
...HAS MATURED A LOT NOW.

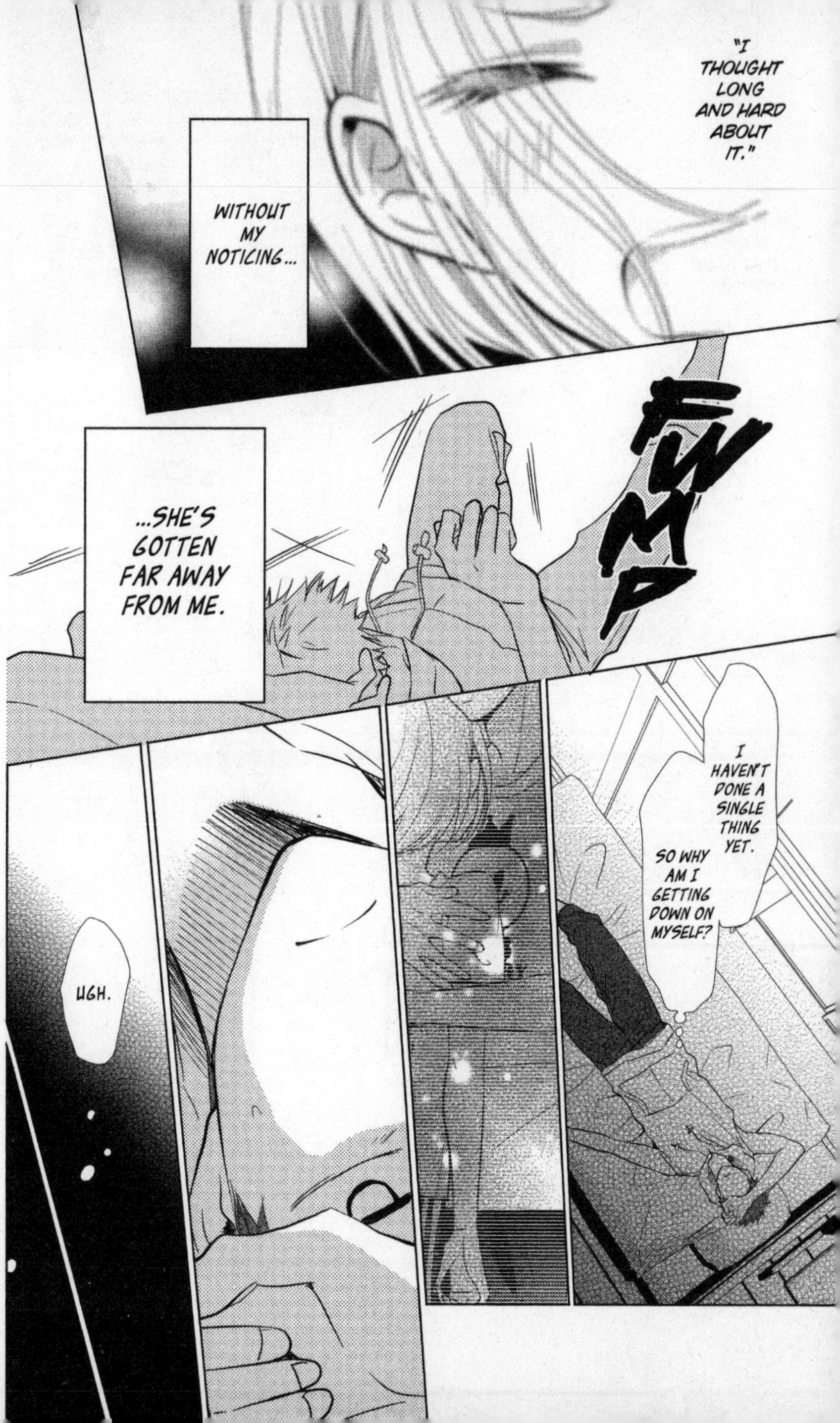
"I THOUGHT LONG AND HARD ABOUT IT."
WITHOUT MY NOTICING...
FWUMP
...SHE'S GOTTEN FAR AWAY FROM ME.
I HAVEN'T DONE A SINGLE THING YET.
SO WHY AM I GETTING DOWN ON MYSELF?
UGH.

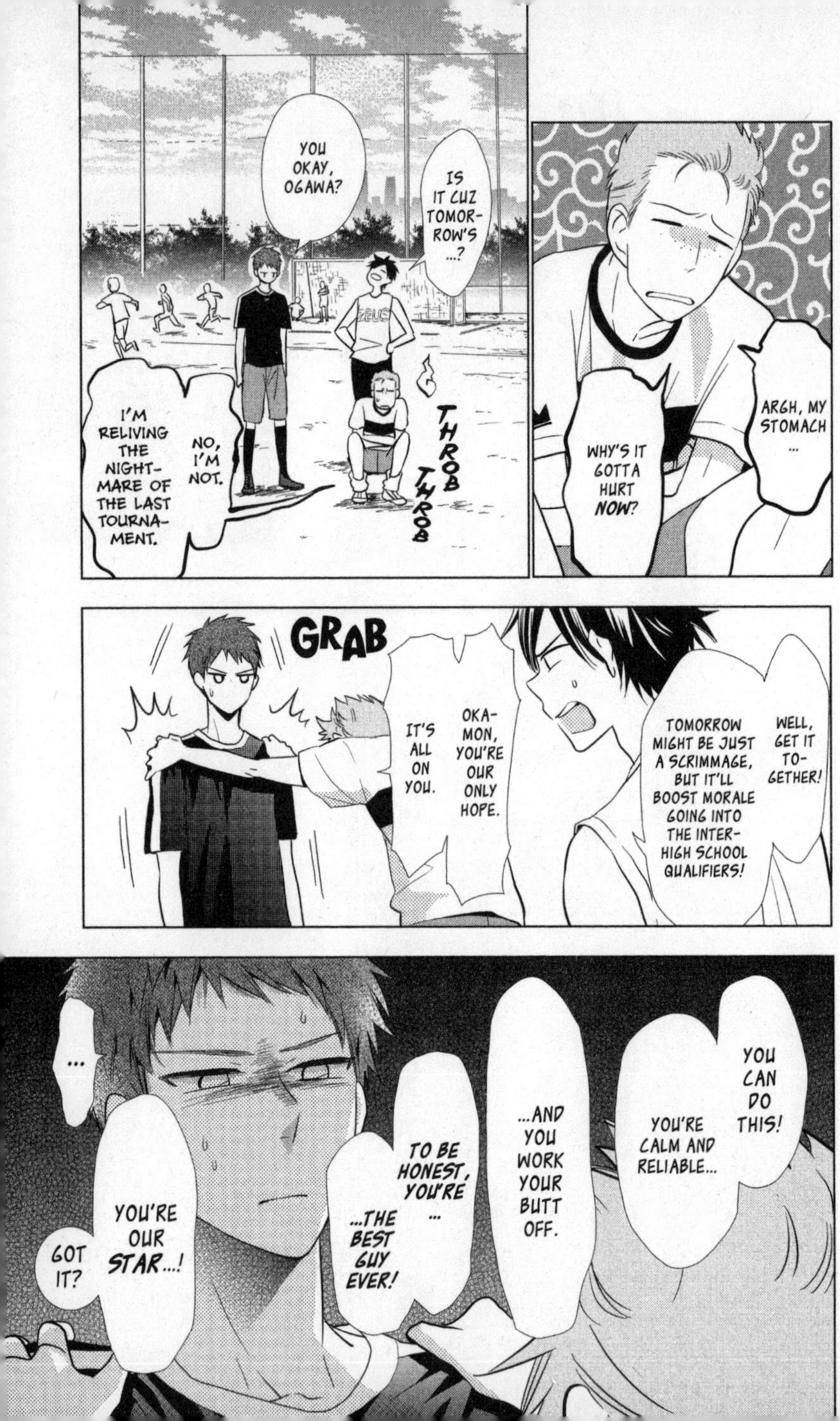

ARGH, MY STOMACH ...
WHY'S IT GOTTA HURT NOW?
YOU OKAY, OGAWA?
IS IT CUZ TOMORROW'S ...?
NO, I'M NOT.
I'M RELIVING THE NIGHTMARE OF THE LAST TOURNAMENT.
THROB THROB
WELL, GET IT TOGETHER!
TOMORROW MIGHT BE JUST A SCRIMMAGE, BUT IT'LL BOOST MORALE GOING INTO THE INTER-HIGH SCHOOL QUALIFIERS!
OKAMON, YOU'RE OUR ONLY HOPE.
IT'S ALL ON YOU.
GRAB
YOU CAN DO THIS!
YOU'RE CALM AND RELIABLE...
...AND YOU WORK YOUR BUTT OFF.
TO BE HONEST, YOU'RE ...
...THE BEST GUY EVER!
...
YOU'RE OUR STAR...!
GOT IT?

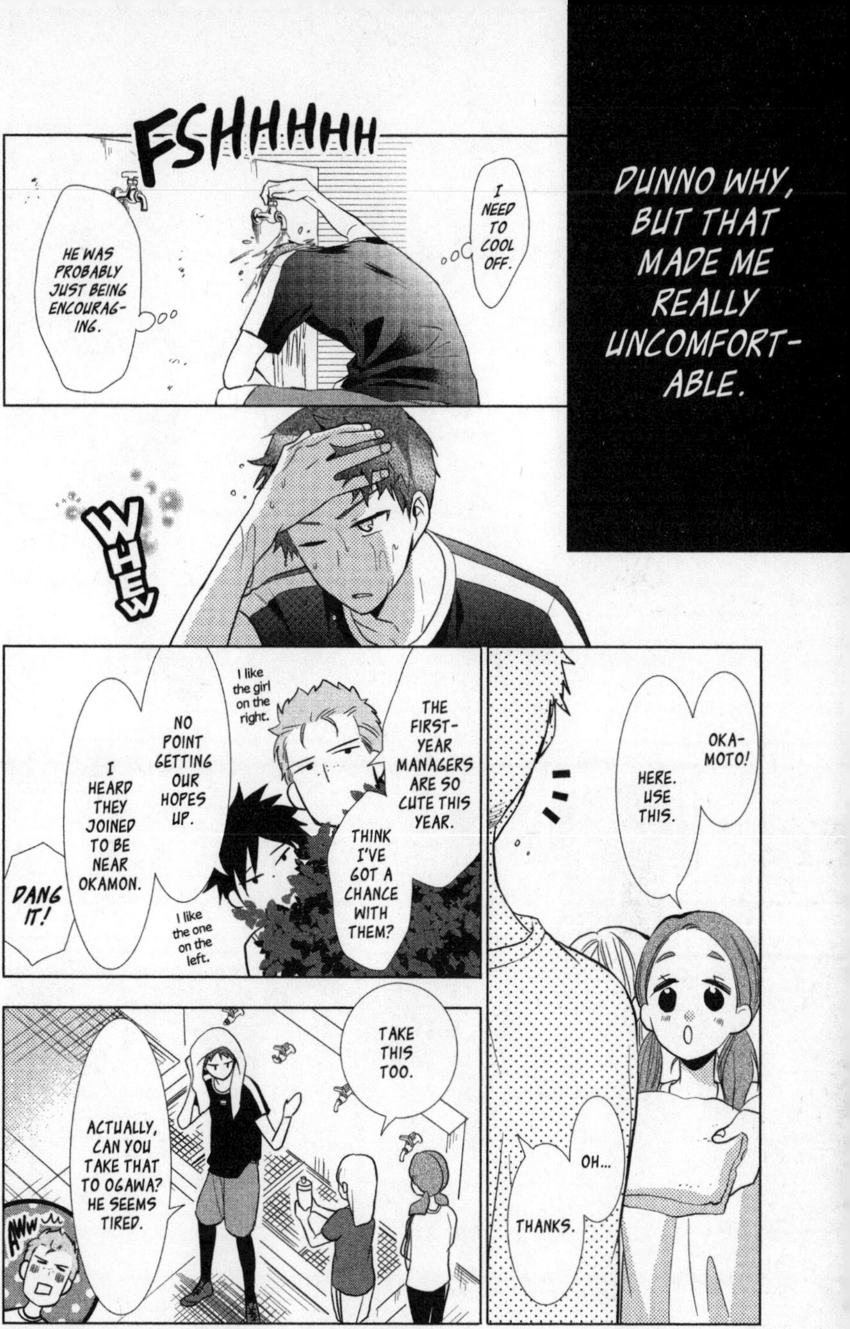
DUNNO WHY, BUT THAT MADE ME REALLY UNCOMFORT-ABLE.
FSHHHHH
I NEED TO COOL OFF.
HE WAS PROBABLY JUST BEING ENCOURAG-ING.
WHEW
OKA-MOTO!
HERE. USE THIS.
OH...
THANKS.
THE FIRST-YEAR MANAGERS ARE SO CUTE THIS YEAR.
I like the girl on the right.
THINK I'VE GOT A CHANCE WITH THEM?
NO POINT GETTING OUR HOPES UP.
I like the one on the left.
I HEARD THEY JOINED TO BE NEAR OKAMON.
DANG IT!
TAKE THIS TOO.
ACTUALLY, CAN YOU TAKE THAT TO OGAWA? HE SEEMS TIRED.
AWW

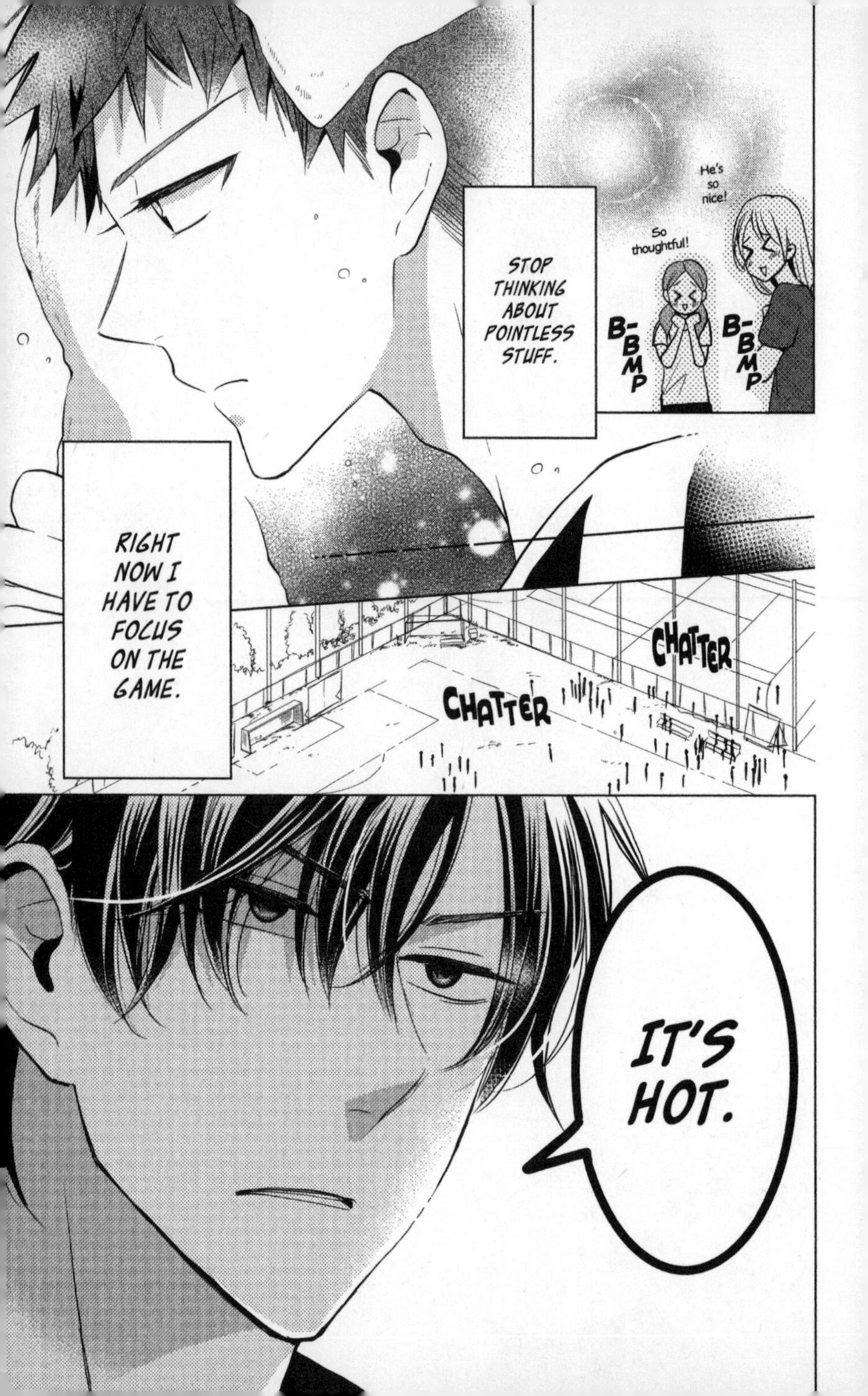
He's so nice!
So thoughtful!
B-BMP
B-BMP
STOP THINKING ABOUT POINTLESS STUFF.
RIGHT NOW I HAVE TO FOCUS ON THE GAME.
CHATTER
CHATTER
IT'S HOT.

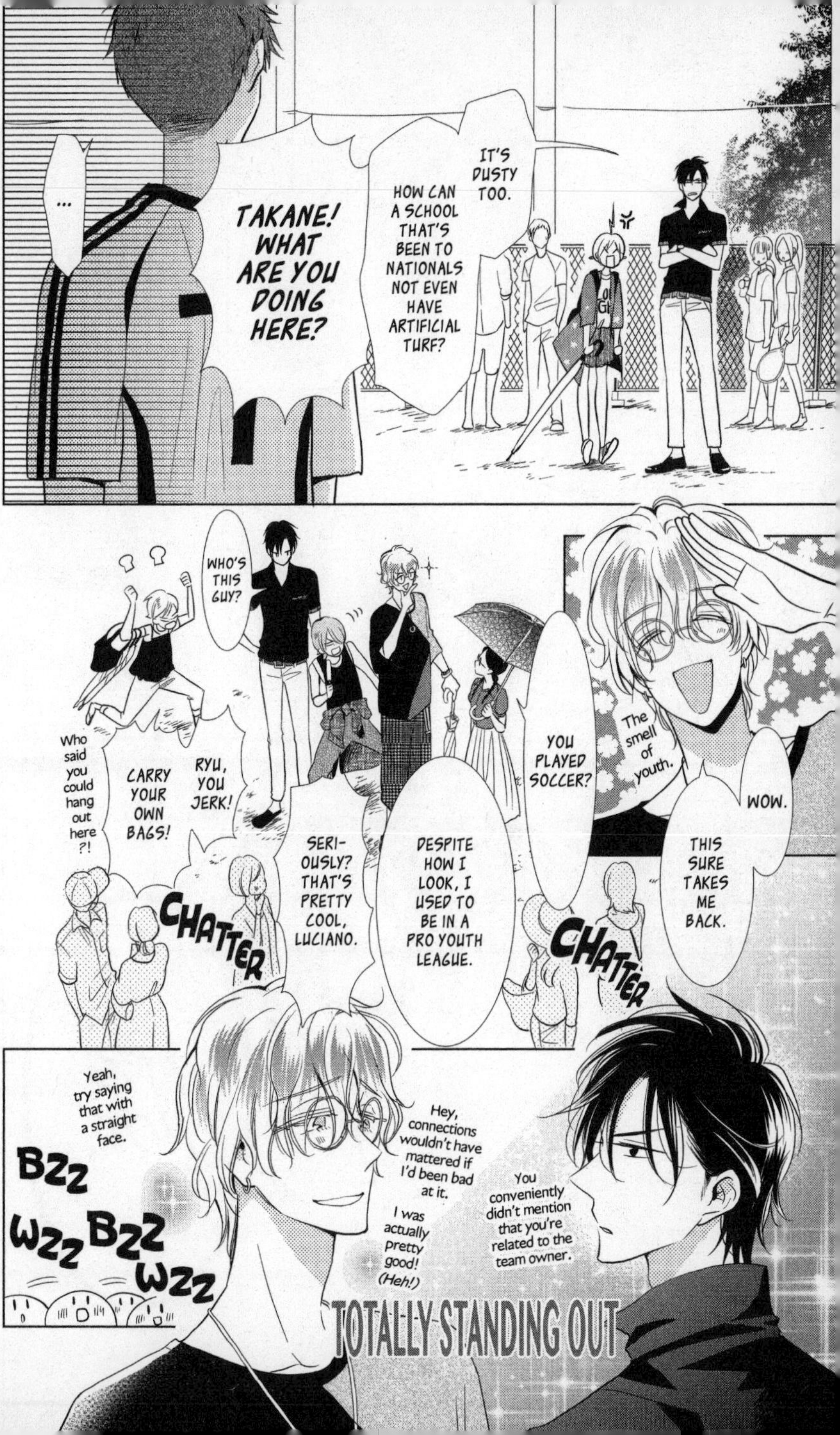
HOW CAN A SCHOOL THAT'S BEEN TO NATIONALS NOT EVEN HAVE ARTIFICIAL TURF?
IT'S DUSTY TOO.
TAKANE! WHAT ARE YOU DOING HERE?
...
The smell of youth.
WOW.
THIS SURE TAKES ME BACK.
YOU PLAYED SOCCER?
DESPITE HOW I LOOK, I USED TO BE IN A PRO YOUTH LEAGUE.
CHATTER
SERIOUSLY? THAT'S PRETTY COOL, LUCIANO.
WHO'S THIS GUY?
RYU, YOU JERK!
CARRY YOUR OWN BAGS!
Who said you could hang out here?!
CHATTER
You conveniently didn't mention that you're related to the team owner.
Hey, connections wouldn't have mattered if I'd been bad at it.
I was actually pretty good! (Heh!)
TOTALLY STANDING OUT
Yeah, try saying that with a straight face.
BZZ
WZZ BZZ
WZZ

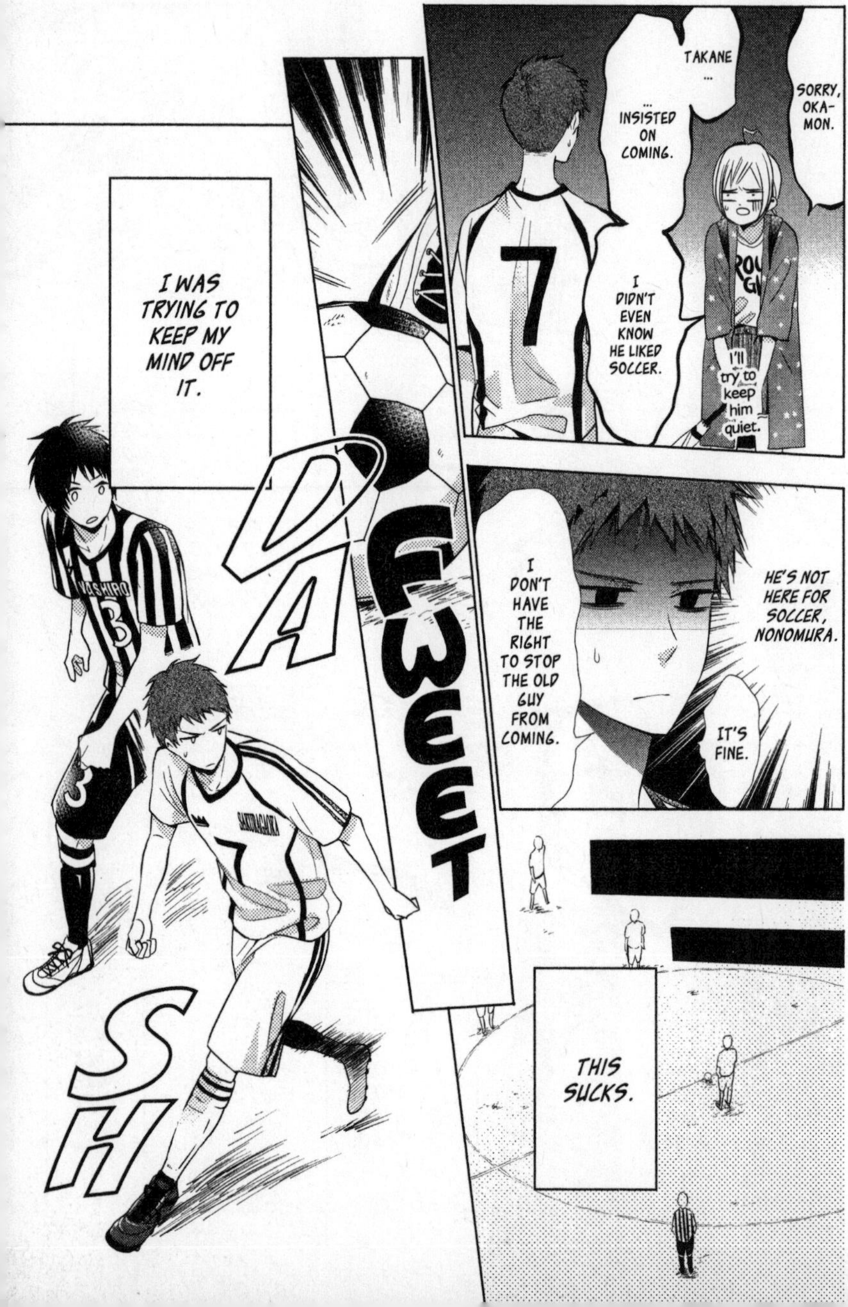
SORRY, OKA-MON.
TAKANE ...
... INSISTED ON COMING.
I DIDN'T EVEN KNOW HE LIKED SOCCER.
I'll try to keep him quiet.
HE'S NOT HERE FOR SOCCER, NONOMURA.
IT'S FINE.
I DON'T HAVE THE RIGHT TO STOP THE OLD GUY FROM COMING.
THIS SUCKS.
I WAS TRYING TO KEEP MY MIND OFF IT.
DA
SH

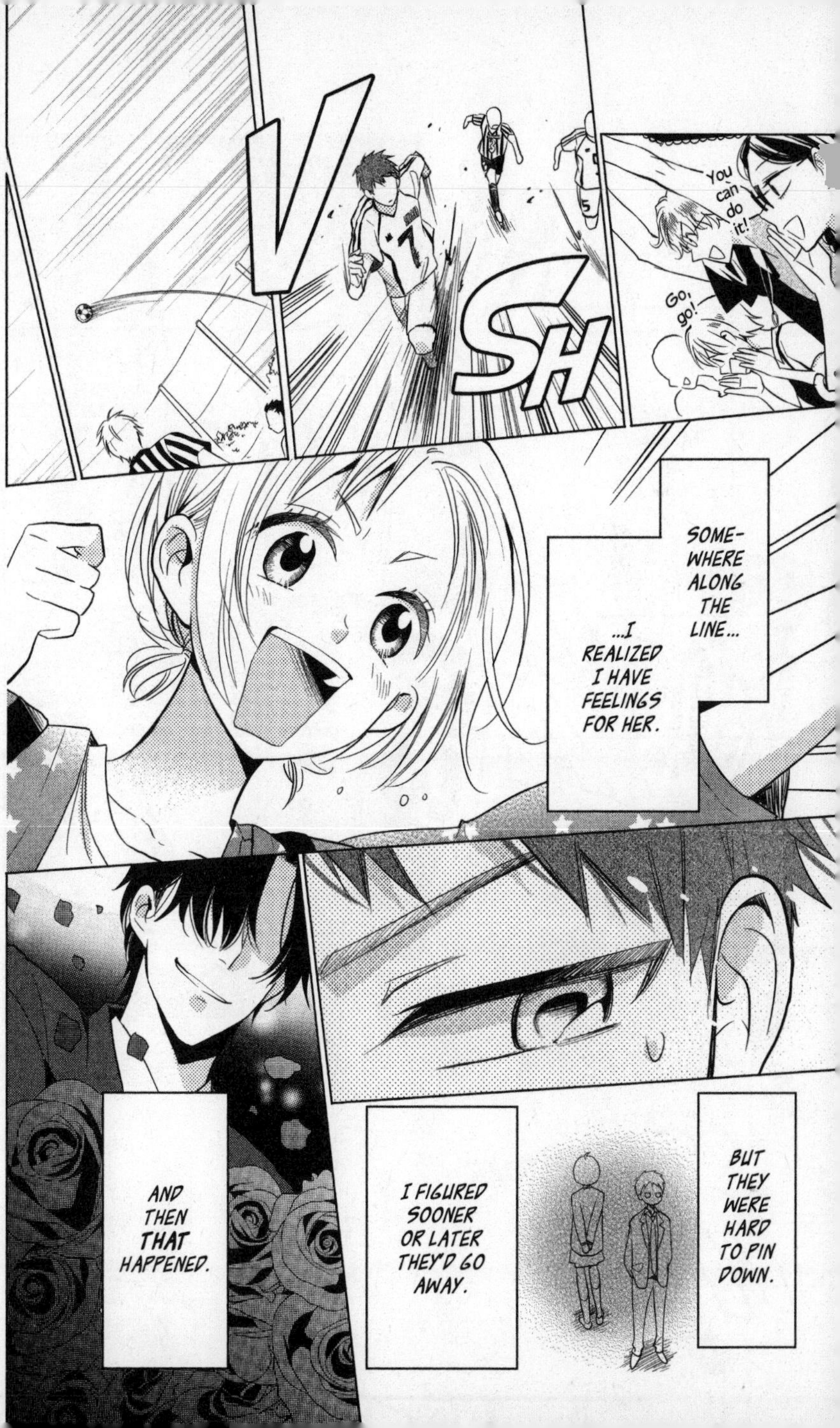

You can do it!
Go, go!
SH
V
SOME-WHERE ALONG THE LINE...
...I REALIZED I HAVE FEELINGS FOR HER.
BUT THEY WERE HARD TO PIN DOWN.
I FIGURED SOONER OR LATER THEY'D GO AWAY.
AND THEN **THAT** HAPPENED.

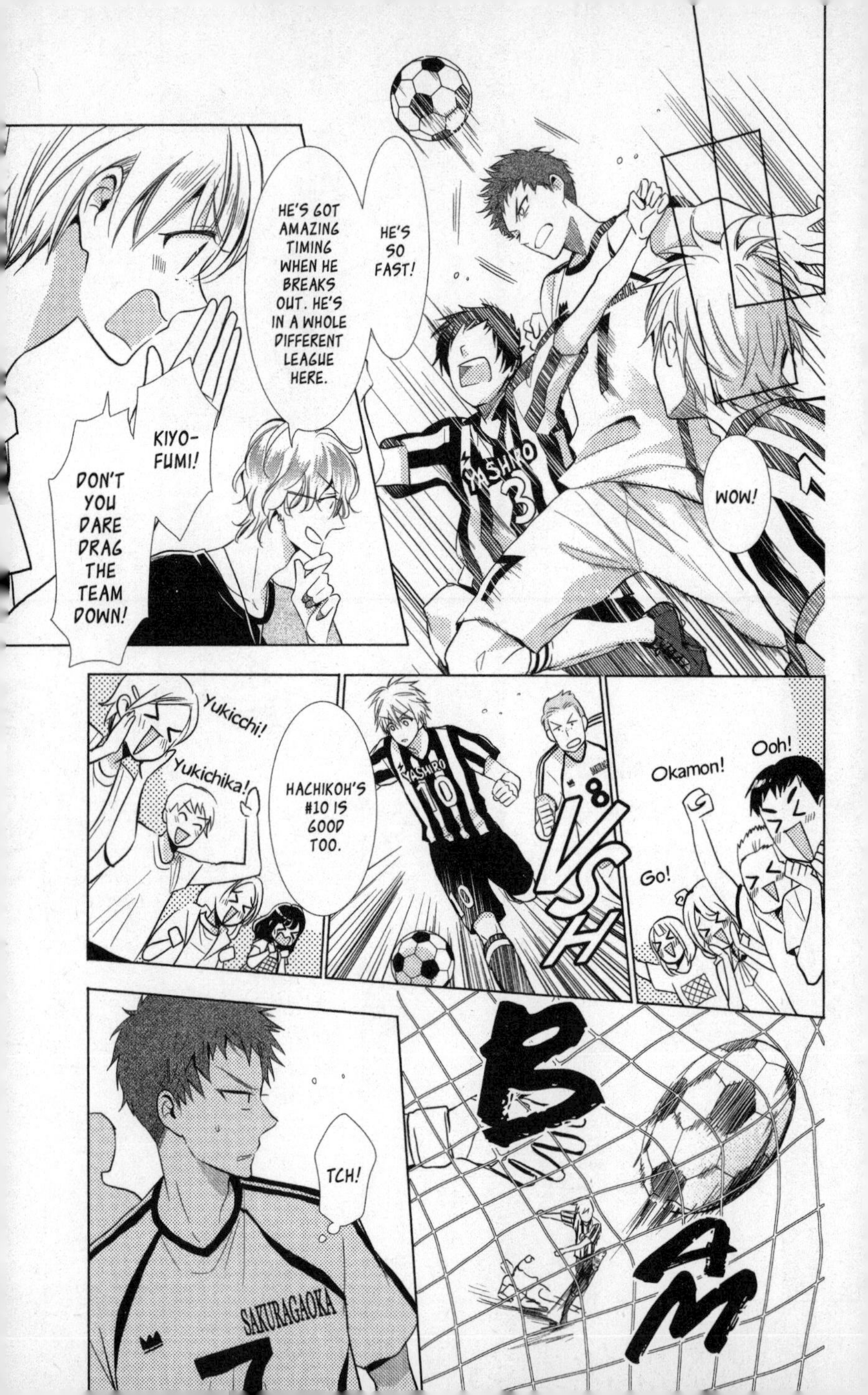
HE'S SO FAST!
HE'S GOT AMAZING TIMING WHEN HE BREAKS OUT. HE'S IN A WHOLE DIFFERENT LEAGUE HERE.
WOW!
KIYO-FUMI!
DON'T YOU DARE DRAG THE TEAM DOWN!
Ooh!
Okamon!
Go!
VSH
HACHIKOH'S #10 IS GOOD TOO.
Yukicchi!
Yukichika!
BAM
TCH!

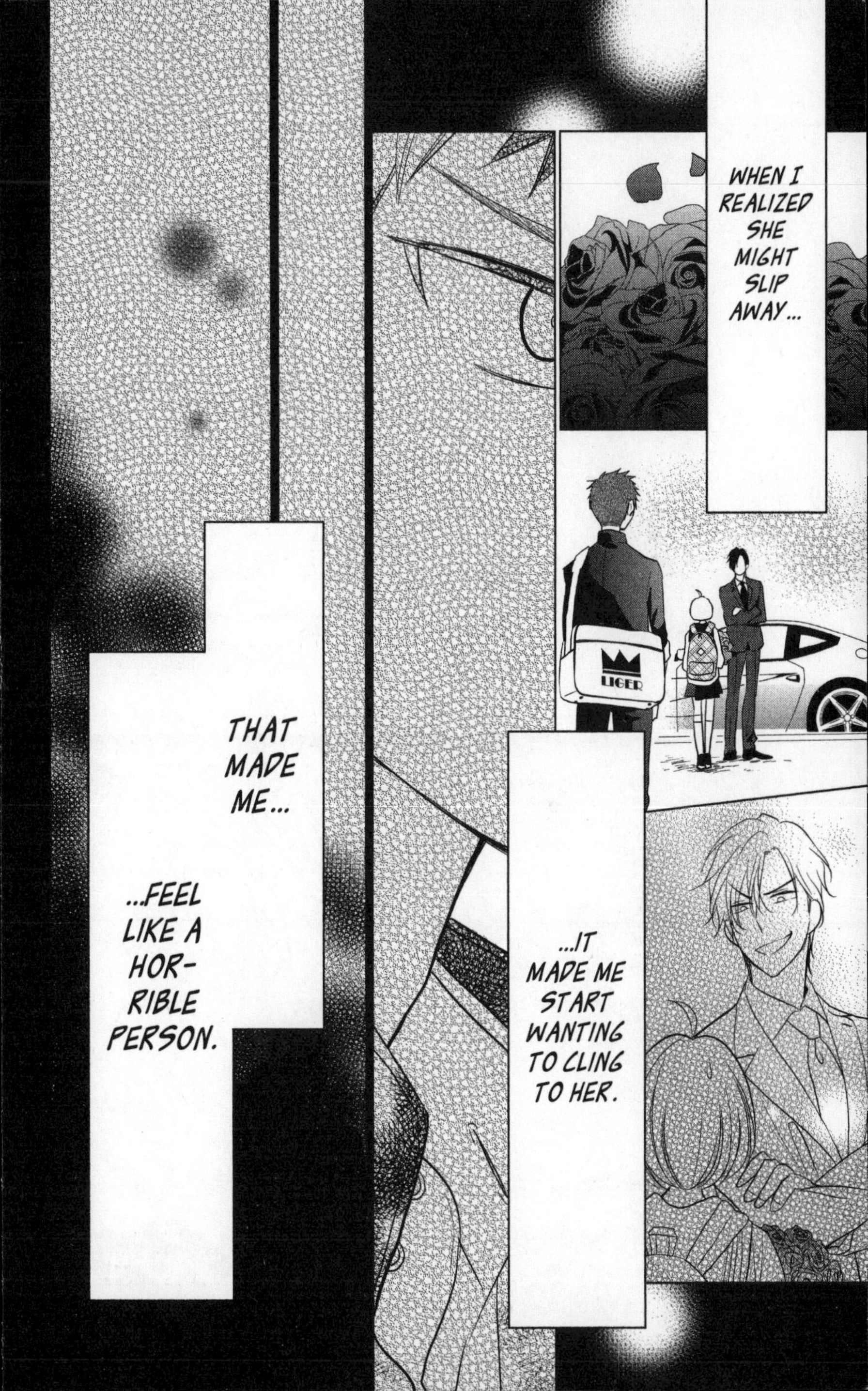
WHEN I REALIZED SHE MIGHT SLIP AWAY...
LIGER
...IT MADE ME START WANTING TO CLING TO HER.
THAT MADE ME...
...FEEL LIKE A HOR-RIBLE PERSON.

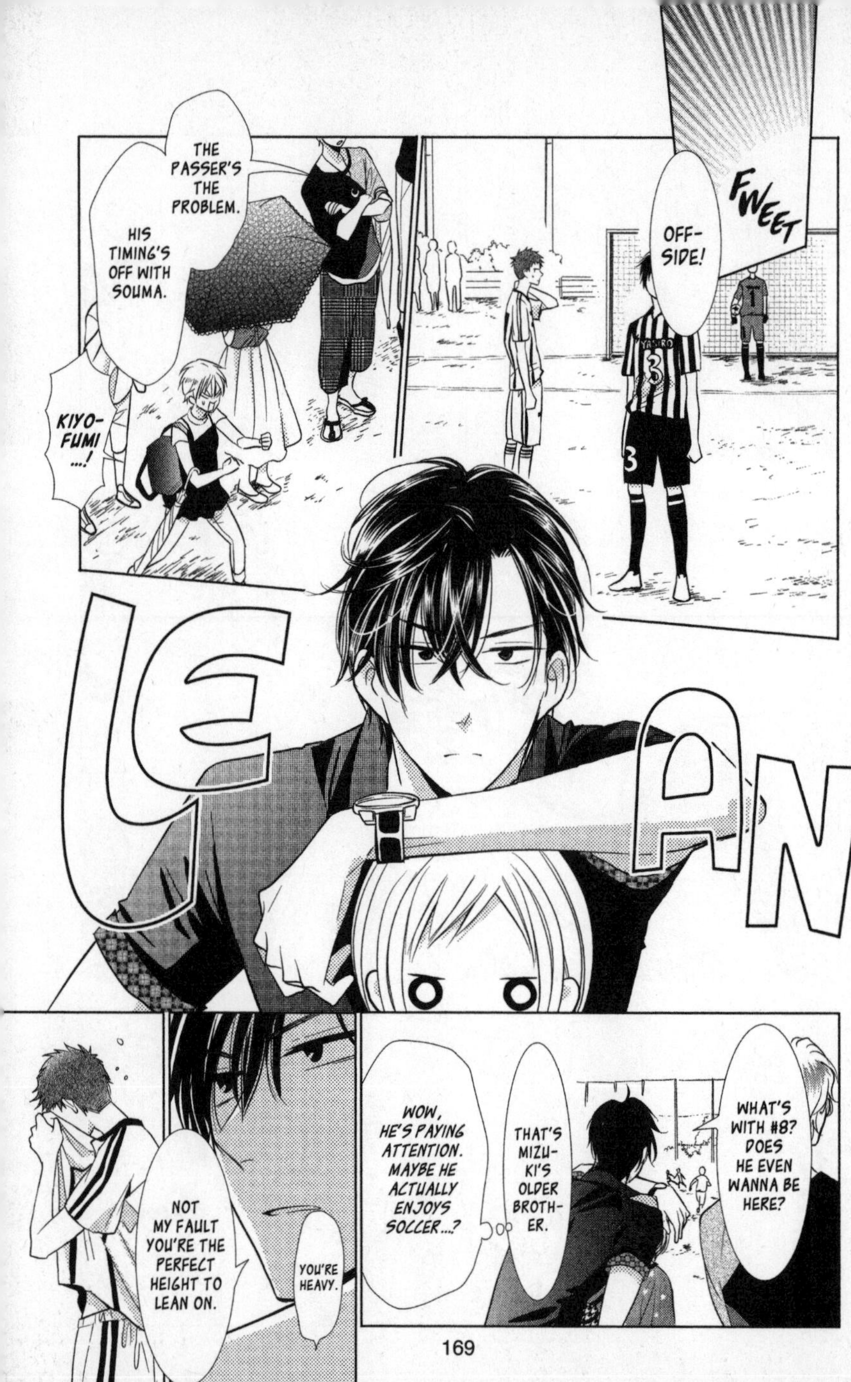
FWEET
OFF-SIDE!
THE PASSER'S THE PROBLEM.
HIS TIMING'S OFF WITH SOUMA.
KIYOFUMI ...!
LEAN
WHAT'S WITH #8? DOES HE EVEN WANNA BE HERE?
THAT'S MIZUKI'S OLDER BROTHER.
WOW, HE'S PAYING ATTENTION. MAYBE HE ACTUALLY ENJOYS SOCCER...?
YOU'RE HEAVY.
NOT MY FAULT YOU'RE THE PERFECT HEIGHT TO LEAN ON.

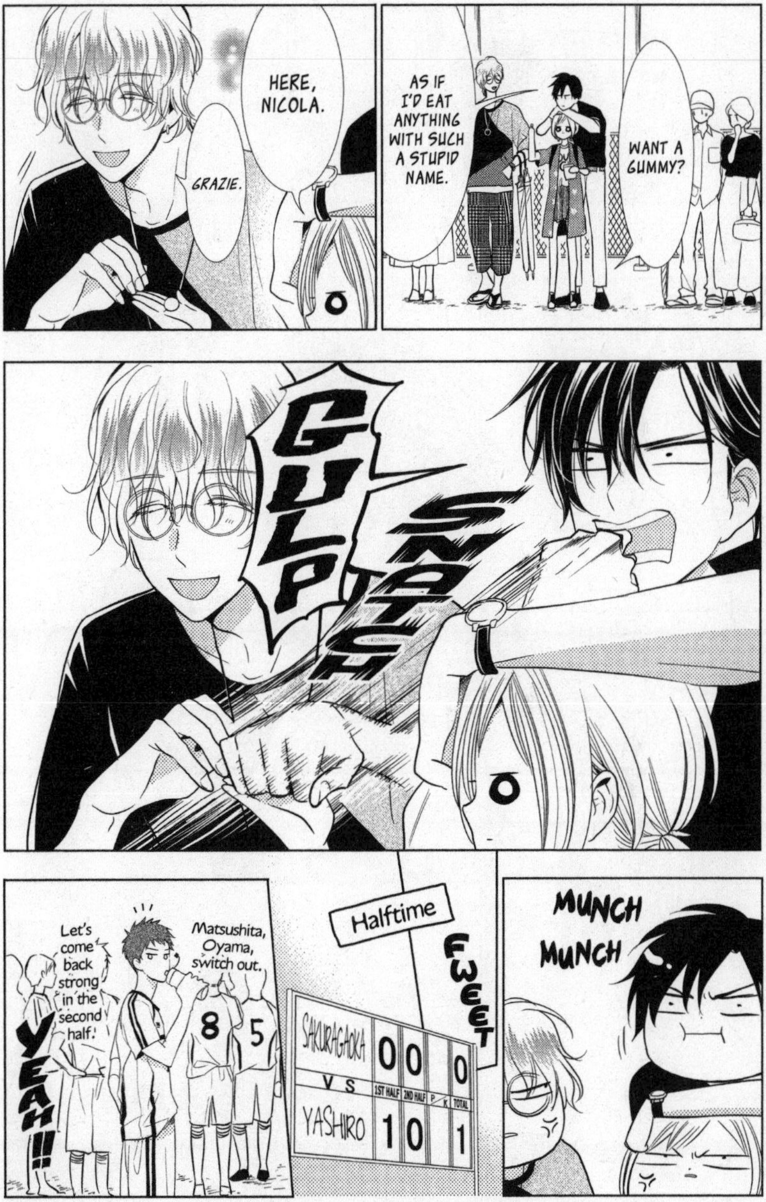
WANT A GUMMY?
AS IF I'D EAT ANYTHING WITH SUCH A STUPID NAME.
HERE, NICOLA.
GRAZIE.
SNATCH
GULP
MUNCH MUNCH
FWEET
Halftime
SAKURAGAOKA 0 0 0
VS
1ST HALF 2ND HALF PK TOTAL
YASHIRO 1 0 1
Matsushita, Oyama, switch out.
Let's come back strong in the second half!
YEAH!!

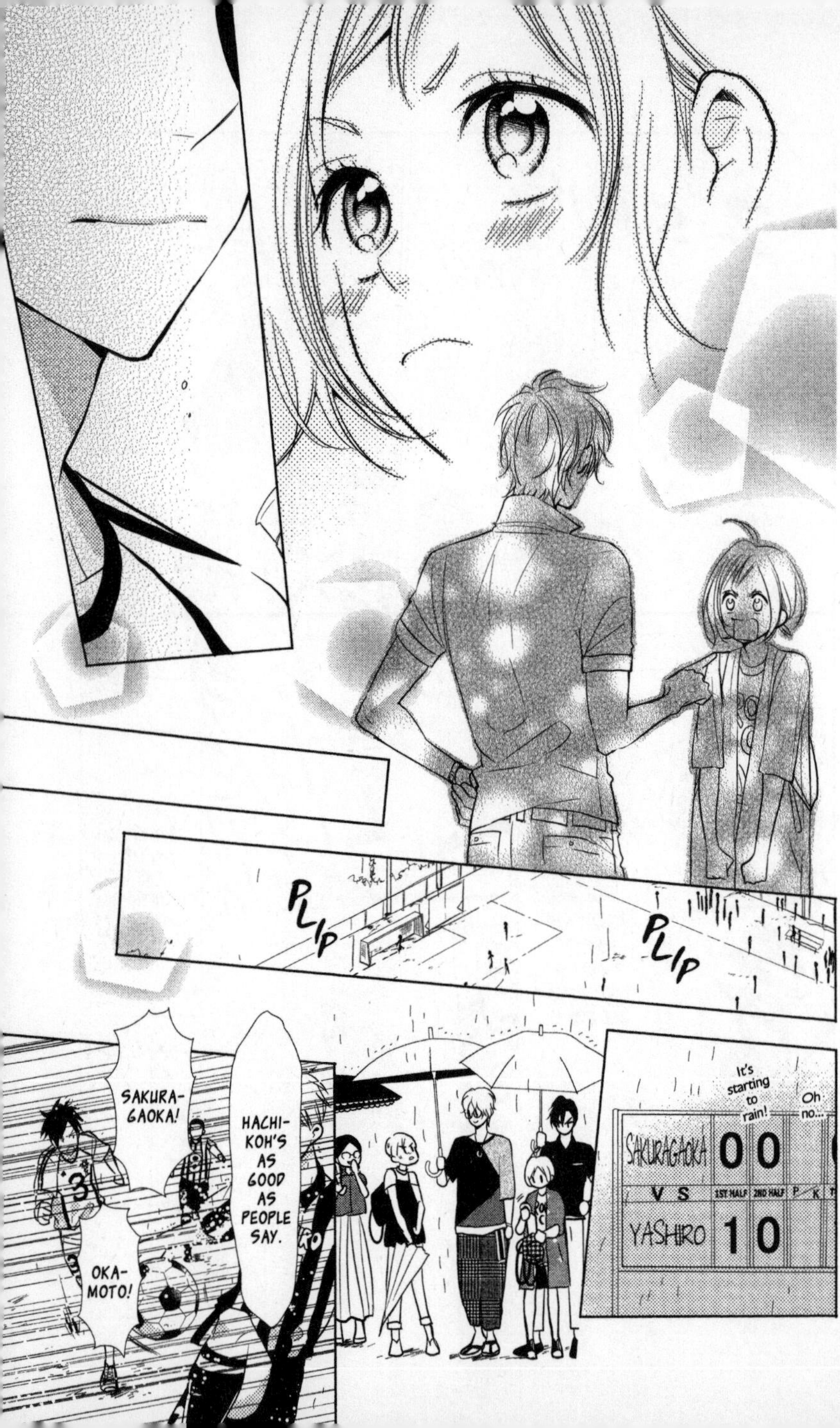
PLIP
PLIP
It's starting to rain!
Oh no...
SAKURAGAOKA 0 0
VS
1ST HALF 2ND HALF P K
YASHIRO 1 0
HACHI-KOH'S AS GOOD AS PEOPLE SAY.
SAKURA-GAOKA!
OKA-MOTO!

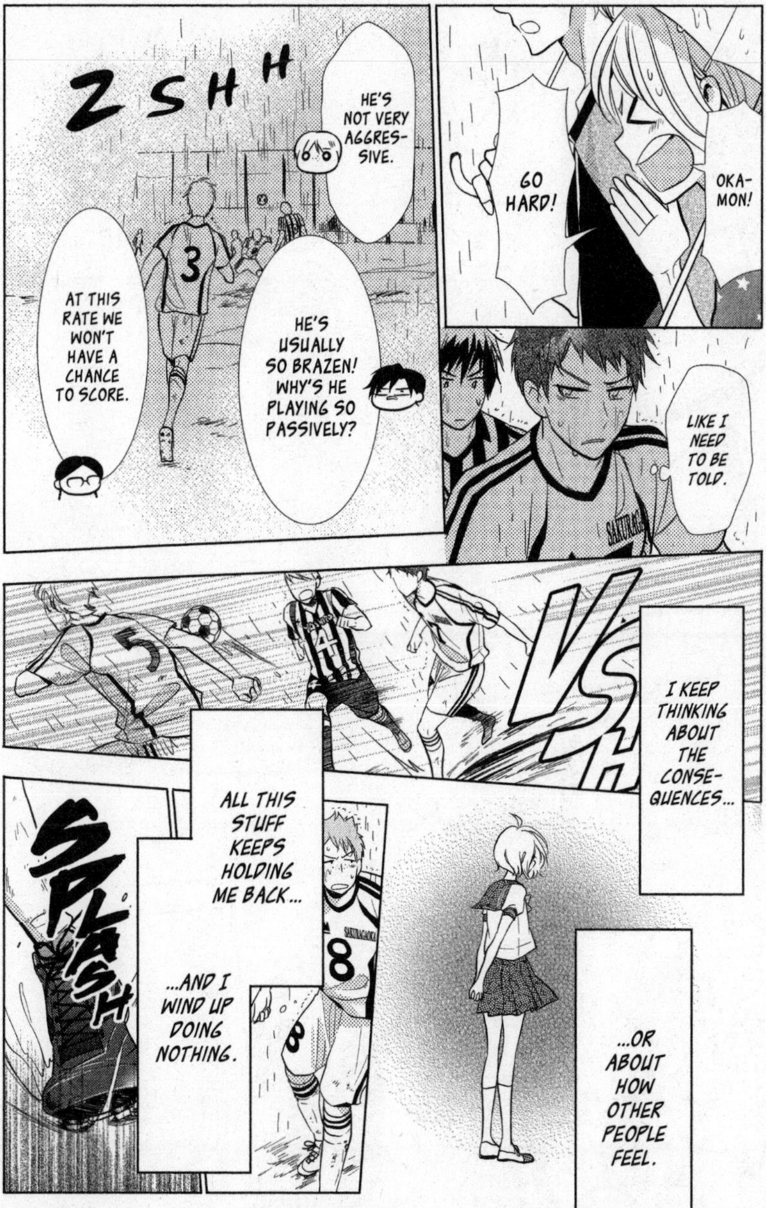
OKA-MON!
GO HARD!
LIKE I NEED TO BE TOLD.
ZSHH
HE'S NOT VERY AGGRES-SIVE.
HE'S USUALLY SO BRAZEN! WHY'S HE PLAYING SO PASSIVELY?
AT THIS RATE WE WON'T HAVE A CHANCE TO SCORE.
VSH
I KEEP THINKING ABOUT THE CONSE-QUENCES...
...OR ABOUT HOW OTHER PEOPLE FEEL.
ALL THIS STUFF KEEPS HOLDING ME BACK...
...AND I WIND UP DOING NOTHING.
SPLASH

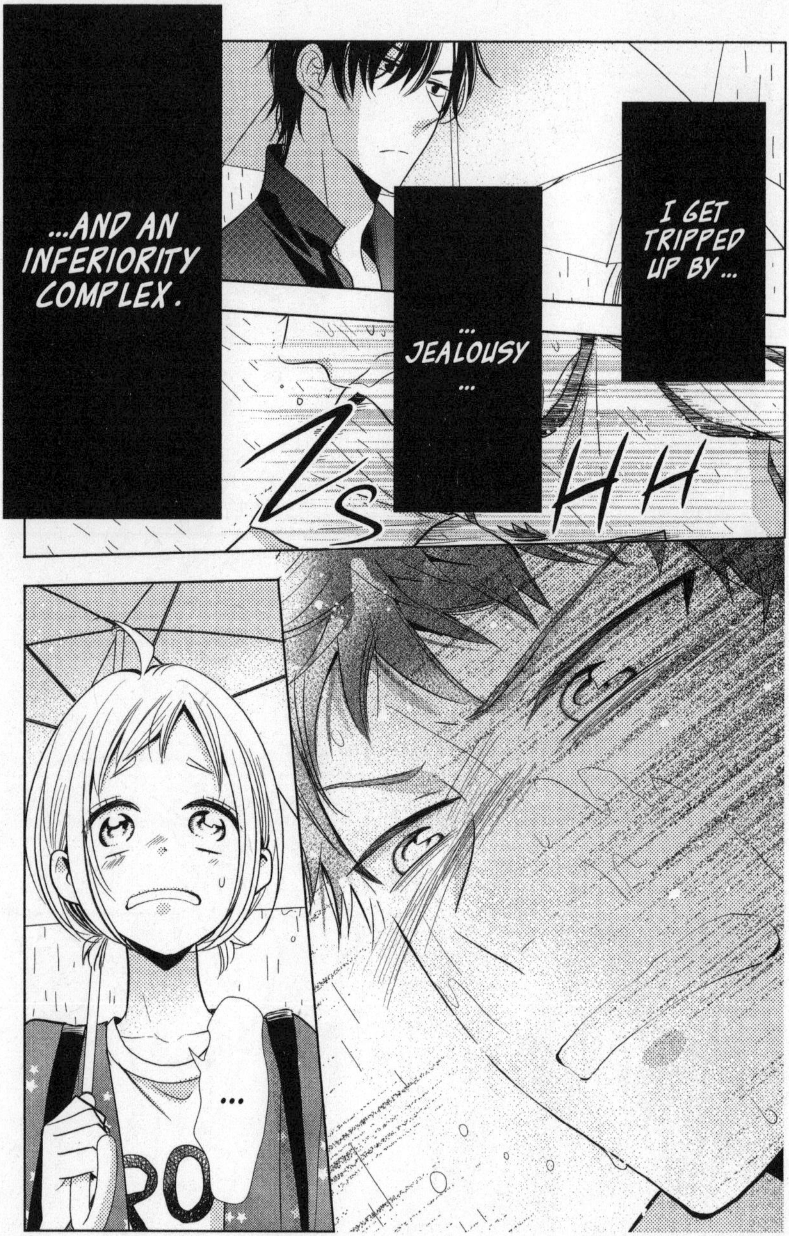
I GET TRIPPED UP BY...
...JEALOUSY...
...AND AN INFERIORITY COMPLEX.
ZSHH
...

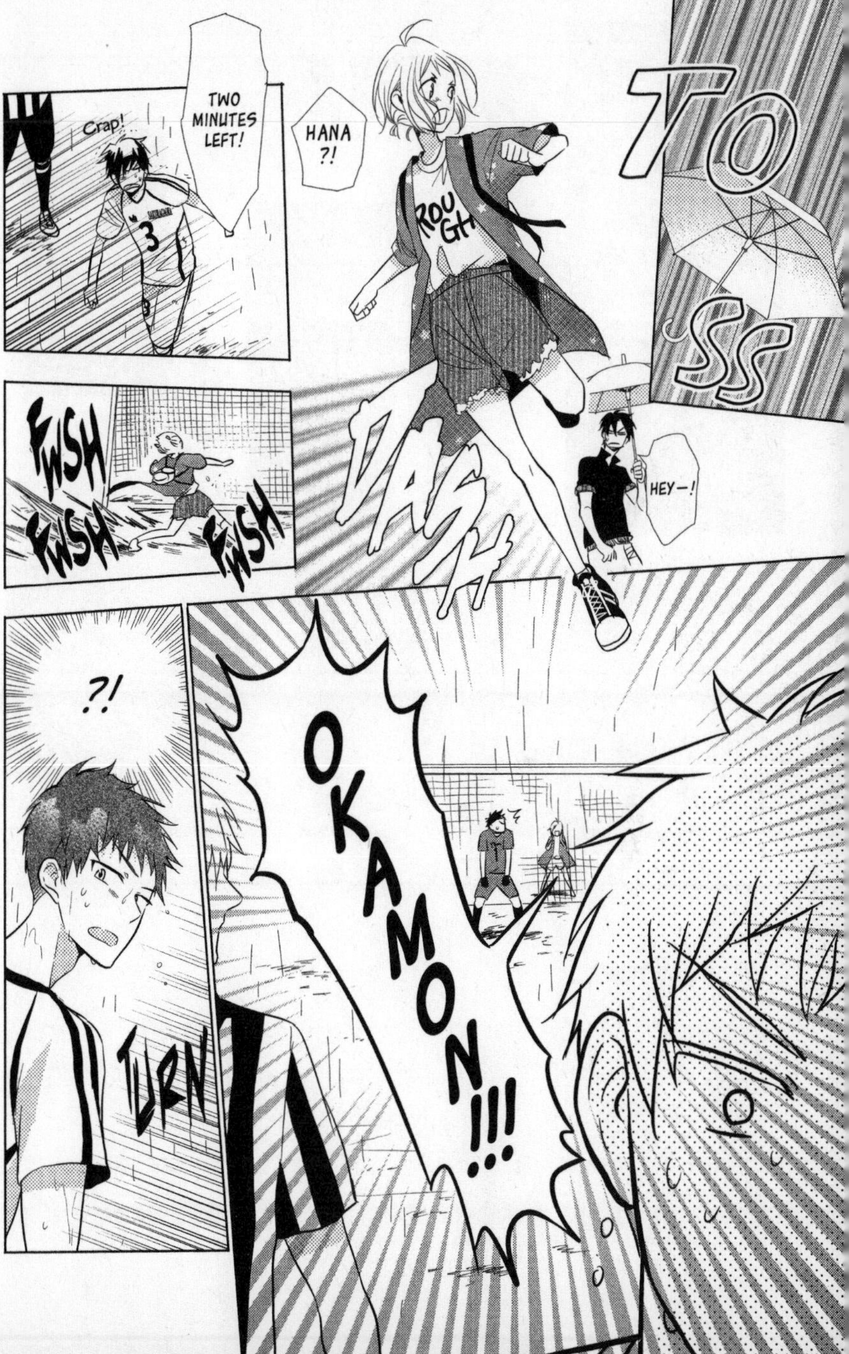
TOSSS
HANA ?!
DASH
HEY—!
TWO MINUTES LEFT!
Crap!
FWSH
FWSH
FWSH
OKAMON!!!
?!
TURN

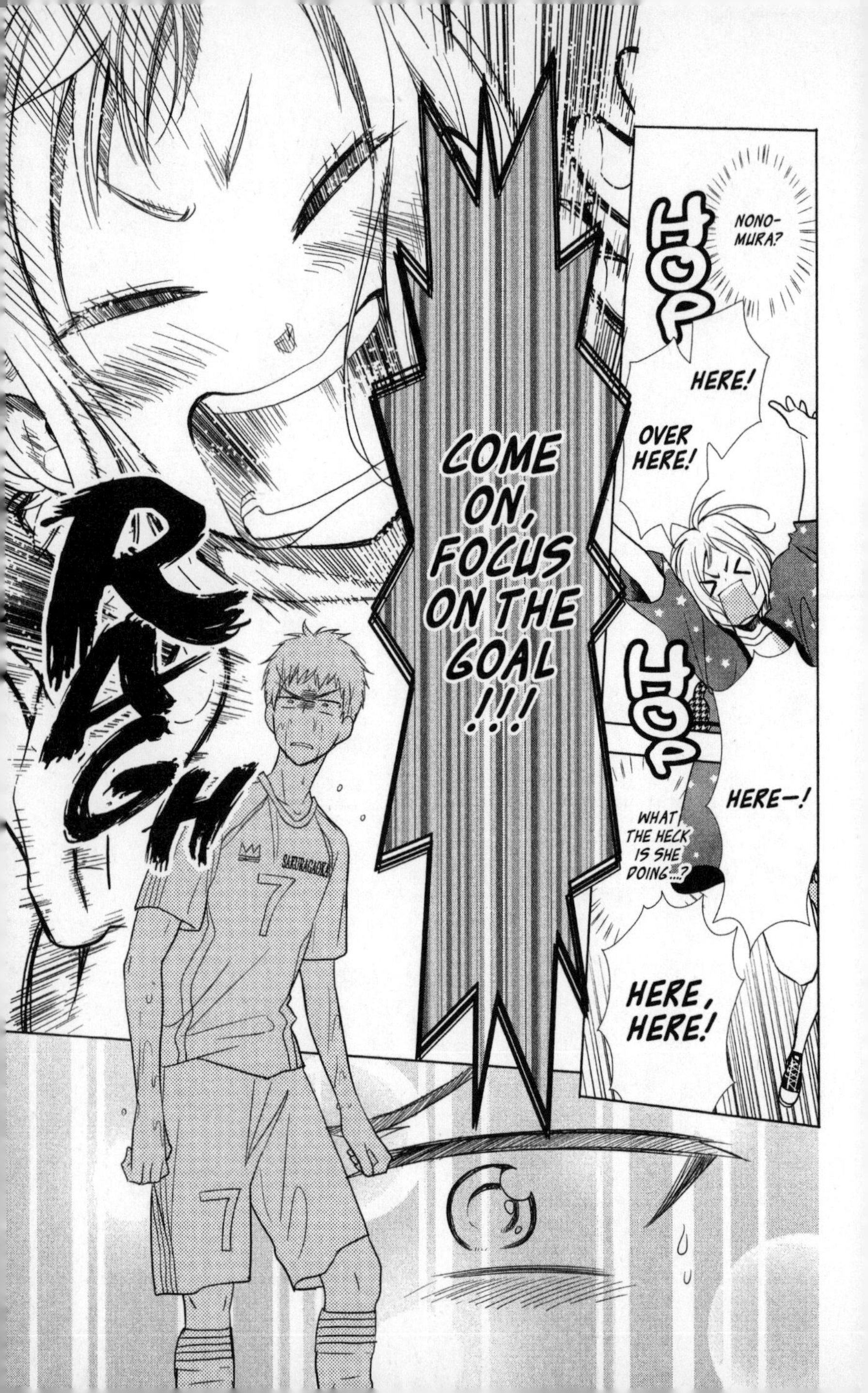
NONO-MURA?
HOP
HERE!
OVER HERE!
HOP
HERE—!
WHAT THE HECK IS SHE DOING...?
HERE, HERE!
COME ON, FOCUS ON THE GOAL!!!
RAGH
SAKURAGAOKA
7

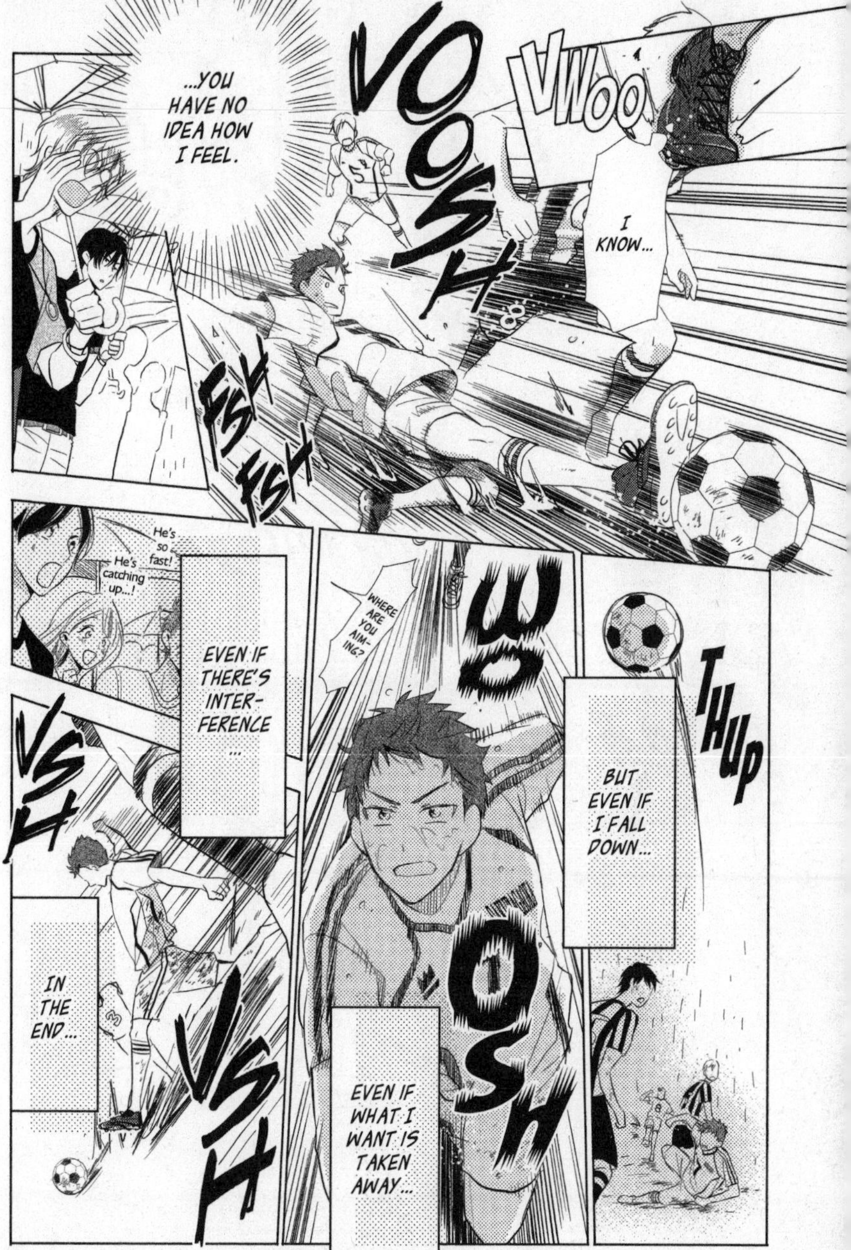
VWOO
VOOSH
...YOU HAVE NO IDEA HOW I FEEL.
I KNOW...
FSH FSH
THUP
BUT EVEN IF I FALL DOWN...
WHERE ARE YOU AIMING?
WOOSH
EVEN IF WHAT I WANT IS TAKEN AWAY...
He's so fast!
He's catching up...!
EVEN IF THERE'S INTER-FERENCE...
VSH
IN THE END...
VSH

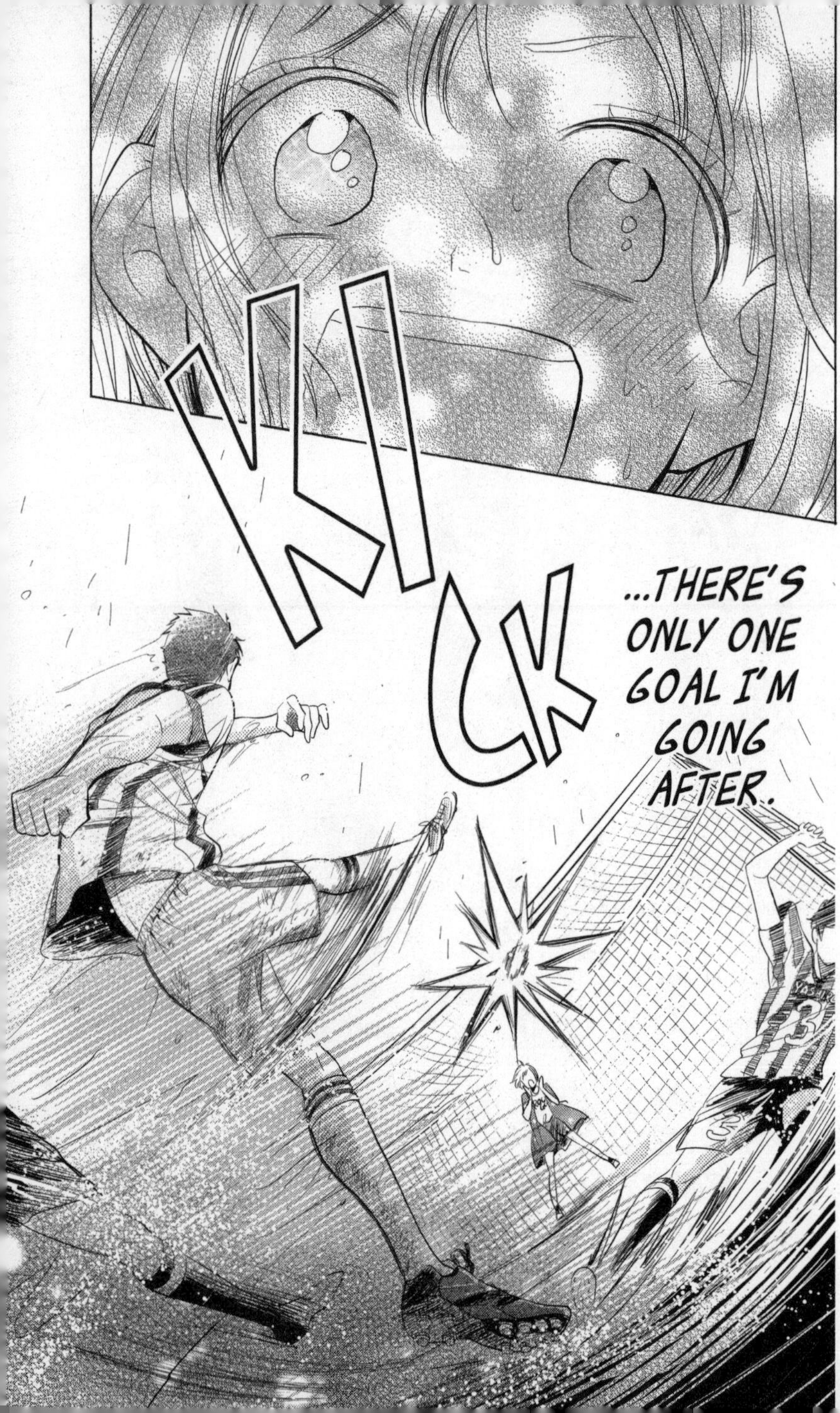
KICK
...THERE'S ONLY ONE GOAL I'M GOING AFTER.

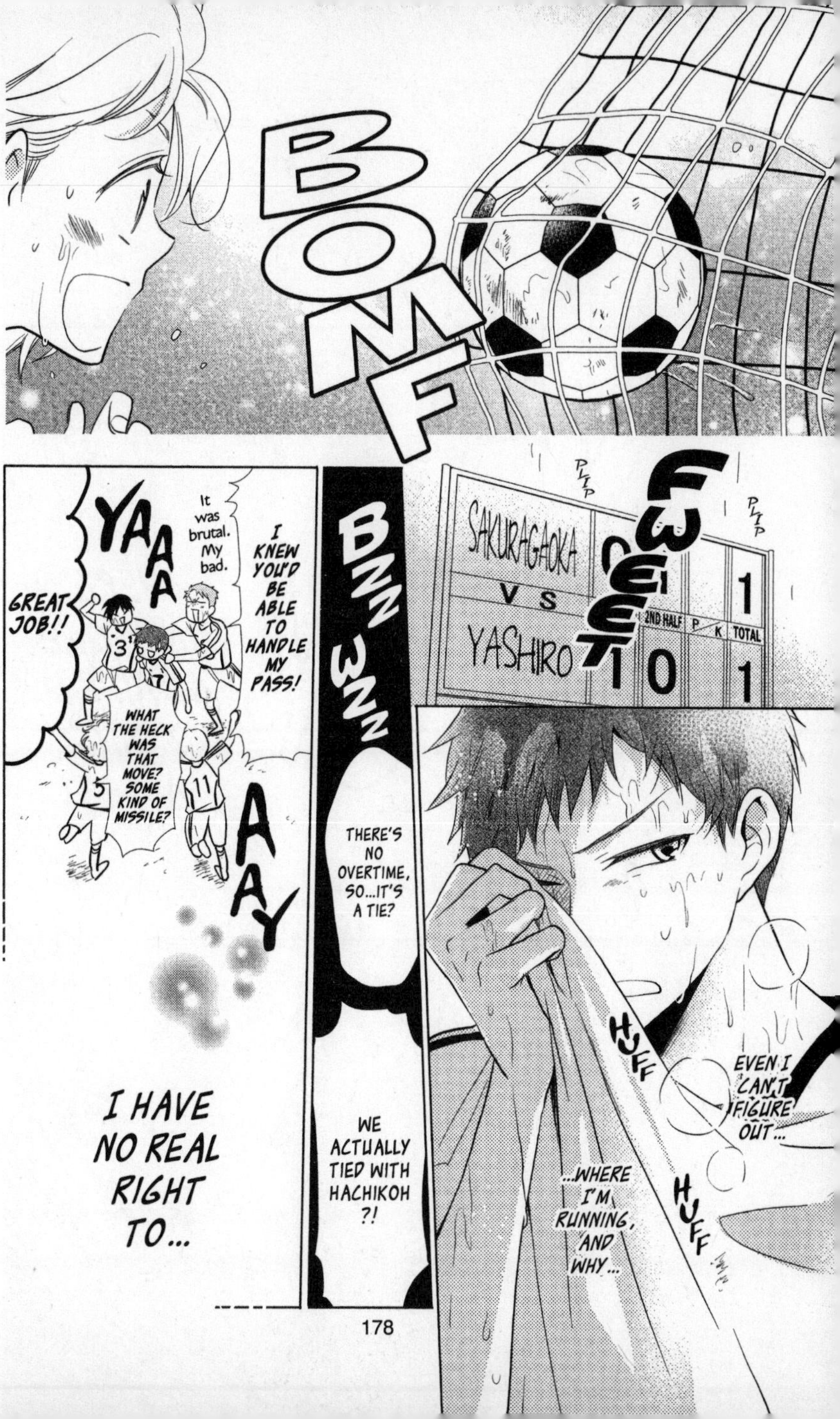
BOMF
PLIP
PLIP
FWEET
SAKURAGAOKA
VS
YASHIRO
1
2ND HALF
P
K
TOTAL
1
0
1
HUFF
HUFF
EVEN I CAN'T FIGURE OUT...
...WHERE I'M RUNNING, AND WHY...
BZZ WZZ
THERE'S NO OVERTIME, SO...IT'S A TIE?
WE ACTUALLY TIED WITH HACHIKOH?!
YAAAAAAY
It was brutal. My bad.
I KNEW YOU'D BE ABLE TO HANDLE MY PASS!
GREAT JOB!!
WHAT THE HECK WAS THAT MOVE? SOME KIND OF MISSILE?
I HAVE NO REAL RIGHT TO...

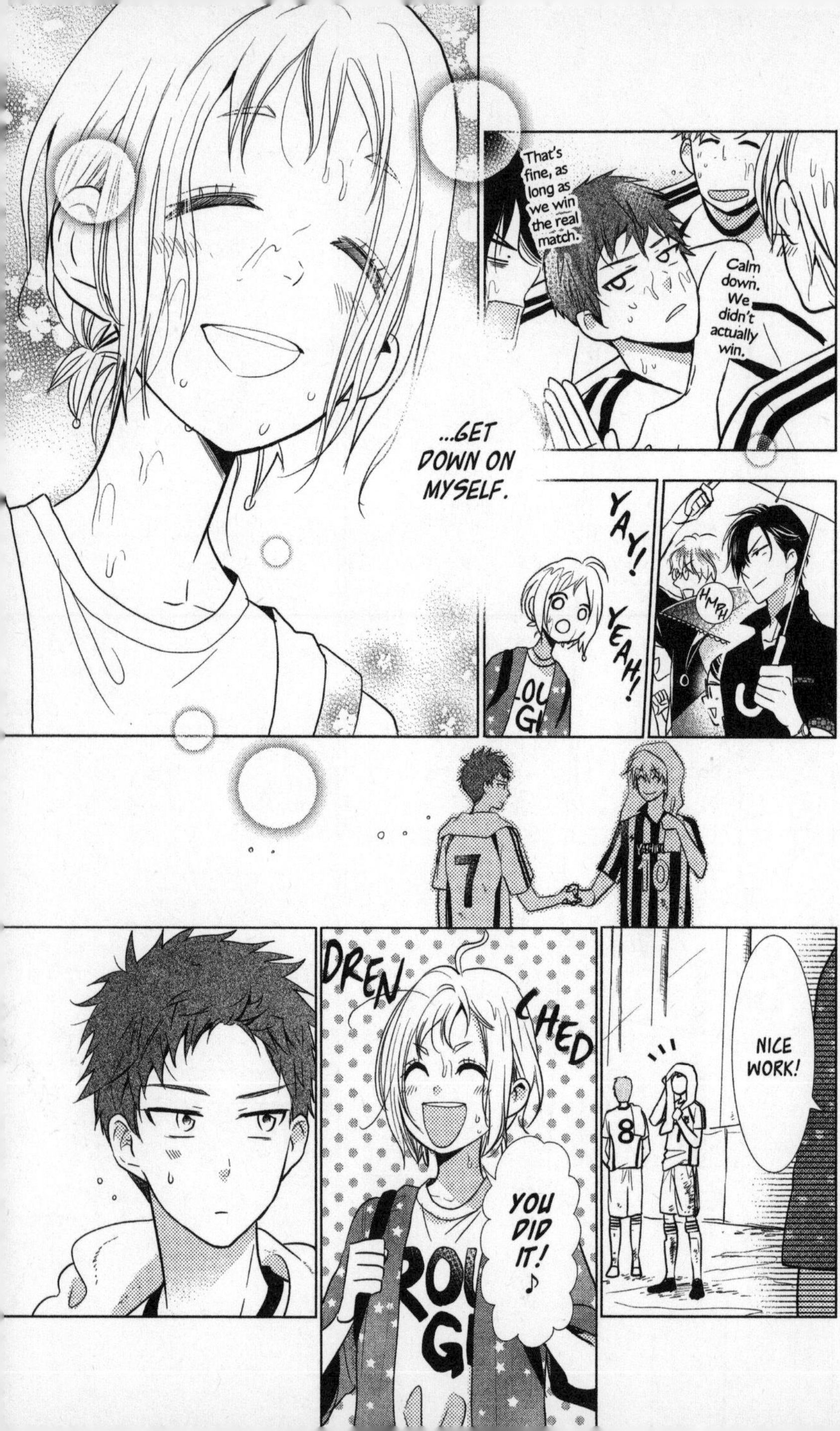

Calm down. We didn't actually win.
That's fine, as long as we win the real match.
HMPH
YAY!
YEAH!
...GET DOWN ON MYSELF.
NICE WORK!
DRENCHED
YOU DID IT! ♪

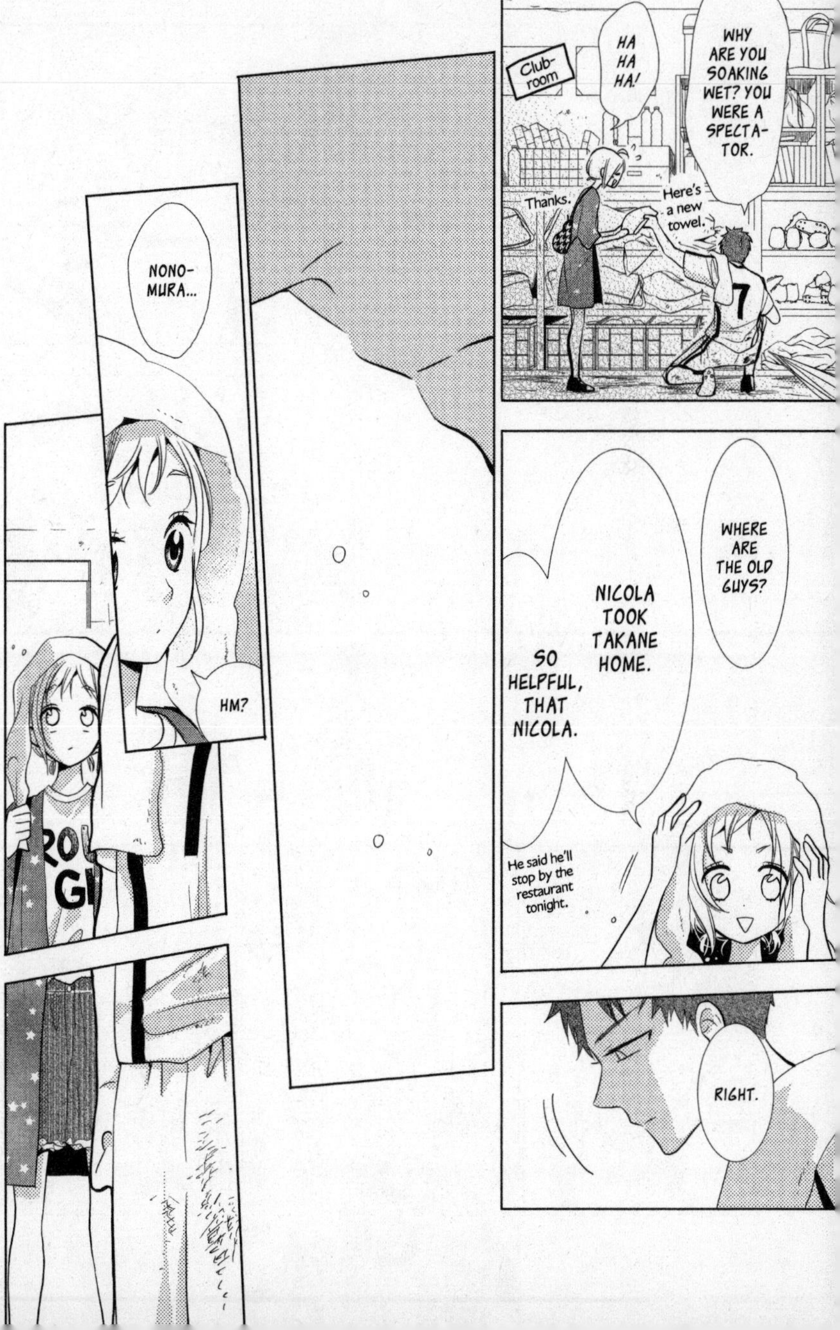
WHY ARE YOU SOAKING WET? YOU WERE A SPECTA-TOR.
HA HA HA!
Club-room
Here's a new towel.
Thanks.
WHERE ARE THE OLD GUYS?
NICOLA TOOK TAKANE HOME.
SO HELPFUL, THAT NICOLA.
He said he'll stop by the restaurant tonight.
RIGHT.
NONO-MURA...
HM?

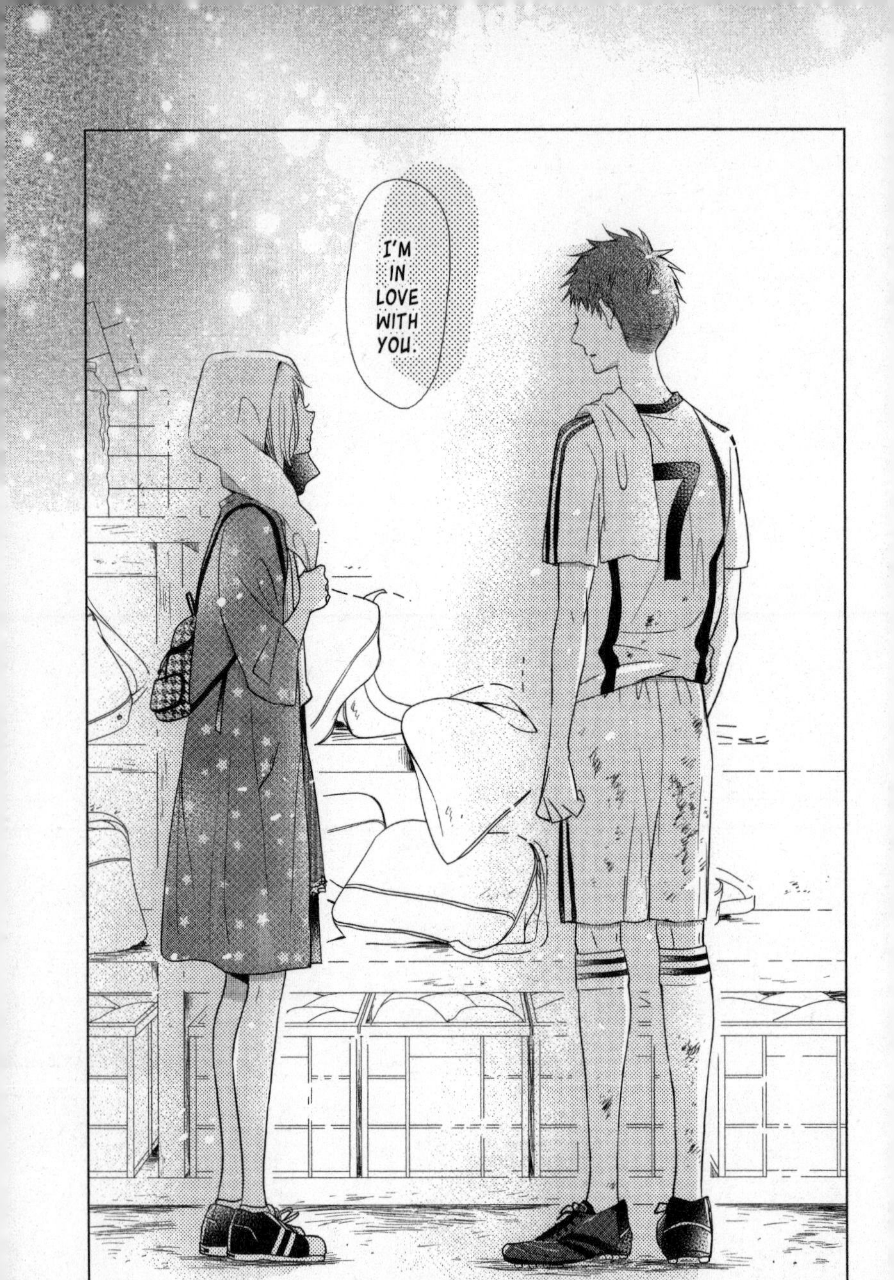
I'M IN LOVE WITH YOU.

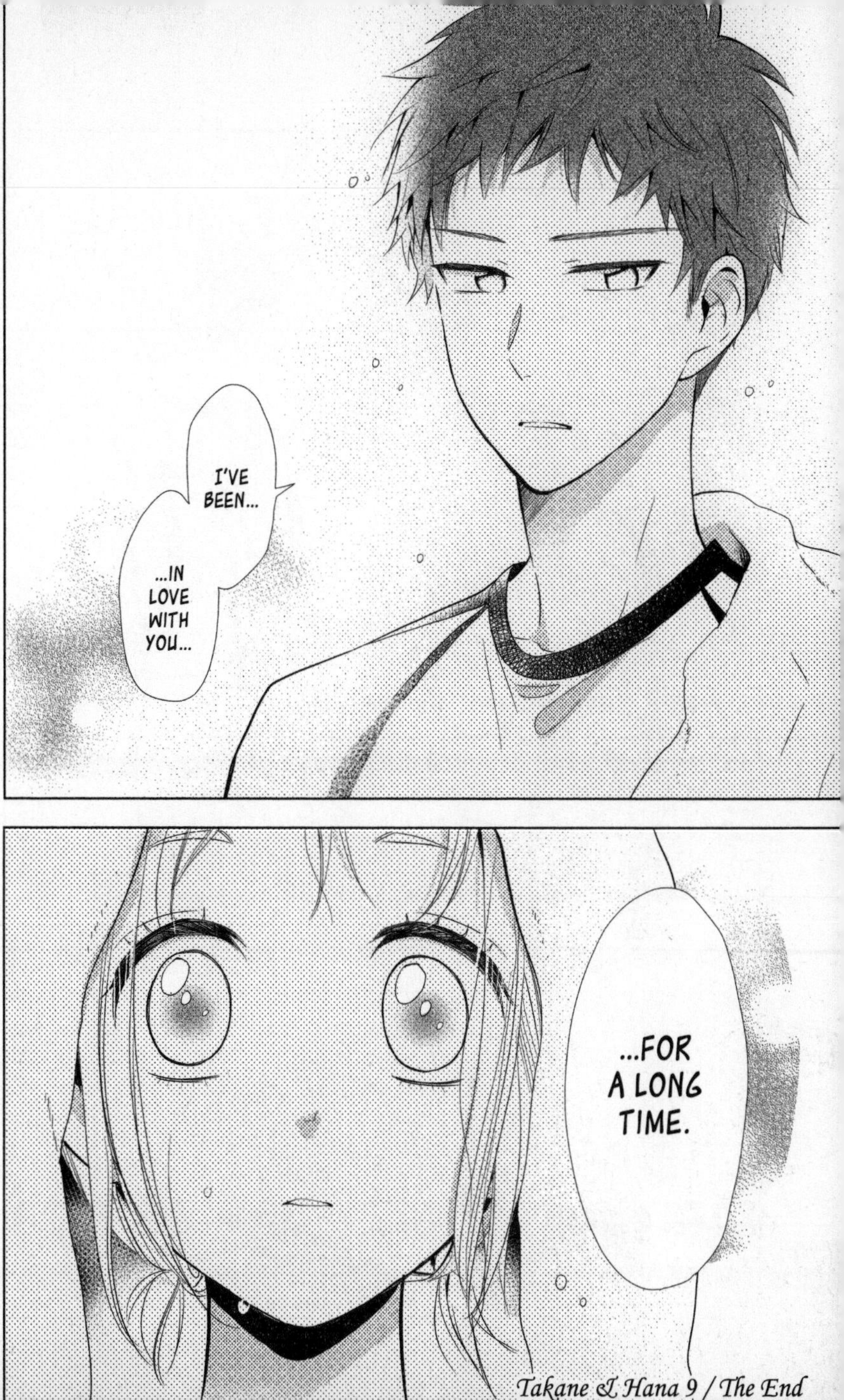

I'VE BEEN...
...IN LOVE WITH YOU...
...FOR A LONG TIME.

Takane & Hana 9 / The End

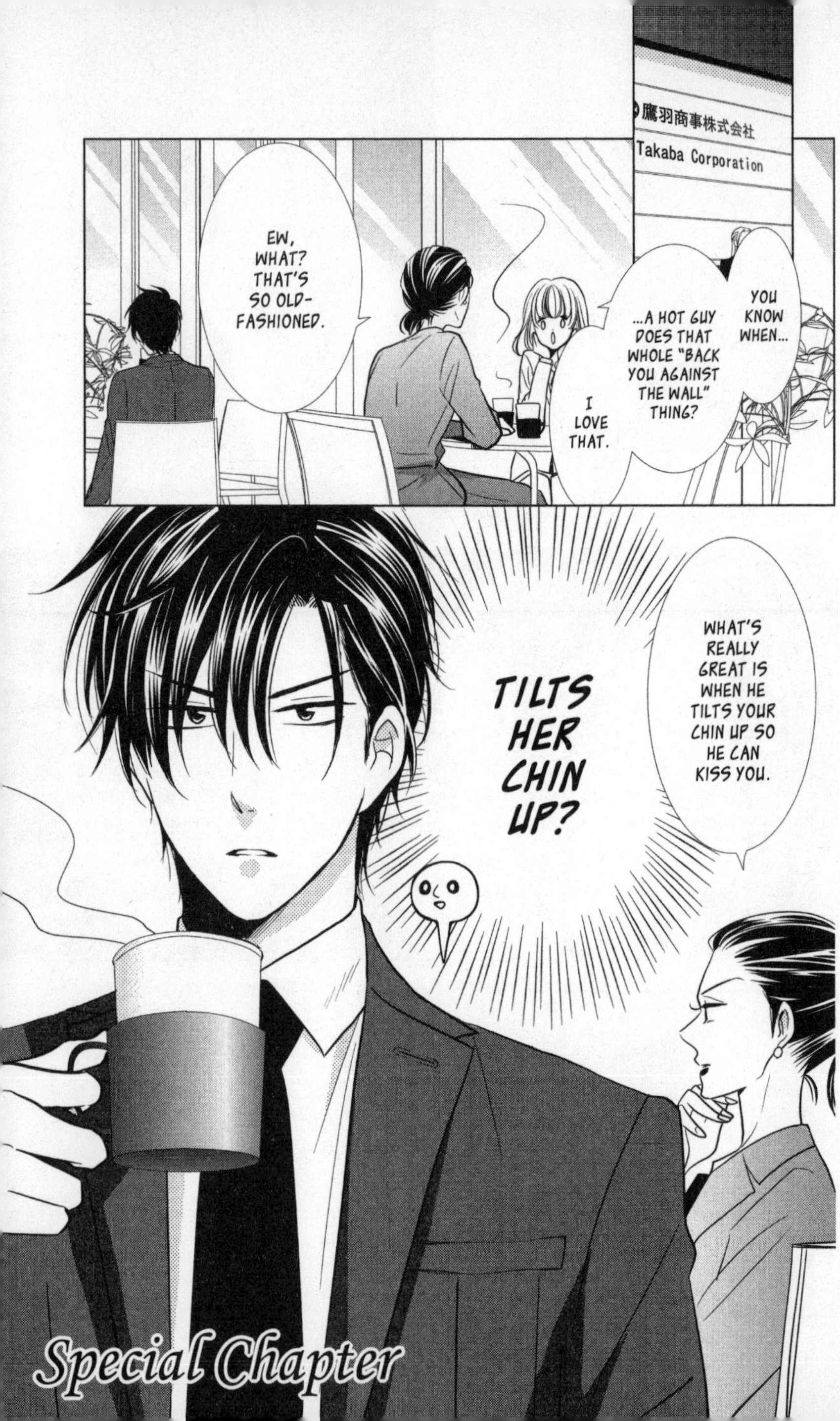
鷹羽商事株式会社
Takaba Corporation
YOU KNOW WHEN...
...A HOT GUY DOES THAT WHOLE "BACK YOU AGAINST THE WALL" THING?
I LOVE THAT.
EW, WHAT? THAT'S SO OLD-FASHIONED.
WHAT'S REALLY GREAT IS WHEN HE TILTS YOUR CHIN UP SO HE CAN KISS YOU.
TILTS HER CHIN UP?
Special Chapter

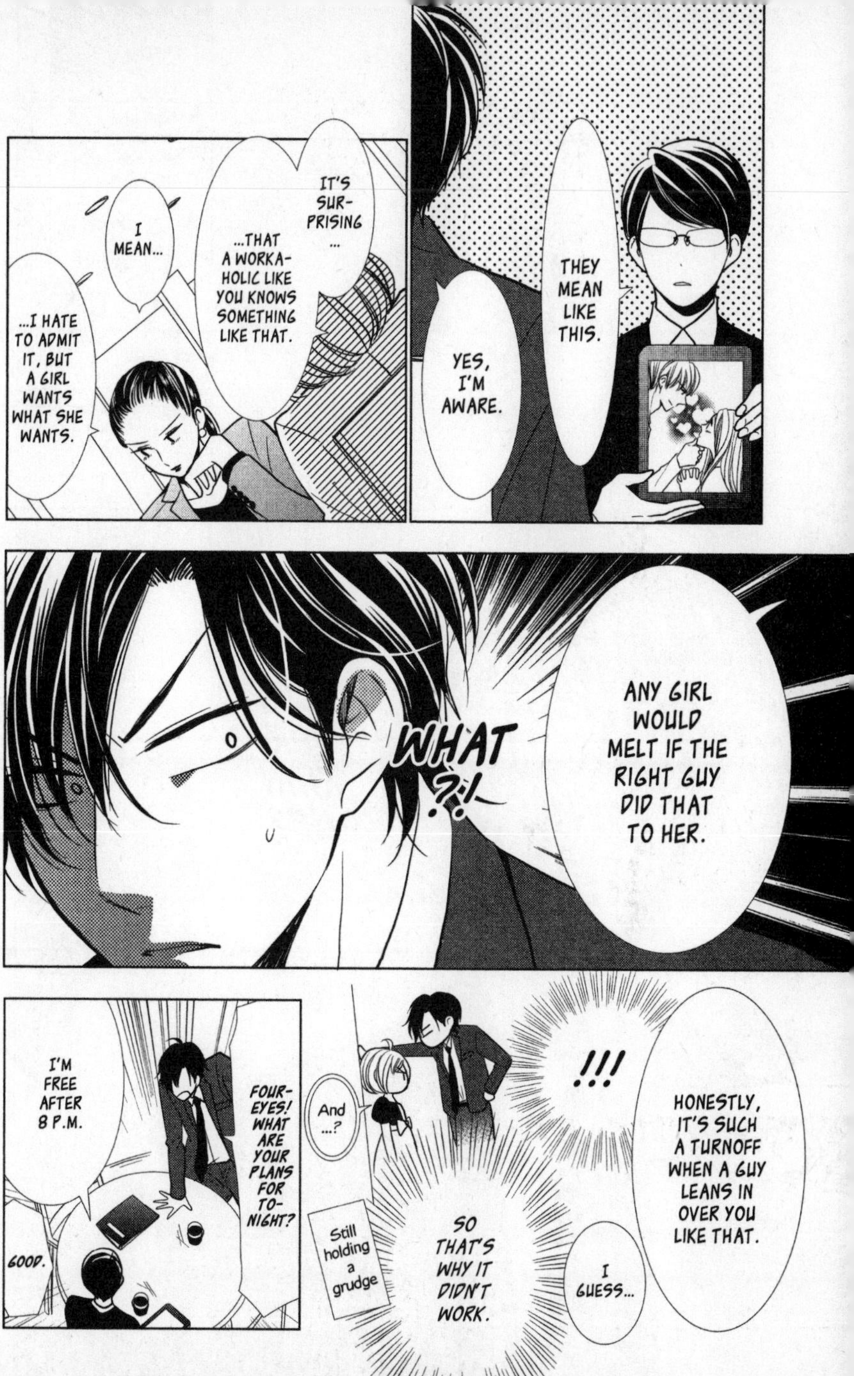
THEY MEAN LIKE THIS.
YES, I'M AWARE.
IT'S SUR-PRISING...
...THAT A WORKA-HOLIC LIKE YOU KNOWS SOMETHING LIKE THAT.
I MEAN...
...I HATE TO ADMIT IT, BUT A GIRL WANTS WHAT SHE WANTS.
ANY GIRL WOULD MELT IF THE RIGHT GUY DID THAT TO HER.
WHAT ?!
HONESTLY, IT'S SUCH A TURNOFF WHEN A GUY LEANS IN OVER YOU LIKE THAT.
!!!
I GUESS...
SO THAT'S WHY IT DIDN'T WORK.
And ...?
Still holding a grudge
FOUR-EYES! WHAT ARE YOUR PLANS FOR TO-NIGHT?
I'M FREE AFTER 8 P.M.
GOOD.

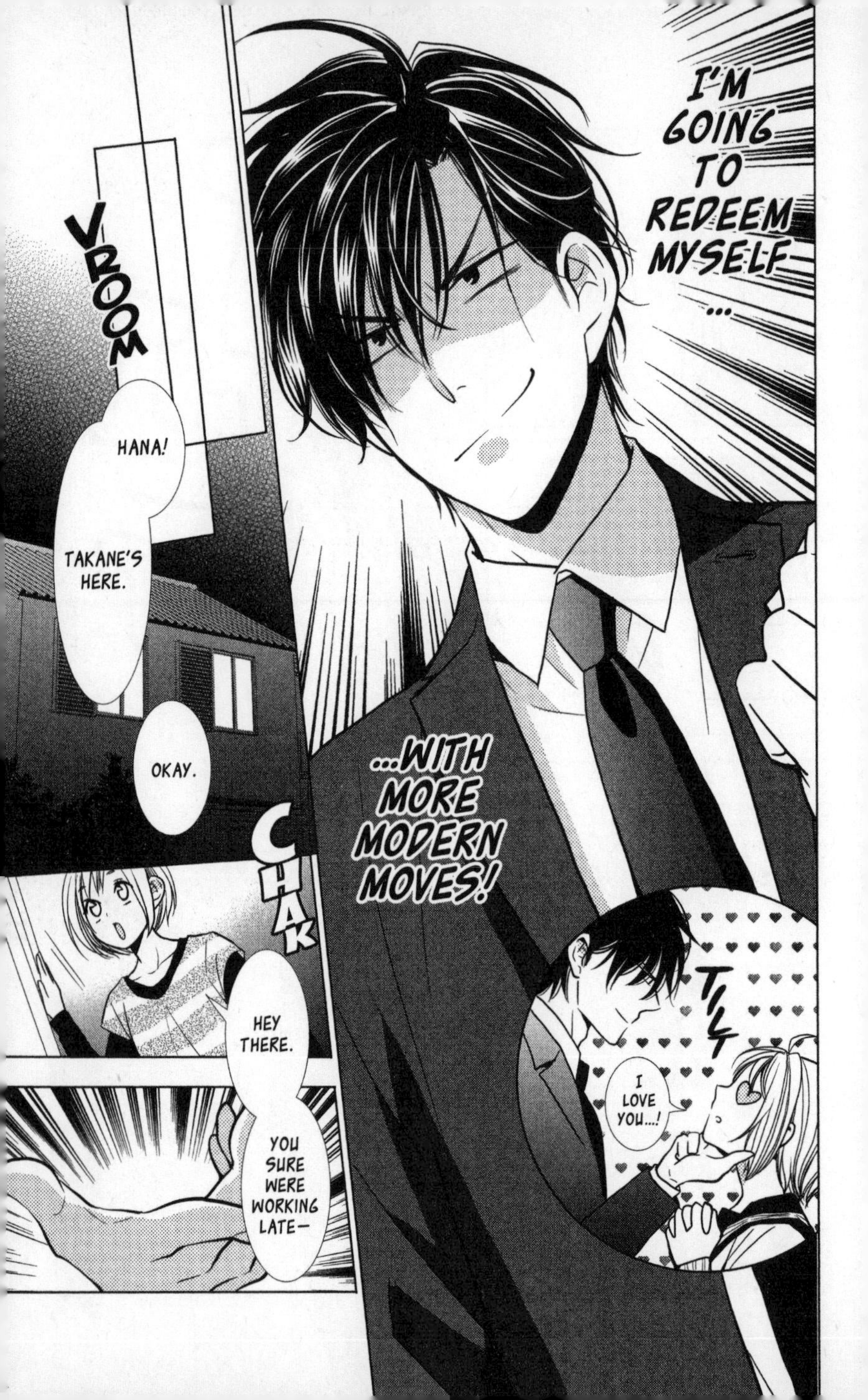
I'M GOING TO REDEEM MYSELF...
...WITH MORE MODERN MOVES!
TILT
I LOVE YOU...!
VROOM
HANA!
TAKANE'S HERE.
OKAY.
CHAK
HEY THERE.
YOU SURE WERE WORKING LATE—

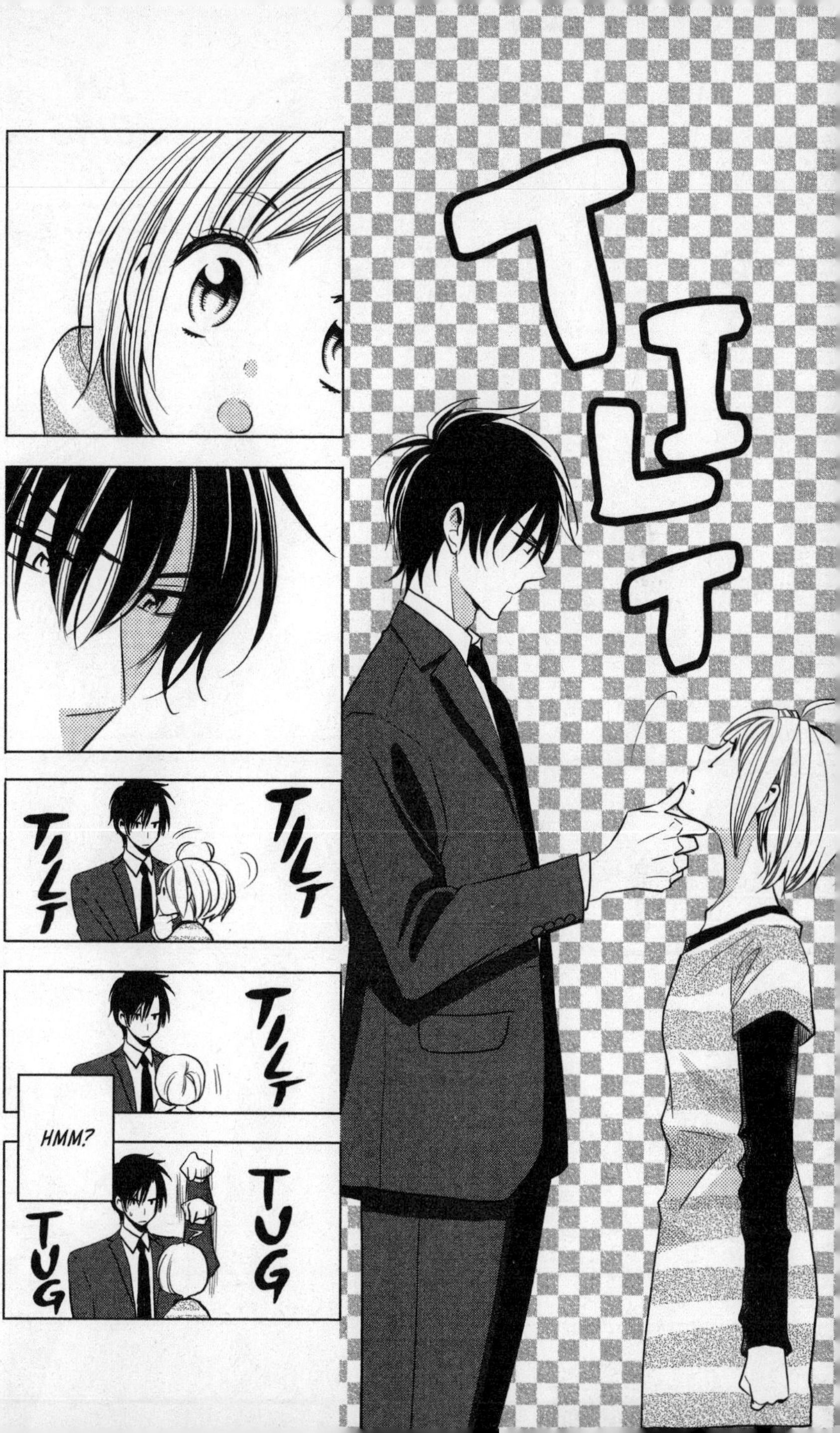
TILT
TILT
TILT
TILT
TUG
HMM?
TUG

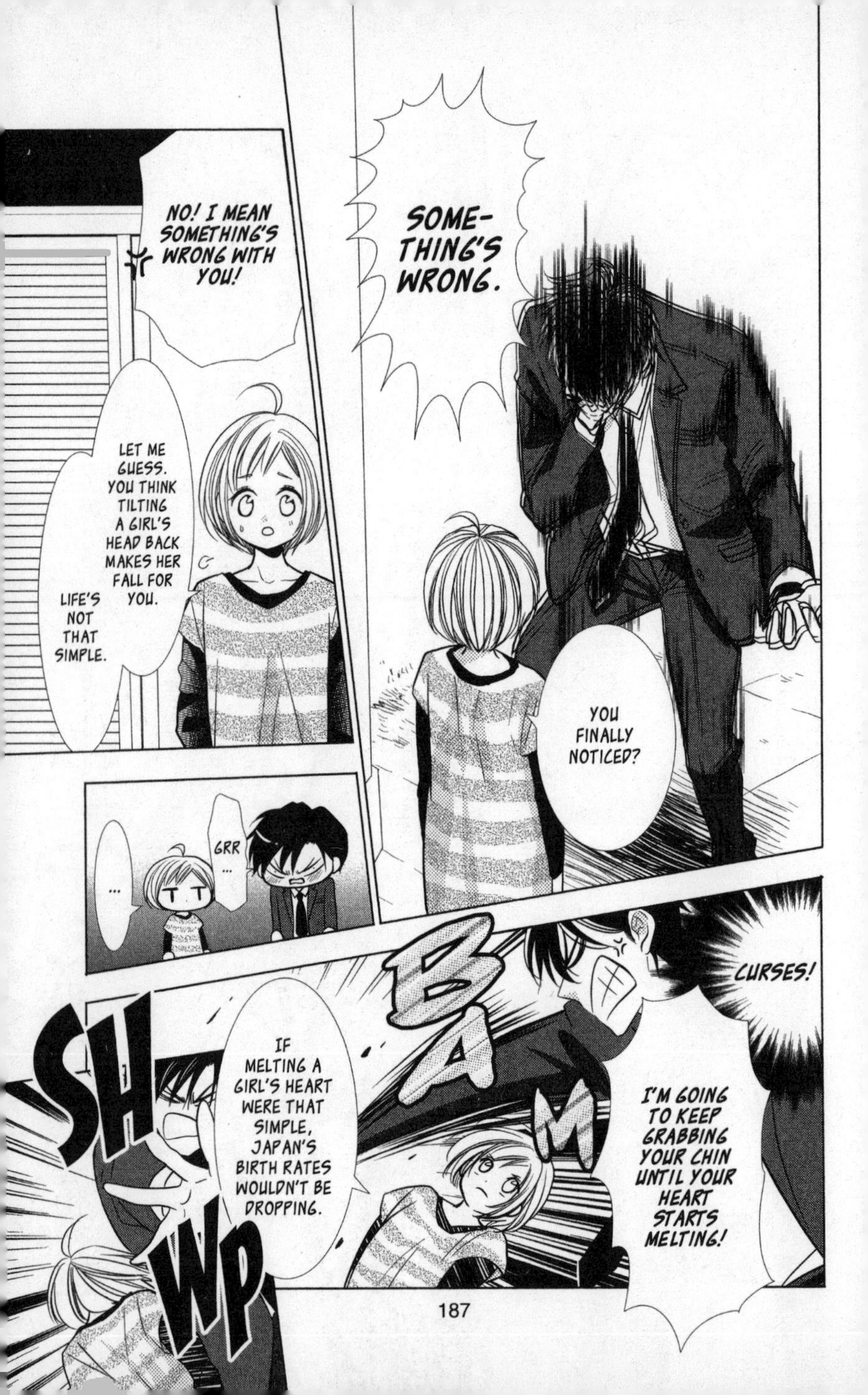
SOME-THING'S WRONG.
YOU FINALLY NOTICED?
NO! I MEAN SOMETHING'S WRONG WITH YOU!
LET ME GUESS. YOU THINK TILTING A GIRL'S HEAD BACK MAKES HER FALL FOR YOU.
LIFE'S NOT THAT SIMPLE.
GRR ...
...
CURSES!
BAM
I'M GOING TO KEEP GRABBING YOUR CHIN UNTIL YOUR HEART STARTS MELTING!
IF MELTING A GIRL'S HEART WERE THAT SIMPLE, JAPAN'S BIRTH RATES WOULDN'T BE DROPPING.
SHWP

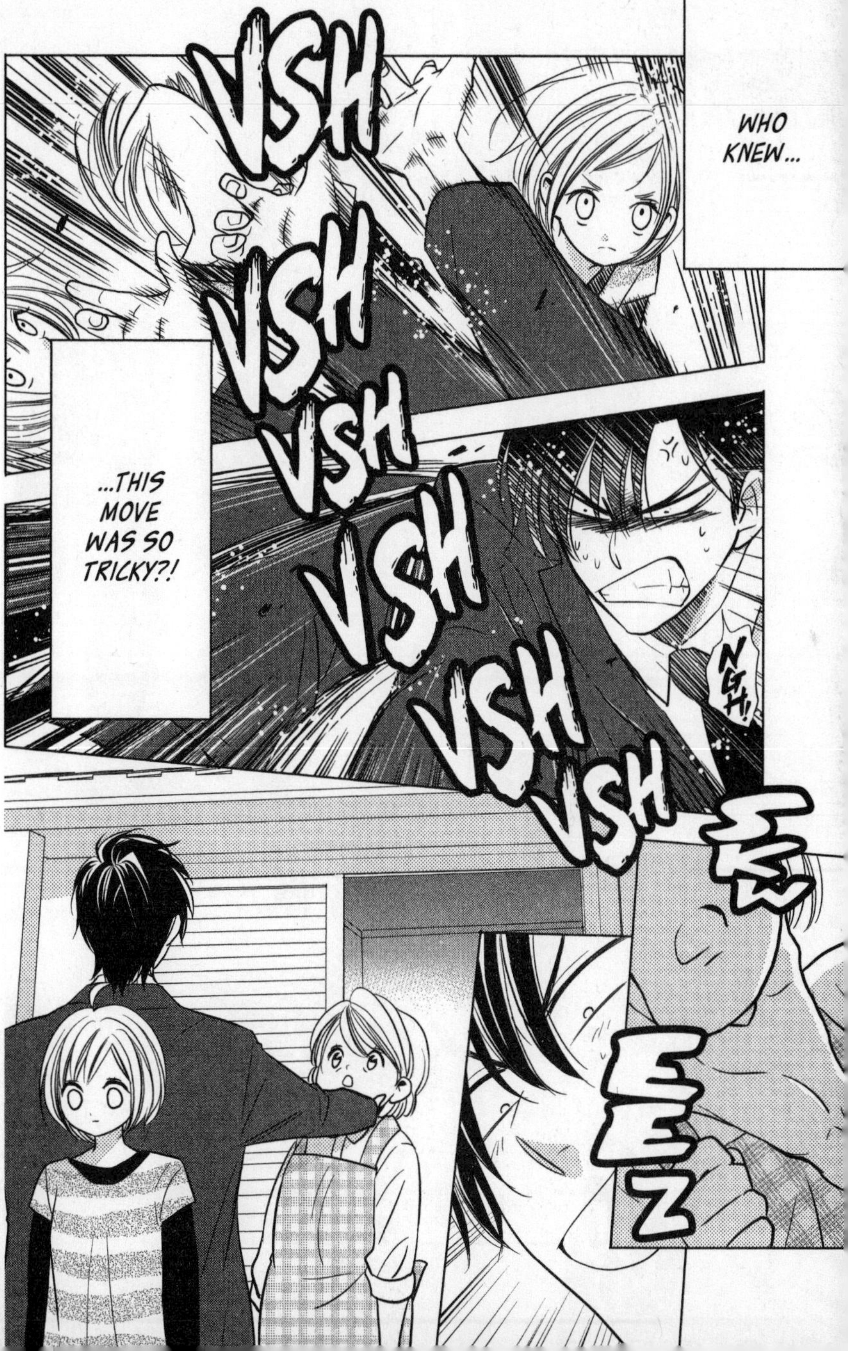
WHO KNEW...
VSH VSH VSH VSH VSH VSH
NGH!
...THIS MOVE WAS SO TRICKY?!
VSH
SKW
EEZ

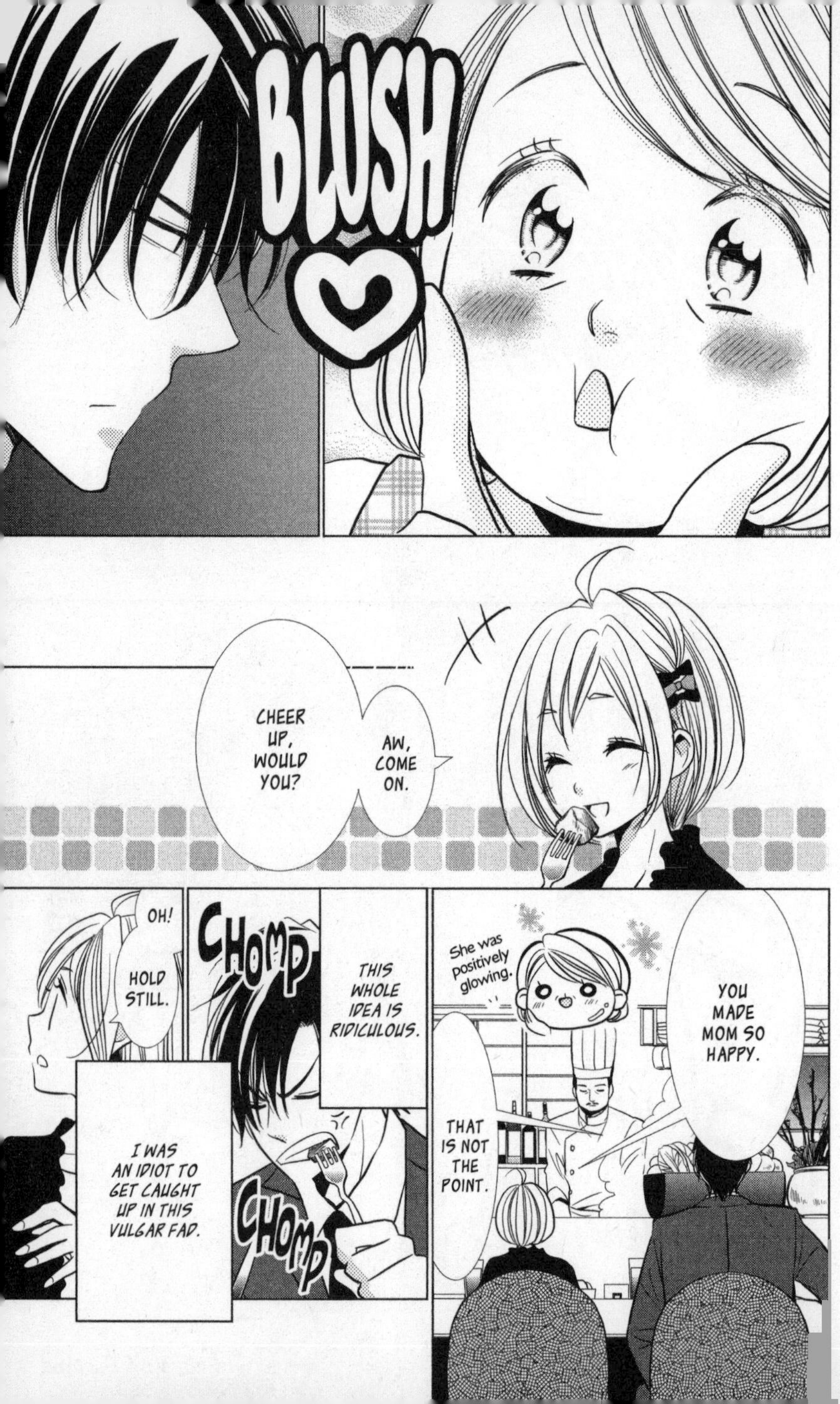
BLUSH
AW, COME ON.
CHEER UP, WOULD YOU?
YOU MADE MOM SO HAPPY.
She was positively glowing.
THAT IS NOT THE POINT.
THIS WHOLE IDEA IS RIDICULOUS.
CHOMP
CHOMP
I WAS AN IDIOT TO GET CAUGHT UP IN THIS VULGAR FAD.
OH!
HOLD STILL.

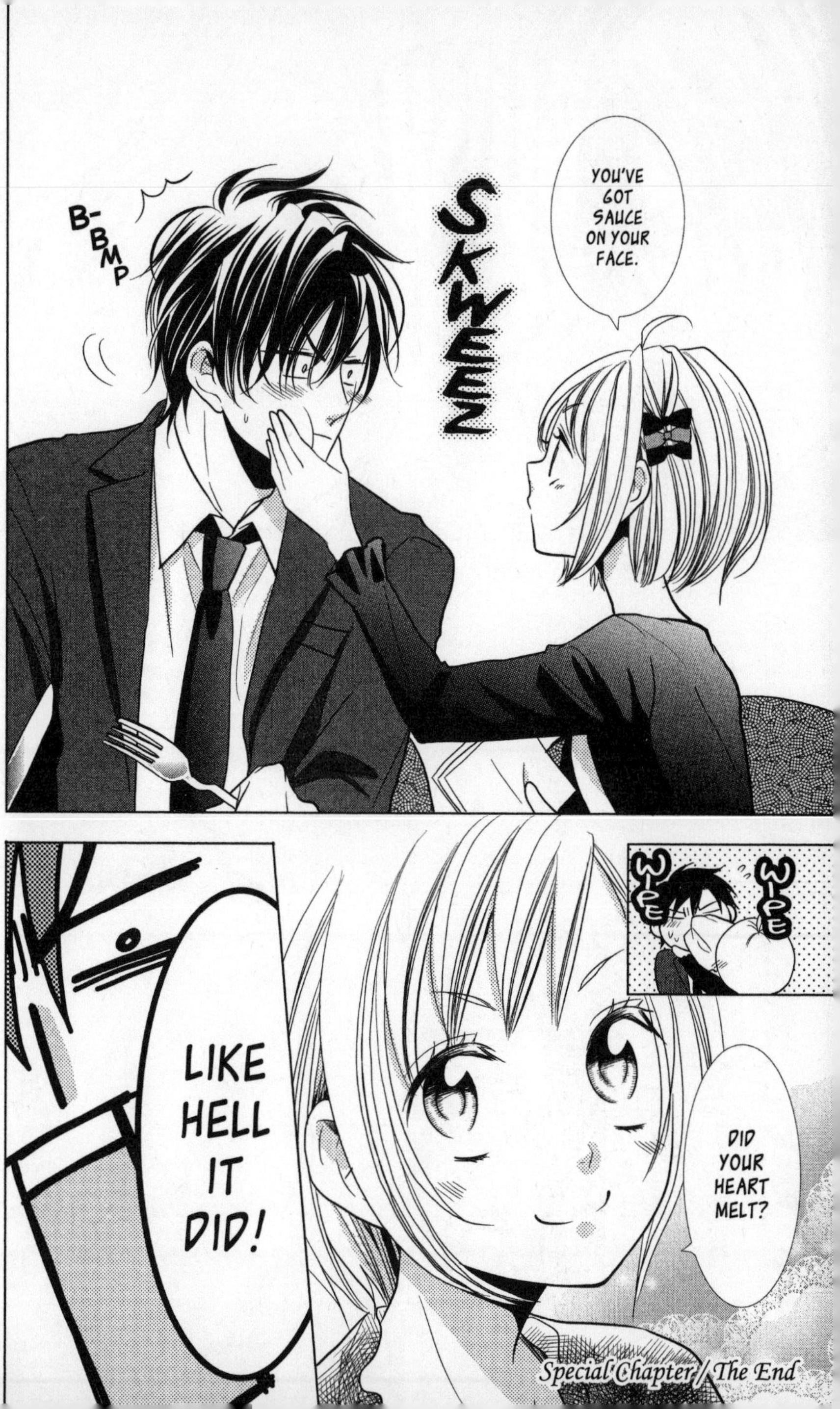
YOU'VE GOT SAUCE ON YOUR FACE.
SKWEEZ
B-BMP
WIPE
WIPE
DID YOUR HEART MELT?
LIKE HELL IT DID!
Special Chapter / The End

The Melt Your Heart Game

YOU KNOW SOME CLASSIC MOVES, BUT DON'T FORGET ABOUT...
...THE ONE WHERE YOUR HEAD LIGHTLY RESTS ON THE OTHER PERSON'S SHOULDERS.
RESTS ...?
LIGHTLY. IT'S A LEAN-IN.
Like this.
RIGHT.
SHING
WILL IT MELT YOUR HEART IF I DO IT?
WHO KNOWS?
WANNA TRY?
IF YOU INSIST.
BONK
YOU'RE TINY.
YOU SUCK AT THIS.

Okamon! Now's your chance to
appear on the cover! Wear your uniform
to commemorate the occasion!

—**YUKI SHIWASU**

Born on March 7 in Fukuoka Prefecture, Japan,
Yuki Shiwasu began her career as a manga artist
after winning the top prize in the Hakusensha Athena
Newcomers' Awards from *Hana to Yume* magazine. She
is also the author of *Furou Kyoudai* (Immortal Siblings),
which was published by Hakusensha in Japan.

Takane &Hana

VOLUME 9
SHOJO BEAT EDITION

STORY & ART BY **YUKI SHIWASU**

ENGLISH ADAPTATION **Ysabet Reinhardt MacFarlane**
TRANSLATION **JN Productions**
TOUCH-UP ART & LETTERING **Annaliese Christman**
DESIGN **Shawn Carrico**
EDITOR **Amy Yu**

Takane to Hana by Yuki Shiwasu
© Yuki Shiwasu 2017
All rights reserved.
First published in Japan in 2017 by HAKUSENSHA, Inc., Tokyo.
English language translation rights arranged with HAKUSENSHA, Inc., Tokyo.

The stories, characters and incidents mentioned
in this publication are entirely fictional.

Printed in the U.S.A.

Published by VIZ Media, LLC
P.O. Box 77010
San Francisco, CA 94107

10 9 8 7 6 5 4 3 2 1
First printing, June 2019

viz.com   shojobeat.com

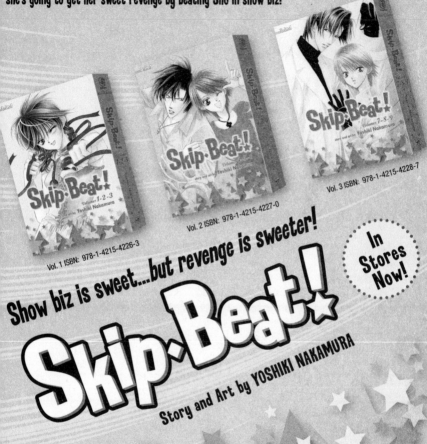

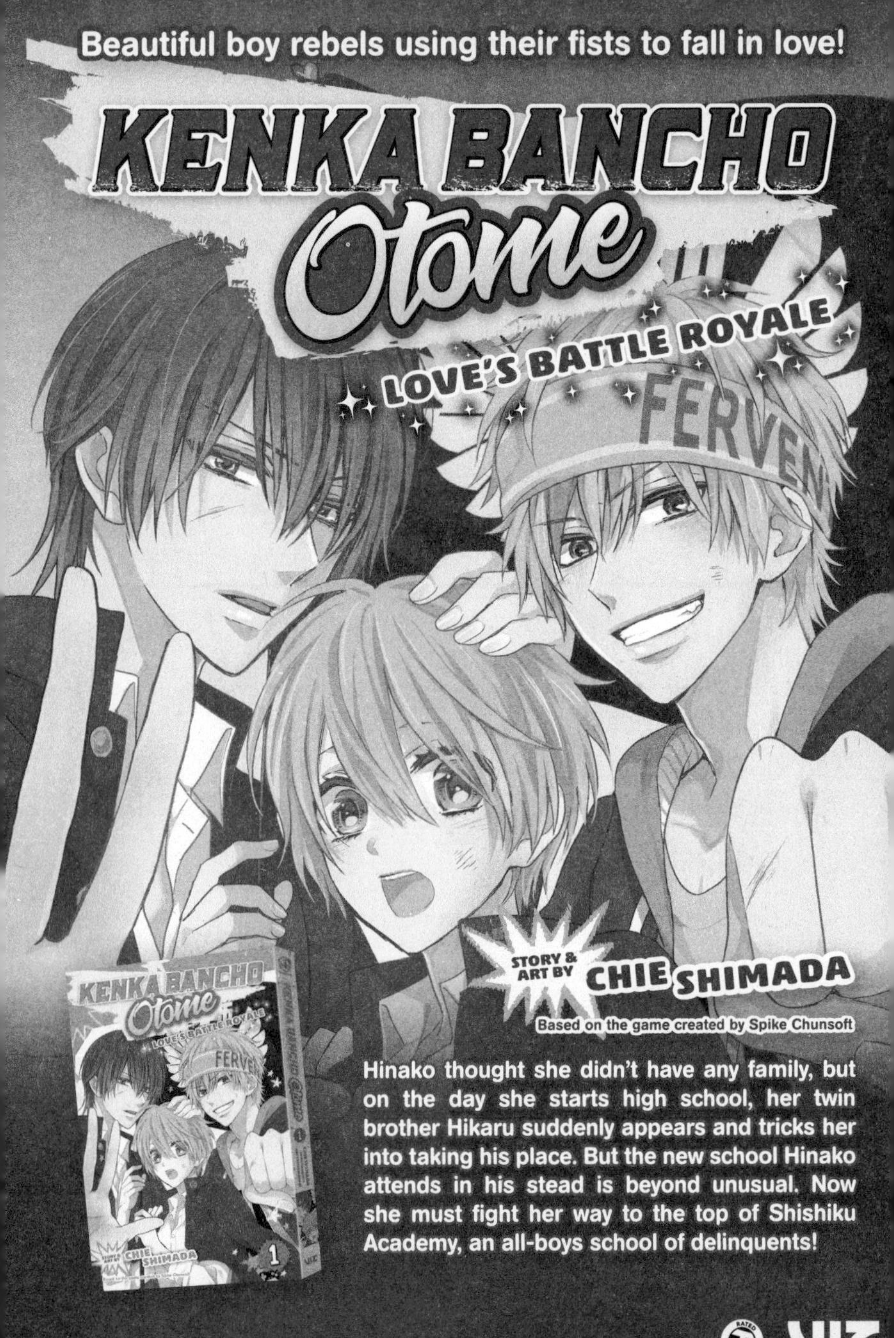
Beautiful boy rebels using their fists to fall in love!
KENKA BANCHO
Otome
LOVE'S BATTLE ROYALE
FERVEN
STORY & ART BY CHIE SHIMADA
Based on the game created by Spike Chunsoft
Hinako thought she didn't have any family, but on the day she starts high school, her twin brother Hikaru suddenly appears and tricks her into taking his place. But the new school Hinako attends in his stead is beyond unusual. Now she must fight her way to the top of Shishiku Academy, an all-boys school of delinquents!
KENKA BANCHO
Otome
LOVE'S BATTLE ROYALE
FERVEN
CHIE SHIMADA
1
VIZ
RATED T TEEN
VIZ
Kenka Bancho Otome: Koi no Battle Royale © Chie Shimada / HAKUSENSHA, INC. © Spike Chunsoft

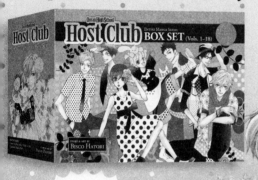

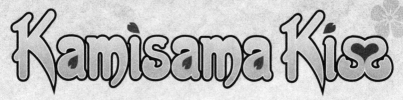

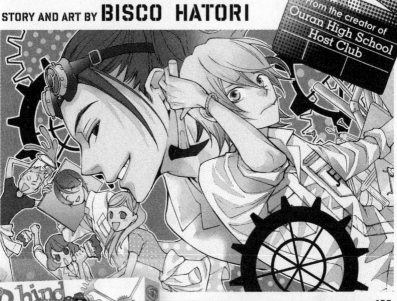
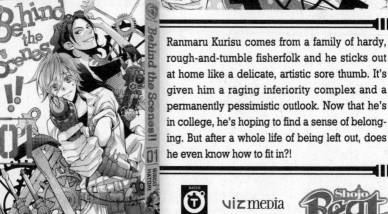

Nino Arisugawa, a girl who loves to sing, experiences her first heart-wrenching goodbye when her beloved childhood friend, Momo, moves away. And after Nino befriends Yuzu, a music composer, she experiences another sad parting! With music as their common ground and only outlet, how will everyone's unrequited loves play out?

ANONYMOUS NOISE

viz media
viz.com

Shojo Beat

Story & Art by
Ryoko Fukuyama

Fukumenkei Noise © Ryoko Fukuyama 2013/HAKUSENSHA, Inc.

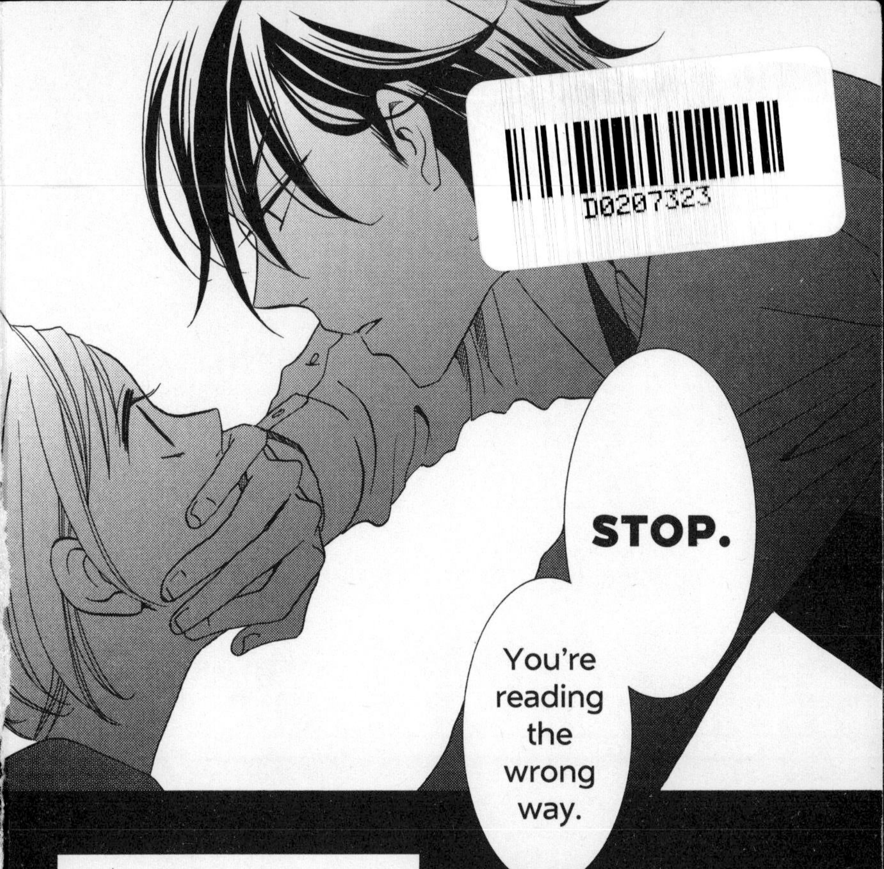
STOP.
You're reading the wrong way.

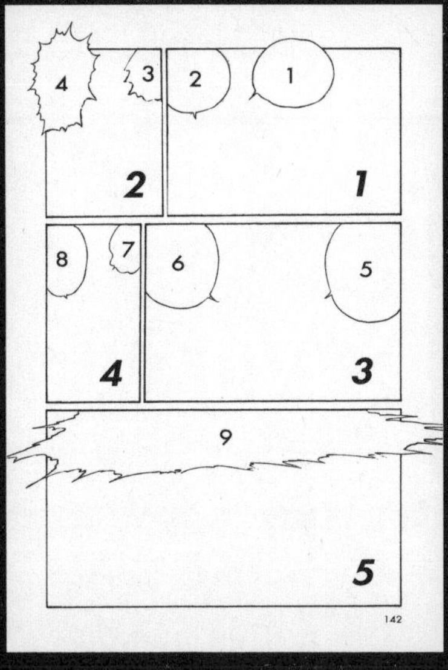
1
2
1
3
4
2
5
6
3
7
8
4
9
5
142

In keeping with the original Japanese comic format, this book reads from right to left—so action, sound effects and word balloons are completely reversed to preserve the orientation of the original artwork.

Check out the diagram shown here to get the hang of things, and then turn to the other side of the book to get started!